May the Secand be good to you.

Very sincerely yours,

John Carn. C89

TO HEAVEN THROUGH A WINDOW

By the same Author :

Teresa of Lisieux : Truly a Lover.
The Ven. Joseph Passerat (From the French).
An Apostle of the Lepers : The Ven. Peter Donders, C.SS.R.
  (From the French).
Christ is All.
St. Clement, C.SS.R., Patron of Vienna.

SAINT GERARD MAJELLA

To Heaven Through A Window

St. Gerard Majella

By

JOHN CARR, C.SS.R.

With Foreword by
HIS EMINENCE CARDINAL GRIFFIN,
ARCHBISHOP OF WESTMINSTER

LONDON

SANDS & CO. (PUBLISHERS), LTD.

1946

Imprimatur:

HUGO KERR, C.SS.R.,
        Sup. Prov. Hib.
        Limerici.
        Die 16 Octobris, 1945.
        In Festo Sancti Gerardi.

Nihil Obstat:

REGINALDUS PHILLIPS, S.Th.L.,
        Censor Deputatus.

Imprimatur:

E. MORROGH BERNARD,
        Vic. Gen.

Westmonasterii.
        die 8a Aprilis, 1946.

CONTENTS

FOREWORD

BY HIS EMINENCE CARDINAL GRIFFIN,
Archbishop of Westminster

St. Gerard is an outstanding example of the power of grace over nature. Grace shone through him from the days of the first awakening of his soul to consciousness. There are some saints, like St. Aloysius, who are sent to us by God for our admiration ; and others for our imitation. In St. Gerard we have both. We can admire the marvellous workings of grace in his soul, the preternatural gifts given him by God, and his power as a wonder worker. We can thank God for revealing His almighty power in the life of this great saint. It is surely an encouragement to us when we are tempted to think that the devil has so much of his own way. He seems to have had a fairly good innings lately.

But St. Gerard is also for our imitation. We should follow him in his love of penance and obedience and, above all, in his marvellous love of God and his neighbour.

I am sure we owe a great debt of gratitude to the author for giving us a modern and up-to-date life of St. Gerard, written in a language which is both simple and attractive. We hope that this life will help to make St. Gerard more widely known and that devotion to him will increase.

His power in this modern world is by no means dead. I know of a small hospital filled with sick children who, for months and even years, lie stretched on planks of wood. They are undergoing orthopædic treatment which is sometimes very painful, wearying and long. Not all of these children have the precious gift of the Catholic faith. But they are the most cheerful children you could ever hope to meet, and I have been frequently asked what is the great secret of their happiness. I like to ascribe it to the devoted care they receive from the good Sisters in charge, but even more, to the power of the prayer and example of St. Gerard, to whom the hospital is dedicated.

I am afraid that St. Gerard suffers from his statues. The death's head is not a cheerful sight for children. Probably it is not meant to be. But it repels. Again, he is made to look so very miserable in his portraits. Now I am sure that he was one of God's brightest children and lovers ; so we designed a special statue for him. He was not emaciated, he always wore a smile, and that smile fell on the crucifix he was holding in his hand. But the death's head had disappeared, and devotion to him through the statue increased. We ought to make the saints lovable. We like to think that they were so in real life but often we write of them and paint them as if they were the most miserable men and women in the world.

There is one feature which stands out in the life of St. Gerard which I feel can be particularly helpful to those who wish to follow him. It is his fidelity to the smallest detail of daily life. Whatever he does, whether it is plying the needle as a tailor ; or, as a lay brother, sweeping the floor, digging the garden, or answering the bell, he does it as well as he can because his every action is filled with the love of God. What a difference there would be in the world if every worker performed his duty, no matter how menial the task may be, after the manner of St. Gerard.

Father Carr has succeeded in presenting St. Gerard to us not only as a great wonder worker; not only as one to be admired; but as one whom we can love and imitate.

Bernard Cardinal Griffin

Archbishop of Westminster

INTRODUCTION

———o———

In a foreword to his large Italian life of St. Gerard Majella, Father Claudio Benedetti addresses the following words to the reader :—" If you delight in reading of the marvellous, here is a life that will please you, for it is full of it. And yet I warn you that when you peruse these pages and meet with scarcely one where you will not read of a miracle, or a prophecy, or an ecstasy, or of some supernatural happening, you will find yourself wondering if it can all be true. Dismiss your doubt. Knowing as we do how wonderful God is in His Saints, particularly in the case of those who were distinguished by their humility and simplicity, we should certainly be prepared to believe wonderful things about them, be they ever so many. When they rest on unimpeachable evidence, what further right have we to question them ? Now we must know that Saint Gerard was most humble and simple of heart, while the credibility of all that is recorded of him can be easily deduced from the sources of our information which we will presently enumerate."

These warning words, addressed primarily to Italian readers of the life of this Italian saint, will be at least as useful for readers of his life in these lands. In the pages of this book there is much that may tax the credulity even of excellent Catholics ; and so I feel I should be making an unreasonable demand upon them if I were to serve them up a profusion of wonders and ask them to swallow it without question. I think it then but fair to my readers that I should set down in some detail an account of the sources from which I have drawn what I have written. And, I add respectfully, I think it but fair to myself and to my subject that they read it.

The three earliest biographers of the Saint were all his contemporaries. Let us see what manner of men they were and what qualifications they brought to their work. First in point of time comes GASPARE CAIONE. Born in Troia, in the Kingdom of Naples, in 1722, he had been practising at the bar for a few years, when the hearing of St. Alphonsus in the pulpit during a mission in his native town and the reading of the Saint's booklet on the religious state drew him, as Alphonsus himself had been drawn, from the law-courts to become a " fisher of men." His holiness and prudence made him one of the Founder's most trusted friends and advisers. Two years after his religious profession he was appointed rector of the house of Caposele, became consultor-general of the Congregation and took part in the general chapter of 1764. He died full of years and merits in 1809.

As soon as St. Alphonsus learned of Gerard's death, he commissioned several Fathers of his Congregation to put in writing all they knew about him. These notes he forwarded to Caione for the compilation of a life. The result was a rough sketch containing all that could then be known about its subject. This sketch Caione fashioned later into a more systematic life, which, however, he would never publish, as he did not consider his book up to the mark from a literary standpoint.

In the course of time this second manuscript got mislaid ;

but as the two other contemporary biographers had already drawn largely from it, its loss was not an irreparable disaster. Caione's first manuscript also disappeared and remained hidden away for long years amongst old papers of no value, until it was discovered in recent times. It should be noted that the second manuscript, though a fuller and more orderly piece of work, was not, strangely enough, so reliable in certain details as the first, with the result that inaccuracies crept into the pages of the two other contemporaries. The discovery of the first manuscript has enabled later biographers to correct them.

The value of Caione's *Notizie* is obvious. They are from the pen of a contemporary of St. Gerard, of one who was an eye-witness of his acts and who eventually became his last superior in Caposele ; they are based on authentic information supplied by other contemporary Redemptorists, including the holy Founder himself ; moreover, they were put together by a learned and very holy man. Unfortunately, I was unable to procure Caione's work either in the original Italian or in a translation, so that my quotations from his pages, though taken from the Italian as found in another life, are necessarily second-hand. In the footnotes I refer to them simply as : *Caione*.

Next comes ANTONIO MARIA TANNOIA, in many ways the Saint's greatest biographer. This Servant of God and pillar of his Congregation was born in Corato about 1724. He entered the Institute when it was fifteen years old and when he himself was nineteen, lived in it for forty years during the lifetime of its Founder, survived him for twenty-one years more, and died in 1808. He was novice master for twenty-four years, became rector, procurator and consultor-general, and likewise took part in the great law-

making chapter of 1764. Tannoia, too, was a most saintly
man as well as a very learned one, and a wise and faithful
counsellor of Alphonsus, to whom the Saint turned in his
many perplexities and cares. More than once, we are told,
he was rapt in ecstasy, and he practised much more austerity
than he preached, going supperless to bed for thirty-three
years. He stood high for his scholarly attainments, not
only amongst his brethren, but in learned circles outside;
and from an inscription beneath a painting made of him
after death we learn amongst other things that in recognition
of his scholarship and literary output he was unanimously
voted into the ranks of the Florentine Academy. Tannoia
is best known to-day for his monumental life of his Founder.
The writer on " St. Alphonsus " in the Catholic Encyclo-
pedia—no mean judge in these matters—speaks of it as
" one of the great biographies of literature," and refers to
its author as " a Boswell in collecting facts." We do know
that two years after the death of Alphonsus, Tannoia visited
every place where the Saint had preached a mission, as
well as Saint Agatha of the Goths, where he had ruled as
bishop.

How Tannoia came to write the life of St. Gerard must
be told in his own words. "It was entrusted to Father Caione,"
he tells us in his preface, " who at the time was rector of the
house of Caposele, where Gerard died. He had in fact
gathered much material for it, but could not see his way
to publishing it in the midst of the unceasing cares that
absorbed him. When reports of the continuous miracles that
were being daily wrought got about amongst the faithful,
many people began to express a wish to read his life. Then
it was that I was set the task in place of Father Caione.
At first this arrangement met with no better success; and

if the book is in print to-day, it is due to Brother Gerard himself, who pledged me to the writing of it by working a miracle. While at S. Angelo dei Lombardi in 1786, I was seized with a mortal illness. I went to Caposele, where the malady grew worse instead of better. In the evening of September 9th, Father Januarius Orlando, seeing I was in great pain, said to me : ' Promise Brother Gerard to write his life and you'll be cured.' As I was wanting in confidence, I did not follow his suggestion. On the morning of the 10th, the thirteenth day of my illness, I was at the point of death. In these circumstances, despairing of any human aid, I turned full of faith to the Brother and exclaimed : ' Gerard, help me ! ' I had no sooner spoken than I was *suddenly . . . . in un subito* freed from all illness. The blessed Brother bestowed this favour on me as soon as I had invoked his patronage ; and this same favour has now compelled me to show my gratitude by writing his life."

Undertaken in these circumstances and under such auspices Tannoia's work could scarcely have been anything but a success. It was printed for the first time in Naples, in 1804, and numerous editions and translations have since followed. Its author is spoken of in the process as " a most learned and virtuous writer . . . who was not only a contemporary, but who lived as a confrère both with St. Alphonsus and the Venerable Gerard, and to whom the holy Founder entrusted the duty, in company with another Father, of scrutinising Gerard's way of life during a certain critical period."—(*Respons. ad Animadvers.* § 213).

Father John Camillus Ripoli, who was superior-general of the Congregation from 1832-1850, and who, with knowledge got first-hand from Gerard's contemporaries, gave the fullest and most invaluable testimony in the process, is very explicit on the merits of Tannoia's work. Ripoli had heard from him, " seated on a bench " (a homely detail) the story of his miraculous cure and the promise to write Gerard's life. He then proceeds in his deposition : " Faithful to his promise, he wrote the life, after having gathered his materials from eye-witnesses, confessors, and such as knew the Servant of God intimately. These were people of marked piety and learning . . . . Never therefore can Father Tannoia be too highly praised for his search after trustworthy persons of proved virtue and knowledge, who had been eye-witnesses of Gerard's doings in their respective localities, with a view to procuring full and scrupulously accurate information. And if he succeeded in his quest, it was due to his remarkable flair for tapping the right sources. He confined himself to recording facts in all their unvarnished truth."— In Apost. no. 3, § 71, 73.

Another Father—Francesco Alfani—who became rector in Pagani, speaks in the same strain both of the author and of his book. The authenticity of the latter he never heard questioned, though he spent forty years in the Congregation. —Ibid. § 76.

It need scarcely be said that there is no discrepancy between the above high commendation of Tannoia's work and the discovery of certain inaccuracies in the light of fresh materials to which he had no access. Though I have not been able to consult any recent edition of Tannoia's life of St. Gerard, I presume that such inaccuracies have been rectified. This should be especially true of the life by Claudio Benedetti for reasons that I will state later on. When all is said and done, none but an inspired historian is exempt from the possibility of such revision.

The only edition of Tannoia's life I have been able to

obtain was the English one published in the Oratorian Series in 1849. As a translation it falls very short of perfection. Fortunately, through the kind offices of confrères of the English province—which I here gratefully acknowledge —I was able to procure the Italian life by Benedetti above mentioned. As this embodies a great deal of Tannoia's original text, I was able to take practically all I needed directly from it. Unless otherwise stated, the footnotes referring to Tannoia's life refer to his original text. The high numbers of the paging in the English edition is accounted for by the fact that the *Life of St. Gerard Majella* forms only most of the second half of the Oratorian volume entitled : *The Lives of the Companions of St. Alphonso Liguori*. In most cases I have ventured to make the language of the Oratorian translation a little more readable.

The third and last contemporary biographer of St. Gerard is JOSEPH LANDI, another man of more than ordinary holiness and culture. As a clerical student of the diocese of Salerno, he entered the young Congregation in the same year as Tannoia and died in it in 1797. Besides taking part in the same general chapter of 1764, he filled the offices of rector and novice master. One of his novices—Clement Hofbauer —was eventually canonised. Landi was, moreover, the official chronicler of his Institute, and his work bears the mark of uncommon industry and thoroughness. His two lives of the Saint were never published and exist only in manuscript. So much for St. Gerard's contemporary biographers. As we shall see, nothing but death prevented St. Alphonsus himself from writing a life of his illustrious son.

Before mentioning the chief modern lives I have used, I must say a word or two about the *Acts of the Ordinary* (*or Diocesan*) *and Apostolic* (*or Roman*) *Processes of the*

Beatification and Canonisation of Gerard Majella. These I have perused in their entirety. Their authoritative value is, of course, unquestionable. They form the basis of the Church's discussion in these matters and on them she grounds her verdict. Nor is she satisfied with knowledge and truthfulness on the part of those whom she calls upon to give evidence : she imposes on them the sacred guarantee of an oath. And this oath she requires each witness to take individually and to repeat as often as he is called upon to give his testimony. By it, moreover, the witness binds himself to declare whatever he knows either directly or indirectly, whether it be for or against the Servant of God, whether it furthers his cause or obstructs it.

Though, when the official inquiry into Gerard's virtues and miracles was opened, there was but one surviving eye-witness, still an unusually large number of people gave their sworn testimony to what they themselves had heard from eye-witnesses. To quote the words of the postulator of Gerard's cause, " although I have seen many ancient causes, I have met with none supported by so many witnesses who had got their information from those who were themselves eye-witnesses and contemporaries of the Servant of God. In the Apostolic process eighty-two witnesses were examined ; in the Ordinary process, excluding such as had given their testimony in the Apostolic, eighty. There were thus one hundred and sixty-two witnesses in all." All my quotations from the Acts I have taken first-hand from their voluminous pages. In the footnotes I refer to the Ordinary and Apostolic processes thus : *In Ord. In Apost.*

To come finally to the later biographies I have used, I am indebted to the same English confrères for an old Italian life and also for the first life of the Saint to appear in French.

The former, printed in Naples in 1847, is from the pen of Father Celestino Berruti, who from 1855-1869 was superior-general of the Neapolitan houses, which circumstances had kept separated from their brethren for some years. Here and there in his pages we come across incidents not found in the older biographies. There is a curious absence of precise dates in his book, as if he almost affected the *In illo tempore* of the Gospel !

The first French life just mentioned is by Frederick Kuntz, a Redemptorist, who conceals his identity on the title-page. It appeared in 1878 and is a careful and orderly work.

Father Claudio Benedetti, to whom we have referred more than once, wrote two lives of the Saint in Italian : a large imposing volume of 500 pages published in Rome on the occasion of Gerard's beatification in 1893, and a smaller one—a compendium of the former—which appeared for the solemnity of the canonisation in 1904. Both have the advantage of being written by the Postulator General of the Congregation of the Most Holy Redeemer, *viz.*, by one officially charged with the furtherance of the causes of its Servants of God. This gives them an authority of a special kind. And this is why I have taken it for granted that whatever the author has taken from Tannoia is correct, or at least has been subjected to correction. The larger life proved invaluable ; indeed I could scarcely have done without it.

Amongst the other modern French lives that I consulted I may mention in particular that by Dunoyer, the sixth edition of which appeared in 1925. It is very full and very readable.

In English St. Gerard has not fared too well, certainly not as well as his popularity deserves or would lead us to expect. To pass over pamphlet lives and the Oratorian translation of Tannoia already mentioned, we have really nothing—at least in these parts—but a translation from the German life by Charles Dilgskron, C.SS.R. and a life by the late Father Vassall-Phillips, C.SS.R. The former, though very full, leaves much to be desired as a translation and, I think, is scarcely obtainable now. The latter is excellent as far as it goes and is deservedly still on the market ; but it is on the short side. We think therefore that a life that will present a larger and fuller portrait of the Saint will be welcomed by his now innumerable lovers in the English-speaking Catholic world. A war-torn Europe closed my way to sources of information that I should have very much liked to have open ; however, what I failed to procure was more of an accidental than an essential nature, and whatever it might have added to the interest of the book, it could have made no change in the veracity of its contents.

J. C.

SAINT GERARD MAJELLA
(1726 - 1755)

CHAPTER I

TWO CHILDREN

IN Southern Italy the scene of our story is laid. Since we entered upon the writing of it, much has happened to that fair and historic land. Blind and inexorable, the destroying hand of the greatest of wars has moved over her face, leaving it torn and bloody. The skies above her and the seas that wash her shores have been made horrible with the sights and sounds of the conflict. Her mountains have been turned into fortresses reverberating to the thunder of great guns ; her fields sown thick with instruments of death ; her vineyards and olive-groves and gardens shot and trampled into a worthless tangle. Her rivers have run red with the blood of contending armies foreign to her soil. Monuments of a distant and venerable past, beautiful in their leisurely decay, have been hurried to their end and stately buildings blasted into premature ruin. Whole populations have been uprooted from the homesteads of their fathers and have fled from towns and villages changed into smoking rubble. And that land that drew the tourists of the world will for years to come draw thousands from other lands to visit places where those other thousands lie, whom Italy never cradled and to whom she has given a grave.

We are not yet able to state with accuracy what
damage has been inflicted on those places associated with
the subject of our biography. The war has brought many
of them into sudden prominence, and many place-names
that would have conveyed little or no meaning to people
beyond the frontiers of Italy have become known to the
world overnight by press and radio in the official *communiqués* from the front and have figured on the war
maps of our papers.

In Southern Italy's province of the Basilicata, on the
site of old Numistri, where, in B.C. 210. Roman Marcellus
and Carthagenian Hannibal once fought an inconclusive
battle, stands the town of Muro. Its situation gives it
charm, and as far as the winds of heaven are concerned,
security. Perched on the lower slopes of the sheltering
Apennines and tucked in on three sides by hills, it looks
southwards across the vast stretch of the Apulian plain
fertile and fair to the eye. The central Apennines cul-
minate in the *Gran Sasso d'Italia* and in a range bearing,
curiously enough, the family name of the saint whose
life we are writing. The *Majella Mountains*, soaring
at their highest over nine thousand feet into the sky, have
been mentioned more than once in the advance of the
famous Eighth Army. They wear their snows right into
July, showing their peaks with a peculiarly delicate and
compelling loveliness against the spotless blue. In this
they are eloquently typical of him whose sanctity so
outsoared that of many holy men amongst whom he
lived and who dazzled his contemporaries with the white
radiance of his soul.

Muro's streets meander carelessly up and down the
rocky ridge on which it is built, and the narrow plateau

on the crest is shared between a beautiful cathedral, the episcopal palace and a mediaeval castle frowning down on the peace and loveliness below. Like most buildings of the kind, the *Castello* has grim secrets. Two of these we now know : Henry, the son of Frederick II and Isabella of England, died within its walls in 1254, poisoned, it is supposed, by his half-brother Conrad ; and one hundred and twenty-seven years later, the same walls echoed the stifled screams of Joan the First, Naples' hapless but un-edifying queen, whose beauty and accomplishments were an inspiration for Petrarch and Boccaccio. While a prisoner of her adopted son Carlo of Durazzo, she was smothered between two mattresses.

Muro has had its good days and its evil. Amongst its major tribulations we read of two earthquakes—the one in 1694, the other in 1857—which wrought great havoc. Each time, however, the little town rose bravely from its ruins. It has been an episcopal city since 1059 ; its see is suffragan of Conza, and in the long line of its bishops we find an Orsini cardinal, the poet Gian Carlo Coppola, and Alfonso Pacello, the founder of a Congregation of priests. The religious needs of Muro were well provided for, and at the time of which we write, the brown of St. Francis' habit was almost part of the local colour-scheme. Besides houses of the Minor Capuchins and the Minor Conventual Fathers, it was also blessed with one of those power-houses of prayer and penance run by the daughters of St. Clare. The atmosphere of the town was thoroughly Catholic and wholesome, and many a young lad, answering the call to higher things, knocked at the Friary door. According to one biographer, the towns-people enjoyed quite a reputation for affability and good manners.[1] But there were exceptions to this, as the hero of our story had but too good reason for knowing.

A bronze statue stands in Muro's town erected to the memory of one of her sons named Gerard Majella, a young man who did not live out his thirtieth year. He did no brilliant soldiering in her defence, dictated no national or civic policy, built up no flourishing business in her midst, made no contribution to his country's literature and art. He just became a saint; and nothing puts a place so precisely and so permanently on the map, in the Catholic world at least, as having been the birthplace of a saint. Within Muro's walls Gerard Majella was born and nursed; from her girdling hills and vales he drew his native air; his first steps abroad were along her streets; within her boundaries he looked for the first time at the great world in miniature; he was registered amongst her children. Muro now is holy ground.

Amongst the eight thousand inhabitants who made up the population of Muro in the early part of the eighteenth century was a man called Domenico Majella, a tailor by trade. He married one Benedetta Cristina Galella, who bore him five children, and in the following order: Brigida; a boy Gerardo, who went home to heaven in a week; Anna Elisabetta; another Elisabetta and, finally, another Gerardo—or Gerard, as we shall henceforth call him—whom the world knows. It is reasonable to suppose, particularly in the case of those saints who are destined to high sanctity from early childhood, that they are given by God into the keeping of parents—

---

[1] *Vie*, par un Père Rédemptoriste, p. 6.

of at least a mother—peculiarly fitted for their delicate
and holy task. After all, the richest soil can lie fallow,
and an enemy may sow cockle, and the birds of the air
may come and eat the good seed up. And a mother
may make or mar a saint. Fortunately there was nothing
to fear on that score in the Majella home. Domenico
was a God-fearing Christian who took his Christianity
and its implications seriously ; Benedetta was in all
things worthy of him and rose at once to the height of
her great calling ; from the meagre details we are given
of the three girls we may gather that they quickly
realised that in their little brother they had a saint in
the making, and a sort of awe of him seems to have
fallen upon them from the start.

When was St. Gerard Majella born ? When was he
baptised ? The year and the month give no trouble :
the year was 1726, the month April. But when we come
to the date, his biographers are obviously in difficulties :
even the earliest of them—Landi and Caione—giving
April 23rd, while Tannoia gives April 6th as the day
of his birth. And little wonder, for they were presented
with the two following certificates of Gerard's baptism.
We translate them literally from the Latin : No. 1. "In
Muro, on this the 6th day of the month of April, in the
year of Our Lord one thousand seven hundred and
twenty-six, the Most Illustrious and Reverend Lord
Felix Coccicone, Archpriest, baptised in the Cathedral
church of the Assumption of Holy Mary the child born
this morning in lawful wedlock of Domenico Majella
and Benedetta Galella, of the parish of St. Mark the
Evangelist, the name of Hierardus Maria having been
given him, and the midwife Beatrix Picinno having

acted as sponsor. Signed . . . FELIX Coccicone, Arch-priest."

No. 2. " Gerard, the son of Domenico Majella, of the district of Baniani and of Benedetta Galella, married, was baptised by the Reverend Felix Coccicone, Arch-priest, on the 23rd of the month of April, 1726, Elisabetta Jacullo acting as sponsor. In the pro-cathedral church of the Most Holy Trinity on this twenty-third day of the month of April, 1726. Signed . . . F. *COCCICONE*, Archpriest."

A few years ago, in the *Analecta, C.SS.R.*, an official periodical published in Rome,[1] Father Palmieri came forward with a solution of the problem created by the discrepancy between these two documents ; it seems to us quite satisfactory. The baptismal registers them-selves from which the documents were drawn were lost in a fire that occurred on June 10th, 1893. Without burdening the reader with details, we briefly summarise Father Palmieri's work. On the 6th April, 1726, Gerard Majella was born. As the infant was alarmingly frail, his parents, fearing a repetition of what had occurred in the case of his tiny predecessor and namesake, rushed their precious burden in the arms of the midwife to the cathedral, there being but one baptismal font in Muro at the time. Everything was gone through hurriedly, with an eye to essentials. As it was Saturday, the name of *Mary* was added to the Christian name, according to the custom of the day. It is interesting to note that on that same day St. Alphonsus Liguori was receiving the diaconate in Naples.

---

[1] Annus XIX, Fasc. i.

As the days went by, however, baby Gerard II, as we may truly call him, had, by means of sundry crowings and a certain liveliness of limb, been intimating to his immediate world that he had come to stay. He waxed strong—never very strong, poor child !—but strong enough to grow into one of God's greatest lovers and to become a canonised saint. As we have seen, the ceremony of April 6th had not been a leisurely affair and accidentals had to be waived. There was no time for sentimental choosing of godmothers, and so the good offices of the midwife had been requisitioned. Even the archpriest seems to have caught the general infection of rush and hustle, calling the infant *Hierardus* instead of *Gerardus*, at least when entering his name in the register. Accordingly, on Easter Tuesday, the 23rd April, the baby was brought, this time to the church of the Most Holy Trinity, whither the baptismal font had been removed, pending repairs to the cathedral. There the full ceremonies of baptism were supplied and by the same Archpriest Felix Coccicone. However, when making this further entry, the good man used undue economy of language, making no mention of the baptism so hastily conferred in the cathedral and thus giving rise to the confusion that have set Gerard's biographers by the ears. Moreover, he seems to have deliberately avoided giving the date of the child's birth, as posterity might be disedified on discovering that in a Catholic town of Muro's standing there were children who were not baptised till seventeen days after birth. This time Gerard was given his true name and, strangely enough, without the *Mary*. This time, too, a godmother was chosen : she was some relative or at least a friend of the Majella family, named Elisabetta Jacullo.

In one sense the baptism of a normal child is recorded in utter darkness ; there is no past to project a ray, however dim and unsure, upon the future, and guess-work is futile. Father Felix Coccicone had neither the time nor probably the taste for indulging in such reflec-tions as he went through the routine work of entering the baptism of that sickly scrap of humanity that was Gerard Majella. He did not know he had written a name in the parish register that would one day be written in the register of the Saints. Neither did he know that amongst the innumerable wonders in the career that had just begun would be this, that, twenty-eight years later, while in the city of Naples—minus telegraph and telephone and radio—Gerard would suddenly announce to his horrified company that a few hours previously the Archpriest Francesco Coccicone, Felix's brother in the flesh and in the priesthood, had been stabbed to death, fifty miles away, in the streets of his native Muro. A letter duly brought the news of the tragedy to Naples : the murder had been committed in the place that Gerard named and on the day and at the hour when Gerard spoke.[1] Father Felix did not know either—nor did anybody know—how closely that infant and the name he bore would be linked in future ages and the world over with the critical dawn of life for thousands of little

---

[1] There can be no doubt that it was Padre Francesco Coccicone who was murdered and not his brother Felice, as some biographers would seem to have it. Benedetti received the following communi-cation on the subject from Mgr. Raffaele Capone, the Bishop of Muro :—
" D. Francesco Coccione succeeded as archpriest his brother Don Felice, who died a natural death on Sept. 7th, 1742. On Oct. 14th, 1754, the innocent man was cruelly done to death by a nefarious personage and was buried in the cathedral on the 15th."—*Vita*, p. 469.

ones and how many of them would be given his name by grateful mothers.

Gerard himself was called after another *St. Gerard*. This holy man was born of a noble family of Piacenza, in the middle of the eleventh century, made his way to Potenza, the capital of the Basilicata, ruled and edified its diocese for eight years and was canonised shortly after his death by Pope Callistus II. He won great renown by his virtues and by the miracles he wrought both during life and after death, and devotion to him went back a long way. His young protégé resembled him in more ways than one, particularly in his great innocence of life and in his untiring prayer. But the " vita mirifica "[1] of St. Gerard of Potenza was destined to be out-distanced by the still more wondrous life of St. Gerard of Muro, as well as by the world-wide allegiance that was to be given him.[2]

The dawn of Gerard's sanctity broke early and re-splendent. He was a precociously holy boy. Now precociously holy boys and girls are not to the liking of many readers, nor apparently to the liking of certain hagiographers, who seem to resent their appearance. Born saints, as they are wrongly called, wearing their halo in their nurse's arms, seem so hopelessly beyond our ken and reach. It is so much easier to consort with

---

[1] From Hymn for First Vespers of Feast, Oct. 30th.

[2] One would think that the following lines taken from the formula for the blessing of water in honour of the holy bishop of Potenza had been written in honour of the holy laybrother of Muro :—

" " Congaudeant aegri, subito veniente salute ;
Pelluntur morbi, febresque fugantur acutae ;
Redduntur claudis gressus et lumina caecis ;
Pelluntur morbi, febresque fugantur acutae."
v. Bollandists, *Acta Sanctorum*, Octob.

those whose feet have walked the same hard human ways as ours, with something of the dust and mire showing on them. And so, reasonably enough, we like to read of saints who began at any rate much as we did, and we listen with a particular relish to what was particularly human in their childhood, from the pranks and gambols of the boy Giovanni Bosco to the dark delinquencies of the boy Augustine. With these as models we feel we have a better chance. Now we must face the fact at once : such human and heartening beginnings have no place in Gerard's childhood. *His* little feet seem scarcely to have touched our soiled earth. And so we hear of no high crimes and misdemeanours in the home, of no infringement of nursery bye-laws, of no impish evasion of maternal authority, of no small boy's unchivalrous behaviour towards big sisters. Such things raise a reminiscent and understanding smile when met with in the lives of the saints in delightful contrast with the towering holiness of their maturity. They throw a homely and familiar atmosphere around them, in which, partially at any rate, we recognise ourselves. Now, as far as Gerard's early years in particular are concerned, we have no such fare to set before the reader. His childhood falls into another category and is rather the emerging of an angel than the growth of a man. In him grace seems indeed to have silenced the instincts of nature, though, as one biographer puts it, he was "heroic from his very childhood."[1]

Even the ordinary games and toys of children seem to have had no allure for Gerard. Not that he was in

---

[1] Berruti, p. 177.

any way gloomy or aloof ; on the contrary, his countenance was always unusually joyous and unruffled, and
the " good odour of Christ " was already emanating
from him. But almost from babyhood his mind, his
heart, his whole being were gripped by God. As soon
as conscious interest in anything was awakened within
him, the little boy was absorbed by what was divine.
When scarcely five, he would trot along gaily by his
mother's side, whenever she went to church. There he
took everything in and on returning home would sing
in his uncertain treble the hymns he had been listening
to and in his own childish fashion piece together the
ceremonies he had witnessed. With him this was no
mere fun, but a serious and elaborate business. He
would set up a miniature altar on a table and deck it
out with flowers and pictures of this saint and that,
St. Michael always getting the post of honour. A few
candle butts coaxed from the sacristan—a relative of
the family—solved the lighting difficulty ; and the little
fellow was soon busy playing the priest at Mass and
Benediction. He had his congregation, too, though he
did not guess it ; he did not see his mother and the girls
—and a neighbour or two at times—with eyes and ears
glued to chinks and keyholes unconsciously repeating
what was said of old : " What an one, think ye, shall
this child be ? "[1] Benedetta especially, like another
Mother long ago, " kept all these words in her heart."[2]

Such were Gerard's pastimes. The fact need not get
on our nerves. Whether it is God or a game, it is all a

---

[1] Luke, i, 66.
[2] Ibid., ii, 51.

question of interest. There is nothing morbid or un-reasonable in a little boy making altars who, as a man, would spend every moment free from duty—ever his dearest devotion—hovering ecstatically about the taber-nacle. We read with delight of a Mozart scribbling harmonies with his baby fingers and of the future victor of Marengo and Austerlitz marshalling his tin soldiers. We look for these intimations of what is to come in the childhood of the world's great men ; why not in the childhood of the saints ? In his monumental work on the *Beatification and Canonisation of the Servants of God* Benedict XIV writes : " In tender years indications of future sanctity are gathered from the disregard of childish amusements and the pleasures of the world."[1] The " Infant Phenomenon " is not confined to the realm of fiction ; he is met with in the realm of fact. And if in the province of music and mathematics and languages, why not in the province of virtue ? If in the world of nature, why not in the world of grace ? The truth is that it is in this particular world of grace that cases of phenomenally early excellence are most frequently met with. The firmament of the Church is studded with these stars. What we would stress from the outset, however, in a life like Gerard's is that the exhibition of God's endowments, be they ever so premature and imposing, puts no saint beyond the pale of imitable sanctity, since no saint has ever been raised to the altars on the score of these endowments alone.

Had Gerard's infant activities been restricted to altar-building and playing the priest, we might well ask whether

---

[1] Vol. ii, p. 395.

there was anything further in them than a child's interest in the sound and stir and colour of Catholic ritual. But this was not the case. Not only did he kneel by his mother in church with a stillness and devotion that drew many an eye, but he loved to pray in the house as well, and they would often come upon him in some quiet corner holding childish but most real intercourse with God. Nor was this all. Even at this early date, this future athlete of the Crucified was already an adept at more than one of the pet performances of the trained ascetic, particularly at table, where he would set aside the tasty morsel or not drink sufficiently to quench his thirst. At times things took a more serious turn when he would fast in a way that awoke a mother's fears. This was going too far and she told him so. At her bidding the future saint of obedience would at once drop his youthful austerities and fall to his meals with a will. Benedetta scarcely knew what to think of it all. It pleased and puzzled the Catholic and the mother in her, and when these early foreshadowings of coming sainthood in her boy were thrust upon her, she could but gaze at him with tenderness and wonder and say : " *Figlio mio, sii benedetto* . . . Bless you, my son."[1] Shortly before her death, when speaking of that son, then a Redemptorist and still living, she would recall the fasting and praying of his childhood and say that her son was indeed born for heaven.

Heaven did not wait long before letting this be known. The plateau crowning the rocky slope on which Muro

---

[1] Benedetti, p. 2.

lies ends abruptly on its northern side, where the ground falls steeply to meet the *Rescio* as it goes thundering through the glen. A narrow pathway rudely cut out of the rock leads precariously down, crosses the stream by the old arch of the *Ponte delle Ripe* and climbs a gentle rise on the other side. From here it traverses fields and vineyards for a distance of about two miles, until it reaches the famous sanctuary of the *Madonna di Capotignano*. This old church enshrines a small wooden statue of the Mother of God—her Divine Child supported on her left arm—venerated and invoked for centuries under the title of *Our Lady of Graces*. It is one of those images of Mary with which Italy abounds, not usually associated with any of the great names in Italian art, but having behind them centuries of trustful supplication on the one side and of answering largess on the other. At its feet generations have laid their sorrows and perplexities, their broken and aching bodies, their stained and ailing souls. On July 2nd, the sanctuary's special feast, great is the forgathering of the pilgrims ; from every side they come, not merely from Muro's town, but from all the adjoining parishes. When Mass is over and devotion satisfied, they disperse and dine in family groups on God's green grass.

Now Gerard, young as he was, knew this sanctuary and the way to it, for Benedetta, like all good mothers in the neighbourhood, had more than once brought her children there. As may be seen, the approach from Muro was none too easy for anybody ; for a small boy of six to make his way there alone was something of an adventure. But saints are daring spirits, even when they are small. Moreover, Guardian Angels are not for nothing, and Gerard's kindred angel knew the treasure he had been given charge over and saw to it that when going down that perilous stairway, the child did not dash his little feet against a stone.

And now we are presented with the first of those wonders in a life that is a glittering chain of them. Scarcely had the child entered the church when the statue of that other Child in His Mother's arms grew animate, smiled him a welcome, and leaving those arms, joined him in mysterious play. When it was over, Mary's Child gave Gerard a little loaf exceeding white.[1] Now that a boy of Gerard's years and temperament should *imagine* he saw the Divine Child smile on him on this one occasion is quite conceivable ; to *imagine*, however, the Divine Child leaving His Mother's arms, approaching him and actually playing with him, and then to *imagine* having received from Him a loaf which he actually carried home and ate would, we must own, demand a powerful imagination indeed. Though, as we shall presently see, the boy did not then realise the greatness either of the Giver or the gift, at any rate his divine Playmate flooded his young heart with an unwonted joy. Hugging his treasure, he trotted home as fast as the rough path would let him to show Mamma what

---

[1] It is interesting, and may be useful, to quote here what we read in the Autobiography of the Little Flower. Recalling the grave illness that seized her when she was ten years old and the agonizing supplications made in her behalf to our Blessed Lady by her sisters, she writes :—

" Suddenly the statue came to life (*s'anima*) ! the Virgin Mary grew beautiful, so beautiful that never shall I find words to convey that divine beauty. Her countenance breathed a sweetness, a kindness, an unutterable tenderness ; but what went to the very depths of my soul was *her entrancing smile*."—*Histoire D'Une Ame*, chap. iii, p. 49.

he got and tell her everything. On being asked from
whom he had got the loaf, he replied at once with the
artlessness and adequacy of truth : " *Da un bellissimo
ragazzo* . . . . from a most beautiful boy."[1] Benedetta
showed her pleasure. Evidently some kind lady had
met him near her house as he was going through the
vineyards. No doubt the little fellow looked tired and
hungry after such a long rough trudge for a child of his
years, and she thought he would be the better of something to eat, of some nice white bread such as she had.
And no doubt she had given her own little boy the
pleasure of handing it to Gerard. It was certainly most
kind of her, whoever she was. And Benedetta thought
no more of it, though the unusual whiteness of the bread
did not escape the housewife's practised eye.

But it was not so with Gerard. The Divine Child did
not stoop to such familiarities without making a divine
impression. That smile, the touch of those hands, the
thrill of that Presence, though but vaguely understood,
could not be forgotten. And surely that little white
loaf, which must have tasted very good, went for something in luring the boy back to Capotignano. And so
morning after morning, for many mornings, he slipped
out of the house and made his way to Mary's sanctuary ;
and each time he brought home a little white loaf, of
which he duly ate. Whether the mysterious loaves were
shared all round—a likely thing enough, Gerard being
what he was— ; whether any peculiarity besides their
unusual whiteness was remarked in the eating of them,
we are not told. But this unusual whiteness and, most

---

[1] In Apost. no. 5, § 49.

probably, an unusually excellent flavour as well aroused
Benedetta's interest. Where were these loaves baked?
Where did they keep coming from? It was time to
look into the matter.

Meanwhile Anna Elisabetta in particular had become
very interested and kept plying her little brother with
questions about the donor of the strange loaves. All
she could draw from him was that he got them from
the son of a beautiful lady. But this beautiful lady
and her son, whoever she and he might be, seemed to
be turning up very often. We do not know for how long
a time or how frequently Gerard went to Capotignano,
but he certainly went there many times and the apparitions were many times repeated. The girl's curiosity
at last became too much for her. One morning, as the
boy left the house, she slipped out after him and followed
at a safe distance, keeping him in view till he reached
the church. There, through the half-open door, she
found herself a dazed onlooker at a repetition of all
the prodigious occurrences of these mornings. What
Gerard saw she saw. Whether she had already surmised
anything of this nature or not, in view of the undoubted
premature holiness of her little brother, there it was
at any rate staring her in the face, as over a hundred
years later similar happenings stared Bernadette
Soubirous in the face,—there it was, a plain indubitable
fact seen by her own two good eyes. There was no
getting away from it. Now at least she knew beyond
all yea or nay who this *bella signora* and this *bellissimo
ragazzo* were. Anna Elisabetta could not get home
fast enough to tell her mother. It was now Benedetta's
turn to be curious; she decided at once to sift matters

thoroughly for herself. She, too, stole out quietly one morning to Capotignano, but before Gerard had left, and took up her station in the church where she could see without being seen. The same astounding sight met her eyes. And what a sight for a mother's heart! According to one witness, Benedetta, on leaving the sanctuary of Capotignano, noticed one of the little loaves under her son's arm and thus became assured of its origin.[1] According to several, it was Our Lady herself who at times presented the little loaf to Gerard, for on one occasion, when visiting the sanctuary with his mother, the boy remarked, as he pointed to the statue : " Mamma, there is the lady who often gave me the bread," adding, as he pointed to the Divine Child, " There is the little boy with whom I played."[2] Twenty years later, when Gerard was a Redemptorist laybrother whose holiness and miracles were in all men's mouths, his sister Brigida went to see him in the monastery at Iliceto. As they chatted about old times and recalled this thing and that of their childhood, Capotignano and all that happened there was mentioned. " Now I know," Gerard remarked with his usual directness and simplicity, " that the Child who used to give me that bread was the Infant Jesus, and I thought He was a child like myself." Then, when his sister roguishly suggested his returning to Muro and seeing the Child again and getting more of the mysterious bread, he replied : " There is no need for me to return there ; I find Him everywhere now."[3]

---

[1] In Ord. no. 5, § 63.
[2] Benedetti, p. 5.
[3] Tannoia, cap. ii.

As the Postulator of Gerard's cause was careful to remind the Promoter of the Faith, or the Devil's Advocate, as he is popularly called, when the latter was throwing a great deal of official cold water on all these alleged favours, Gerard was far from being the first or the only child amongst the saints to be thus privileged. From numerous instances he selected one—the well-known case of Blessed Hermann Joseph—and quoted in detail similar wondrous occurrences as he finds them set down in the pages of those most sober-minded and scholarly hagiographers the Bollandists.

It was not in Capotignano alone that these two children —Jesus and Gerard—were thus visibly and miraculously associated. Just outside Muro was a large well-wooded park, the property of the De Cillis family, which was evidently thrown open to children. Gerard often went there with such companions as he could induce to share in his pious pastimes. He would marshal them in processional order and lead the way round about the trees in prayer and hymn, in imitation of Church ceremonies. One evening, while so engaged, all at once he stopped in front of an almond tree, and fashioning a rude cross from two sticks, fixed it in some way to the trunk and called upon his youthful company to venerate it. Even at this early date his sanctity had a subduing power and they readily acquiesced. As the children prayed, the tree was suddenly lit up, " looking like an altar covered with lights," as one eye-witness puts it.[1] So great was the brilliance that it was seen outside the precincts of the park, in the whole neighbourhood and even in parts

---

[1] Benedetti, p. 5.

of the town. Everybody saw the light. Gerard saw
more. From the midst of this refulgence emerged his
Divine Playmate of Capotignano. Down from the tree
He sweetly floated, bearing in His hand the now familiar
little white loaf. This He gave to Gerard as Benedetta
and Anna Elisabetta had seen Him give it before. The
boy evidently ate it there and then, for on being asked
by his mother that evening why he had let his supper
go untouched, he replied that he had already eaten, as
the Child had given him the bread. It was the Child
again. According to the sworn testimony of a priest,
Gerard was not the only one to see the Divine Child
on this occasion. He states : " The Archpriest De Cillis
used to tell me that he was an eyewitness of the Child
Jesus descending from the illuminated tree " ; and he
adds : " The Archpriest De Cillis, with many others
from the neighbourhood, ran to see the illuminated tree
and were struck with amazement."[1]

Nor was this all. More than once, as the boy knelt
by his mother's side at Mass, he was given to see the
same Divine Friend of his childhood, in the guise of
a little child, in the hands that held aloft the consecrated Host, and when the Child disappeared at the
Communion of the priest, Gerard was heart-broken.
What took place at this part of the Mass perplexed
him sorely ; and one morning, on meeting the celebrant
afterwards in the sacristy, where Gerard had gone,
perhaps to renew his supply of candle butts, he remarked with pained surprise : " That's a nice thing
you did to eat a little child . . . . . *un piccirillo !* "[2]

---

[1] In Apost. no. 5, § 7.
[2] *ibid.* § 10

According to one witness, he was heard bewailing the fact that the priest had eaten ' *un bel bambino* '.[1] [2]

We have already mentioned Gerard's precocious abstemiousness and the alarming lengths to which it sometimes went. May we not suppose that the little white loaves, whatever heavenly vitamins they contained, went for something in keeping the child alive and well ? It would be idle to speculate on their nature.

---

[1] *Ibid.*, § 73.

[2] Here perhaps we may anticipate the possible objection that Gerard alone was the witness of such visions. Mgr. Farges writes (*Mystical Phenomena*, P. II, i, p. 399) : " We have no right to reject the vision of one alone, presuming that it has all the marks of authenticity . . . . under the pretext that he is the only seer and all the others present have heard or seen nothing. It is obvious that an apparition might quite well have shown itself to one whilst remaining invisible to the others. In fact, as history proves, this is what happens in the greater number of cases, St. Paul, Bernadette . . . . "

How such Eucharistic apparitions come about is explained by St. Thomas Aquinas as follows : " Such apparition comes about in two ways, when occasionally in this sacrament, flesh, or blood, or a child is seen. Sometimes it happens on the part of the beholders, whose eyes are so affected as if they outwardly saw flesh, or blood, or a child, while no change takes place in the sacrament. And this seems to happen when to one person it is seen under the species of flesh or of a child, while to others it is seen as before under the species of bread ; or when to the same individual it appears for an hour under the appearance of flesh or a child, and afterwards under the appearance of bread. Nor is there any deception there, as occurs in the feats of magicians, because such species is divinely formed in the eye in order to represent some truth, namely for the purpose of showing that Christ's body is truly under this sacrament ; just as Christ without deception appeared to the disciples who were going to Emmaus . . . . But it sometimes happens that such apparition comes about not merely by a change wrought in the beholders, but by an appearance which really exists outwardly. And this indeed is seen to happen when it is beheld by everyone under such an appearance, and it remains so not for an hour, but for a considerable time ; . . . . "

Summa, III, Q. 76, art. 8.   (Dominican transl.)

However these Eucharistic apparitions are explained, that they sometimes did occur is plainly admitted by the great Doctor and evidently causes him no surprise.

How they tasted ; what was thought of them by mother
and sisters, with whom they were surely shared ; whether
they were analysed or preserved in part we do not know.
This much we feel justified in saying, that these literally
God-given loaves symbolized another Bread that came
down from heaven. And surely, too, the bread of
Capotignano, whatever it was, created in the soul of
that angelic boy an early devouring hunger for the
Bread of angels. He had now learnt what the Mass
meant. He now knew of the transcendent prodigy of
the Consecration, and we are told that when the priest
raised aloft the sacred Host, he would bow his face
to earth and remain thus for an appreciable time.

These two little ones—Mary's son and Benedetta's—
had, during all these months of amazing intimacy, grown
in mutual love in a way altogether extraordinary. Whatever Gerard may have thought of the *bel bambino* of
Capotignano at that time, he had now been told what
Communion was, and he yearned for It only as a child
could yearn who had had his ravishing experiences.
Alas ! he had not yet reached the age required in those
days : he should be ten, and he was only eight !

Now one morning he was at Mass as usual. The
moment came for the faithful to receive, and communicants moved towards the altar rails. The celebrant
came down bearing the ciborium. Gerard watched and
hungered. It was more than he could bear, knowing
what he knew and loving as he loved. Driven by an
impulse he could no longer master, he left his place
and knelt at the rails. The priest came along distribut-
ing the sacred particles. He reached Gerard. He glanced
at the child, recognised him and passed him by. The

little boy remained kneeling for a few dazed moments
and then, realising it all, slowly rose and returned to
his place weeping bitterly. But all the hungering love
and all the frustrated yearning were not on Gerard's
side. Long ago, in the Garden of Gethsemane, when
men forgot for the moment who He was, Jesus said :
" Thinkest thou that I cannot ask my Father, and he
will give me presently more than twelve legions of
angels ? "[1] His Father could do the same now. This
time His Father gave Him one angel, and an archangel
to boot. That same night St. Michael, Prince of the
angelic host, overriding all the laws of Church and
nature herself, bore the Body of his Lord to him of
whom Leo XIII speaks as follows : " An angel seems
to have come down from heaven and appeared amongst
men."[2] Small wonder if, as the sequel will show, the
great Archangel had henceforth a special corner in
Gerard's heart all the days of his life. Here is how the
boy himself related the incident the following day to
a family friend : " Yesterday the priest would not give
me Communion, and last night I was given Communion
by St. Michael."[3] Berruti gives us an additional detail
which contains a spice of exultant rebuke which is not
without its charm on Gerard's childish lips. He writes :
" Early in the morning, Gerard full of joy after receiving
such a grace, went to the same church, entered the
sacristy, and seeing the priest who had turned him from
the altar, with delightful simplicity thus addressed him :

---

[1] Matt. xxvi, 53.
[2] *Litt. Apost. super Beatific. Ven. S. D. Gerardi Majella*, Romae.
1893.
[3] In Apost. no. 5, § 48.

' You turned me away from Holy Communion, and
Jesus Christ gave me Communion last night by means
of St. Michael.' "[1] We are not told how the priest received the little speech.

Now we wonder how many of our readers have already
made up their mind about this incident. We feel we
are not wronging them by supposing that they have
already dismissed it as the pretty dream of a holy child,
for one need not be a cynic or a poor Catholic to jump
at the conclusion. The Devil's Advocate jumped at it
—officially anyhow—when Gerard's amazing story was
being scrutinised by that most unemotional and objective
board of examiners in the world : the Sacred Congregation of Rites. Yet the obvious explanation of the
occurrence—the dream theory—was ruled out.[2]

Let us look at the incident for a moment. When it
occurred, Gerard had already shown unmistakably to
all who had eyes to see that he was no ordinary child
and that God was treating him in no ordinary way. A
child of his years who could pray and fast as he did and
whose one overmastering interest in life was God was
undoubtedly a phenomenon. Now such an unusual
interest in God on Gerard's part argued a correspondingly unusual interest in Gerard on the part of God.
Already he had been favoured to a rare degree and

---

[1] Pp. 19-20.
[2] The language employed by this personage during the process is
worth quoting : " The Apostolic Censors are not unreasonably of
opinion," he argued, " that all these pretty visions should be attributed
to the imagination of the Venerable youth ; and that when the
witnesses heard of them, they were led away by a hasty credulity
and related them as real facts." The most sceptical could not better
that. Yet the Devil's Advocate lost his case ! *Respons. ad Nov.
Animadvers. R.P.D. Promotor. Fid.* § 16, p. 34.

had been made the object of a most uncommon intervention on the part of Heaven. What had happened in the church of Capotignano and in the park near Muro had been witnessed by others and had later been attested to on oath. These supernatural events clearly pointed to an extraordinary destiny for the child. A continuance of them therefore would be reasonably looked for. In technical language there was an antecedent probability in its favour.

Again, though this miraculous Communion had no other witness but Gerard himself, who was then a little boy of eight, still we have his own statement that it did take place, and his testimony is by no means to be lightly set aside. At this time he was old enough to know what he was saying and what he was doing. It is admitted on all hands that he was a boy intelligent quite beyond his years, and he was clearly able to distinguish between a mere dream and an objective happening. We have all had realistic dreams, so realistic at times that, on awakening, we have wondered for a few bewildered moments if they were not true. But the first swift intake of familiar objects by returning consciousness was usually enough to shatter the illusion and assure us beyond all yea or nay that the supposed incident unquestionably had not happened. Like shadows before the sun, the persons and places of our dream melted away and as quick as thought receded into the realm of unsubstantial things. They were soon forgotten. But Gerard did not forget. All his life he remembered that miraculous Communion as something that had *happened, really happened,* and it awoke within him a new and quite remarkable devotion to the great Archangel which grew with his growth and accompanied him to the end.

Moreover, the boy was already a marvel of precocious sanctity, and anything like a lie on his lips would be unthinkable. Benedetta had not waited for the priest and the schoolmaster to instruct her child in his religion, and he had long since been grounded, not only in its mysteries, but in its moral obligations. It was not yesterday that the sinfulness of lying—no uncommon fault in childhood—had been driven home. He told what had occurred in simple unembroidered speech, and he told it to more than one. But, what is still more vital, when he was at the close of his life, and when his consummate holiness would have recoiled in horror from the shadow of a sin, he was given an obedience by his confessor to reveal the secrets of his soul, and amongst these secrets the miraculous Communion at the hands of the Archangel found a place. Caione, Landi and Tannoia, his three contemporary biographers, who all knew Gerard personally, soberly chronicle the event. Tannoia writes of it : " Such a signal favour would have remained unknown if Gerard's holy simplicity had not led him to reveal it to D. Alexander Piccolo, the goldsmith, who was his godfather, and to Catherine Zaccardi, his nurse. He also mentioned it to his director after he joined us. This was the origin of the great devotion which this holy brother entertained throughout his life for St. Michael the Archangel."[1] We need but add that Pope Leo XIII, in his Brief of Beatification, thus records the miraculous occurrence :

---

[1] English Edit., pp. 243-244.

" As Gerard was at prayer in his room that evening, St. Michael, to whom he had a most special devotion, stood before him shining with a most brilliant light, and, approaching the boy, gave him the Sacred Host and straightway returned to the choirs of the Blessed."[1] What is recorded in such a document is surely deserving of more than ordinary respect.

It was in truth a miraculous occurrence ; but they who are not prepared to meet the miraculous in the life of Gerard Majella have no business reading this book. There is a temptation, particularly nowadays, when the critics are abroad in such numbers, with their scalpels poised pitilessly over every page, to dismiss all such pretty stories with a smile and a shrug. It is too true that in the field of hagiography—as in other fields of history—the cockle of legend has been abundantly oversown amongst the wheat of fact, not indeed by an enemy but by injudicious and over credulous, if well-meaning friends. Historians and hagiographers are right in not waiting for the Day of Judgment to separate the two, and we are grateful to them for doing so. At the same time, in their admirable eagerness to sift the one from the other, to let us know where fact ends and legend begins—they may forget the danger of rooting up the wheat with the cockle, fact with fiction.

Before we leave this subject of Gerard's miraculous Communion, we would remind the reader that similar privileges have been recorded more than once in the lives of the saints. We read that St. Barbara, St. Juliana Falconieri, St. Mary Magdalen de 'Pazzi, St. Bona-

---

[1] *Litt. Apost. super Beatificat. Ven. S.D.Gerardi Majella.*

venture, St. Stanislaus Kostka and others received the
Eucharist in various miraculous ways. We are told,
for instance, that sometimes the Host flew from the
altar to the lips of St. Catherine of Sienna.[1]

When all is said and done, does the occurrence contain
anything intrinsically improbable or strange? If Our
Lord in His incomprehensible love, as far beyond our
fathoming as any other of His attributes, thought it
worth His while to give Himself miraculously to souls
and remain miraculously in their midst, even when His
doing so involved coldness, indifference, abandonment
and often appalling sacrilege, is it so far beyond belief
that once in a while He would work a further miracle
to satisfy His yearning for union with a heart that
yearned for union with Him as yearned the Saints,
as yearned a Gerard Majella? Obviously it is not a
question of His power, but of His love, and after all
that that love made Him do at the Last Supper, we
are prepared for any conceivable display of it. It is
just a question of more or less.

And seemingly it was to be a question of still more.
What Our Lord did not suffer His priests to do He
did Himself: as long ago in that Supper-room, where
one breathed nothing but miracle and love, He gave
Himself in Communion to His chosen followers with
His own hands, so did He now favour His little friend
and playmate. We have sworn testimony to the fact
that one day a priest found Gerard kneeling at the foot
of the altar. On asking what he was doing there, he got
the reply: " A little boy came out of the tabernacle

---

and gave me Communion."[1] It was the Child of Capotignano and of the park in Muro again. Whether this happened more than once is not stated.

All these favours seem to show Our Lord's wish to satisfy periodically, even at the cost of a miracle, Gerard's hunger for the Bread of life, until the day should come when the laws of the Church would allow him to receive It regularly. Two years had yet to pass. Long years they were, and many a time, as he assisted at Mass and watched the come-and-go of communicants, hot tears fell. At last, when Gerard reached his tenth year, the day of days arrived. We can scarcely call it his First Communion, in view of those that had gone before ; it was rather the official inauguration of a lifelong series. Thenceforth he would have loved to make daily Communion his daily joy ; to go a few times in the month, however, was all he was at first allowed : such was the ruling in those days. A little later authorities showed themselves more lenient by allowing him to receive twice or thrice a week, as well as on Sundays and festivals.

It goes without saying that after all this miraculous wooing of Gerard's heart on the part of his Divine Friend, devotion to His Eucharistic Presence became at once a marked feature of the boy's spiritual life. Never had the tabernacle a more ardent or unwearying visitor, and never, as we shall see, was friendship repaid so gloriously and so generously in kind. Even thus early in his career the little boy took every occasion to slip out and make his way to the parish church of St. Mark close by. Getting as near as he could to the tabernacle,

---

[1] Benedetti, p. 9.

he would spend hours on end in that divine company and, as in later years, he had literally to tear himself away. On hearing the bell ring for evening devotions, he would rush from the house and sweep along in the wake of his own enthusiasm any of his youthful comrades whom he chanced to meet, saying : " Come ! let us go and visit Jesus Christ our Prisoner . . . . . *il nostro carcerato,*"[1] thus summing up in a word the origin and end of the Real Presence in our midst.

When Gerard first met the Child Jesus, that Child was in His Mother's arms. It was from those blessed arms that Jesus came to him in Capotignano ; and surely that Mother must have looked down with a new delight on the novel scene : Jesus of Nazareth and Gerard of Muro playing their wondrous play. As we have already seen, from Mary too did Gerard receive the precious loaves. Strange it would have been had Mary not loved the child of Benedetta ; stranger still had Gerard not loved Mary. But love her he did with all the fresh exuberance of his young heart. He loved saying her Rosary and singing her hymns and keeping her festivals ; a generous increase in his prayers and penances was always an essential part of his preparatory programme, and when the days themselves came round, he would be in remarkably high spirits. Mary responded lavishly. Not far from Muro, in Caposele, in the Archdiocese of Conza, there was another sanctuary of the Madonna called *Materdomini*, of which we must here say a word. *Materdomini* is the name given to a stone statue of Our Lady, of no artistic value, which

---

[1] Benedetti, p. 9.

was discovered by shepherds in the fifteenth century on a solitary hill overlooking the sea from a height of 1,936 feet and girt by far loftier mountains. From its summit the eye embraces in a wide sweep the lovely valley of the *Silari*. This river takes its rise at the foot of the hill and gives its name of *Caposele*, or *Caput Silari* to the neighbourhood. To-day the source of the *Silari* yields 1900 gallons of excellent water per second and irrigates the whole of Southern Italy on its Adriatic side. *Materdomini* is also the name given to Our Lady's sanctuary, which, in 1746, was handed over to the care of St. Alphonsus and his sons, as well as to the hamlet of some two hundred souls that has grown up around it. A monastery was built beside the shrine, and its first superior, appointed by St. Alphonsus himself, was the Venerable Caesar Sportelli. Two other Venerable Servants of God—Father Paul Cafaro, Gerard's first director, and the student Dominic Blasucci—died in it. But what interests us most to know and what has given *Materdomini* its world-wide appeal is the fact that Gerard Majella passed from it to heaven as a saint, leaving his precious remains within its walls for the veneration of countless thousands.[1] To *Materdomini*, then, Benedetta or some relative of the family once brought Gerard when he was still very young. The boy had scarcely entered the church when he fell prostrate before the miraculous image and there remained rapt and motionless for a long time. What he then saw or heard we are not told.

Needless to say, Gerard, even as a child, had to do

---

[1] *Analecta C.SS.R.*, Annus viii, p. 292.

other things besides pray. His schooling had to be
seen to ; and so to the primary school he was sent
when he was seven or eight. All we know about his
school days is that he was an apt and industrious pupil.
As Tannoia puts it, " he was soon able to read and write
and express himself with ease, for he spent all his time
there trying to improve himself[1]." Not only was he a
model in all things to the other boys, but the schoolmaster, Donato Spicci, seems to have completely lost
his heart to the little lad. With Gerard away his class
was never the same, and whenever he failed to put in
an appearance, another boy was despatched to find out
what might be amiss.

As was to be expected, religious truth he assimilated
with peculiar promptitude and ease. In view of the
amazing infused knowledge of divine things of his adult
days, the question is how much of this knowledge he
possessed as a child. Benedetta had already done her
part with all the zeal and thoroughness of a mother who
recognised from the outset that she was fashioning the
mind and heart of a saint. As we read in the process :
" She spared no pains to sow in the heart of her little
boy the seeds of the choicest virtues, which struck roots
that were never to be torn up."[2] The same process
tells us that from his tenderest years he had a " cor
senile."[3] Perhaps we had best translate this as a " mature
heart." And there is much in that. The fruit of his
sanctity, already ripe, was breaking rather through a
blossom than through a husk.

---

[1] English Edit. p. 244.
[2] *Informatio super dubio*, § 7.
[3] *ibid.*, § 9.

Thus did these two children—Mary's son and Benedetta's—love each other in a way not often given to see. The stupendous intimacies we have just recorded, which have been soberly set down by Gerard's contemporaries, are indeed most rare. While they amaze, they need in no wise disconcert. It is so easy to think of God in terms of our own puny and niggard selves. Christmas night explains everything and contains in embryo every miraculous display of the love of God for man, however perplexing and phenomenal. So great a rending of the heavens took place when God came down and put on our " muddy vesture " and walked our ways that no outpouring of His goodness need shake our faith. What He has already done leaves no room for further surprises. " The Incarnation," writes Newman, " is the most stupendous event which ever can take place on earth ; and after it and henceforth, I do not see how we can scruple at any miracle on the mere ground of its being unlikely to happen. No miracle can be so great as that which took place in the Holy House of Nazareth ; it is indefinitely more difficult to believe than all the miracles of the Breviary, of the Martyrology, of saints' lives, of legends, of local traditions, put together ; and there is the grossest inconsistency on the very face of the matter, for any one so to strain out the gnat and to swallow the camel, as to profess what is inconceivable, yet to protest against what is surely within the limits of intelligible hypothesis. If, through divine grace we once are able to accept the solemn truth that the Supreme Being was born of a mortal woman, what is there to be imagined which can offend us on the ground of its marvellousness ? . . .

When we start with assuming that miracles are not unlikely, we are putting forth a position which lies embedded, as it were, and involved, in the great revealed fact of the Incarnation."[1]

Such was Gerard's childhood. It was a lovely dawning, with the light of heaven playing about his cradle, and the glitter and sparkle of supernatural happenings, and the beating of angels' wings, and the coming and going of visitants from another world in the air. It was a childhood of sweet visions and welcoming smiles and rich and mysterious gifts : it was the childhood of the little white loaves. But God's heroes grow, not on the white loaves of divine endearments, but on the hard black bread of suffering and combat. Gerard was now to eat of this.

---

[1] *Present Position of Catholics in England*, viii, 7, pp. 305-306.

CHAPTER II

APPRENTICESHIP

WHEN Gerard was in his twelfth year, there occurred in the Majella home that event which more than any other dislocates the domestic body, shattering dreams, thwarting purposes, bringing the machinery of daily life to a momentary standstill and calling for an immediate readjusting of its several parts : the bread-winner was suddenly taken away. After a brief illness Domenico Majella died a Christian death. What the girls were called upon to do to ease the situation we are not told ; but it was now a question of daily bread, and the widow had to turn unwilling eyes to her youngest child. What dreams the mother had been dreaming for her boy we are left to guess. The astounding predilection shown him by God would certainly seem to suggest a religious career of some sort ; on the other hand, utter lack of means ruled out all thought of the priesthood. Gerard's own dreams had been very definite. With Heaven arriving so early in the field of his young heart, earth had but slender hopes of capturing it. Whether he was of an age or not to appreciate the obstacles that lay between him and the sanctuary, this nursery ritualist and altar-builder must surely have looked forward to the day when the holy pastimes of his childhood would become in some shape or another serious and sacred realities.

But the serious and sad reality of his father's unexpected death had now to be dealt with. Benedetta saw nothing for it but to get Gerard, young as he was, to step at once into his father's shoes and fit himself as fast as might be to become what his father had been before him—a tailor. It was the natural thing for him to turn to. Tailoring was in the family, and the boy must have picked up, even unconsciously, a thing or two about it in his father's workshop. Besides, Benedetta reasonably argued, he could hope in due course to pick up his father's customers as well. As may be surmised, with Gerard himself no arguing was needed. He was already master of the theory that his mother's will in such matters was the Will of God. He was accordingly taken away from school, much to the regret of his teacher, and apprenticed to one Martino Pannuto, a master tailor in Muro, from whom he was to learn to ply the needle instead of the pencil. And Gerard was to ply many a needle before he died. As was the practice in Muro, the apprentice was supposed to give a helping hand in housework as well.

Now Pannuto was a good man, and the extraordinarily good qualities of the new apprentice were not lost on him. In fact it was not long before he had to recognise that he had under his roof something uncommonly like a saint. Besides being a model of conscientious industry, the boy seemed to be always praying. However busy his hands might be, his heart was evidently in heaven. At times indeed that heart would draw those hands along with it and Gerard would fall into what seemed to be an ecstasy. It happened unwittingly on occasions that his work suffered on this account ; but the apprentice never failed to make good the loss. Beyond giving him leave to go to Mass and devotions at will, Pannuto said nothing.

When St. Alphonsus, lying like a corpse on his bed, was informed that there were holy coachmen in Naples, he was seized with a rapture and cried out in amazement : " Holy coachmen in Naples ! *Gloria Patri* ! " [1]

Without exactly bringing on a rapture, Gerard's unusual sanctity must have produced much the same effect on Pannuto. An apprentice who crept under his work-table the better to give himself to contemplation and who entered into ecstasies was something so altogether new in his establishment that it was well worth a little falling off in output and even the risk of the loss of a client or two. A saint on his premises was a rare and valuable phenomenon. So thought Pannuto, who, as we have said, was a good man.

But now behind the pleasing figure of the master there soon arose the figure, sour and sinister, of his foreman, whose thoughts about the newcomer ran in quite a different direction. There seems to be no getting away from the fact that this foreman was a brutal ill-tempered fellow. How he found his way into Pannuto's employment and how he managed to stay in it, in spite of his unlovely nature, is not easy to see. No doubt he did his work well and saw to it that those under him did likewise ; and when employees are efficient and are duly paid, a blind eye is turned on what are often other serious shortcomings. It may be, too, that when this personage exhibited his ugly qualities to his subordinates, he got as much as he gave, thus restoring the balance of power and averting open war. In little Gerard the

---

[1] Berthe, *Saint Alphonse De Liguori*, vol. ii, p. 581.

bully found a victim for the first time in a saint. And saints fall easy victims to their persecutors.

From the outset this foreman seems to have taken an instinctive and tell-tale dislike to the new apprentice. He had no time whatever for all this praying and piety. These things were but the dodges of a shirker. The boy's job was to work, not to pray. The fellow was seemingly far from being a saint himself, and Gerard's example preached a sermon he had no wish to hear. He began with ridicule and abuse, which were soon followed up by blows. In the fashioning of His heroes the Lord uses instruments of all shapes and sizes, some of them indeed seeming better calculated to mar than to make what He has in hand. He has not to go far to fetch them, as they are usually found near the material He purposes to work. The instrument He now took in hand for the fashioning of a Saint Gerard was none too delicate or keen : in fact we might best describe it as a bludgeon.

One day this foreman—his name has not been handed down to us—spied the little apprentice giving himself to his devotions under the work-table. There, Gerard thought, he would be less likely to be disturbed by wagging tongues. The fellow dived at him, dragged him out and beat him cruelly. At times the brute would strike the child—Gerard was barely in his teens—full in the face with his clenched fist. In these days of organised labour, with its trade unions and sympathetic strikes, such savagery is almost beyond belief. When we read it in cold print as an incident in a saint's life, and especially when we look at it against the luminous background of his present glory, it is easy enough to see in it a provi-

dential ruling and recognise in those foul blows the
divine chiselling of a masterpiece. But it was quite
another thing for Gerard to realise then what is now so
evident to us. Yet realise it he did ; and though his own
canonisation never crossed his mind at the time, the
hand of God he most certainly recognised. The days of
Capotignano, with its white loaves and its divine petting
and playing, when he was treated as the darling of
Heaven itself, seemed very distant now—they might
have almost been a dream—and the bread of pain and
humiliation very hard indeed and very black. In a way
the amazing virtue shown by this little boy in the face
of downright persecution presents a bigger test to our
belief than all the heavenly visions and all the glorious
gifts that marked his early childhood. After all, one
need not be a saint to see a vision—sinners have seen
them—and the smallest act of virtue is in a sense a
greater thing than any heavenly visitation. Gerard had
already travelled a long way in the spiritual life and had
climbed steeper and more rugged paths than the path
that led to Capotignano.

What was the key to his fortitude and forbearance ? It
is a commonplace of Christian spirituality that we should
see the Will of God in all things, sweet and bitter, fair
and foul. It is a lesson most of us take a lifetime to
learn, and perhaps some of us never learn it at all. And
no truth can be more inexorable in its implications. This
child had already mastered it. " God wills it " was to
be the slogan of his life ; it would make him deaf and
blind to all personal considerations ; it would make him
impervious to any logic but the logic of its demands ;
it would make him embark airily on any undertaking

regardless of ways and means ; with it the impossible
never crossed his mind. We shall have much to say of
this in a later chapter ; but even now, on the threshold
of his career, he is true to this fundamental principle of
all spiritual activity, and true even to the point of heroism.
When blows and curses rained on him, he would groan
in his anguish : " My God, Thy Will be done."[1] God
willed it ; he pushed this truth unpityingly to all its
consequences, and behind the hand that struck him he
recognised and worshipped the Hand of God. On one
occasion he put the stark fact into blunt unmistakable
words.

During his apprenticeship Gerard continued his visits
to Capotignano. Heaven knows he needed its consola-
tions sorely, though they were far from being the con-
solations of his early days. It was his favourite sanctuary,
and little wonder. One morning, as a result of his devotions, he turned up a few minutes late for work. We
can well understand how little at times clocks and watches
meant to Gerard when he was at his prayers. The
foreman met him with thunder in his face. The boy
stammered out an explanation and an apology which
he feared too well would carry little weight with such a
taskmaster. Gerard's excuses were sneered away. There
was a rush at him, and hard words and harder blows were
soon dealt out freely. Suddenly the little victim was seen
to smile. The infuriated foreman could see but one
meaning in that smile : the boy was making fun of him.
He told him so and insisted on knowing the cause of his
merriment. Then he got an answer which is as wonderful

---

[1] Benedetti, p. 14.

as anything in Gerard's life : " I am smiling because
God's Hand is striking me . . . . *Rido, perchè mi batte
la mano di Dio.*"[1] It took keen eyes to discern God
through the murk and uproar of that storm and to
trace His loving hand through the ruffian hand that
struck him. The words were no doubt reported by
another less tractable apprentice or perhaps retailed
as a good joke by the foreman himself. Yesterday sweet
loaves ; to-day the bread of suffering. It was all one to
this child ; the same Hand dealt out both. When the
wife of Job—that wise and patient man—sought to
shake him out of what seemed to her his silly apathetic
composure, she got this answer : " Thou hast spoken
like one of the foolish women. If we have received good
things at the hand of God, why should we not receive
evil ? "[2] It was thus, too, that Gerard reasoned.

Gerard Majella was neither a stick nor a stone nor
in any way a senseless thing. He was human, and his
south Italian nature was as quick to resent and retaliate
a wrong as was this ferocious man to inflict it. But in
his young heart there was already kindling the fire of an
all-devouring passion, a love for his Lord, for his Crucified
Lord, together with an uncontrollable yearning to
express that love by imitation. On another occasion,
accusing Gerard of being a slacker at his job, the foreman
cuffed him savagely out of the work-room. Again the
bully was met with that exasperating smile. " You're
laughing, are you ? " he hissed, and seizing the nearest
thing to hand—an iron measure it chanced to be—he

---

[1] *Benedetti*, p. 15.
[2] Job, ii, 10.

struck him. At once the boy fell upon his knees and spoke these words : " I forgive you for the love of Jesus Christ."[1] He then quietly resumed his work. " For the love of Jesus Christ." His meaning is plain : the smarting blows, the maddening injustice of the man stung the boy's nature and whipped it into momentary revolt ; but at once the image of his Lord similarly struck and wronged for love of him arose before him through the mist of tears, appealing irresistibly for forbearance, and for the love of Him and of Him alone Gerard forbore, as from his lacerated heart and through his quivering lips there came the words with Christian heroism in every syllable : " I forgive you for the love of Jesus Christ." That love and that love alone could lay a restraining hand upon his heart and turn back the rising tide of his anger.

And now, it may reasonably be asked, what of Pannuto ? Is it possible that he was aware of all this cruel tyranny going on in his own establishment ? One thing is sure : whatever complaints the foreman made about Gerard, Gerard uttered not an incriminating word about him. Others perhaps, sympathetic witnesses of these distressing scenes, reported what had happened to their master. It may be that they were not believed and were told to mind their own business. It may be that they were cowed into silence by the bully and that the master heard nothing. On one occasion, however, Pannuto was given to see things for himself. One day, as a climax to a torrent of abuse, the fellow had sent the little boy with a blow reeling to the ground. Suddenly

---

[1] Tannoia, English Edit., p. 245.

Pannuto came upon the scene. He entered a charged atmosphere. The rack of the storm was trailing across the foreman's face and the growl of the receding thunder was in his voice. The boy's cheeks were flushed with a suspicious red. Pannuto demanded an explanation. The coward bully, knowing he could rely on Gerard not to give him away, pointed to his victim with a shrug, muttering : " He best knows himself what to answer." The man reckoned aright. In modern parlance the boy showed himself a sport, again for the love of Christ. " Master," he said quietly, " I fell down."[1] He satisfied the truth by stating the effect ; he satisfied charity by withholding the cause. For the actual facts we are indebted either to Gerard himself, who had to reveal everything at a subsequent inquiry, or to an eye-witness of the scene, who spoke when speaking was safe. It is not likely that Pannuto was by any means satisfied.; but for the moment he kept his counsel and tolerated his suspect but efficient foreman. Meantime he kept a sharp eye on the comings and goings of his extraordinary apprentice. Pannuto was an honest man himself and had fallen under Gerard's spell, as the schoolmaster Donato Spicci had fallen before him.

He was aware of the boy's frequent visits to the church of Capotignano, and he did what Benedetta and Anna Elisabetta had done half a dozen years before : he followed him there unseen. His legitimate curiosity was richly rewarded. After spending a long time at his prayers, the apprentice performed an act of penance that would no doubt give an unpleasant jolt to our

---

[1] Benedetti, p. 14.

northern nature to-day, but which, in Gerard's time, was much favoured in Southern Italy by devout and generous souls : to make reparation for sins of the tongue, particularly those of blasphemy, so horribly rife amongst his countrymen, he went on all fours and dragged himself on his knees to the altar, drawing his tongue the while along the floor. This accomplished, he forthwith entered into ecstasy. Pannuto had seen enough. He left the church with his mind made up. After due investigation the foreman was dismissed. This particular bludgeon in the hands of God had done its work, though God had not yet done with the bludgeoning.

Capotignano itself was the occasion of another encounter for Gerard with an angry man and of another display on his side of heroic patience. His master owned a vineyard quite close to the famous sanctuary and had one day sent his apprentice there to give a helping hand. Before returning home, the boy paid a visit to his beloved shrine and then took a bypath across the fields to the town. As he was making his way along a hedge he unwittingly frightened away a bird that happened to be in range of a sportsman's gun. The latter, baulked of his prey and showing very poor sportsmanship indeed, vented his vexation on the hapless boy and passed rapidly from words to blows. Gerard, taking the precept of his Divine Master literally, and unconsciously making amends for those who do not heed it at all, without more ado duly presented the other cheek to his assailant. The sportsman read new wrongs into this rare and to him unintelligible exhibition of Christian forbearance, and the blows fell thicker. Happily Pannuto's son Joseph Anthony unexpectedly presented himself and succeeded in pacifying the man. Reason and grace combined to bring him to a sense of his folly and injustice. He slunk away striking his forehead and bemoaning the fact that he had maltreated a saint. We will give him the credit of not knowing how literally this was true. He had in truth struck a saint, and he preached Gerard's virtues to all comers.

As we can see, the apprentice was striding swiftly forward, not in tailoring alone, but in holiness. Though miracle-working is neither a science nor an art and so cannot be acquired, yet we may say that in Pannuto's establishment Gerard began his apprenticeship as a wonder-worker also. Miracles indeed—in other words, supernatural external signs of heavenly approbation—were to be looked for in a life already outstandingly holy.

When the grapes in Pannuto's vineyard had become tantalisingly ripe, thirsty thieves were to be reckoned with ; and there was evidently no way out of it for a man in his circumstances but to do the policing of his own property and sometimes at least keep watch during the night from a workman's hut on the premises. On one occasion he took Gerard with him ; they could thus watch and sleep in turn. Now on reaching the vineyard, Pannuto discovered to his chagrin that he was short of oil for the lantern. It was late and dark and he could not in fairness ask the little boy to walk back the two odd miles to Muro to fetch some. Gerard, however, needed no asking. Seeing his master's difficulty, he told him he would go, and in a moment he was off. He had scarcely gone when he was back again with the needed oil and asserting, moreover, that he had got it in Pannuto's house. Covering such a distance with such speed was, humanly speaking, quite impossible. As we shall see later on, this miraculous agility and annihilation of space were amongst Gerard's most spectacular prodigies.

Obviously Pannuto could not do the watching every night himself; so on one occasion he entrusted this duty to his son Joseph Anthony. He sent Gerard with him. Such an excursion was a windfall for the holy apprentice, as it provided him with ample opportunities for prayer. Now, while his companion snatched a little sleep, Gerard left the hut, where he had spent quite a time at his devotions. With a lighted reed in his hand he was giving expression to his piety in characteristic fashion by making the round of the hut softly singing the *Miserere*, when suddenly a spark from the reed alighted on the thatch, and in an instant the roof was ablaze. Joseph Anthony awoke and rushed out in terror, exclaiming: "What have you done, Gerard, what have you done?"[1] Gerard knew well what he had done, but he also knew what God could do; and raising the reed over the burning hut and using words that were to become his formula, so to speak, in the working of countless miracles, he said calmly, as he made the sign of the cross over the flames: "*Non è niente* . . . It is nothing.[2]" Instantaneously the flames went out.[3]

---

[1] Benedetti, p. 18.

[2] *Ibid.*

[3] In the process the Promoter of the Faith relates the incident as follows: " (Gerard) did what he had seen people do when making supplication to God . . . There was no wide empty space in the vine-yard except where the hay was stacked. In order not to pass the night doing nothing, or to keep himself from being overcome by sleep, he took to his prayers, accompanying them with physical movement.

Gerard was soon an adept in the twofold craft of tailoring and the sanctifying of his own soul. The tailoring was now to cease for a while, and the sanctifying was to continue, though no longer in a work-room, but within the walls of an episcopal palace. The apprentice became a bishop's boy. A change of air sought by two delicate prelates brought this about.

Muro's own pastor, Monsignore Delfico, spent much of his time recuperating in his native Teramo, the capital of the Abruzzi province and the ancient *Interamna*, while at this particular period, Monsignore Claudio Albini, the Bishop of Lacedonia, was convalescing with his family in his native Muro. Now this episcopal absenteeism was not helpful to Muro, and it explains why Gerard did not receive the Sacrament of Confirmation till he was in his fifteenth year. Monsignore Delfico now profited by his confrère's presence in his diocese to ask him to confer the Sacrament in his stead, and amongst the youthful candidates who thronged the church of *S. Maria del Carmine* attached to the Poor Clare convent, on the 5th June, 1740, was Gerard Majella. For him it was no mere ceremony. To the close of his days, devotion to the Holy Ghost was to hold a very definite place in his spiritual life. Every Pentecost saw him filled with rapturous joy and his face glowed with an inner fire. We are told that even the tepid who drew

---

For the twofold purpose of avoiding obstacles in the dark and of ritual of light to his devotions, he took a reed, fashioned it into the form of a cross, kept it alight by means of a piece of wax, and thus to the singing of a hymn went round the stack of hay . . . ." The miraculous ending is recorded in the same terms by all the saint's biographers.—*Resp. ad Nov. Animad.*, § 90.

near him caught this glow. Not a day, not an hour passed in which he would not seek the strength and guidance of the Holy Spirit, either for himself or for others. He was soon to need them sorely.

Whether Gerard's reputation had gone before him— a likely thing enough in a town of Muro's size—or whether he made the impression there and then on the occasion of his Confirmation, certain it is that he captured the officiating prelate's heart so completely that the latter asked him to enter his service. No doubt his full and accurate answering at the preliminary examination struck his Lordship. And then saints quickly betray themselves and the " good odour of Christ " soon gives them away.

Though we credit the good bishop with the best of intentions, we cannot help thinking that the milk of human kindness was not altogether unadulterated and that other reasons, too, nearer home inspired the proposal. Monsignore Claudio Albini was in many ways a remarkable man. He was an exceptionally good canonist, and before he got the mitre, his wisdom and learning were much in demand here, there, and everywhere. After having filled the office of Vicar-General in more than one diocese, he became Bishop of Lacedonia in 1736. But now it so happened that Monsignore Claudio Albini was remarkable for something else besides his knowledge of Canon Law ; the fact is that this holy man had a most unholy temper. Indeed it was notoriously bad. He had made the servant problem so acute for himself—and incidentally for his servants—that these came and went at an alarming rate. None of them was known to have survived more than a few weeks, some being quite willing to forgo arrears in wages in order to get away as fast as they could. According to one witness—who, we presume, is speaking figurat'vely—his Lordship was *il martello* . . . the hammer or scourge of his servants.[1]

No doubt the poor man's nerves were frayed. His health was none of the best. Then, though he came of a wealthy family, little of the wealth made its way to the palace, and he was hard put at times to meet his liabilities. Now he saw clearly how matters stood and in asking Gerard to go with him, he must have jumped at the idea of having a saint in his service, naively oblivious of the fact that his own well-known failing must enter largely into the fashioning of a saint of anyone who would have virtue enough to stay on with him. In making his offer was he led chiefly by the hope that in this unusually patient and holy boy he would at last find one who would bear with him and see it through ? Did he shrewdly divine that he was making a good bargain ? We can only guess.

Gladly and gratefully Gerard accepted the proposal, agreeing to go to the bishop in a year, when his time with Pannuto would have been served. As soon as word of his intention got about amongst his friends, there was no end to the advice he got not to accept. Hair-raising pictures of what it would mean were drawn for him ; for the numerous failures in the prelate's service lost no time in spreading the bad news. Did he know what he was doing ? Was he a fool ? Gerard knew what he was doing, and he was not a fool. He knew well

---

[1] *Resp. ad Nov. Animad.*, § 90.

what it would mean, and what was meant to scare did but allure this youthful stalwart of Christ.

Gerard was in his sixteenth year when he entered the episcopal household of Lacedonia. He made the longest record look ridiculous by remaining in it for three years. All the dark and direful prophecies of his well-wishers were now fulfilled. These three years were years of thankless unremitting drudgery. Not blows exactly now —to give his Lordship his due, he did not go that far— but words, angry, scolding, nagging words ; orders and counter-orders, biting comments on his work, mountains made out of molehills, penalties and penances of all sorts, threats of dismissal—if it was not one thing, it was another. It was an unending series of squalls in the palace, under which the poor lad had to bow his head ; the barometer never seemed to rise ; and as he had to give a hand in the kitchen as well as being his Lordship's valet, the area of atmospheric disturbance was fairly wide. Indeed, according to Tannoia, he " did all the work of the house."[1]

As we might expect, and as we may conclude from his lengthy stay, Gerard fell an easy and a willing victim. Never a sullen look, never a rude retort, never even a deprecating word did his irate master get from him. As soon as the storm had blown itself out, he would quietly resume his work without a thought of what the next hour might bring. Quoting eye-witnesses—for these distressing scenes had eye-witnesses—Tannoia writes : " His humility and silence while receiving the severest unmerited reprimands . . . showed what a deep

---

[1] English Edit. p. 255.

root Christian patience had struck in his heart."[1] Other
members of the household, as well as visitors—priests,
businessmen and the like—frequently fell in for these
displays of heroic meekness and forbearance. They could
scarcely understand it, especially when they recalled
how many of his predecessors they had seen come and go.
From this time they looked upon the boy as a saint.
Their criterion could not have been more orthodox and
unerring. Many advised Gerard to leave. Here was the
reply they got, as his biographers report it : " His Lordship wishes me well, as if I were his own son, and as
far as I am concerned, I mean to serve him to the best
of my ability till he dies."[2] He kept his word.

Here again it was no lack of character in this boy that
made him bend so compliantly under the petty tyranny
of his strange master. It is so easy to read behaviour
of this kind amiss. When all is said and done, the patient
man bends to the demands of grace, the angry man
to the demands of nature ; and it is not hard to see
which is the more humiliating compliance of the two.
Gerard showed character to a supreme degree by showing
the character of a follower of Christ. Again he was
driven on by something very positive and strong : it
was the same love for Jesus Christ and for Him Crucified,
the same yearning for resemblance which began almost
in his infancy and was to be the all-subduing passion
of his life. It made him strong enough to beat back
resurgent nature when it rose against the calculated
brutalities of Pannuto's workshop ; it strengthened him

---

[1] Cfr. Benedetti, p. 22.
[2] *Ibid.*, p. 23.

now to bear the prolonged if comparatively milder and far less malevolent unpleasantness of constant pin-pricking in the episcopal palace of Lacedonia.

We need scarcely add that all the other elements of Gerard's growing sanctity were of a piece with his heroic patience. Cardinal Newman has said : " The moral growth within us must be symmetrical, in order to be beautiful or lasting."[1] Perhaps it is in this that the best of us differ from the saints : our spiritual growth is not symmetrical ; we practise certain virtues, it may be with something like heroism ; the saints were heroic in them all. And thus it was with Gerard even now. His soul was growing symmetrically to the likeness of Christ. One would have thought that these endless harassing encounters with the bishop would have been penance enough for him without adding others of his own devising. But he had long since grasped the relation between suffering and love, and the more he loved his God the more he longed to suffer for Him. Already his health, never normal, had begun to give trouble, and when the doctor one day took him by surprise and examined his chest, he came across a hair-shirt. Now that he was more or less a free agent and out of range of his mother's anxious eyes, he indulged his ascetic tastes liberally. He gave himself the minimum of food and usually made his fare of vegetables and dry bread. Whenever tit-bits came his way from a kind-hearted cook, they were invariably set aside for some poor sick person. His prayer was in keeping with his penance. There was daily Mass of course and almost daily Com-

---

[1] *Oxford University Sermons*, iii. p. 47.

munion in the cathedral hard by. Whatever leisure
he had was given to his Eucharistic Friend—now so
fast a friend—and members of the local clergy have
testified that the bishop's boy often knelt motionless
for hours at a stretch before the tabernacle. No wonder
the whisper went about : " Gerardiello is not a man,
but an angel ; he is a saint."[1]

As was to be expected, God let men see that as far
as sainthood was concerned they were right. One day
the bishop went out for a walk, leaving the key of his
room in Gerard's keeping. The boy stayed in to put
things in order. This done, he locked the room and
taking the key with him, went to fetch water from the
well in the palace grounds. However it happened—
whether he had the key in his hand or in the pocket of
his coat—it slipped into the well as he bent over the
edge. There was a moment's dismay, as he exclaimed
with something like consternation in his voice : " What
will his Lordship say ? Won't he be upset. ! "[2] The poor
boy had only too good reason for guessing what his
Lordship would say, as he had got many a round rating
for far less. He clearly foresaw the storm. However,
his perplexity was shortlived. Suddenly the terror
faded out of his eyes and they kindled with a bright
idea. Without a word to the bystanders—the well was
evidently available to the public—off he ran to the
sacristy of the cathedral. He was soon running back
again carrying a little wooden statue of the Divine
Infant that was kept there for Christmastide. The

[1] Benedetti, p. 23.
[2] *Ibid*.

memories of Capotignano with all its wonderful intimacies and gifts were still green with him. The Friend of his childhood Who had done a greater thing would surely now do a lesser. By this time quite a crowd had gathered ; for the bishop's boy had begun to make a name for himself and so they were prepared for anything. Fastening the statue to a rope that was used for drawing the water, he let it down into the well, turning to his statue and saying : " You alone can get me out of my difficulty. His Lordship will be vexed with me ; but it is for You to recover the key."[1] Tannoia adds a detail which, we think, goes to the root of Gerard's distress. According to him the boy said : " You must recover this to prevent his Lordship from sinning by impatience."[2] After all, if Gerard were to be consistent, he would rather welcome another brush with the bishop in which nothing would please him better than getting the worst of it ; but sin, even the smallest and even in another, he would give the world to avoid. Nor did he think a miracle too drastic a way out of the difficulty. Necks were now craned, and the crowd held their breath as Gerard slowly drew the statue to the surface. The Bambino of Capotignano did not let His former playmate down : the statue re-appeared bearing in its hand the precious key. Awe fell upon the onlookers. The news of the prodigy spread like wildfire ; soon the whole town was talking of it, and crowds gathered about the well to hear details from eye-witnesses and especially to see Gerard. We are not told where he went ; most likely he lost no time in entrenching himself behind the

---

[1] Benedetti, p. 24.
[2] English Edit., p. 254.

privacy of the episcopal precincts. The well henceforth bore the name of *Pozzo Gerardiello* or *Gerard's Well*. Berruti, writing in 1847, states that it still went by that name in his day.[1]

The same biographer records another wonderful incident which occurred while Gerard was still in the service of the bishop. We insert it here as an early example of a supernatural power which in later years he was destined to display to an extraordinary degree. Berruti writes : " Having noticed in the cathedral a man who was about to approach the altar with his soul stained with grave sin, he called him aside, threw himself at his feet and with tears in his eyes showed him what a great wrong he would have been guilty of by communicating unworthily. Stirred by his words, the man prepared for confession and bore witness ever after to the obligation he was under to Gerard."[2]

On June 25th, 1744, while visiting his metropolitan the Archbishop of Conza, Monsignore Claudio Albini unexpectedly died. He was only forty-seven. Gerard's assurances of fidelity to the end read like a prophecy. He was the prelate's sincerest mourner and wept bitter tears at his passing. While those about him looked on the bishop's death as a good riddance for the boy, the latter was heard exclaiming : " Alas ! I have lost my best friend, for his Lordship really wished me well."[3] All we can say in explanation is that the saints viewed these matters from an unusual angle.

Gerard now returned to Muro and to his home with

---

[1] P. 44.
[2] Pp. 306-307.
[3] Benedetti, p. 24.

the intention of setting up for himself as a tailor. He was eighteen years old. Though we have no further knowledge of his inner life during his stay in Lacedonia, what we have recorded is abundant proof that his spiritual growth had already far outpaced his years. Even now he was nothing short of a great saint, and evidently God thought as much.

No doubt his knowledge of his craft had been put to the fullest use during the past three years and many a neat little job had been done on various articles in the episcopal wardrobe, thus cutting down episcopal expenses. Realising, however, that he had grown rusty at his work, he spent some time—we are not told how long—rounding off his apprenticeship under another master—one Vito Mennona—a young tailor who was being largely patronised in the locality on account of the excellent quality of his work. In this establishment Gerard fared well, though not perhaps according to his own ascetic ideals. He was treated as a member of the family. His sanctity was at once recognised and appreciated, and when Mennona had become a very old man, he would glow with enthusiasm as he spoke of Gerard's virtues. He often visited his former apprentice, then a laybrother in Caposele, and sought comfort and counsel at his hands. Gerard Majella now felt justified in advertising himself as a fully qualified tailor, probably towards the end of 1745. Heaven had long since been advertising him as a fully qualified Christian.

CHAPTER III

THE TAILOR OF MURO

THE newly-qualified tailor who opened his establishment to his fellow-citizens of Muro, towards the close of 1745, was not yet twenty. He had not long to wait for patronage. Old clients of his father returned, to be followed by new ones in evergrowing numbers, not merely from the town but from the neighbouring district of Castelgrande. Had Gerard not given satisfaction as a tailor besides giving edification as a saint, he would scarcely have done such a good business. But his sanctity was reared on strong foundations, and before springing into the altitudes of great holiness, he planted his feet firmly in the solid earth of daily duty conscientiously fulfilled.

Apart from the charm and courtesy of a saint, what drew his clients first and foremost was the blessed and satisfying fact that he was an honest man. And they were sure of it. From young Majella they got their money's worth, each and everyone and at all times. In business transactions he was scrupulously straight ; in his eyes no dishonesty was small enough to be trivial. As one witness put it, " he never defrauded anyone of as much as a piece of thread."[1] Then his prices were as low as he could in reason make them, and from those

---

[1] In Ord. no. 6, § 99.

who were really hard up he would take nothing at all.

One day a poor man brought him a piece of material for a garment. Gerard saw at a glance that it was altogether too small for the purpose and told him so. The poor fellow was very upset and said he could not afford to buy any more. Then once again we hear the words that will usher in the working of so many prodigies : " *Non è niente, non è niente ;* it is nothing, it is nothing." Taking the piece of cloth, the tailor thereupon proceeded to stretch it this way and that until in his holy hands it grew to the requisite dimensions. A few days later, the man was given his garment together with a miraculous surplus. It is not of miraculous loaves only that one may " gather up the fragments."[1]

After providing for the upkeep of the home, Gerard divided what remained of his earnings between the poor and the souls in Purgatory. Pity for suffering in any guise revealed itself very early in his life and is a feature of his sainthood that has made the Catholic world take him to its heart in a more than ordinary way. Now that he was earning his own money, he was in a better position to follow the dictates of his charity. The poor—" God's poor "—as he always spoke of them, he loved as only Christ's saintly followers have ever loved them. Alms-giving was one of the joys of his childhood, and it grew old with him.

And he had compassion, too, on that other multitude whose pleading reached him from another world : the souls in Purgatory. " And they, too," he would say, " are poor creatures and are calling out for help."[2] He

---

[1] John, vi, 12.
[2] Tannoia, cap. iii.

went generously to their rescue himself. All he could spare of his weekly returns went in Masses for these unseen sufferers, and often at no small cost. Once, in a gush of uncalculating pity, he diverted a whole week's takings—about six and a half lire to-day—to this charity, though it meant subsisting on a little bread himself the following week. Tannoia writes: " If now and then business was none too brisk, what alone distressed him and broke his heart was that he would be unable to help these poor holy souls."[1] There were times indeed when Benedetta would look askance at all this pious prodigality. She would quietly call a halt to it and try to awaken her son to the harsh realities of their home. " Mamma," would come the invariable reply, " God will provide for our needs. He will never suffer us to want for necessaries."[2] Coming from him, with the memories of Capotignano thronging to her mind, the reply was crushing. She let him be.

Though tailoring for a livelihood entered in no uncertain way into the making of the saint in Gerard, there were other elements as well. We have seen how his yearning for intercourse with God pursued him into Pannuto's work-room and more than once betrayed him into trouble. Now, with a mother to support and clients to attend to, he had to hold his straining soul in leash and fix his thoughts on such unspiritual things as a needle and thread ; but he gave to prayer all the time it was his to give. Every morning at daybreak he made his way to the cathedral, where he heard and served

---

[1] Tannoia Cap. III.
[2] Benedetti, p. 27.

all the Masses he could and where he received the two
or three Holy Communions a week his confessor allowed
him. At times, when his work admitted it, he would
take a day off and give himself a spiritual holiday in the
country church of *Santa Maria del Soccoro*. This practice,
however, grew rarer with him, as the Blessed Sacrament
was not reserved there. The head sacristan of the
cathedral—no doubt the same who supplied him with
candle butts when he was a little boy—was, as we have
said, a relative of the Majella family and from him the
young tailor would sometimes get the keys of the church
at night. " Then," writes Tannoia, " he would lock
himself into the holy place and there in the presence
of his beloved sacramental Lord give vent to the longings
of his heart, and scourge himself and bewail the ingratitude shown his beloved Lord by men, particularly
at night."[1] According to his anonymous French Redemptorist biographer, if at times the sacristan in his concern
for Gerard's health, withheld his co-operation in these
nightly vigils and refused him the keys, the young tailor
would manage in some manner—love is so fertile in
expedients—to make his way into the sanctuary of the
Blessed Sacrament by the campanile.[2]

Nor did these prolonged intimacies with his Lord and
Lover content his heart. Nothing into which God enters
can be small and no moment can be short which can
have its repercussions in eternity. Gerard knew it, and
with the greed of a miser clutching at his gold, he snatched
at every chance the day offered of hastening to the

---

[1] Cap. iv.
[2] *Vie*, p. 47.

tabernacle. Every visit forged a new link in the chain
that bound his young heart to the Heart he had so learned
to love and that so loved him.

Such was Gerard's life in Muro for nearly a twelvemonth. What was Muro thinking of it ? After all, a
tailor of twenty, in their very midst, who was always
spying out opportunities of breaking away from his work
in order to pray ; who spent his nights in church ; who
was absurdly honest in business and flung his earnings
away on others, and who seemed to be uncommonly near
starving himself, was a phenomenon, even for an Italian
population. People had to think one way or the other
about him : the boy was clearly either a fool or a saint.
Each theory had its adherents in Muro. Many had no
difficulty in recognising the saint. Many more set Gerard
down as a fool. Some of these were unthinking youths,
others were such as read into the tailor's holy life a
condemnation of their own. " The sensual man per-
ceiveth not these things that are of the Spirit of God.
For it is foolishness to him."[1] So the Apostle tells us ;
and now this strange youth was eminently of the Spirit
of God. And so jeers and stinging names followed him
freely in the street. Some went further and drove home
their abuse with blows. The bludgeoning again ! The
poor lad should be used to it now. Here was too good a
chance of imitating his Divine Lover. He seized it and
was silent. At most he would say pleadingly to his
tormentors words which sound like an echo from the
court of Caiphas : " O God, and what have I done to
you ? "[2]

---

[1] I Cor., ii, 14.
[2] Caione.

An unexpected change in his fortunes occurred towards the close of 1746 or the beginning of 1747. About that time of the year the civic authorities made it their business to revise the rates and taxes. Whether they acted through malice or relied on inaccurate information is not clear, and in the circumstances either explanation is possible ; but they taxed the young tailor out of all proportion to his income. Gerard felt he could not meet the demand and decided to leave Muro and set up elsewhere.

Providence was looking after him and in more ways than one. A fellow-townsman—Luca Malpiedi by name —had opened a high-school for boys in October, 1746, in a place called San Fele, some five or six miles outside Muro. He advertised for a resident tailor. Gerard applied for the position and got it. He saw the hand of God in this as in everything else ; it was harder perhaps to see that hand in what his new surroundings were to entail.

It was a strange school and a strange schoolmaster he had come to serve. It was clear from the outset that discipline and decorum were utterly excluded from the curriculum. Gerard was soon found out and at once fell victim to the evil ingenuity of the pack of rowdies who masqueraded as students. One of them, who afterwards made good and eventually became a priest and entered the Redemptorist novitiate, has stated that his schoolfellows expended all their powers of pitiless mischief on the young tailor. The amazing thing about it all was that their master, far from calling off his unmannerly charges, himself took a hand and led the way, even when they proceeded to blows. It was the old bad days in Pannuto's establishment over again, only now Gerard was twice the age and his persecutors were many. Let us hear the headmaster's very candid confession as recorded by Caione. He writes : " A schoolmaster of San Fele testifies that while Gerard worked in his house as tailor for more than a month, he never gave way to impatience or ill-humour ; he was never seen to be anything but cheerful and patient ; moreover, when he was severely whipped by the boys in the master's absence, he showed no sign of anger or displeasure. On one occasion he was beaten when he had actually gone to bed and beaten most painfully ; without defending himself in the least or losing his patience, he merely said : ' *Finitela mo!* Do stop ! ' At other times the said master would divert himself after school by whipping poor Gerard, who bore it all with the utmost patience and even with joy, to use the master's own words."[1]

When we bear in mind Gerard's position in this establishment, we must admit that all this makes curious and nauseating reading, especially to our ears. It reminds us of *Dotheboys Hall*, with the roles slightly reversed. Truly these young gentlemen, too, considered Gerard either a fool or a saint, and it is more charitable to suppose that they thought him a fool. If he courted suffering and humiliation, the Lord certainly made ample provision for his desires. What he did *not* seek amongst men—honour and glory—would come in due course and in overwhelming abundance.

Towards the end of January of the following year

---

[1] Caione,

1747 Gerard was home again. Whatever his motive was in leaving San Fele, it was scarcely to seek a respite from persecution, for now, instead of becoming a victim of Malpiedi and his bullies, he became his own. During the Lent of this year he spent much of his leisure reading a book entitled: *Anno Doloroso*, by Fra Antonio dell' Olivadi, on the Passion of Christ. As we have seen, a love for his Crucified Lord which sought to express itself in imitation had long since possessed and absorbed his soul. This new reading fanned it to a flame. Feeling that all our readers may not appreciate what is to come, we think that a word or two will not be amiss.

Great saints are God's resounding counterblast to great sinners. Their seeming extravagances in virtue are a glorious and comforting offset to the too real extravagances of vice, and the riot of iniquity which goes on without restraint and almost without comment the world over, finds its blessed counterpart in the holy riot of generosity and sacrifice that distinguishes the great servants of God. Abnormally wild deeds of wicked men, outstripping commonplace wrongdoings and shaming our common nature,—deeds of monstrous lust, of murderous hate, of stony-hearted greed—confront us from time to time in our daily papers. If now and then they are matched in their rarity and strangeness by deeds of charity and renouncement, we thank Heaven for it. It is our solace and our pride that if our fallen humanity has given birth to evil abnormalities, it has likewise produced prodigies of good.

And there is something else. Gerard read that book of Fra Antonio with the eyes of a saint. " God died for me " : there was the fact that pursued him relent-

lessly, gripped him, shook and swayed his soul, dazed
his mind, set his heart aflame and drove him into all
the holy excesses and seeming eccentricities of a saint's
love. God—with all the infinities the word connotes—
died for him, for Gerard Majella, the tailor's son, of
Muro. God died for him after having been humbled
and gashed and broken. And God need not have *died*
for him, for He who did immeasurably more might
have done immeasurably less. And He did it through
sheer love for Gerard, but through love raised to the
white heat of the divinity. And He did it as though
Gerard had been alone to die for ! These overwhelming
mountainous facts bore down on Gerard and swept him
into all the glorious recklessness of his tremendous love
for his tremendous Lover. He would give love for love,
humiliation for humiliation, pain for pain, if possible
life for life. Since anything he could ever do for his
Crucified Love must fall infinitely short of what that
Love did for him, he would at least go to the full length
of his poor human nature and do all he could. Our
cold hearts may not find it easy to understand the
fierce onslaughts on himself made by this young man.
St. Augustine gives us the key : " *Da amantem, et sentit
quod dico . . . Si autem frigido loquor, nescit quid loquor :*
Give me a lover and he knows what I am saying . . . .
If I speak to one who is cold, he knows not what I am
talking of."[1]

And so the Lenten season, which for most of those
about him was just a time for a little more piety with
a judicious admixture of penance, became for Gerard

---

[1] *In Joan. Evangel. Tract.* xxvi, 4.

E.

an inspiration to reproduce in himself as far as might be the physical and moral agonies of his Beloved. With all the sacrilege and brutalities of Christ's scourging before his eyes, he lashed his own unoffending flesh. Long since this had been one of his favourite penitential practices; but now, when the drama of the Passion was being lived through in thought once more by the faithful, it became fiercer and more frequent. And now, too, Gerard went further and enlisted the services of another. The name of this strange benefactor was Felice Farenga. He tells us how, having bound the holy youth to a stake, he would scourge his bare shoulders with wet and knotted cords; and when Gerard noticed that his friend could not bring himself to continue, he would implore of him to keep on till the blood flowed. It was no morbid fanaticism that drove him on, but sheer unthinking love, the love for Jesus and for Him Crucified. Between the dervish of the desert and the Christian ascetic lies a world.

During this season of official fasting Gerard could be heard repeating : " The time of the death of Jesus Christ is now at hand. If He died for me, I wish to die for Him."[1] Had he been allowed to die in such a cause, he would have done so joyfully a thousand times. But this he could not do. However, he gave the minimum to his body and gave it grudgingly. So little did he eat during these days that he seemed to live by miracle. Bread dipped in water was not an elaborate menu, and whenever more substantial and appetising fare was forced upon him, it usually found its way to the sick

---

[1] Benedetti, p. 35.

and poor. He often distributed his earnings amongst the needy and not rarely went without necessaries himself to help the distressed. At times he would go three whole days without food. The tasty element in whatever he eat was effectively eliminated by the use of bitter herbs. He always kept a goodly supply of this penitential commodity about him.

Naturally this sort of thing did not make for an abundance of health and reflected itself in his thin and wan appearance. His good mother did not like it and said so. The only answer she got was : " Do not worry, I am quite satisfied and I don't need anything to eat just now."[1] That seemed to end matters. Tannoia tells us that one day, during this Lent of 1747, a lady named Eugenia Pasquale sent for Gerard in the hope of inducing him to eat. She got the same answer : " I have quite enough." He then informed her that he always carried eatables about with him. Donna Eugenia had her doubts and suddenly slipping her hand into his wallet, she pulled out an assortment of roots and herbs. She tasted them and found them most bitter. On her asking what these might mean, Gerard replied : " By eating these one loses all appetite."[2] A gourmand could have truthfully said as much about the rarest delicacy. The poor saint must have been hard put at times to soothe the anxieties of inquisitive sympathisers while adhering to the truth.

There was one aspect of Christ's Passion, one incident in it that aroused Gerard's pity and indignation in a

---

[1] In Apost. no. 6, § 19.
[2] Cap. iii.

unique way : it was the humiliation to which his Lord
was subjected by Pilate's soldiery. It shocked and
horrified and wounded him even more than any of the
physical sufferings Christ had to go through. The stark
awful blasphemy of all that happened then stood out
before him in revolting detail. He saw that divine
Figure rigged out in the makeshift trappings of mock
royalty : he saw the diadem of twisted thorn, the scarlet
rags, the hollow reed. He saw the spitting and the
ruffian blow. He heard the taunting queries and the
hoarse chant of sham allegiance. He saw and heard
it all and remembered that the object of this blasphemous
burlesque was the uncreated Wisdom and Sanctity of
his Incarnate God. And the remembrance struck deep
into Gerard's heart and stung him into the doing of
something that would be a loving if a feeble effort to
atone in his own poor person before men and angels
for this crowning wrong. Christ allowed men to make
a fool of Him for their sake : Gerard would induce men
to make a fool of Gerard for the sake of Christ. Nature
revolted at the thought more than at any bitter herb
or bloody scourge. There is nothing we cling to more
tenaciously than our reputation for sanity. A man will
shout the fact that he once had an illness or met with
an accident that brought him to death's door and willingly regale his friends with his experiences ; but that
he was once in a mental home will always be the skeleton
in the cupboard. What Gerard now proposed doing was
a hard hard thing ; but love suggested it and love would
strengthen him to see it through. Nothing else he could
devise would, he thought, go as near making adequate
amends for the incalculable profanities of the Passion.

Gerard had not been the first to make such amends. Another saint—St. John of God—whose name is inseparably linked with that very sane Catholic charity, the nursing of the sick, had been before him in this heroism. Having listened to a sermon by the Blessed John of Avila, he was so fired with a longing to pay back love for love in the same hard coin that he rushed from the church into the public street feigning madness. He went through the town tearing his hair, beating his face and rolling in the dust. So admirably did he succeed in his acting that he was committed to an asylum and there underwent the harsh treatment which in those days passed for the only remedy for obstreperous lunatics : he was soundly whipped. It was only when the preacher whose eloquence had started the trouble, and who happened to be the saint's director, had heard of it and had ordered his penitent to desist, that he was set free.

Perhaps Gerard knew nothing about this act of St. John of God. Anyhow, he needed no model to encourage him. No doubt the poor lad had not much difficulty in playing the part. His childlike simplicity and candour, his superhuman patience under every sort of insult and cruelty, his amazing fasts, his aloofness from the world and its ways, together with his gaunt and abstracted air, gave ready colour to the belief that young Majella the tailor was not right in the head. He now made it his business to confirm this belief. This was also in the Lent of 1747. And so he feigned a silly unnatural delight when jeered at in the streets. And he would beg of people as a favour to strike him. Uncomplimentary to our human kind as it may sound, perhaps this is the easiest part any of us can play. Any fool can feign folly. We need go so very little out of our ordinary course. The most delicate deflection from the normal in our daily behaviour will suffice to make our friends become suddenly and painfully interested in our welfare. Yes, poor Majella the tailor was mad, clean mad. It was sad of course but obviously true.

It was not long before he reaped the harvest, and an abundant one it was. Good-hearted folk felt for the boy and prayed for him, and gave him a wide berth. They knew it would come to that. There was the result of saying too many prayers and taking things too seriously and trying to be better than one's neighbours. And they thanked God that they were sensible Catholics who did not say too many prayers, and did not take things too seriously, and did not try to be better than their neighbours. But there were others : there was the younger irresponsible sort for whom a fool was a windfall ; there were also those to whom Gerard's life was a reproach. To such as these he fell an easy unresisting victim. His appearance in the street was a signal for all the roughs and urchins in the neighbourhood to swarm about him, yelling delightedly. They did more than yell : they spat at him, they pelted him with clods and stones, they tripped him up in the mud, they dragged him through the street. One day they knocked him down in the snow and almost buried him alive. Suddenly his mother came upon the scene and bitterly reproached the young ruffians with their heartlessness. Gerard, however, rose in the best of humour. Similar scenes were of frequent occurrence ; far from avoiding them he would say : " Now I am happy and satisfied."[1] Love put a new complexion on it all.

Nor did he wait for such treatment to come to him ; he went to meet it and challenged it. He played his part to the full ; and when he succeeded only too well, no one was better pleased than himself. Once when in Castelgrande, some distance from Muro, he met a knot of young fellows laughing and joking hilariously. They were on the look-out for something new in the way of diversion, and he was just in time. He accosted them with these words : " Hello ! we have been having fun ourselves ; what about doing something to give pleasure to the Lord ? "[2] Suiting the action to the word, he lay down on the ground and told them to tie his feet together and drag him through the street, which happened to be very stony. The youngsters asked for nothing better. Here was a fool indeed on his own showing and as such their legitimate prey. They lost no time in getting to work. Gerard insisted on being drawn to the appointed spot ; but when they saw his poor head and shoulders bruised and bleeding, they found their hearts again and some of them cried. Gerard, however, seemed to be in his element, as of course it became a fool to be. This particular incident took place in front of the house of the Carusi family, where a few years later God would glorify His servant before men's eyes by exhibiting his supernatural wisdom.

Even now God gave him a glimpse of what was to come. On one occasion, after a rough handling on the

---

[1] Benedetti, p. 34.
[2] In Apost. no. 6, § 43

part of a number of mischievous boys, Gerard suddenly
changed his attitude of meek submission and assumed a
new dignity ; inspiration illumined his eyes, as he said
solemnly to his tormentors : " You now despise me.
There shall come a day when you will think it an honour
to kiss my hand."[1] That day would come indeed—a
day when his fellow-citizens would gather reverently
around him ; when Muro's religious communities would
think themselves honoured with his presence ; when
lay and ecclesiastical dignitaries would vie with one
another in escorting him and having him beneath their
roof. Nor was that day so very far off. Referring to
Gerard's words on this occasion Benedetti writes : " He
undoubtedly spoke thus the better to give colour to
his pretended idiocy ; though his words were prophetic,
as the sequel shows."[2] Such a purpose on his part,
however, is not incompatible with conscious prophecy.

And thus this fool for Christ's sake went on with his
fictitious folly. We do not know for certain how long
he persisted in his heroic self-humiliation ; it was probably
during the first two or three weeks of the Lent of 1747.
What we do know is that after some time it was forbidden him by his confessor and was dropped with the
same readiness with which it had been taken up ; just
as St. John of God gave over his feigned insanity at the
bidding of Blessed John of Avila. Had Gerard had
his own way, it would have gone on to the end. But
he must have long relished the twofold pleasure of
doing God's Will by obedience while still being treated
as a fool, since it surely took him many a day to catch

---

[1] Tannoia, cap. xxx.
[2] P. 35.

up with his pretence and convince people that he was really sane.

Such was the tailor of Muro in 1747. He was already in his twenty-first year, and before he should have completed his thirtieth he would die as a Redemptorist laybrother, leaving behind him the reputation of a saint and the wonder-worker of his age. Though there are canonised saints in every walk of life, and though we have reason to believe that had Gerard Majella remained in the world he would have gone on as he began, still it was to be expected that in the case of one whose life was so angelic, who aimed at so complete an imitation of Christ Crucified and yearned so strongly after a life of intercourse with God, the call to religion would be early and imperative. And such it was. If he had not long since left the world, it was certainly not for want of trying. More than once he had tried, even during the years of his life we have already chronicled. Let us briefly retrace our steps.

Gerard made his first attempt soon after his confirmation. There was a Capuchin convent at San Menna, a short distance from Muro, and here the boy presented himself as a lay postulant. He had an uncle in the community, a theologian of note named Fra Bonaventura, on whose support he naturally relied. However, his age and his appearance told against him : he was only sixteen and he looked wretchedly delicate. In any case his application was put down to a fit of passing fervour. Father Guardian would not accept him. Partly to console his nephew, partly to supply an evident need, Fra Bonaventura presented him with a new coat. He did not guess how slight such a consolation was. Gerard had scarcely left the precincts of the Friary when he was accosted by a beggar appealing piteously to his charity. Surely there would be something for a poor man in the pockets of such a coat as that. In a trice Gerard and the coat had parted company and the beggar was arrayed in it, no doubt to his own astonishment. What had happened was soon reported. This treatment of his gift did not in the least commend itself to Uncle Bonaventura. The offending nephew was sent for and given a lecture. According to Berruti he appeared in the beggar's rags before the good Father, who administered a hiding before the lecture.[1] Anyhow, having heard his uncle out with his customary meekness, he replied : " Don't be vexed with me, uncle. I gave the coat to one of Jesus Christ's poor who needed it more than I."[2] The son of *Il Poverello* could say nothing to that. Anyhow, the incident must have set him thinking hard. Boys of sixteen did not usually behave in that manner. Thus ended Gerard's first attempt to be a religious.

He made a second when he was eighteen, on his return from Lacedonia, after the death of its bishop. It proved equally abortive. Again he knocked at a Capuchin door, whether at the same one or at that in Muro itself does not seem to be certain. Though older now, his looks still betrayed him. His chances of being physically fit for the strenuous duties of a laybrother were unmistakably too slender, and this time the refusal was final. It was clearly God's Will that for the present at least he should remain in the world and continue his tailoring. Had God not destined him to be the son of St. Alphonsus,

---

[1] P. 25.
[2] In Apost. no. 6, § 79.

we cannot help thinking that, with his simplicity and detachment and personal love for Our Lord, he would have made a worthy follower of the Seraph of Assisi.

The old craving, however, never left him. Gerard was not at home in this bustling world of men. Its cloying perishable things had no meaning for him. While his hands cut and sewed, his thoughts flew upwards and his heart sighed for God.

At last, when he was twenty-one, he got an idea. What about being a hermit ? In our ears no doubt the notion would sound fantastic. In these parts we have come to associate hermits with remote days and terrifying solitudes. In Italy, however, hermits living isolated lives of austerity and prayer had been very numerous in the preceding century, so that in Gerard's day a hermit was not the phenomenon he would be in ours.

In Gerard's case the plan had much to recommend it. Religious life was obviously ruled out : it was not God's Will, as far as he then saw, and that was enough. As a hermit he would be a burden on nobody, in spite of his poor health, and then he could do a great deal of what religious do for God and for their own souls. Evidently he must have made some arrangement to counteract any loss his enterprise would involve for the family. We are not told whether he sought his confessor's approval for the venture ; it may be that he intended just making a trial of the life before committing himself definitely to it.

He took a young friend into his confidence who was of a sort to appreciate the move. Not only did he approve of the project but actually offered himself as a companion. The next step was to find a hermitage. That presented no difficulty. Gerard's idea was, not to attach himself to any particular church and live on the charity of the neighbours, as hermits commonly did in those days, but to retire to the mountains and the woods and choose some solitary spot where he would be completely severed from the world like the anchorites of old. Such a spot was easily found.

And so, one fine morning in the spring, he and his generous companion left Muro and men behind and were soon installed in their hermitage in a wood some distance from the town. What the family said or thought about it we do not hear. They had already seen too much of God's extraordinary dealings with Gerard to be surprised at anything he attempted, or to question its feasibility or wisdom.

The new life was taken up with deadly earnestness. Prayer, penance, work and holy conversation were to make up the day ; prayer again a good part of the night. There was to be the minimum of sleep. Whatever they could pick from the ground or the bushes was to be their fare.

After two or three days Gerard's companion gave up. The spirit indeed was willing but the flesh weak ; and the fasting beat him. Not so Gerard. He was no novice at austerities. He saw no reason why he should be influenced by this defection ; in a way it but served to make his solitude and severance from men the more complete. But it was not to be. His confessor intervened and some days later the anchorite returned to Muro and to his workshop. One thing told against his continuing the life and reconciled him to the decision of his director : receiving Holy Communion meant going backwards and forwards to the town, and that did not make for solitude. Meanwhile, whatever Gerard thought about his chances of being a religious, God had it all arranged, and events which seemingly had nothing to do with the holy tailor of Muro now began to fit into the divine scheme of things and play their part in the shaping of his subsequent career.

In the May of 1746, the great Founder of the Redemptorists, St. Alphonsus Maria de Liguori, with a number of his disciples, gave a mission in the little town of Caposele. When the saint founded his Congregation Gerard was six years old. Alphonsus had already spent thirty years in this world when Gerard was born; he was destined to spend thirty-two years more after Gerard's death. So rich had been the fruits of this mission and so glowing the accounts that were coming in of Redemptorist activities throughout the archdiocese that its pastor, Monsignore Nicolai, thought he could do nothing better than perpetuate the good work, as far as might be, by asking Alphonsus to establish a Redemptorist house in Caposele itself, offering them that very sanctuary of *Materdomini* where Gerard had been so favoured as a child. The saint gladly accepted the offer.

As the funds needed for the new foundation were greater than the Fathers were in a position to supply, an appeal had to be made to the charity of the people in other towns within and outside the archdiocese. Furnished with a letter of warm recommendation from the archbishop, Father Francis Garzilli, accompanied by the laybrother Onufrio, set out on their begging tour. In due course they appeared in Muro. It was in August,

1748. They were the first Redemptorists to set foot in the town, and they and their Institute were utter strangers to Gerard. Whether he had met them in his tailor's shop in the course of their rounds or seen them in the cathedral, he felt irresistibly drawn to the visitors. He followed them about, made contact with them, and had a long chat with Brother Onufrio. He inquired about their Rule and their various exercises of piety. He was particularly keen on finding out how matters stood with regard to practices of penance. He heard enough and at once acquainted his informant of his decision to become a Redemptorist laybrother. Brother Onufrio was sympathetic but gave him no encouragement. Once again poor Gerard's appearance played him false. The Brother knew from personal experience what he would have to go through and did not mince matters. Early rising, hard and constant work, rough fare—and perhaps none too much of it at times—minute and exacting rules. Infant Orders—unlike other infants—are not reared on delicacies. The picture was sombre and discouraging, and it was meant to be so. Then came the retort which must have nonplussed the good Brother and made him look close at this young man. "Why," said the would-be postulant, "that's just what I am looking for."[1] For some unstated reason the matter ended there.

In the following year 1749, at the request of the bishop and clergy, the Redemptorists were back again in Muro, this time not to quest but to give a mission. The good news of their success in the archdiocese had crossed the

---

[1] Tannoia, cap. vi ; Caione.

border. It was obviously meant to be a thorough business, as fifteen of them came. Amongst them was Father Garzilli. Amongst them were also Fathers Carmine Fiocchi, Francis Margotta and Paul Cafaro, the leader of the band and the superior of the new foundation in Caposele. These three eminently holy men will often make their appearance in subsequent pages. Of Paul Cafaro we just say here that he was one of the most eloquent missionaries of the Institute. St. Alphonsus, who wrote a sketch of his life, says of him : " When in the pulpit, he spoke with wonderful fervour and energy. It was admitted on all hands that his sermons made an extraordinary impression and were different from those of anybody else. Even in the familiar discourses which he delivered to us at the weekly chapter his words were like arrows that pierced us through ; he uttered them with such penetrating energy that we all felt that they came from the depths of his heart. When speaking of eternity especially he made all his hearers tremble."[1]

On April 31, the first Sunday after Easter, the great campaign against the world the flesh and the devil opened simultaneously in Muro's three parishes. Muro was a very religious town in those days and we can imagine how it was stirred. Whether the preachers, especially Father Cafaro, took any particular notice of a tall gaunt youth standing morning after morning and night after night near the pulpit we do not know. But we do know that the tall gaunt youth took particular notice of them and listened—held, fascinated,

---

[1] *Vita di D. Paolo Cafaro*, vide *Opere di S. Alfonso M. de Liguori*, vol. iv, p. 657.

shaken to the depths of his soul by the great truths
of religion as only the saints are shaken by them. As
we have said, there was more than one preacher of
uncommon sanctity amongst the missioners and " deep
calleth on deep."[1]

Gerard could not see enough of the Fathers. He
shadowed them everywhere, followed them to the church,
to their lodging, offered his services in every way, was
hardly ever out of their sight. As the mission drew to
a close, he had his mind made up to enter the Congregation and already began making remote preparations by
severing every tie that bound him to the world. The
little he still had he gave to the poor. His possessions
now consisted of a spare shirt and two pairs of drawers.
These went to a needy friend. Thus denuded he presented himself to Father Cafaro as a postulant. The
saintly superior looked pityingly at the long lanky
youth and the bloodless emaciated face and the great
eager eyes—" *piu spettro che uomo* . . . more a ghost
than a man," as a witness describes him.[2] He thought
of the laborious life to which Gerard wished to dedicate
himself. He was convinced of his sincerity—who would
not be ? He admitted and admired his virtue. But he
had his Congregation to consider ; and he could never
think of burdening a community with such an un-
promising subject. He refused to accept him and told
Gerard to put the thought definitely out of his head.
Renewed appeals met with renewed refusals, until the
youth had at last to leave, still unconvinced that he
was not called by God, still hoping against hope.

---

[1] Ps. xli, 8.
[2] In Ord. no. 7, § 442.

Meantime Benedetta and the girls had got wind of it. Every arrow in the quiver of a mother's heart was now shot at his purpose. Surely he would not cause her this sorrow. Surely it was clear that his health would never stand the life. Did he not see that any further effort he would make would end only in further disappointment ? Why not stay on with his mother, who would always look after him ? After all, one can serve God and work out one's salvation anywhere. So the mother argued, as many a mother and many a good mother, too, has argued before and since ; and fond sisters' supplications were soon ranged on her side.

Gerard was unshaken. Then Benedetta called on Father Cafaro and implored of him to espouse her cause. With an exaggeration born of her grief she stressed her poverty and the need in which she stood of her son. " The desire to keep her beloved son," writes Benedetti, " induced Benedetta to overstate her poverty when speaking to Father Cafaro ; but with Gerard she never alleged such a motive. The truth is that she never experienced want : during her three remaining years she lived as before on the work of her hands, and her daughters were able to support her at need. Besides, had the mother been really indigent, St. Alphonsus would never have admitted her son to the novitiate."[1] But indeed the mother's tears and eloquence were not required and she was but forcing an open door, as Father Cafaro had not the slightest intention of receiving the boy. And with this assurance he dismissed her. One little piece of advice he thought it well to give as he showed her out : it might be just

[1] P. 51.

as well to turn the key on Gerard in his room when the
Fathers would be leaving Muro.

Benedetta took this hint. When the missioners were
departing, Gerard happened to be in his room. She
turned the key and left him. It was a drastic move, but
it was quickly checkmated by another. The prisoner,
realising at once how matters stood, saw that there was
no time to be lost in argument or appeal. Whipping the
sheets off the bed, he made them fast to the window-sill,
lowered himself to the ground and was away at top
speed in pursuit of the travellers, without any member
of the family becoming aware of his escape. In true
runaway fashion he left a note behind him on the table
to the effect that he had gone off to become a saint and
requesting all concerned to think no more about him.
Anybody who fancies that sanctity knocks the character out of a man will get a rude shock. In this runaway for Christ's sake we scarcely recognise the meek
submissive apprentice of Pannuto's work-shop, the
bishop's boy and the resident tailor of Malpiedi's high-
school.

Meanwhile the missionary band had got a good start
and was well on its way. Gerard knew they had taken
the road to Rionero, in the diocese of Melfi, where they
were to give a mission. The way was rough and mountainous and unfamiliar. After having covered a good
twelve miles, at last he saw them ahead of him. Running
feet and a voice crying tearfully, " Do wait for me,
Fathers,"[1] made them look back and soon brought them
to a halt. In their breathless pursuer Father Cafaro

---

[1] Benedetti, p. 51.

quickly recognised his obstinate postulant. He thought
he had seen the last of the pale-faced tailor of Muro,
and now here they were at grips again. Entreaties and
refusals began afresh. Again Father Cafaro told the
kneeling youth what he had told him over and over
before, that he was unfit to be a laybrother in the
Institute. Again he bade him return home. The
other members of the band now joined in with their
superior. It was a strange and moving scene there on
that country road, on that May afternoon in the year
of grace 1749, with that little knot of Redemptorists
gathered sympathetically about that wretched-looking
lad arguing and appealing frantically, gesticulating as
only an Italian can do it, with all the devils listening
fearfully and all the angels of heaven looking expect-
antly down. Little did the Fathers know that they were
using all their powers of persuasion to keep out of their
Institute him who was to become one of its greatest
glories. At last the party moved on. Gerard moved
on with it. The arguing continued on both sides. Every
appeal to him to go home was met with the retort :
" Try me ; you can then send me away."[1] Thus Rionero
was reached, the arguing and counter-arguing continuing
the while. The Fathers arrived at their lodgings. Gerard
clung to them. They went in. Gerard went in. They
could not shake him off, they could not eject him. He
stayed on and practically forced his services upon them.
For the first time in his life the holy youth showed off,
now giving a hand in the kitchen, now doing various
jobs with the needle and making himself useful in every

---

[1] Tannoia, cap. vi.

way he could devise. All the while he never let slip a
chance of renewing his request, only to meet with the
same refusal. The Fathers marvelled at his persistency,
but could do nothing.

At last, Gerard one day suddenly threw himself at
Father Cafaro's feet and with streaming eyes spoke thus :
" If you will not receive me as a laybrother, I will take
my place amongst the poor begging for bread in your
hall."[1] He had shot his bolt. This time it struck home.
This youth had clearly a vocation of some sort. In any
case a trial seemed reasonable enough. He would be
given a trial. Father Cafaro accepted him, "rather
to get rid of him," as Tannoia puts it, "than from any
wish to receive him."[2] It was indeed "because of his
importunity."[3] He sent Gerard to our house at Iliceto
with a letter to the rector, Father Lorenzo d'Antonio.
In it we read : "I am sending you another Brother,
who will be useless as far as work is concerned, since
he has a very delicate constitution ; but I could not do
anything else in view of his persistent entreaties and the
reputation for virtue the youth enjoys in the town of
Muro."[4] As Tannoia says again laconically : " this, then,
was the way in which Gerard Majella was admitted
into the Congregation."[5] How near that Congregation
was to keeping him out ! When Gerard escaped so
dramatically from his mother's home on that May day,
he darted in pursuit of holiness and heaven, and darted
literally through a window.

---

[1] In Apost. no. 7, §. 33.
[2] English Edit., p. 259.
[3] Luke, xi. 8.
[4] Berruti, p. 48.
[5] English Edit., p. 259.

CHAPTER IV

THE "USELESS" LAYBROTHER

AMONG the many place-names that ring sweetly familiar in the ears of Redemptorists the world over is that of Iliceto.[1] Iliceto is a little town in the diocese of Bovino, situated in the heart of Apulia. About three miles outside it, on the fringe of a dense wood and clinging to a hillside stands an ancient church dedicated to the Blessed Virgin. The place had long been hallowed and historic ground. In the early centuries the wood had given shelter to many a persecuted Christian and a grave to many a martyr. Centuries later, about the year 1460, the Blessed Felix da Corsano, a Hermit of St. Augustine, of the Congregation of St. John a Carbonaro, had built the church, together with an adjoining monastery for a community of the primitive observance, thus making it the mother house of the *Riforma Ilicetana*. Over the high altar he had placed an unusually appealing picture of the Mother of God under the title of *Our Lady of Consolation*. The shrine soon drew ever-increasing crowds from the town and surrounding country, and miracles quickly stamped their approval on the popular devotion.

Nearly two more centuries rolled by, and then the

---

[1] It is now called officially *Deliceto*. We will retain the old and more familiar form.

community, too small to fulfil its purpose of strict observance, was suppressed by Innocent X, in 1652. Since that date, in spite of individual effort and good-will, the history of the shrine, up to the time of which we write, had been one of comparative oblivion and eclipse. One interesting relic of the holy past was a grotto hewn out of the rock, close to the monastery, to which the saintly reformer would betake himself for prayer and penance.

Towards the end of the year 1744, when Gerard Majella was eighteen, St. Alphonsus, with four of his best missioners, including Father Cafaro, was giving a mission in Iliceto. Naturally he visited the famous shrine. It was love at first sight. The surrounding solitude and peace, the venerable church and monastery to which so many sacred and touching associations clung,—above all, the haunting loveliness of Mary's storied picture, delighted him. And there was something else that struck another cord. He was told, amongst other things, that when winter was at hand, some 50,000 shepherds would come down the mountains to watch their flocks upon the plains, while there was none to shepherd the shepherds themselves to the Fold of Christ.[1] And so, when it was suggested that the Redemptorists should take permanently over the ancient church and monastery and be the guardians of Mary's shrine and put their sickles into this teeming harvest of abandoned souls, the future *Most Zealous Doctor* of the Church and author of the *Glories of Mary* could not hesitate. Generous friends came forward, difficulties were smoothed

---

[1] 50,000 may seem a high figure ; but in those days the sheep ran into millions.

over, and on the 24th December, 1744, the Fathers
entered into possession, to the great joy of the whole
diocese and particularly of its saintly pastor Monsignore
Lucci.

The holy Founder himself ruled the community for
the first two years. He loved this house of Iliceto and
within its silent and sequestered walls wrote his *Meditations on the Passion* and worked at the first edition
of his *Moral Theology*. The saint goes into practical
details about the place. In a letter to Father Xavier
Rossi, dated December 19, 1744, he writes : " The
country is fertile and produces everything : wood, wheat,
vegetables, good wines, excellent cheese, and an abundance of good fruit. There are cows, sheep and goats
here, and a certain kind of cheese the like of which I
have not tasted before. The air is very good and mild.
In one spot there is water in the place that seems to
come from paradise itself, with a spring dedicated to
the Madonna and a fish-pond by which we can water
the garden at all times and keep it green."[1] It is refresh-
ing to hear this great ascetic dilating with such evident
gusto on all these pleasant and homely things. Father
Cafaro strikes another note : " In this new house of
Our Lady of Consolation in Iliceto," he writes, shortly
after the foundation had been made, " I seem to be
enjoying the solitude enjoyed by the hermits of Egypt.
When we return here after the spring and winter missions,
we are so peaceful and secluded and are so withdrawn
from the tumult of the world that we never know what
is going on in it. We are cut away from all intercourse

---

[1] *Lettere di S. Alfonso Maria de'Liguori, Corrispond. General.* vol.
I, p. 100.

with men. We are in a wood where the air is good and the view pleasing. It rivals the Pedroso of St. Peter of Alcantara. Blessed be God Who has led me hither."[1] So was another to express himself soon after.

The foundation of Iliceto was little more than four years old when, most probably in the evening of Saturday the 17th May, 1749, the door-bell rang. On opening, the porter found himself face to face with an unusual-looking visitor : a young man in his early twenties, tall, ominously thin, with the flush and grime of long hard journeying upon him. It was Gerard. And long and hard the journeying had been. On receiving Father Cafaro's letter of introduction—his oddly-worded passport into the Congregation—he thought the moment would never come until he had delivered it. Iliceto was a good day's walking from Rionero, and hard going at that, and the roads were vile. However, nothing counted with him now but to get there, and love lent wings. His packing was not complicated. When a young man parts with a superfluous shirt his luggage is not likely to be heavy. Probably the most substantial part of it, and in his eyes the most important, was the whole ascetic armoury of disciplines, hairshirts and other dreadful-looking devices for self-torture, which, as Tannoia definitely tells us, he brought with him into the Congregation.[2] Apart from these possessions Gerard brought little to the community beyond his own incomparable self.

---

[1] From a letter to a priest quoted by St. Alphonsus in his *Vita di D. Paolo Cafaro*. Cfr. *Opere di S. Alfonso*, vol. iv, p. 660.

[2] English Edit., p. 265.

He asked to see the superior and handed him the letter. Father d'Antonio read it and glanced at the bearer. " I am sending you another Brother, who will be useless as far as work is concerned, since he has a very delicate constitution." So the letter ran. It was a strange reference for a prospective laybrother. Father Cafaro had evidently anticipated the rector's reactions, for he added by way of apology, " I could not do anything else in view of his persistent entreaties and his reputation for virtue." His " uselessness " was but too obvious : the sunken cheeks, the tell-tale pallor behind the passing flush, the frail slender frame assured him of that. And what would Father Minister say to this new recruit to the ranks of his workers ?[1] At the best of times it had been hard to balance the budget at Iliceto, in spite of the glowing picture drawn by St. Alphonsus. Performance had lagged sadly behind promise in the matter of gifts, and most of the pilgrims to Our Lady's shrine showed a tendency to being beggars rather than benefactors. From the very outset the house had to struggle against stark destitution. So much so indeed that not so very long before St. Alphonsus had written from it : " If God does not provide I shall be obliged to disband my companions, for want of a livelihood. Although we have eaten nothing but beans and drunk nothing but water, we are already sixty ducats in debt[2]." And now here was another mouth to

---

[1] The Father Minister, or Bursar, enjoys a special authority over the Laybrothers in the Institute.

[2] According to the *Oxford Dictionary* (1940) the ducat was a gold coin valued about 9/- of our money.

feed, with no likelihood of getting anything in return ! Virtue was all very well, but the community could not live on air. Work had to be done—and there was plenty of it—and the Father Minister had to keep a steady eye on results.

Meantime the postulant was kindly received. Gerard himself was in the third heaven. He wept for joy. He kissed the walls. He thanked God and men for taking him out of the world and into His own holy house. Iliceto was new to him, and when he was told he had entered one of our Lady's own sanctuaries, the heart of this young lover of Mary leaped within him. And with good reason, for more than once Mary had been associated with great moments in his life and had mothered his soul with more than her wonted mother's love. From Mary's arms the Divine Child had descended at Capotignano, when he was a little boy of six, to play with him and enrich him with the precious loaves. While still a child himself, he had held that mysterious converse in her shrine at Caposele ; and now yet again he finds her, this time installed as Queen, in the very spot that had been the goal of all his longings and all his prayers. Kneeling before her image he renewed his resolve to spend his days in Iliceto under her protecting hand. Most of his brief remaining years were indeed to be lived there, though he was destined elsewhere to die.

Gerard came to Iliceto to be a Redemptorist laybrother. It will not be amiss to let our readers know what this precisely meant. There are Redemptorist laybrothers to-day in the four quarters of the known world, sons of its many races, speaking its differing tongues, exhibiting all its various racial characteristics ; but in the pur-

suance of their religious vocation and of the special
sanctity with which it is identified, they are told to
turn their eyes to one who typifies most fully everything
they have in view. In the general constitutions of the
laybrothers of the Congregation of the Most Holy
Redeemer we read : " They should always have before
their eyes St. Gerard Majella, whom Pius IX solemnly
declared to have been given them from heaven as their
Patron and Model."[1] Gerard is now their ideal, for he
realised supremely in himself the ideal set before him
in his Rule.

The word " laybrother " best tells us all we wish to
know. The laybrother is not a priest, and he knows
and never forgets that as far as spiritual dignity and
power are concerned, there lies between him and the
priest a distance that nothing can ever bridge. But if
he is " lay," he is a " brother," and this means everything to him. Though he has come to serve his Congregation in material things, he is far indeed from being
a mere servant in its ranks. To begin with, he is a
religious and as such is bound by the same obligations
as the Superior-General himself and is equipped with
much the same means of discharging them. However
onerous or multiplied his external occupations may be,
they are never allowed to clash with the fulfilment
of his specific duties as a religious and with the attain-
ment of his specific end. Spiritual fare, either in the
form of prayer or sacraments or instruction, is ever
to be had in abundance. Not only does he take part
in most of the spiritual exercises of the community,

---

[1] *Constitutiones et Regulae C.SS.R.*, no. 1556.

but he can pray—and he is taught so to pray—even in his busiest moments. The spirit of prayer acquired in the oratory can overflow into any and every work of his hands outside of it, penetrating and saturating and transmuting it into itself.

Moreover, if prayer is what we all believe it to be and what the age-long history of the Church and her saints have proved it, the laybrother who prays much and well is no mean asset to the apostolic army. The Judgment Day will surely have astounding revelations to make on this head, when the divine assessment of merit and glory will take place. Working behind the lines, as it were, in the war against the powers of darkness, the laybrother can lead a far more sheltered life than his missionary confrères, facing few of their dangers and shouldered with none of their dread responsibilities. There is something else. To say nothing of the stupendous fact that the same roof covers the laybrother day and night and his Eucharistic Lord, he is housed with a family of priests whose priesthood is literally every moment at his beck and call. And thus St. Alphonsus would have it : " They are the sailors who work at the oars," he would say, " while the pilot and others are busy in the interior of the vessel. If they help us in temporal matters, it is but right that we help them in spiritual matters."[1]

Not only is the laybrother a " brother " of the priests in his religious status and obligations and opportunities, but he is such in other ways as well. Though he always ranks after the chorist members of the Institute, whatever

---

[1] Berthe, *Vie*, vol. i, p. 648.

be his merits or his years, still he is a member of the same religious family and shares its material as well as its spiritual goods, even to partaking to an iota of the same fare in the same refectory.

Of course manual work is the specific duty of the laybrother, that thus the workers in the Vineyard may be released to perform their own. His Rule bids him " be always mindful that they have come to serve."[1] Idleness must be shunned ; when their allotted task is done, they must either pray or seek another. Obedience must be their watchword. They are taught to realise that constancy and thoroughness in the discharge of daily duties is the first and not rarely the most painful of austerities ; that no duty can be small and that sin alone degrades ; that the most menial service, if done for God and done aright, is a prayer ; that in God's sight the least duty is of equal import with the greatest ; that it is not the " what " one does in His service that matters, but the " why " and the " how " ; that whatever is done for His glory will receive good payment on the Accounting Day. Writing from Nocera, January 13, 1756, to the laybrothers at Iliceto St. Alphonsus says : " Humility is the virtue most proper to the laybrothers . . . the virtues most necessary to make you saints are humility, obedience and patience ; without suffering there is no sanctity."[2] We can easily see how a life such as this, not only secures salvation for the Redemptorist laybrother, but opens a door to consummate sanctity. And no wonder his Rule begins with these words : " The Brothers should have always before their

---

[1] *Constitutiones et Regulae C.SS.R.*, no. 1544.
[2] *Lettere di S. Alfonso*, vol. i., pp. 321-322.

eyes the great favour of their vocation."[1]

The Congregation which Gerard had entered was still very young. It had not yet completed its first score of years, and already more than one of its laybrothers had fulfilled this programme and distinguished himself for outstanding holiness. Thus there was Joachim Gaudiello, who, when the world tried to bar his path to the cloister, swept it aside saying: " I mean to become a saint."[2] He kept his promise, entering the Institute at the age of eighteen and dying in it in the odour of sanctity at twenty-two. The Venerable Cæsar Sportelli, one of St. Alphonsus' early companions, in a letter dated May 16, 1740, called him " our little angel." And an angel in the flesh was Gaudiello, who none the less waged against that flesh of his a savage unrelenting war. His biographer Tannoia says of him that " his every breath seemed a prayer " and that " Joachim himself owned that the community meditations seemed to him to last but a moment."[3] With him the remembrance of God's presence was literally unbroken. But Gaudiello did more than pray. It was a maxim with him that " the love of work is the true test of the virtue of a laybrother."[4] " I work by the piece," he would also say, " and my profits grow with my weariness."[5] The keenest eyes could never detect a wilful fault in him. " Joachim teaches us many a lesson," St.

---

[1] No. 1543.

[2] Tannoia, *The Lives of the Companions of St. Alfonso Liguori*, p. 458.

[3] Tannoia, *ibid.*, p. 460.

[4] *Ibid.*, p. 461.

[5] *Ibid.*, p. 462.

Alphonsus often remarked.[1] And the same saint wrote his epitaph in Latin, of which the following is a translation : " Brother Joachim Gaudiello, rich in every virtue, yearning after the likeness of Christ, moulded his life in all things according to his Model, and by his patience in illness, meekness in trial, and striking obedience, showed forth with unchanging constancy the life of Jesus Christ to the eyes of all. Not on the wood of the cross, but with a longing for the cross and in the embrace of the Crucified, he was the first amongst us all to secure the crown of the glory of heaven."[2] Gaudiello was in fact the first to die in the Congregation. He was, as Tannoia puts it, " the first sheaf from the field of our Congregation to be garnered for heaven."[3] As he put it himself on his death-bed, " I am the standard-bearer."[4]

Then there was Vito Curzio, whose life Alphonsus himself has sketched. This young gentleman, secretary to the Marquis of Vasto, had displayed very few of the qualities of an angel, except it be of a fallen one, for up to his twenty-sixth year, he seemed possessed by a very devil of pride. His temper was ferocious. He admitted that his only objects of devotion in the world had been his sword and pistol, and he was quick with them. He fought several duels which nearly cost him his life. He shot at a doctor on one occasion and at a military officer on another, but happily missed them

---

[1] Tannoia, *The Lives of the Companions of St. Alfonso Liguori*, p.466.
[2] *Ibid.*, p. 475.
[3] *Ibid.*, p. 457.
[4] *Ibid.*, p. 473.

both. Grace called him to enter the new Congregation
as a laybrother, when it was one week old. On his
arrival he was ordered to serve at table. Then the crisis
came, that ' tide in the affairs of men,' that pregnant
moment in some men's lives when they are poised
between heroism and abject surrender, between ultimate
triumph and failure abysmal and complete. On hearing
the order to serve, his proud soul sprang back erect
and resolute. He to serve ! He—Signore Vito Curzio—
secretary to the Marquis of Vasto ! He—with a brother
a canon and another a doctor ! His first reaction was
to settle matters violently with him who had given the
order. But grace came to the rescue, first without and
then within. It turned his eyes towards a postulant
of social standing doing what he—Signore Vito Curzio
—had been told to do and whispered the words it
whispered long ago to the shrinking Augustine : " Can not
you do what these men have done ? "[1] That was the
end of Signore Vito Curzio. That same day Brother
Vito served quietly at table. After this initial triumph,
he leaped from summit to summit in the ways of God.
Obedience became the favourite virtue of this once
proud man. So fervent was his prayer that he was
often bathed in tears. St. Alphonsus writes in a sketch
of his life : " He received such light when meditating,
especially on the mysteries of the Birth and Passion
of Christ, and he was so moved that he could not keep
from bursting into tears and sobbing in such a way
that it seemed as if the violence of his love for God
would really suffocate him. This was particularly the

---

[1] *Confession.*, lib. viii, cap. xi, 27. ·

case when he received Holy Communion, which he
did almost daily. I often witnessed this myself and
had to wait some time before he could receive the sacred
Host. His tears and sighs would also last for a good
while after he had communicated."[1] He died at Iliceto
less than four years previous to Gerard's entrance there.
" A saint is dead " was heard on all sides when the
news got out. St. Alphonsus sang his Requiem and
broke down with weeping.

Again there was Francis Tartaglione, that " model
of true humility,"[2] as his biographer Tannoia calls
him, another holy tailor, a very gay and handsome young
man and once a Jesuit postulant. The same Tannoia
says of him that " he ate little and slept less "[3] and that
" his aspirations were so frequent as to form one
continuous prayer "[4]; that " this good Brother's patience
and good-humour amidst the poverty and misery we
then endured served as a model to us all, and his example
incited us to aim at the highest perfection."[5] His
good looks once urged the unchaste world to throw itself
upon him in its vilest way and made of him another
Joseph. Francis entered the Congregation twelve years
before Gerard and outlived him a score. We shall
meet him again.

Lastly, there was Januarius Rendina, who entered
in 1732 and died at an advanced age. He relates of
himself : " When I entered the Congregation our founder
said to me : ' Brother, do you wish to become a saint ?

---

[1] *The Lives of the Companions of St. Alphonsus Liguori*, p. 482.
[2] *Ibid.*, p. 491.
[3] *Ibid.*, p. 494.
[4] *Ibid.*
[5] *Ibid.*, p. 493.

If you do, welcome; but if not, return whence you came.'
And when I would go to him on later occasions to complain of my troubles or sufferings, he never failed to
reply : ' Ah ! Brother, so you don't wish to become
a saint ! ' "[1] These words became the constant subject
of his meditations. Gerard loved this old Brother
and he became a saint ; and perhaps the first fact had
much to do with the second. He died with the reputation of great holiness, which Heaven seems to have
confirmed in no uncertain way. Such were some of the
earliest Redemptorist laybrothers, and the list is far
from being exhaustive.

We need scarcely say that the laybrothers of the
rising Institute had by no means the monopoly of great
holiness. One clerical student must get a passing
mention. Dominic Blasucci, in whose case both the
diocesan and the Roman process have been happily
terminated, has been called the ' Aloysius ' of the Congregation. Born with it in 1732, he was a novice at
eighteen, a student at nineteen, and dead at twenty.
" I know of only one fault in Blasucci," once remarked
St. Alphonsus, " he mortifies himself too much."[2] After
his death, Father Cafaro wrote thus to the saint : " I
may say that Brother Blasucci was a saint worthy of
canonisation . . . . There was such perfect and universal
rectitude in all he did that the greatest saint could not
well have surpassed him . . . . I look on him as a saint
and have kept a piece of his habit as a relic."[3] Shortly

---

[1] Berthe, *Vie*, vol. i, p. 171.
[2] Tannoia, *Lives of the Companions*, p. 209.
[3] *Ibid*. pp. 225-227.

before his death he was sent for a change to Iliceto.
There Dominic and Gerard met and for a few brief
months their souls were knit in the closest friendship.
They promised each other a daily prayer till death.
On All Souls' Day of the following year Dominic died.

Alphonsus did not stand alone among the Fathers.
During his life as a Redemptorist, Gerard had much
to do with superiors and directors of eminent sanctity.
One of these calls for immediate notice : Father Paul
Cafaro, the man who nearly lost him to the Congregation
and who finally made him the bearer of that paradoxical
letter of introduction.

In 1741, almost eight years before Gerard entered,
a long lean man, in his thirty-fifth year, threw himself at the feet of Alphonsus and begged admittance
as a postulant. A native of Cava, in the province of
Salerno, and the son of a father who taught the members
of his family how to make mental prayer ; a saint from
childhood whose toys at the age of thirteen were the
penitential paraphernalia of great ascetics ; an habitué
of graveyards who would ponder on death and eternity
for hours amongst the tombs ; a parish priest at twenty-
eight who slept in his clothes when on duty in order
to answer sick-calls without delay ;—such Paul Cafaro
had been before he became a Redemptorist. His bishop
so resented his departure from his diocese that he no
longer employed the services of the Congregation. St.
Alphonsus could not say too much of Paul Cafaro.
As he put it, he was " always heroic in his actions."[1]

---

[1] *Vita Del Rev. Padre D. Paolo Cafaro, Opere di S. Alfonso*, vol.
iv., p. 667.

His soul battened on the strong meat of suffering. " The seal which binds me," writes the saint, " does not allow me to reveal it, but if I were free to write, I should move the very stones to pity. It can be said that during those (last six) years he suffered a martyrdom more cruel than that endured by any martyr of Jesus Christ." He remained unshaken through it all. One of his brethren, quoted by St. Alphonsus, used to say that if he had to summarise the virtuous life of Father Paul, he would have to represent him on a marble pillar, with the inscription : *Semper idem : Always the same.*[1] Not satisfied with God's chastening hand, he tortured his own gaunt frame with instruments of penance that were truly terrifying. He had not been three years in the Congregation when Alphonsus chose him to be the guide of novices who ran rather than walked the ways of sanctity. But perhaps the best compendium of all this man's merits is the fact that the holy Founder himself chose him for his own director, bound himself by vow, even when Superior-General of the Institute, to obey him, wrestled with God for his recovery when he was told of his illness and wept bitterly at his death. Such was Paul Cafaro and such was the man who was destined to be the greatest and most famous director of St. Gerard Majella. His cause has reached the same stage as that of Dominic Blasucci. He assisted in the foundation at Iliceto, was twice its rector and left it, in 1751, to rule the community of Caposele. Though Gerard had to choose another confessor, he continued to be directed by him. As a director

---

[1] *Vita*, p. 660.

the Father took his stand on the axioms and examples
of the saints. War on the passions by every lawful
and prudent means : such was his stern and unrelenting
programme. " This severity," he says himself, " few
wish to embrace, and fewer still have the courage to
persevere in it ; because to pursue it one has to make
up one's mind to mortify everything that comes from
nature and make a complete sacrifice of one's own
will."[1]

It was into this perfervid atmosphere of great holiness
that Gerard stepped on that Saturday evening in May,
1749. Such was the background of heroic virtue against
which we shall see him moving. The Congregation was
young, with all the vigour and enthusiasms of youth.
Ideals were high and were being aimed at and reached,
not only by the great saint himself who had set them
up, but by numbers of his sons—Fathers, students,
novices, laybrothers—several of whom had already died
or were to die in the odour of sanctity. Even in the
community of Iliceto itself it was not at all going to
be a question of Gerard's sanctity towering in isolated
splendour from a plain of mediocre virtue ; it was not
to be a question of the one-eyed being king amongst
the blind. He was to be no triton amongst minnows.
It is well to bear this mind ; Gerard's stature will grow
in our eyes.

Now so far we have adhered with fair exactness to
the chronological order in the telling of our story. We
are now going to depart from it. The rest of Gerard's
biography, in the usual sense of the word, involving

---

[1] *Vita.*, p. 667.

changes of place and fortune and environment, is easily
told ; unlike his confrère St. Clement Hofbauer, he was
identified with no great public movements or events ;
he moved in a comparatively restricted sphere ; he was
not to complete his seventh year in the Congregation
before he died ; and as we wish to present him to our
readers under the various aspects in which we see him
during his short but wonderful sojourn in this world,
we must cast chronology more or less aside and look
backwards and forwards as our need demands.

It is nowhere stated definitely when Gerard was
clothed in the habit of the Congregation. As we have
seen, he entered in May, and we know that Father
Cafaro returned to Iliceto as rector in the following
October ; that he forwarded to St. Alphonsus the verdict
of the community on the new postulant, and that the
saint gave orders that he should be received. It was
the rule then, as it is still, that the postulancy of a
prospective laybrother should last six full months, and
even longer if the circumstances demanded it. In view,
then, of Father Cafaro's action, it is very likely that
Gerard was received towards the close of 1749, that is,
six or seven months after his arrival. According to the
ruling in those days, the lay novice began immediately
his first novitiate of six months. After a longer or shorter
period of probation, he made his second novitiate, at
the close of which he was admitted to profession. Now
at this time this period of probation had been considerably lengthened, and St. Alphonsus was very slow
to make individual exceptions. However, an appeal
on the part of a canonical visitor induced him to shorten
the time in the case of this very exceptional novice ;

Gerard began his second novitiate early in January, 1752, and became a professed Redemptorist laybrother on July 16, of the same year, a date which by a happy coincidence was simultaneously the feast of the Most Holy Redeemer and of Our Lady of Mount Carmel. Thus this lover of Jesus and Mary began his religious career under their twin auspices.

After this event, the newly-professed wrote as follows to his Superior-General, St. Alphonsus : " Jesus et Maria. May the grace of divine love be ever in the soul of your Paternity, and may the Immaculate Mother keep it there. Amen. My Father, prostrate at the feet of your Paternity, I thank you most heartily for the kindness and charity you have shown me, without any merit on my part, by accepting me and receiving me amongst the number of your sons. Blessed for all eternity be the goodness of God Who has shown me so many mercies, though so undeserving, and amongst them that of making my holy profession on the feast of the Most Holy Redeemer, and thus consecrating myself to God. O God ! and who was I, or who am I that I should dare to consecrate myself to God ? I should like to speak fittingly of the greatness and goodness of God ; but no, it would be useless on the present occasion and you would call me a foolish man. Father, for the love of Jesus Christ and most holy Mary send me your holy blessing and place me at the feet of His divine Majesty. Kissing your hand, I remain, Your Paternity's unworthy servant and son, GERARD MAJELLA, of the Most Holy Redeemer."[1] The vows Gerard then made for

---

[1] Berruti, p. 175.

the first time he renewed every morning before the Blessed Sacrament.

Gerard Majella was now a professed Redemptorist laybrother, and the rest of his short external life can be chronicled in a few words. Apart from two visits to Naples, the first in 1754, the second in 1755, he spent his religious life chiefly at Iliceto, where he began it, at times accompanying the Fathers on their missionary tours or going into the surrounding country on other business. Towards the end of his career circumstances brought him to Caposele, where he died.

And now let us look at Father Cafaro's " useless " laybrother. Even though the contents of that un-flattering letter had never got out amongst the community and had reached only official ears, the whole physical appearance of the new postulant made his success as a laybrother very questionable. Iliceto was a compara-tively new foundation and, as we have seen, an extremely poor one at that. Moreover, the state of neglect and disrepair into which the old house had fallen during a long course of years insured the com-munity against unemployment. It was a hive, with no place for drones. The newcomer's goodwill was undoubted, but for the duties of a laybrother strong arms are as necessary as a stout heart, and the " use-lessness " of Gerard, so bluntly stressed by Father Cafaro, was naturally taken for granted. However, he had asked for a trial and the trial was given. In any case his exuberant attitude on being admitted was not likely to last and he would then settle matters himself by departing. Perhaps a little less exuberance on his part would have given more hope of ultimate success.

Whatever had been thought about him and his chances, the fact is that in a few days he had won over the entire community, and it was not long before the Fathers and particularly the laybrothers, with whom Gerard was naturally brought into closer contact, began to exchange glances. Little exclamations of approval and surprise soon made themselves heard. In every department where he was called upon to give a hand, whatever were the facts about the qualifications of the worker, there could be but one opinion about the quality of the work. No doubt poor Gerard, for a second time in his life, deliberately showed his paces on every occasion, for the menacing spectre of dismissal haunted him everywhere. It was indeed a spectre conjured up by himself when he laid down the condition of his acceptance : " Try me and you can then send me away."

We may here anticipate a little and give his worker's programme as we find it in the list of resolutions written at a later date. It was his programme from the outset : " My God, for Thy love I will obey my superiors as if I beheld Thyself in them and as if I were obeying Thine own divine Person . . . . As soon as I see any Father or Brother in great need, I will leave everything to help him, provided obedience does not forbid me. I will never meddle with anybody else's business, so as to say that such a one has done such a thing badly or the like. Whenever I am told to help others in their work, I will obey him who is in charge most exactly and without any demur ; nor, if I am given an order, will I ever dare to say that such a thing is not being done properly, or not to my liking. When I know from experience that certain things are not done as they should be, I will give my advice, but never in the tone of a master. Whenever I am working with others in any employment, no matter how trivial or menial it may be, such as sweeping, carrying things and the like, I will make it my rule never to be the first to secure the best and most convenient place, or the most suitable instrument for that work ; I will leave the best and most convenient place to others, taking for myself what God may leave me. Thus others will be pleased, and myself as well. I will never put myself forward for any office or anything else, without having first got orders from another.''[1]

On the occasion of his first retreat, in preparation for his clothing, he put in writing the following solemn words of warning addressed to himself : First : " *Posuit me Deus in paradiso voluptatis.*[2] Know, O Gerard, that God has snatched thee from the world and has placed thee like another Adam in this paradise of the Congregation for the one purpose of working and carrying out the precepts and counsels of His Gospel as thou hast them in the Rules. Woe to thee if thou neglect it ! '' Secondly : " I will take care to observe minutely every point of the Rule, to persevere and keep growing in perfection and to set myself to acquire silence, patience and especially union with God.''[3]

As we shall now see, these grave words were to remain no dead letter. The " useless '' laybrother was soon found to be capable of turning his hand to anything

---

[1] Benedetti, pp. 266-268.
[2] Cfr. Gen., ii, 15. *The Lord took man and put him into the paradise of pleasure*.
[3] Benedetti, pp. 58-59.

and everything. What Tannoia wrote of him at a later
date was true from the beginning : " Every kind of
employment suited him : whether he was cook or baker
or porter, he was indifferent to everything, for in every
employment, as he would say himself, he recognised
the good pleasure and will of God."[1] That we can
please God and do His holy Will in every office was a
principle with him.

It was not long before the whole community woke
up to the fact that they had a treasure in the house.
How long Father Cafaro expected Gerard to remain
when he sent him to Iliceto we do not know. Neither
do we know whether he was surprised to find him still
there on his return six months later as rector. But
whatever his own thoughts and feelings were, he was
greeted on his arrival by a universal chorus of Gerard's
unstinted praises. The laybrothers especially, who
were in a particularly good position to observe and
appreciate and who would be the first to detect a conscious or unconscious slacker, declared that he " did
the work of four . . . . *valeva per quattro nella fatica.*"[2]

As though the Lord had destined him to serve as
model for every class of worker, especially in a monastery, Gerard, during his brief life in religion, was in
turn gardener, sacristan, cook, tailor, refectorian,
infirmarian, carpenter and porter. Shortly before his
death, he was clerk of works during building operations
in Caposele, but a clerk of works who did not restrict
his activities to giving orders and looking approval.

He began in the garden. It was a new and violent

[1] Cap. xxvi.
[2] In Apost. no. 12, § 76.

change over from the needle to the spade, particularly
in the case of one who had but slender reserves from
which to draw for the large-scale exercise of physical
strength such work entailed. Gardening in a monastery
is not usually the dainty and diverting hobby it is with
spinsters and elderly gentlemen. It may be that this
duty was assigned to him just to test his powers of
body and will alike. It is likely enough, too, that Gerard
made of it a much more laborious business than it was
ever meant to be. Anyhow, the zest and thoroughness
he put into the plying of the needle he now put into
the plying of the shovel and the hoe. Whenever he
had finished his allotted task before the others—which
generally happened—he would run over to his companions
saying gaily, " let me go on with it, I am younger."[1]
In his eagerness to help he almost snatched work from
the hands of others. But it did not follow that he was
stronger, and one day Father Cafaro, looking into the
garden from the monastery window, saw Gerard working
in the best tradition of the black. The gardener was
clearly overdoing it. He called him and forthwith made
him sacristan.

Great was the joy of the Little Flower when, as
sacristan, she was allowed to touch the sacred vessels
and prepare the altar linen on which Our Lord was
to be laid.[2] Gerard would have understood that joy.
We do not need an unusually vivid faith to recognise
that a sacristan stands apart from all other workers
in a religious house, or an unusually strong imagination
to realise that he is most literally the bodyguard of his

---

[1] In Apost. no. 17, § 4.
[2] *Histoire D'Une Ame*, chap. viii, p. 140.

sacramental Lord and custodian of His earthly palace, and this even in a truer and more permanent manner than the priest himself. Had Gerard been driven by obedience to choose his office as a laybrother, he surely would have chosen the one with which he was now entrusted. When we recall the prodigious intimacies with his Eucharistic God that sweetened and illumined his early years, we can guess the holy thrill that shot through his pure and ardent soul on being given a duty that brought him into such close and constant touch with the Divine Companion of his childhood. With such a faith and such a love as his he seemed more like an angel hovering round the tabernacle than a human worker doing human if very holy work. And none but Jesus and the hovering angels themselves could see the love he put into it. Never had the church of Our Lady of Consolation a better sacristan. " All the old Fathers whom I met and who formed part of that community of Iliceto, used to tell me," says Father Camillo Ripoli in his deposition, " that the Venerable Gerard, when sacristan in that church, kept it so spotlessly clean and neat that never since have they found a sacristan to equal him in the wonderful thoroughness he brought to his work."[1] Half a century afterwards people still spoke of him.

As was to be expected, Gerard's proficiency in tailoring was often turned to account. A skilled workman in any line is always a welcome recruit to the ranks of the laybrothers in a religious community : the only alter-

---

[1] In Apost. no. 7, § 174.

native being for the worker to acquire his skill within
by practising on his brethren. In his tailor's shop Gerard
was naturally quite at home, making and mending ;
and at Iliceto there was much more mending than
making, as the house was so poor and in the clothing
department, as elsewhere, very little had to go a long
way. Here he had ample opportunities of being generous
with others at his own expense, and he never missed
them.

Perhaps no official in a religious community stands
a better chance of canonisation than a flawless porter.
A porter in a busy convent must either be a holy man
himself or contribute not a little to the making holy
men of his brethren.   No office calls with such merciless
persistency for virtue on the part of him who holds it.
The porter is at the beck and call of every member of
the community and must serve them in all his humours
and in all theirs as well.   Not rarely he has to try to
be at the four points of the compass simultaneously
and bilocate without the gift of bilocation.   He has
to try to look sweet on all occasions, even when he is
strongly tempted to look sour. To display consistent
unruffled efficiency in this office is sheer heroism. Gerard
rose at once to this heroism and never fell short of it.
Towards the end he was made porter in Caposele. On
accepting the charge, he said : " This key must open
the gates of heaven for me."[1]   He was under no delusions about the nature and demands of the charge and
realised its import for eternity.   We shall have more

---

[1] Benedetti, p. 299.

to say about the porter of Caposele.[1]

When speaking of the religious life of a laybrother we emphasised the fact that his daily work, whatever form it may take, is characterised by prayer and union with God. With Gerard's past in mind, we need hardly say that he combined the two supremely well. " With Gerard," writes Tannoia, " the spirit of prayer was never divorced from work. If by day he spent himself in manual labour, by night he would retire to the church and there melt into tears before the Blessed Sacrament. As the exercises of piety prescribed by rule were not enough for his heart, he made up at night and would be found in the morning where he had betaken himself the evening before. Moreover, for him everything was prayer, since no matter how preoccupying his duties were, he never lost sight of the presence of God. His recollection was profound, his aspirations frequent and most fervent. Jesus and Mary were ever in his heart and on his lips, and at times he was so lost in God that he would be seen stopping up in the midst of his work."[2] " Whether he was travelling or at home," says a witness, " whether he was discharging the duties of his office

---

[1] Here we may quote what a former Superior General of the Congregation of the Most Holy Redeemer (Raus) wrote in a letter addressed to the Italian periodical *Il Beato Gerardo Majella*, November 18th, 1901 :—

‘ If this devotion (to St. Gerard) was always useful, we must say that it is most useful in our own day, when wicked men are striving in every way to corrupt the unhappy working-classes. On religious and social grounds they badly need to have set before them the example of a young man of their own class, who, by his humility and patience and industry not only acquired holiness for himself, but did good to his neighbour by his prayers, his example, and his kindness towards the needy. If many workers were to imitate Blessed Gerard, how happy they would be and what a blessing they would bring upon society ! "

[2] Cap. vii.

or happened to be in the house of some benefactor ; whether he eat or spoke ;—in a word, whatever he was saying or doing, it was clear that his thoughts were busy with God and heavenly things ; so that many a time, when put some indifferent question, he would give an answer concerning Christian perfection, or heaven, or God made flesh for the love of man and the like. At other times he would break off a conversation and speak of the mysteries of the faith or the love of Mary ; and most frequently, while speaking or working at something, he would fix his gaze on some object of his burning love, such as an image of the Blessed Virgin or of the Passion of her divine Son. He would then remain silent and motionless or be seen fainting away or rapt in ecstasy."[1] As another witness describes him, he was "a man made entirely for God, unable to remain a single instant without God."[2] Father Giovenale—another great servant of God, who had been chosen by Gerard as confessor after Father Cafaro's departure and had been appointed temporary superior by St. Alphonsus—relates how once, at the chapter of faults, Father Cafaro, for some reason of his own, forbade Gerard in the presence of the whole community to think any longer of God. It was one of the most difficult prohibitions he was ever given, and as he went along the corridors or bent over his work, he could be heard repeating : " *Non ti voglio, non ti voglio* . . . I do not want Thee, I do not want Thee."[3]

---

[1] In Apost. no. 11, § 82-83.
[2] In Ord. no. 8, § 54.
[3] Landi, Appendix.

Towards the close of his short life he was once the guest of the archpriest of Oliveto, D. Angelo Salvadore. One evening after supper he and Gerard had been indulging in holy conversation far into the night. The archpriest evidently felt sleepy and remarked to his guest : " My dear Brother Gerard, it is very late. Talking of God and His concerns is very pleasant, but God wishes us to give our body its necessary repose." Gerard sighed profoundly. On being asked what this might mean, he replied : " Oh ! how wretched we are ! during all the time we give to sleep we cannot think of our dear God ! "[1]

For Gerard indeed the difficulty lay in keeping his attention sufficiently fixed on external things. The reader will remember what tricks this rare weakness amongst mortals played on him when he was a mere child and apprenticed to the tailor in Muro. These tricks were now repeated, at times with interesting consequences. We give an instance or two.

One day he was marshalling some retreatants to the dining-room. As the party descended the staircase, Gerard's eyes happened to fall on a picture of Our Lady Immaculate hanging on the opposite wall. The pious gentlemen suddenly found the traffic held up for a considerable time by their guide, who had risen in ecstasy ! We may be sure that there was not a member of the party who did not agree that the rare sight more than compensated for the delay in the serving of the dinner.

On another occasion, it was Gerard's duty as refectorian

---

[1] Caione.

H.

to lay the table for several young clerics who were making their retreat in Iliceto for their ordination. As he proceeded with his work, an image of the *Ecce Homo* caught his eye and straightway, as on the previous occasion, he rose in ecstasy. Another Brother who was passing gazed on the unusual sight. Gerard was raised from the ground, his gaze fixed, his arms extended, holding a fork in one hand and a napkin in the other ! Surely an excellent symbolic figure of the mixed religious life : action and contemplation. The other Brother, seeing that the table was not yet ready and that time was pressing, called Gerard, but to no purpose. He called louder, but in vain. On hearing the voice, other Brothers arrived upon the scene. These, however, met with no better success. Father Cafaro was finally called in, and a touch with a formal word of command brought the ecstatic refectorian immediately to earth. After receiving a severe rebuke he quietly resumed his work. These lapses, however, if we may so paradoxically call them, were exceptional, for he was an efficient and all-round worker.

And now, in speaking of Gerard as a worker, we must speak in some detail of one of his outstanding virtues as a laybrother and a saint, viz., his obedience. Its extraordinary nature and the miraculous circumstances often attending it call for a few prefatory words.

Obedience is one of those religious virtues which even a world that does not worry overmuch about religion has no difficulty in understanding. From servants in its homes, from employees in its offices and shops ; above all, from those who serve in its armies and man its fleets it exacts an obedience as unquestioning and prompt as any exacted in a monastery. The necessity of this obedience is recognised, its demands accepted, its violation never tolerated. An employee may disobey : he will be told to seek employment elsewhere. On a warship, in the barrack square disobedience will be dealt with more sternly. On the battlefield it may mean courtmartialling and death. However far private interpretation of an order is allowed to go in military life, there have been historic acts of obedience which have been held up to posterity as superb, if unthinking heroism

One such act on a Crimean battlefield wrote six hundred names at a single stroke on England's register of heroes, and the nation's poet sang of them : " Theirs not to make reply, theirs not to reason why, theirs but to do and die . . . Noble six hundred." Though *they knew* " someone had blundered " and had given *an unreasonable* order, they obeyed it *without reasoning*, though not necessarily without reason, and went *blindly* to their death. Whatever we may think about the intelligence displayed by these men, they were certainly looked upon as heroes.

On the evening of the 22nd June, 1893, along that north African coast which recent events have made so familiar, the *Victoria*, the flagship of the Mediterranean fleet and the acme of naval construction at the time, was engaged in summer manoeuvres. Suddenly Admiral Tryon gave an unintelligible order to another unit, the *Camperdown*, which would inevitably involve disaster. It was the joint verdict of her officers that its execution was impossible, and they signalled back : " Order not understood." The captain of the *Victoria* twice drew

the admiral's attention to the fact. He made no reply.
There was nothing for it but to obey. In the ensuing
collision the *Victoria* went down carrying with her 359
men. On the part of the admiral it was evidently a
mental lapse or a grave error of judgment; but the
order was obeyed and the captain of the doomed ship
was acquitted.

Now while in religion obedience has none of these
harsh characteristics, based as it is more on love than
fear, still it must be none the less unquestioning and
prompt. Whatever we may think of the incidents just
recorded—whether they are worthy of a cheer or a
sneer, whether they are stupid or sublime—their counterpart is not normally met with in a monastery. *Blind*
obedience is indeed looked for; but we hasten to add
that blind obedience in religion has excellent sight.
An order is given. It may appear unreasonable to the
subject and against *his* judgment. To this he will
indeed be blind, but other considerations he will see
quite well, making his obedience the most reasonable
thing in the world. He will bear in mind that most
likely he is unacquainted with all the pros and cons
of the case; that there is a common as well as his
individual good; and that superiors as such speak in
the name of God, have His authority on their side, and
are presumably favoured with a guidance not vouchsafed to their subjects. St. Alphonsus could write in
a letter to Father Tannoia (Nocera, February 22, 1760):
" The orders of superiors should be obeyed *without
knowing the reason why . . . senza sapere il perchè.*"[1] At

---

[1] *Lettere, Corrispond. General.*, cccxxvii.

the same time, taking orders literally, regardless of consequences, like the sailor or the soldier, is not normally met with in religious communities. Nor is it expected. Christian prudence must play its part even in obeying, and to lay possibly unforeseen difficulties before superiors has always been recognised as in keeping with the most perfect obedience in religion.

Now it is here that Gerard and Gerard's obedience come in. He was a saint, a very great saint, and for that reason was not to be judged by normal standards. He received immensely more than the usual graces from God and corresponded with them with far more than the usual generosity. He was lifted high above the plane of ordinary mortals and led along a higher path in an unusually detailed and intimate way. He was raised up by God to be a shining example of humility and submission to His Will before the eyes of a proud and recalcitrant world. And so, if at times we see Gerard, in this matter of obedience, behaving in ways that seem strange and even stupid and eccentric, we must bear all this in mind. This sort of obedience was well understood by all the saints.

Speaking of the Carmelite nuns of Toledo, St. Teresa writes : " So mortified and obedient were the nuns that while I was there, the prioress had to consider continually what she was saying, for the Sisters did what she told them, though she might be speaking without reflection. One day, when looking at a pond in the garden, the prioress said to them : ' What will happen if I tell her ' —meaning a Sister who was standing close by—' to throw herself in ? ' She had no sooner spoken thus than the Sister was in the water, and so much wetted

that it was necessary to change her habit. How many
similar instances did I not see and how many acts of
virtue did I not admire in those fervent religious !"[1]
These words from a saint and a woman of Teresa's
intelligence are remarkable.

One further consideration is important. The great
name of Benedict XIV was cited (Lib. iii, cap. xli, n. 20)
for the assertion that " the prodigies worked by God
on the occasion of any singular action on the part of
the Servants of God should certainly be regarded as
an approval of that action, stamped upon it by an
unimpeachable divine testimony."[2] As far as Gerard
is concerned, the bare fact that his exhibitions of extraordinary obedience were usually accompanied by this
miraculous intervention clinches the matter. God spoke
His approval ; miracles are His resounding language
which all can understand. Indeed Gerard deftly attributed
all his miraculous cures to the power of obedience.

So striking in its heroism and simplicity was Gerard's
obedience that Father Camillo Ripoli has deposed as
follows : " Speaking with me of the obedience of the
Venerable Servant of God, Fathers Tannoia and Negri
assured me that Brother Gerard so distinguished himself in this virtue that he might be called *il Santo dell'
ubbidienza* . . . . the Saint of obedience."[3] And indeed,
were the Church ever to cast about for a patron saint
of this virtue, she need not look beyond St. Gerard
Majella. One superior said that the like of his obedience
was not to be found in the world and that it was the

---

[1] *The Book of the Foundations* (Lewis), chap. xvi, p. 102.
[2] *Resp. ad Nov. Animadv.* no. 32.
[3] In Apost. no. 7, § 143.

chief explanation of all his miracles.[1] " He was commonly spoken of by all his rectors as a miracle of obedience " ; writes Berruti, " and Father Cafaro, when extolling this virtue of the Servant of God, used to say that God had raised him up in all things above other men and that his obedience made his life one unceasing miracle."[2]

To begin with, he obeyed his Rule. Whether it was by dint of reading and studying it continually, or whether he literally got it by heart, it was said that he knew it so well that if ever it came to be lost, he could restore it without missing a comma. It is not known whether he bound himself under pain of sin to its observance ; but had the infringement of the smallest rule involved grave sin, his fidelity could not have been greater. The word of the Holy Ghost : " He that contemneth small things shall fall by little and little "[3] was one of his basic principles, and the following prayer was often on his lips : " Lord, grant that I may keep Thy holy law, for if I depart from it a little, I may depart from it further ; for Thou dost suffer him who offends in lesser things to fall into greater sins."[4] " Why," he would ask, " why lose the merit of obedience even in little actions ? "[5] For him no rule and no violation of rule was trifling.

Then came his prodigious obedience to superiors. It was a maxim with him that obedience should lead him

---

[1] Berruti, p. 342.
[2] *Ibid.*, pp. 337-338.
[3] Ecclus., xix, i.
[4] In Apost. no. 14, § 133.
[5] *Ibid.*, no. 13, § 44.

to paradise.[1]   Amongst his resolutions is the following :
" My God, for love of Thee I will obey my superiors
as if I saw Thy very self in them and were obeying Thine
own divine Person. I will live as if I were no longer
mine own but Thine by conforming myself to the judgment and the wishes of him who commands me."[2]   A
witness declares that he would not do the slightest
action, though good in itself, without the approval and
leave of his confessor or superior ;[3] and this leave he
always sought even for the doing of the best and holiest
actions, for he dreaded being deceived. As we have
just seen, when all else failed, the voice of obedience
was always enough to take him out of the profoundest
ecstasy.

Indeed had Jesus Christ in person given him a command, it is hard to see how Gerard's obedience could
have been more ready or exact. He would say that
a subject should be ready to go through fire if the superior
so willed it.[4]   He very nearly went through fire on one
occasion to obey a superior, as we shall see in a moment.

A superior one day told Gerard to wait for him at a
certain place in the house, and subsequently forgot all
about his injunction. Late that night he recalled it.
Knowing Gerard for what he was he went to the rendezvous, and sure enough there he found him.

Superiors had to be extremely cautious in issuing
orders, as this extraordinarily obedient youth took them
at the letter, exactly as if they had come straight from

---

[1] *Ibid.* no. 13 § 44.
[2] Benedetti, p. 266.
[3] *Ibid.*
[4] In Apost. no. 14, § 115.

the lips of Christ Himself, and acted accordingly. At times superiors forgot to be cautious and interesting complications ensued.

One cold day, when Gerard was porter, the rector—again Father Cafaro—told him he should drop everything at once the moment he heard the door-bell ring and run and open it, so as not to keep the people waiting outside. Shortly after, Gerard was in the cellar drawing wine. The door-bell rang. Leaving everything as it was, he was off with a half-filled decanter in one hand and the stopper of the wine cask in the other. On the way he met the rector. The latter asked him where on earth he was going with such articles in his hands. Gerard told him and told him why, reminding him of his own orders. Father Cafaro then made use of a curious expression : *"Va t'inforna* . . . . Go and put yourself in the oven ! "* The two Italian biographers—Berruti and Benedetti—make no comment on the words, which seems to suggest that the expression was a familiar one. In his deposition Father Ripoli says : " It had become a habit with this rector to say to anyone who disagreed with him : " *Va t'inforna.*"[1] At any rate, whether the holy man was in bad humour at the moment, or in a particularly good humour and spoke in jest, or whether he was distracted and did not advert to what he was saying,[2] as another witness suggests, there was but one meaning in the words for Gerard : " to put yourself in " meant " to put yourself in " and " the oven " meant " the oven." He took the words literally

---

[1] In Apost. no. 7, § 182.
[2] In Ord. no. 14, § 152.

and forthwith went literally into the oven.[1] Shortly after the Brother baker came along to make it ready for his baking. On opening the door he was mightily astonished to find Brother Gerard squatting inside serenely and saying his prayers ! Half angrily and surely half laughingly he told him to get out. Gerard, however, would not budge without Father Rector's leave and acquainted the Brother with the injunction he had received. Obedience alone could surely have put him in : obedience alone could get him out. The baker ran off to get the leave. On hearing where Gerard was, Father Cafaro exclaimed, distressfully clasping his hand to his forehead : " *Ah! mio Dio*, we must then weigh every word we say when dealing with this man, for he obeys every order blindly."[2] Then, suddenly recalling his encounter with the Brother, and the objects he had in his hands, he sensed the possibility of further complications and told the baker to go at once to the cellar and look after the wine cask. The baker did so to find that though the stopper had not been replaced, not a drop of wine had fallen to earth ! He ran breathlessly to tell the rector. The latter, accompanied by other Fathers of the community, went down and verified the prodigy for themselves. Raising his eyes to heaven, Father Cafaro remarked : " In truth God is jesting in a strange way with this man. We must only let him follow the guidance of the Spirit, else there is no explain-

---

[1] Perhaps the phrase corresponds to our " Go to Hong Kong " and " Go to Jericho." Had an English-speaking Superior given Gerard such an order, we wonder if he would have made an immediate bid for those distant places, unless he were stopped in time !

[2] In Apost. no. 14, § 82.

ing this wonderful prodigy."[1] He could never cease speaking of this extraordinary act of obedience. We are not told anything about the temperature of the oven when Gerard got into it. Had it been heated and had the saint been miraculously preserved from burning, the biographers would surely have mentioned it. One thing is certain : had the oven been heated and had Gerard been told to enter it, it would not have made the slightest difference to his obedience. And had Gerard been a soldier instead of a laybrother, and had he lost his life in a similar act of blind obedience, would it be too much to expect that he would have been awarded a posthumous decoration ?

Now we are quite prepared to see in spirit many a questioning smile—if not more—on the faces of some who read all this. For their sakes we relate the following : " While I was out questing," a laybrother who was a great admirer of Gerard tells us in the process, " the Marchesa Granafe asked me to tell her something about the life of Venerable Gerard. I told her of the very great obedience and simplicity he showed in the incident of the oven . . . Whereupon she said : ' Oh, I see he was a stupid saint . . . *un santo sciocco.*' ' Signora Marchesa,' I replied, ' God forbid you should ever be obliged to have recourse to this stupid saint.' Oh, how wonderful is God in His saints ! Two months had not passed since I had given this answer, when I received in Caposele a letter from the Marchesa informing me that after my departure . . . she had been seized with a mortal illness, the nature of which she did not disclose.

---

[1] In Apost. no., 14 § 82.

Seeing she was given over by the doctors, she turned to the Venerable Servant of God, saying : ' If you are really a saint, let me know it and I will contribute to the cause of your beatification.' She had scarcely uttered the words when she was out of danger and wrote that letter to me three days later, enclosing a cheque for a hundred ducats for the cause of the beatification and apologising for having called Gerard a ' *santo sciocco* . . . a stupid saint.' "[1] This fact happened at the beginning of the nineteenth century ; the witness did not remember the precise year. As we read in the process, " what means that open cask from which not even one drop of wine had fallen if it does not point to God's own approval of his heroic and unique obedience ? for God has certainly never yet ratified or confirmed anything wild or crazy, especially by miracles, which are His undoubting and evident verdict."[2]

As sacristan Gerard once needed a new silk cover for a ciborium. A lady whom he knew, with much piety and money to back it up, promised to supply the material. The quondam tailor of Muro would do the rest. Not finding what she wanted, she generously made up her mind to cut the requisite material out of her wedding-dress. The following day, Gerard met her and before she could utter a word, protested against her spoiling her precious dress and told her to look again, when she would surely find little pieces of silk for the purpose. His remark naturally amazed her, as she had not breathed a word to anybody about her intention. Her amazement grew on finding, when she returned home, what

---

[1] In Apost. no. 22, § 99-100.
[2] *Resp. ad Animadv.*, § 27.

she had been unable to find high or low before. When the rector saw the silk, he told Gerard to make two covers out of it instead of one. The lady had evidently cut liberally. He made one and then realised that, however he managed, he could not possibly make two. He told the rector so. To test the Brother's obedience, the latter insisted on his orders being carried out. Gerard took up the piece of silk without question or demur and began anew. There happened to be a priest in the room at the time, who was a witness of what took place. Again Gerard failed. Then the priest himself, laying down a book, took the silk and having measured it in every way according to the pattern, concluded that no one is bound to do the impossible. He had yet to learn with whom he was dealing. " I must obey," retorted Gerard, " and do it at once ; as it is for Jesus Christ, it is for Him to come to the rescue."[1] Kneeling down and raising his eyes to heaven, he prayed for about a minute ; then he rose, took up the scissors and piece of silk once more and this time produced a second beautiful cover.

Gerard literally took every word of command that came from a superior's lips as if it had issued straight, without any intermediary, from the lips of Christ Himself. If he were told to do seemingly impossible things, that was none of his business : it was Our Lord Who told him and it was for Our Lord to make them possible. He no more thought of questioning or interpreting a superior's order than did the Apostles at the Last Supper when they were given the seemingly absurd and

---

[1] Landi.

impossible command to change bread and wine into the Body and Blood of their Master. "When the superior spoke," writes Benedetti, " Gerard out of love for this virtue (obedience) became as it were incapable of reasoning. His natural judgment was then in a sense suspended and his entire will came under the sway of a sort of passion to wish for nothing but what God wills."[1]

Here is an incident which for the delightful disregard and naivety with which he brushes aside even the ordinary laws of nature and brings them under the yoke of obedience to superiors is not easily paralleled. Father Giovenale, in an appendix to Father Landi's Notes, tells the story : " I remember how, during one of his illnesses, I was called to him by a Brother. I went to his room and found him in a state of high fever. As the patient was under my direction at the time, I gave him an obedience to put an end to the illness at once and get up and go back to work. He obeyed and got up ; the fever had disappeared. As he knew that I was due to leave for the missions immediately, he came to me and said : ' *Padre, non ho più da stare ammalato* ? . . . Father, am I not to be ill any longer ? ' ' It is my wish that you keep well,' I replied, ' till I return from the missions. ' And so it fell out."[2]

It was the same with every order he got, no matter how strange or unreasonable it might seem to be. To see how far Gerard's obedience could go, Father Cafaro one day told him to make his account of conscience to

---

[1] P. 99.
[2] Landi, Appendix.

another laybrother. It was certainly going very far, but Father Cafaro evidently knew his man. He was not mistaken. Gerard ran off at once to the laybrother and made his account of conscience cheerfully and with as much fulness and precision as he would to his own director. We do not hear how the laybrother took it all ; it was probably a far more trying ordeal for him to play such an unwonted *rôle* than it was for Gerard and to receive such confidences than it was for Gerard to deliver them.

His promptitude in obeying was in keeping with everything else. On one occasion he was told to go immediately (a dangerous word to use when dealing with him) to Ascoli, a township near Iliceto, to transact some business. He was on the road at once, without having changed the large unfashionable-looking shoes worn in the house by the laybrothers. On his reaching the square of the town, a crowd of youngsters quickly discovered the shoes and gathered round the wearer. They were highly amused. And Gerard was in his element.

He worshipped the very thoughts of his superiors. What is more, he knew these thoughts, knew them when no human agency could have possibly revealed them. Orders given mentally and from afar he promptly carried out. Three years after his entering the Congregation, Father Fiocchi, another saintly Redemptorist, who died in the odour of sanctity and whose body was found incorrupt four years later, succeeded Father Cafaro as Rector of Iliceto. He had not been long in office before it was suddenly and dramatically brought home to him what manner of man Gerard was where obedience was concerned. He had sent the Brother with a letter for the archpriest in Lacedonia. He was well on his way when the rector suddenly remembered that he had inadvertently omitted a most important item and devoutly wished the messenger back. Gerard returned at once. On seeing him Father Fiocchi showed surprise and asked him why he had come back. The messenger said nothing but looked at the rector and smiled knowingly.

Berruti relates a striking instance of this knowledge which occurred when Gerard was in the house of Caposele. He writes : " Father Rector called him one day to send him on a message. Gerard was going off without even waiting to hear what it was. The superior looked surprised and began to rebuke him for setting about his commission without knowing its nature. The servant of God, however, meekly replied that he was carrying out the order exactly. The rector then knew that Gerard was acquainted with his purpose even before it was expressed in words."[1]

Similar incidents convinced Father Fiocchi that it was quite enough to issue orders mentally to ensure obedience. And he—and other superiors likewise—made liberal use of this supernatural and extremely economic telephony. After all, saints like Gerard Majella did not arrive every day. Towards the end of March, 1752, Father Fiocchi was preaching a novena in Melfi, where he was the guest of the bishop, Monsignore Teodoro Basta. One day the conversation turned on Gerard and the rector regaled his host with stories of

---

[1] Pp. 190-191.

his gifts and virtues. His Lordship was profoundly interested and expressed his desire to meet him and keep him for a few days in the palace. He then suggested sending a messenger to fetch him. Thereupon the rector replied that there would be no need for that, as he had only to bid him mentally to come and he would come at once. His Lordship could then see how far his obedience could go and how much he was favoured by God. Father Fiocchi then recollected himself for a moment and mentally issued his orders. At that precise moment—this was easily checked afterwards— Gerard knocked at the door of the Father Minister's room in Iliceto and informed him that he had to leave at once for Melfi in obedience to a summons from his rector. He left immediately. When he appeared in the episcopal palace, Father Fiocchi, feigning ignorance and surprise, said rather tartly : " And what brings you here ? " " The obedience Your Reverence gave me," Gerard quietly replied. " I didn't summon you by any messenger or letter," retorted the rector. " You did by giving me the obedience in his Lordship's presence, as he wishes to see me." Then turning to the bishop, he went on : " And who am I but a worm of the earth, a sinner, a wretched man who stands in need of all God's mercy."[1]

During a stay he had been making in the town of Corato, Gerard one evening suddenly decided to return to Iliceto, saying he had been summoned home. Nothing could stop him. Yet no verbal or written message had

---

[1] In Apost. no. 7, § 302.

come. Father Fiocchi confided later to a priest that that same evening, at that same moment, he had sent Gerard a mental order to return.

Landi records the following incident, which is not without its comic element : " When Gerard lay ill, this wonderful thing happened which I have heard from more than one of our Fathers. Father Rector Major (St. Alphonsus himself) happened to be in the refectory, when suddenly the Brother presented himself before him, half-dressed and wrapped in a bed-sheet. On being asked by the Father why he was going about in that ridiculous fashion, Gerard replied : ' I came because Your Paternity called me.' He thus revealed that he had miraculously received a mental command from the Father." In truth may we say of Gerard in the words of the Holy Spirit : ' An obedient man shall speak of victory.'[1]

While it in no way takes from the heroism and perfection of Gerard's obedience, we must admit that all his rectors—they were not so many in his brief life— were eminently holy men who themselves were very near and dear to God and through whose lips God evidently spoke. We will conclude this chapter with a word about one temporary superior in whom the divine was not at all apparent. Gerard had not been a twelvemonth in the Congregation when in response to a request of the Bishop of Melfi, nearly all the Fathers, including Father Cafaro himself, left Iliceto to give a mission in that town. The rector handed the care of

---

[1] Prov. xxi, 28.

the house over to a certain young Father named Matteo Criscuoli, an odd and capricious man, though these defects of character had not sufficiently developed at the time to disqualify him for authority. In any case, in the circumstances there were not many to choose from. St. Teresa tells us that Our Lord sometimes allows the blunder of putting such people in authority in order to perfect the obedience of those whom He loves. And so it was now. The community soon discovered to their cost the failings of the temporary superior. But poor Brother Gerard was his chief victim. It was the Bishop of Lacedonia over again, only worse. Indeed the temporary superior approached nearer Pannuto's foreman than Monsignore Albini. Reproaches, penances of all sorts, rigid fasts, and—what mattered infinitely more to Gerard—the frequent deprivation of Holy Communion, nothing was wanting to this strange persecution. But never a look, never a word of impatience or resentment. Tannoia, who was a student in the house at the time, writes : " Not a shadow of repugnance could be discerned on his countenance. My confrères and myself, who were witnesses of it all, never ceased admiring such virtue and we would say to one another : ' Brother Gerard is a saint.' " The same Tannoia once expressed himself in this way : " Either this Brother is a fool who does not realise the unwarranted mortifications inflicted upon him, or else he is a saint who has attained a high degree of the love of God."[1] The fact is that Gerard was both one

---

[1] Cap. vii ; Landi.

and the other : a saint and a fool—with the folly of the Cross. It is but fair to add that the superior who had so much to do with Gerard's sanctity and foolishness eventually left the Congregation.

Such, then, was Gerard's obedience, and such was Father Cafaro's " useless " laybrother.

CHAPTER V

THE SECRETS OF A SAINT

A SHY reticence cannot be said to characterise the ephemeral celebrities of our day. Magnates of industry and commerce, the literary lions of an hour, film stars and beauty queens, champions and record-breakers in the world of sport have no difficulty in favouring us with their confidences. What they are pleased to call their life-story will be given prominence in our Sunday papers and magazines ; and radio talks will share with us, not only the secrets of their achievements, as far as these may conveniently be told, but their views on current topics and events, even when these are not necessarily valuable by reason of the specific eminence of those who hold them. A man standing on a sand-hill does not necessarily see over the mountain.

Now it need hardly be said that the saints were not given to this advertising of themselves. Unless God's glory or their neighbours' good demanded it, they kept in the background ; but when such a demand was made, then they leaped unhesitatingly to the fore. They gave mere interviewers and newsmongers as short a shrift as charity and courtesy allowed. They shunned the house-tops, and one of their biggest problems must have been to do all the good they could without drawing the world's approving glances on themselves.

Consequently, we are not as rich as we should like to be in autobiographies, personal memoirs and life-stories written by saints. Those that we possess were called forth by circumstances that made speech better than silence, and self-glorification had no part at all in the designs and wishes of the writer. Augustine flung his immortal *Confessions* into the world in a vain attempt to stop his praises in the mouths of men. The two Teresas—of Avila and Lisieux—bared their beautiful souls in obedience to authority.

St. Gerard Majella left behind him no autobiography, no intimate and lengthy record of his spiritual experiences. A word, a sign from a rector or a confessor, and he would have rushed to it. However, one day, Father Giovenale, whom we mentioned in the preceding chapter as Father Cafaro's successor in the keeping of Gerard's conscience, got a holy and a happy thought. On the plea of testing his penitent and desiring to find out whether he was guided by self-love or by the Spirit of God, he bade Gerard commit to writing the secrets of his spiritual life : his aims and aspirations, his resolutions, his mor-tifications—in a word, all that went on behind the scenes in the sanctifying of his soul. The result was a manuscript of great interest and no meagre usefulness.[1] A detailed study of it deserves a chapter. The secrets of any man's success are valuable ; the secrets of a saint's sanctity are precious. And if we be allowed the paradox, perhaps we shall be surprised to find that the secrets of the saints were no secrets at all, that we

---

[1] In Apost. no. 7, § 591-598.

possessed them ourselves, but that while the saints remembered, we forgot.

Towards the end of June, 1754, in circumstances we shall soon relate, Gerard was sent to Caposele in company with Father Giovenale, and it was during his short stay there that he penned the document we are going to discuss. We have taken it straight from the Italian text as found in the *Acta*. Gerard begins: " May the grace of God be ever in our hearts and may most holy Mary preserve it for us. Amen.

" My Father, Your Reverence wishes to know all the mortifications I practise ; and you wish me to put them in writing, as well as my other desires and resolutions, together with the precise explanation of the vow I have already made. Here I am, then, ready to give a full account, not only of my external actions, but also of all that passes within me, so that I may be more closely united to God and walk with greater security in the way of my eternal salvation."

Such is the straightforward business-like preamble. He has been asked an intimate, searching and comprehensive question by one who has authority to ask it, and he proceeds to answer it. There are no deprecating apologies, no bashful demurring at the inherent difficulties of the task. He replies to the question with the sincerity and simplicity of a child, as if God Himself had asked it. First of all, he sets down the rather terrifying enumeration of his penances. These we reserve for the next chapter. He then proceeds to state what he calls his " desires," the habitual yearnings of his soul. Here they are :—

" DESIRES. To love God much ; always to be united

to God; to do all things for the sake of God; to love everything for God's sake; always to conform myself to the Will of God; to suffer much for God."

We are here confronted with a programme which, taken broadly, could result in a spirituality of a nebulous insubstantial kind, but which, taken literally and carried conscientiously through, can only issue in consummate sanctity. By Gerard it was taken literally and completely fulfilled. It was a tremendous undertaking: God and God alone; the utter elimination of self, except when self can love God and suffer for Him. In these "desires" of the saint we see the ruthless logic of love: love, union, conformity of will, sacrifice. We must pause here to examine at some length the first three links in the chain, as we see them in his life. We will deal with the fourth—his sacrifice for God—later on. What we are going to speak of now is really the key to all the rest, the key to Gerard's life in many ways so bewildering, the key to Gerard himself.

To begin with Gerard's love for God. According to one witness, his love was regarded as "a prodigy."[1] In the vivid speech of another, "his heart was a volcano of the love of God."[2] The silly hyperbole of the language of human love seemed literally true of his love for God: he was madly in love . . . "*un pazzo innamorato*."[3] On one occasion he happened to be the guest of the mayor of Castelgrande, where a few years previously he had allowed himself to be dragged through the streets for the sake of Christ. One evening, after

---

[1] In Apost. no. II, § 147.
[2] *Ibid.*, § 113.
[3] In Ord. no. 9, § 75.

supper, the love of God was under discussion. Gerard's eyes were raised to heaven and in the words of his host, "his cheeks were as red as roses."[1] We read that "his fervent discourses, accompanied with incessant sighs, turned continually on Jesus in the Blessed Sacrament, on the Passion, on the generation of the Word, on the Incarnation, on the virginity and maternity of the Blessed Virgin . . . . His face then became as it were fire and light, so that he seemed to be an angel from paradise."[2] To put it all in the beautiful words of a witness : " God alone was the food of his heart . . . . *il pabolo del suo cuore.*"[3]

As we shall see in a special chapter, he was brought into unusually close relationship with nuns, and these were particularly fortunate in witnessing the exuberance of this extraordinary love. A Carmelite community once crowded to the grille to hear Gerard discoursing on the great topic. When he came to the words from the Canticle of Canticles : " He brought me into the cellar of wine : he set in order charity in me,"[4] he fell into an ecstasy, during which the parlour and adjoining entrance-hall were seen by all the nuns to shine with a sudden and unearthly brilliance.

On another occasion, in the same parlour, Gerard was conversing on the same subject. Again he rose in ecstasy, and again the room grew luminous. His face was aflame. In the rapture of his love he seized the grille, and its solid iron bars bent like wax in his

---

[1] Landi.
[2] In Apost. no. 9, § 89.
[3] *Ibid.*, no. 10, 32.
[4] Cant. ii, 4.

grasp. The good Mother Prioress was not prepared for this particular effect of divine love and woke Gerard to realities by loudly calling his attention to the damage he was doing. Coming to himself and recognising it, he told her with delightful simplicity that he would have it seen to. The prioress accepted the offer, telling the workmen to leave some of the bars still bent, in commemoration of the incident. The damage had evidently been extensive. As late as 1853, when investigations were being made with a view to Gerard's beatification, the twisted bars still bore mute testimony to his love for God.

There was a convent in Foggia (of which we shall have more to say later) where a number of young girls were being educated. Among them was little Geltrude de Cecilia. One day the nuns took her with them to the parlour to hear Gerard discoursing on holy things. When he had done, he turned to the child and asked her to sing a hymn. Now Geltrude was particularly shy and had not bargained for this. Gerard, however, pressed his suit and coaxed her into singing. Unsuspecting she sang an air to the words of a poem by the contemporary Italian poet, Pietro Metastasio, which contains the verses: " *Se Dio veder tu vuoi* . . . If thou desirest to see thy God."[1] They happened to be an old favourite with Gerard, and the little girl had scarcely begun when he was ravished in ecstasy. Geltrude, encouraged no doubt and thrilled by this altogether

---

[1] *Se Dio veder tu vuoi,*
Miralo in ogni oggetto,
Cercalo nel tuo petto.
Lo troverai con te.

novel and unlooked for effect of her singing, sang the four verses of the hymn right through, leaving Gerard still in his rapture. Never before had she been given such a reception.[1]

Nor was this the first time he had been wrought upon by Metastasio. He had been commissioned to go to Melfi to look after three of the Fathers whom doctor's orders had sent there to take the waters. They were staying in the house of a pious widow named Vittoria Bruno, a devoted friend of the Congregation. Now Gerard could both sing and play tolerably well and often did both to cheer his invalids. One day at recreation he was invited to sing the same verses. He asked for nothing better. The effect was instantaneous and this time took a rather violent turn. Jumping up, the performer flung his arms about one of the Fathers— Stephen Liguori by name—and in a rapture of joy and love whirled him round and round as if he had been a straw. In vain poor Padre Stefano struggled to get free ; he had to dance out the ecstasy. The company were vastly astonished and lost no time in spreading the news of it through the town.

No doubt all this will perplex some of us. It looks so odd, so dreadfully odd. And yet we fancy we can

---

[1] Many years later a member of this same community of Foggia testified as follows in the apostolic process : " When I first entered this monastery, I got my first account of Gerard's eminent sanctity, virtue and miracles from the old decrepit Sister Donna Maria Geltrude De Cecilia . . . . She had known and conversed with the Saint."— In Apost. no. 3, § 110. As the members of the community who had witnessed that memorable scene in the parlour long years before dropped one by one out of her life, that old decrepit Sister must have often been called upon to describe it to a younger generation who knew not Gerard, and perhaps even to sing once again in the thin and tremulous accents of age the song that sent Gerard into ecstasy.

recall instances of people, otherwise sane and sober, giving similar demonstrations of fantastic behaviour in moments of unusual exaltation. On the announcement of some great national victory, for example, or even of some triumph in the more restricted world of finance and sport, men who have been utter strangers to one another and who had never been given to maudlin displays of their emotions, have been known to throw their hats in the air, to shake one another by the hand, to clap one another on the back, and to indulge in mutual familiarities usually associated with meetings between beloved and long-lost brothers. And all this seemingly without consciousness of any breach of the proprieties. The truth is that if we all loved God as Gerard loved Him, we should all probably behave as he did. In heaven, when we shall be "inebriated with the plenty of his house and . . . . drink of the torrent of his pleasure,"[1] we shall understand these holy if freakish exhibitions of those who were given to taste of its anticipated joys. That is how Gerard loved God.

Now love seeks for union, and because Gerard loved God as only the great saints have loved Him, his life was a continual straining upwards to the divine object of his love. Among the resolutions he penned on entering the novitiate was that of practising union with God. No resolution was better kept. He had no difficulty in keeping his mind on God; as we have seen in the last chapter, his difficulty lay in the other direction.

It is a truism of Christian spirituality that loving God does not consist in ecstasies and raptures. No one

---

[1] Ps. xxxv, 9.

understood this better than Gerard. Identity of wills: there is the acid test of love. Willing what God wills, unreservedly, absolutely, utterly: there is sanctity in brief. And there is what Gerard did. And we are safe in saying that in the long roll of the Church's canonised men and women there is not one in whom this complete identifying of one's will with the Will of God is more gloriously marked. To do the Will of God always, everywhere, in all imaginable circumstances and conditions, in the smallest as in the greatest of its demands —there was Gerard's supreme devotion, the ruling passion of his life, the sum and substance of his holiness. It was not so much that he brought his own will into line with God's, to run parallel with it ; rather did he make his own will identical with that of God. And he admitted it : " O Will of God ! . . . O Will of God ! . . . Thou and I have become one and the same thing."[1] In a word, in every detail of his life Gerard willed *with* God. It mattered not in the least who or what the mouthpiece of that Will might be. As he wrote in a letter to a nun : " The kernel of the true love of God consists in yielding oneself to God in everything, and in conforming oneself to the Divine Will in everything, and in being rooted therein for all eternity."[2] " O Will of God ! O Will of God ! " he was often heard exclaiming, " happy is he who wishes for nothing else but the Will of God."[3] In another letter we read : " Great is the Will of God ! O hidden and priceless treasure !

---

[1] In Apost. no. 10, § 21.
[2] Undated letter to Sister M. Baptist of the Most Holy Trinity, of the Carmelite community of Ripacandida. In Ord. no. 7, § 567.
[3] In Apost. no. 9, § 95.

Ah ! if I understand thee aright thou art worth as much
as my dear God Himself.   Who can understand thee
except God ? . . .   What the angels are doing in heaven
we wish to do on earth.   May the Will of God be done
in heaven, may the Will of God be done on earth : then
paradise will be in heaven and paradise will be on
earth."[1]

Nor was Gerard a mere theorist in this matter, a
signpost pointing the way but never following it. Even
when young in years he was already a practised hand.
We have not forgotten his reply to Pannuto's infuriated
foreman who had asked him why he was smiling : " I
am smiling because God's hand is striking me." All
through life, without the cloister and within, whenever
he was subject to authority of any sort, he looked
straight at God in every superior, and in their every
command, nay in their every desire, he heard none
other voice but God's.   We shall see in a moment how
doing the Will of God was to be the *Alpha* and *Omega*
of all his resolutions.

When Gerard was porter in Caposele an extraordinary
incident took place. Amongst the poor who crowded
for alms at the monastery door was a blind man, Philip
di Falcone by name, who played the flute really well
and—what is perhaps a rarer accomplishment in itinerant
musicians—sang excellently. Now Philip and his dog
were well known to the warm-hearted porter and were
always sure of a welcome and a bit to eat. One day
Gerard appeared at the door. He was in a particularly
mirthful mood. Spying Philip in the crowd, he cried

---

[1] To Mother Mary of Jesus, Prioress in Ripacandida. Cfr. Benedetti, p. 216.

To face p. 143.

out to him to play something. " And what do you wish me to play ? " asked the blind man. Gerard asked him to play an Italian air set to the words of a hymn written by St. Alphonsus and beginning thus :[1]

" Il tuo gusto e non il mio
Voglio solo in te, mio Dio . . . "

" 'Tis Thy good pleasure, not mine own,
In Thee, my God, I love alone . . . "

The hymn was a popular composition of the holy Doctor and fortunately was in Philip's repertoire.[2] Philip began at once. The crowd listened. It was too much for Gerard. The mere words " Will of God " in any connection usually thrilled him ; but now, sweetly sung to sweet music, they reacted on him in an extraordinary way. Clapping his hands and literally dancing with joy, he kept repeating the lines : " *Il tuo gusto* . . . 'Tis Thy good pleasure . . . " Then suddenly the words died away upon his lips. He grew quite calm, and with his eyes turned heavenwards and his arms extended, he rose several feet from the ground in full view of the crowd of beggars as well as of the community doctor, who happened to be standing at the door at the time. A painter has reconstructed the scene in a well-known picture.[3] Philip is seated on the steps, bewilderment

---

[1] Its composition was called forth by the death of his beloved Father Cafaro.

[2] Benedetti, pp. 313-314.

[3] After Gerard's beatification, Gagliardi's painting was duly presented to Leo XIII, who ordered it to be given a place in one of the Vatican galleries amongst the outstanding examples of modern art. Here it remained till 1900, when it was transferred to the Lateran gallery, where it draws many admiring eyes.

and inquiry in his sightless face.   He has heard Gerard's
ecstatic repetition of the words of the hymn and the
exclamations of wonderment and delight all about
him. He has lost his audience and ceased his fluting,
and in reply to his eager questions they tell him what
is happening. Contemporary biographers, as well as
the apostolic process, have recorded this event.[1]

It is of course comparatively easy to do God's Will
when it supposes no suffering and coincides with our
own desires ; it is quite another matter when it means
carrying the cross. We shall soon see in detail that
it was all one to Gerard.

Such, then, were what Gerard calls his " desires."
He now passes on to what he terms : " *Sentimenti piu
vivi del mio cuore* . . . The most ardent sentiments of
my heart." The transcendent triumphs of many of
the world's great men may often be resolved into very
simple elements. Their secret often lies, not so much
in any outstanding intellectual endowment, as in habits
and principles of work, in unremitting industry, in
consistent thoroughness and accuracy, in method and
thrift, in the greedy snatching of minutes frittered away
by others often more gifted than themselves. Not rarely,
however, the most potent element in success is the swift
recognition of opportunity and the wholesale and
immediate seizure of ways and means. Captains have
won historic battles because of it, and captains of
industry, too, have dated their fortunes from the moment
when they saw as in a flash that there was money in
some commodity, while it escaped the notice of their
less discerning fellows.

---

[1] In Ord. no. II, § 122.

And so it seems to have been with the great men and women of God. Setting aside their special destiny and its accompanying gifts and graces, we must admit that the starting-point in their holy career was the sudden vivid realisation of opportunities and their quick and thorough exploiting of graces which, in the main, lie within the reach of all. And so Gerard writes :—

" THE MOST ARDENT SENTIMENTS OF MY HEART. I have one good chance of sanctifying myself, and if I lose it I lose it forever. And if I have this chance of sanctifying myself, what is wanting for my sanctification ? Every favourable opportunity for sanctifying myself is mine. Come then ! I will sanctify myself. Oh ! how much it matters that I should sanctify myself ! Lord, what folly is not mine ! Others provide me with the means of sanctifying myself, and do I complain ? " He proceeds :—

" Brother Gerard, make up thy mind to give thyself entirely to God. Henceforth be firmly convinced that thou shalt not sanctify thyself merely by remaining in prayer and contemplation. The best prayer consists in being just as God pleases, in doing God's Will un-reservedly, that is, in spending thyself unceasingly for God. This is what God demands of thee. Be not a slave either to thyself or to anything in the world. It is enough to have God alone present in thy work and to be always united to God. Truly everything we do is a prayer, if only it is done for God. Some follow this business, others that ; my only business is to do the Will of God. Nothing is painful when it is done for God."

Now we know what part prayer played in Gerard's days and how his love for it lured him more than once into unwitting oblivion of earthly duties and surroundings. But with all his contemplative yearnings, he was no unpractical visionary, and his attitude towards such things as recollection and union with God was flawlessly orthodox. No saint was ever more profoundly convinced that all authentic holiness consists, not in pious and pleasant dreaming about God, but in doing His Will, no matter what abject or unlikely form the doing of that Will might assume. Gerard was destined by God to be the greatest wonder-worker of his age. He was a mystic richly gifted with every gift that has made sanctity resplendent. He passed through this world more like a disembodied spirit than a creature of flesh and blood. But Gerard Majella was called to be a lay-brother and it was vital he should never forget it. He never did forget it. Never had he one moment's delusion about the relative value of God's gifts to him and his duties to God. He understood that as far as his own eternal meriting was concerned, it was an immeasurably greater thing to sweep a corridor or wash a dish out of obedience than to work a miracle or see a vision. Had it been in his power, he would have unhesitatingly shaken off an ecstasy to answer the door-bell as porter, or left a heavenly visitant to look after the dinner as cook. There is a curious inclination to dissociate great men of any kind in our thoughts from the normal everyday activities of human life and picture them as constantly engaged in the exercise of their abnormal endowments. Yet Napoleon was not always fighting battles, nor Beethoven always composing symphonies, nor Shakespeare always writing plays. It was the same with the saints. It is easy, when reading Gerard's life, crowded as it is with mystical and miraculous phenomena, to picture him as being in an almost unbroken ecstasy or working unintermitting wonders. Numerous as these undoubtedly were, they were after all but isolated incidents in days filled with commonplace but much more important things done with supreme excellence because done to the last iota absolutely and solely for God.[1] Gerard continues :—

"On the 21st September, 1752, I realised better the following truths : Had I died ten years ago, I should have sought for and aimed at nothing. To suffer and not to suffer for God is a grievous torment ; to suffer everything and to suffer it for God is nothing. I wish to act in this world as if God and myself were alone in it. Many tell me I am deceiving the world. O God ! and what would there be wonderful in my deceiving the world ? The wonder would be if I were to deceive God."

In this passage Gerard recalls certain definite moments in his religious life when certain definite truths struck home. He may have been making his retreat on that 21st September. He may have been in the oratory, in the privacy of his cell, in the garden, anywhere busy with his work, or just going from one place to another in the house. Holy and serious thoughts were the staple food of his thinking, and he could think of them in all

---

[1] " We should be much surprised," certain Canons one day remarked, " if our bishop (St. Francis de Sales) were one day to be found in the catalogue of the Saints. It is true that he discharges all his duties well ; but, after all, he lives like others, he entertains his canons and other people royally ; he even goes boating with them to share in their pleasure."—Hamon, *Vie de Saint François de Sales*, T. II, p. 474. We feel that Gerard would have had a thing or two to say to those Canons, had his opinion on the subject been asked.

places and at all times. He had already often heard
these truths ; but this time, on a certain date and in
a certain setting, they had been grasped as never before.
Even thus had Christ's words about gaining the whole
world and losing one's soul been heard many a time by
Francis Xavier before Ignatius recalled them ; but in
Gerard's case as in the case of Francis they now struck
home. On that 21st September Gerard saw, perhaps
as he had never seen, the swift flight of time and the
need for haste in the holy work to which he had set
his hand. He was to die just three years later, and there
is nothing to indicate that the time of his death had
been thus early revealed to him.

In the next place, in two brief sentences, Gerard gives
us the pith and essence of all we need know about the
cross : " To suffer everything and to suffer it for God
is nothing. To suffer and not to suffer for God is a
grievous torment." His attitude towards suffering is
quite sane and quite human and not at all what perhaps
we might have expected it to be. There is no morbid
fanatical hugging of the cross for its own sake, as if
suffering were a good in itself, to be prized and loved
and sought after apart from God. He has no time for
the Stoic. But let the daily crosses of life be touched
by the Cross of Calvary, then, however thick and fast
they come, they are sweet and treasurable things.

" I wish to act in this world as if God and myself
were alone in it," he writes. A startling attitude surely
to assume towards life and this little world of ours.
Indeed it seems to make of Gerard what we should
call to-day an " isolationist," looking with a lofty aloofness at the petty doings and concerns of men. But

we know that he was nothing of the sort. His words embody quite a number of fundamental things. He reminds himself that God is his first beginning and last end ; that God is most intimately present to him and that on God he depends for every instant of his being ; that to God he is ultimately responsible for every item of his moral life ; that God fulfills all possible aspirations of his soul and satisfies all his possible needs ; that God died for him as if he had been alone ; that, consequently, his individual soul is subjectively of greater import than the world of souls about him ; and that in this sense therefore his soul is alone and should be alone with God, since God alone necessarily counts. And so Gerard understood it. He never meant it to entail any self-centred isolation from his fellow-men ; quite the contrary, for it urged him to work for the glory of God and, as we shall see, fired him with an insatiable zeal to procure this glory by working unstintly for the souls of others.

Gerard says : " Many tell me I am deceiving the world." When he penned these words, he had already tasted of the treatment meted out to God's servants by jealous uncomprehending men. He is prepared for this. God sees his heart and he goes his way in peace.

Under the heading : " *Riflessione :* REFLECTIONS," Gerard now puts on paper one of those elemental truths —one of those eternal platitudes, if we will—which periodically are dinned into the heads of the rank and file of the faithful at missions and retreats, but which, we may fancy, were beneath the consideration of the great saints and mystics. He writes :—

" If I am lost, I lose God ; and with God lost, what

remains for me to lose ? " These fundamental common-
places were clearly, we may imagine, not Gerard's
thoughts. Yet the possible loss of God and the eternal
and all-embracing finality of that loss had obviously
gripped and swayed him as it gripped and swayed all
the saints. And still it is so hard to imagine this angel
of the earth and intimate of God ever losing Him. Then,
as if clinging half in fear, though wholly in love to his
Eucharistic God, he writes :—

" Lord, grant me a particularly living faith in the
most holy Sacrament of the altar."

Gerard now approaches his resolutions and draws a
picture of himself strung up by all these reflections for
the taking of a serious step. There is a sublime and
touching artlessness in his words :—

RESOLUTIONS. " My Lord Jesus Christ, here I am
with pen and paper in hand, ready to write down and
make the following resolutions in the sight of Thy Divine
Majesty, which I have already taken but which I now
ratify anew by virtue of holy obedience."

He is about to write his resolutions, and he feels that
there is something final and irrevocable in the act.
Scripta manent. What we write remains to be seen,
if not by others, at least by ourselves. Written resolutions are hostages for our fidelity ; they bear witness
against us, even when read by no other eyes than
our own. However, Gerard is under no delusions. He
knows human nature, particularly his own, and mistrusts
it. He is not forgetting the warning words of Christ :
" Without Me you can do nothing."[1] Had anybody

---

[1] John, xv, 5.

told him, as he took his pen in hand that day, that even he could become a castaway, nobody would have been less surprised than himself. And so he writes:—

"May it please Thee, my Lord, to grant that I may keep all the promises I now renew. Alas! I cannot trust myself, for I know that I am incapable of any undertaking; but I trust solely in Thy infinite goodness and mercy, for Thou art the infinite God and canst never be unfaithful to Thy promises. O Infinite Goodness, if I have failed in the past, it was from myself the failure came. Henceforth I will that Thou shouldst act in me. Yes, Lord, grant that I may observe all with the greatest exactness. I firmly hope for everything from Thee, Thou inexhaustible Fount. Amen."

He now formally invokes the Holy Ghost and proceeds to enlist all the heavenly helpers he can:—

"I choose the Holy Spirit to be my only Comforter and Protector in all things. May He be my defence and help me to overcome all my passions. Amen.

"And Thou, my only joy, Immaculate Virgin Mary, Thou also art my protection and my comfort in all that befalls me, and Thou art my only advocate with God, that I may be faithful to these my resolutions.

"And I call on you also, all ye Blessed Spirits, and beg of you to help me and be my dear advocates with the one common Creator of us all. It is in your presence that I am writing all this, that you may read it from heaven and read it well, and that you may intercede with the Divine Majesty to enable me to be faithful to everything. May your prayers be efficacious. Come then! Thus do I bind myself and promise the Most High God and Most Holy Mary and you all. But especially may I be helped unfailingly by St. Teresa, St. Mary Magdalen de' Pazzi, St. Catherine of Sienna and St. Agnes."

Before setting down his resolutions in detail he makes a covering resolution concerning them. What he is about to write is to remain no dead-letter. He knows himself and is going to take no chances. And so he provides against fickleness and forgetfulness by resolving to arraign himself periodically before the tribunal of his own conscience. He writes :—

" I will examine my conscience every fortnight in order to find out if I have been unfaithful to what I am here writing down."

His pen is poised. He is about to write, when once again the solemnity of what he is going to do and its eternal import grips him afresh. Again he apostrophises himself and in touching and emphatic words asserts his distrust of his own strength :—

" Alas ! Gerard, what art thou about ? Dost thou know that what thou art now writing shall one day be brought against thee ? Be mindful, then, to fulfil it in all things. But who art thou that dost thus reproach me ? Yes, thou sayest well and sayest truly ; but thou knowest not that never have I relied upon myself, that I am not relying upon myself, that I will never rely upon myself ; because, knowing my own wretchedness, I always fear to trust myself ; and did I not do so, I should certainly have lost my head."

At last, with a final casting of himself and his holy enterprise on God, he takes the plunge :—

" Therefore it is in God alone I hope and trust, for I have placed my whole life in His divine hands, that

He may do with me what He pleases. Thus, I live, though without life, since God is my life. In Him alone do I trust, and from Him alone do I hope for help to keep the promises I am now about to make. Live Jesus and Mary!"

Then follow his resolutions. According to the *Acta* they are thirty-nine in all. The first three concern the doing of God's Will and its often difficult but inevitable consequence, obedience. We give the thirty-nine in full :—

1. "My dear and only love and my true God, today and forever I give myself up to Thy divine Will, and so in all the temptations and tribulations of this world I will say : *Fiat voluntas tua!* I will embrace everything with my whole heart, never ceasing to raise my eyes to heaven to adore those divine hands of Thine that shower down on me the precious gems of Thy divine Will.

2. "My Lord Jesus Christ, I will do everything commanded me by my holy Mother the Catholic Church.

3. "My God, for love of Thee, I will obey my superiors as if I saw Thy very self in them and were obeying Thine own divine Person. I will live as if I were no longer mine own but Thine by conforming myself to the judgment and wishes of him who commands me.

4. "I will be most poor in all pleasures of my own seeking and rich in every discomfort.

5. "Amongst all the virtues that are dear to Thee, my God, what I love best is purity and spotlessness in God's sight. O infinite Purity, I trust in Thee to keep me from every impure thought, even the least,

which I in my wretchedness might conceive in this world."

This resolution we shall soon have occasion to recall in connection with a most painful and a most heroic moment in his life. With the exception of no. 11 : " I will be an enemy of all singularity," nos. 6-12 deal with the use of the tongue. They run :—

6. " I will speak only in three cases : when what I have to say concerns the glory of God, the interests of my neighbour, or some personal need.

7. " At recreation I will speak only when spoken to, except in the above cases.

8. " For every word I might wish to say to God's displeasure I will substitute an aspiration : My Jesus, I love Thee with my whole heart.

9. " I will speak neither well nor ill about myself, but will act as if I were not in this world.

10. " I will never excuse myself, even though I have every possible reason. It will be enough for me if no offence to God or harm to my neighbour follows from what is said against me.

12. " I will never answer back when blamed, unless I am told to do so.

13. " I will never accuse anybody or speak of the faults of others, even in jest.

14. " I will always excuse my neighbour, seeing in him the person of Jesus Christ Himself unjustly accused by the Jews. And I will do this especially in his absence.

15. " Should anyone speak ill of another, I will warn him of his fault, even though he be our Father Rector Major himself.[1]

---

[1] As the Father Rector Major was St. Alphonsus himself, it is not likely that Gerard was ever called upon to proceed to this extreme.

16. " I will most diligently avoid causing any annoyance to my neighbour.

17. " When I notice my neighbour committing a fault, I will be careful not to correct him before others, but in private, with all possible kindness and in a low tone of voice." What a different world we should live in if all its tongues were governed by such rules !

With the exception of no. 19, nos. 18-23 deal with his external work in the house. We have already quoted them in the preceding chapter. No. 19 runs thus : " I will visit the sick several times a day, always with the requisite permission."

24. " I will not look about me at table, unless my neighbour's good or my duty demands it.

25. " I will take from the board at meals the plate that is nearest to me, without looking at the others.

26. " I will be careful not to yield hastily to un-reasonable disturbance.

Now we can scarcely help noticing that these fore-going resolutions of a very great saint are remarkable for what we may call their obviousness. Indeed the one extraordinary thing about them is that they are so ordinary. At one time or another, in one guise or another, we have all surely made them. Many of them form the stock-in-trade of our resolving at retreats and other periods of fervour. Which suggests that one difference between our resolutions and those of the saints, even of the greatest, is that while we make resolutions and break them, the saints make them and keep them. When all is said and done, there is nothing exceptionally new or bold in Gerard's code of laws that are to govern his dealings with his neighbour :

it is simply the practical application of Christ's words addressed to all about loving one's neighbour as we love ourselves and doing as we would be done by. Which suggests that if we were to go in the practice of virtue with the saints, even with the greatest, as far as we are bound to go as ordinary Christians, we should go a considerable distance. St. Gerard Majella is indeed a striking instance of exalted sanctity reared on the sure and solid basis of perfect compliance with the ordinary calls of duty. He climbed high, but in climbing his feet rested firmly on every rung of the ladder, even on the lowest. Before he was a great saint, he was a thoroughly good Christian.

To return to his resolutions. In nos. 27-30 he reverts to his first, which sums up everything. He tells us so :—

27. "My supreme resolution is to give myself entirely to God. For this reason let these three words be before my eyes : *deaf, blind* and *dumb*.

28. "Let these words never be mine : *I will, I will not ;* for I will only that *in me sint vota tua, et non vota mea*.[1]

29. "To do what God wills I must no longer do what I will myself. Yes, *io, io, io* . . . I, I, I wish for God alone, and if I wish for God alone, I must detach myself from everything that is not God.

30. "I will refrain from seeking my own ease in anything.

He resolves to give himself "entirely to God." What is often but a vague formula for us, bringing us nowhere, is for Gerard something to be taken with a literalness

---

[1] *May Thy wishes, not mine, be accomplished in me.*

tremendous and heroic. He means it. " I wish for God alone," he says. The original Italian is strikingly emphatic: " *Si, io, io, io, voglio solo Dio.*"

In nos. 31-39 he enters into certain practical details about piety and virtue :—

31. " During the whole time of silence I will occupy my mind with the thought of the Passion and Death of Jesus Christ and the sorrows of most holy Mary.[1]

32. " All my prayers, communions, etc., shall be for the benefit of poor sinners, for whom I will offer them up to God with the most precious Blood of Jesus Christ.

33. " When I know or hear of anybody who is being greatly tried by the Divine Will and has no longer courage to suffer and ask for the divine assistance, I will pray to God for him and for three whole days at least offer up all I do in order to obtain him from the Lord holy conformity with the Divine Will.

34. " When I receive the superior's blessing, I will look upon myself as if I were receiving it from Jesus Christ in person.

35. " I will not ask permission for Holy Communion overnight, except there is great need ; I will ask it only at the moment before going to receive, that thus I may always keep myself in readiness for It. If leave be refused, I will make a spiritual Communion when the priest communicates.

36. " My thanksgiving shall last until after midday, and my preparation for next day from midday until six o'clock in the evening.

---

[1] This refers to what is called the "little silence" of the rule, beginning at the end of the midday recreation and lasting three consecutive hours.

37. " PRACTICE FOR THE VISIT TO THE MOST HOLY
SACRAMENT.   My Lord, I believe that Thou art present
in the Most Holy Sacrament.   I adore Thee with all
my heart, and by this visit I intend to adore Thee in
all places on earth where Thou art present in the Sacrament, and I offer Thee all Thy Precious Blood for all
poor sinners, with the intention also of receiving Thee
spiritually by that act as many times as there are places
in which Thou dost dwell.

38. " ACTS OF LOVE.   My God, I intend to love Thee
with as many acts of love as have been offered Thee
by most holy Mary and all the Blessed Spirits from the
very beginning, as well as by all the faithful on earth,
together with that love which Jesus Christ bears to
Himself and all His loved ones, multiplying the aforesaid acts each time.   And the same for most holy Mary.

39. " Henceforth I will treat priests with all possible
respect, as if they were the very person of Jesus Christ,
although they are not such, bearing in mind their great
dignity."

Such are Gerard's resolutions.   Having stated them,
he proceeds to explain with minuteness and precision
a vow he had made, after the example of St. Teresa
and other saints, always to do what he considered the
most perfect thing.   It was a vow, not a mere resolution,
by which he bound himself.   That he so understood it
and that he regarded its violation as very grave may
be gathered from the careful wording of the conditions
under which he took it.   He writes :—

" EXPLANATION OF THE VOW.   By this vow I have
bound myself always to do what is most perfect, that
is, what seems to me to be the most perfect thing before

God. It covers all my actions, even the smallest, and obliges me to do them all with the greatest self-renunciation and perfection, as I see it before God. That I may proceed with safety, I will always suppose myself to have a general permission for this from your Reverence.

" RESERVATIONS WITH REGARD TO THE SAID VOW. 1. All those actions performed by me in moments of distraction or through inadvertence, and that are against this vow, do not come within the scope of the vow. 2. I shall not be acting against my vow in asking for a dispensation from it from anybody when out of the house. This is in order to avoid all confusion and scruple which might hamper my actions. I also retain the power to ask my Father confessor for a dispensation from this vow, and on his side he will be always free to liberate me from it whenever he wishes."

The comprehensive and unrelenting heroism of such a vow, having no truck with half-measures, ruling pitilessly out every concession to fallen nature, flogging on its fickleness and sloth is too obvious to need any comment. When we think of them, its implications are terrifying.

Finally, this childlike and obedient man tears away the last vestige of the veil that covers the inner work of his sanctification by detailing certain little prayers and pious practices that are usual with him. He even goes the length of giving Father Giovenale the names of all his holy patrons ; and a goodly company they are. We feel our readers would like to know them. It is interesting to learn to what saints the saints themselves prayed. Little did Gerard think, as he humbly and lovingly called upon them in his daily needs, how many thousands the world over would call upon himself and insert his canonised name in the list of their intercessors and friends ! Little did he think how many children would be given it in baptism in his honour and how many of Christ's cloistered spouses would love to bear it !

" DEVOTION TO THE MOST HOLY TRINITY. I declare that I will always practice this little devotion, viz., a *Gloria Patri* each time I see a cross or a picture of any of the Three Divine Persons, or hear them named, and whenever I begin and end any action.

" TO MOST HOLY MARY. I will act in the same way towards most holy Mary, and whenever I see women, I will say an *Ave* in honour of her purity."

Then follows the lengthy list of his Patrons :—
" St. Michael the Archangel and all the Blessed Spirits, SS. Joachim and Anne, St. Joseph, St. John the Baptist, St. John the Evangelist, the Saint of the day, the Patron Saints of the year and of the month, the Saint of the day on which I was born and of the day on which I shall die, St. Francis Xavier, St. Teresa, St. Mary Magdalen de' Pazzi, St. Philip Neri, St. Nicholas of Bari, St. Vincent Ferrer, St. Anthony of Padua, St. Augustine, St. Bernard, St. Bonaventure, St. Thomas Aquinas, St. Francis of Assisi, St. Francis de Sales, St. Francis of Paula, St. Felix the Capuchin, St. Pascal, St. Vitus, St. Aloysius Gonzaga, St. Mary Magdalen, St. Catherine of Sienna, St. Agnes, SS. Peter and Paul, St. James, and the Venerable Sister Mary of the Crucified."[1]

---

[1] According to Berruti (p. 290), the Saint also cultivated a special devotion to the Forty Martyrs of Sebaste, earnestly begging God to grant him the grace of dying for His love. Cfr. In Apost. no. 9, § 104.

It looks as if he set them down in the order in which they came into his head; otherwise it would be hard to account for the low place given to some of the Apostles. After having given this list, he characteristically hastens to add, as though he had forgotten it and felt bound to insert it :—

"Before and after meals three *Gloria Patris* in honour of the Most Holy Trinity and three *Aves* to most holy Mary. Each time I cut a slice of bread a *Gloria Patri ;* when I drink wine another *Gloria Patri ;* when drinking water an *Ave Maria.* The same each time the clock strikes."[1]

Then follow these burning words, which show how his thoughts are running ; " AFFECTIONS. O my God, would that I might convert as many sinners as there are grains of sand in the sea and on the land, as there are leaves on the trees, blades of grass in the fields, atoms in the air, stars in the sky, rays in the sun and moon, creatures on the whole earth.

" When rising and retiring I will make the acts of thanksgiving customary in the community ; at night and in the morning before Communion and before dinner and at night I will examine my conscience and make the act of contrition.

" Live Jesus and Mary, Michael, and Teresa, Pazza and Aloysius.   Ad M.D.G.   Amen."[2]

---

[1] It is not easy to see whaf Benedetti's version means here : *Net dividere il pane ed il vino, un altro Gloria Patri.* The Ac ta have it thus : *Nel dividere il pane ad ogni fetta un Gloria Patri. Nel bere il vino un altro Gloria.*

[2] Whom Gerard is here invoking under the strange name of *Pazza* is not clear. If it be a misprint for *Pazzi,* it must refer to St. Mary Magdalen de' Pazzi, who figures in the list of his patrons given above. No doubt he deal as familiarly with the Saints as with his Lord.

CHAPTER VI

TO CHRIST CONFORMABLE

DURING his first stay in Naples, Gerard one day happened to be in the workshop of a man who made crucifixes and other objects of piety. While there, there slouched into the establishment a member of the notorious fraternity of Neapolitan beggars called *lazzaroni*. Seeing Gerard, whose patched habit and unfashionable hat probably awoke feelings of kinship in his heart, he approached the saint and at once began indulging in rude though not ill-meant familiarities. He tweaked him by the nose and covering Gerard's eyes with his hands, stood back to look at him in mock admiration, exclaiming: " My jewel, but you're a beauty ! "[1] Gerard submitted without a word or a stir. Not so the onlookers. Italian tempers leaped from their scabbards. Angered at the fellow's insolence, they would have handled him roughly had not his victim stood between saying : " 'Tis nothing, 'tis nothing. I am a sinner and a wretch. What harm has he done ? He just wanted to have a little sport with me." Meantime the beggar had taken to his heels.

But Gerard had been making himself acquainted in that workshop with something besides the rough-and-

[1] Landi.

ready good-fellowship of the *lazzaroni*. He had already spent many an hour watching with an unusually interested eye the carving and moulding and painting of crucifixes and other images of the Passion. We know what the Crucified meant to Gerard. He now longed to learn the art of making crucifixes. He would know well what to do with them. The owner of the establishment was a great friend of the Congregation and gladly offered his services. The pupil soon became a master. He brought home several models and to the end gave much of whatever leisure he had to the making of crucifixes, *Ecce Homos* and images of Our Lady of Sorrows, many of which, we are told, were most touching and striking in their realism. Writing about 1780, Father Landi says: "Even to our own day several of these works from Gerard's hands are preserved with great veneration." And Berruti, whose biography appeared in 1847, tells us that one of his crucifixes was to be found in Vietri.[1] Gerard's first French biographer states that one of his best productions was a crucifix on which the saint was working when death took him.[2]

However, Gerard's masterpiece in representations of his suffering Lord was his own soul, his own crucified self. His conformity with Christ Crucified was indeed so consummate an achievement that the Church in her collect for his feast singles it out as the truest epitome of his life. She prays: "O Almighty and Everlasting God, Who didst draw to Thyself the Blessed Gerard, even from his tenderest years, making him conformable to the Image of Thy Crucified Son, grant, we beseech

[1] P. 219.
[2] *Vie*, p. 383.

Thee, that imitating his example, we may be made
like unto the same Divine Image, through Jesus Christ
Our Lord. Amen." The austerities of St. Gerard
Majella may truly be said to rival those of the most
renowned penitents in the Church's history. As his
short years went by, " on looking at him one was
reminded of Jesus Crucified," to use the words of the
same French biographer just quoted ; " the unceasing
thought of the Passion had imprinted the likeness of
the Man of Sorrows on his very features."[1]

He had set early to work upon his masterpiece, almost
as soon as he had first laid eyes on a crucifix and heard
the story of the Divine Sufferer at Benedetta's knee.
We can recall the little boy's extraordinary abstemiousness, which called forth more than one protest from
a worried mother. We remember how greedily he ate
the bread of suffering as an apprentice to Pannuto and
a bishop's boy in Lacedonia. We have not forgotten
the austerities of his maturer years in the world, his
fastings and watchings, his scourgings, his fictitious
madness—all to make himself like unto his Divine
Master and so prove his love. Tannoia writes of him :
" The Passion and Death of Christ made the most vivid
impression on Gerard's heart, even at this early period.
It is in the nature of love ever to be in motion and never
to rest, till it becomes conformed to the object of its
affections. And so it was with this fervent servant of
God who, in contemplating the torments suffered by
Jesus Christ, was not satisfied till he became conformed
to His likeness."[2]

---

[1] *Ibid.*, p. 152.
[2] English Edit., p. 248.

We may here relate an incident of his life in the world which we have reserved for this chapter. In the Lent of 1749, some weeks before Gerard entered the Congregation, a sort of Passion Play, consisting of a series of *tableaux vivants*, was staged in the cathedral of Muro for the devotion of the faithful. Its organisers were casting about for an appropriate " Christus." Gerard heard of it, offered himself and was accepted. However, he meant business and had no notion of being merely the central figure in a show. By some sort of holy bribery he induced the " executioners " to play their part as seriously as possible, not to be niggard of their blows and to fasten him to the cross in as painful a manner as they could. In any case they knew their man and took him at his word. In spite of his silent endurance, the sufferings of the " Christus " were obviously so great as to draw pitying tears from the spectators. Amongst these was Benedetta. She had heard nothing of her son's intentions, and when she saw him literally agonising on the cross, she fainted. Gerard was delighted with himself : from his point of view he was a great success. He was in high spirits on his return home and met his good mother's expostulations by merely remarking that all he endured was nothing and that he must suffer for Jesus Christ.

With all this in mind we can well understand his answer to Brother Onufrio, who tried to frighten him away from the Congregation by detailing the austerities of its Rule : " That's just what I am looking for." Had Gerard had the founding of an Order that would embody his own spiritual ideals, he could scarcely have bettered his choice of one whose specific end was to imitate the virtues and example of Jesus Christ the Redeemer.

He was not well in the novitiate when he was into his stride. To ponder on the mysteries of Christ's Passion was his delight and the source of all his strength. " The Crucifix was as it were a bundle of myrrh," writes Benedetti, " ever clasped against his heart, whose heavenly perfume he delighted to inhale during the scraps of time his duties left him."[1] To hear the Passion spoken of or see it represented in art would at times throw him into an ecstasy. But there was something more than sharing Christ's sufferings in thought, and his devotion to the Passion took other forms besides that of ecstasy. Tannoia tell us that Gerard's longing to share in the sufferings of Jesus Christ did not go unrewarded, and that it pleased the Crucified to favour him with a grace He has bestowed on but few of His servants, viz., that of experiencing in themselves the sufferings endured by Christ in His Passion. " This grace Gerard had earnestly asked for and received. While he looked comparatively strong and well on the preceding Thursday, at the approach of Friday he looked worn out with pain, noticeably weak and like a man in his agony. On Fridays his hæmorrhages were often copious. His interior sufferings and desolation of soul were so painful and agonising that he could not express them. At the approach of Saturday, he would be quite himself again and fit to attend to his duties."[2]

Gerard treated his own poor body very badly, even though nature had already treated it none too well.

---

[1] P. 69.
[2] Cap. viii.

As a French biographer puts it, " while he was nothing but milk and honey towards others, he was nothing but gall and wormwood towards himself."[1] " All Fridays," writes Tannoia, " and especially those in March, as they were consecrated to the Passion of his Divine Master, were days of torture for Gerard. Thistles, little chains, scourgings to blood, nightly vigils, everything was put in operation for self-martyrdom. These were days of bread and water only, if not altogether fast days ; and he ate kneeling or seated on the ground.

" Holy Week was the most sorrowful of all the Lent for him. He seemed to be in his agony and to be barely alive. He seemed to be laid with Christ in the tomb. ' Jesus Christ,' he would then say, ' died for me, and I do not die for Him Who gave His life for me.' "[2] " If the days devoted to the Passion of Jesus Christ were sad days for Gerard," writes Tannoia again, " it was not so with the glorious days which the Church solemnises with repeated alleluias. He then communicated his festive gladness to others and the exuberance of his joy overflowed on those about him."[3]

Gerard's principle concerning the intimate connection between the love of God and bodily mortification was a principle with all the saints ; so much so indeed that Benedict XIV has written : " We read the history of no saints in the Church and find no Bulls of Sovereign Pontiffs for the canonisation of holy confessors and virgins in which the great desire of mortifying and

---

[1] *Vie Abrégée*, p. 42.
[2] Tannoia, cap. viii.
[3] Ibid. cap. ix.

subduing the flesh is not commended."[1] And again : " No progress can be made in the causes of those servants of God who are confessors, unless their spirit of mortification be thoroughly established,"[2] The saints were true to type, and St. Gerard was no exception.

We have mentioned Gerard's health. Poor health can be a great austerity and the patient bearing of it no mean heroism. But like many another saint, Gerard never allowed the ills that flesh is heir to, to cancel out the gratuitous infliction of penitential pains and privations. These were of all sorts. The revolutionary changes in the methods and weapons of war we are witnessing on so vast a scale to-day are never likely to be introduced into the warfare of the spirit against the flesh. Apart from certain often ingenious details, the weapons used against themselves by the latest canonised saints have been in service from the beginning, and they are not likely to grow obsolete.

Fasting is a tried and efficient weapon, and Gerard used it well. " He had mortification of the palate greatly at heart," Tannoia tells us, " and practised it rigorously to the end of his life. ' The love of God,' he would say, ' does not enter the soul if the body is full.' "[3] There must have been ample room for that love in the soul of Gerard. He fasted as often and as much as was allowed him. Perhaps the part of the house he entered with the greatest reluctance and left with the greatest relief was the refectory. " He ate so

---

[1] *Heroic Virtue*, vol. i, p. 322.
[2] *Ibid.*, p. 374.
[3] Cap. vii.

sparingly," says a witness, " that his fast might be said to be unbroken."[1] He would have fasted every day had he been allowed. It must be added that the dire poverty of those early days played into his hands. " He did not take as much as two ounces of bread," writes Tannoia, " and when through obedience he had to eat of the little that was served up for the community, he made it bitter and almost poisonous with aloes and centaury. Even during meals . . . . he was seen many a time rapt in ecstasy and abstracted, with a mouthful at the end of his fork. Brother Januarius Rendina testifies to having seen him at table in an ecstatic state, with his eyes suffused with tears."[2] For three years he had earnestly besought God to deprive him of the sense of taste, and the grace was given him. In his last illness the doctor had ordered an appetising delicacy. " Doctor," said the patient, " there is no need to order delicacies for me, as vegetable marrow would mean just the same as pigeon pie."[3] Then the secret came out.

This grace, however, did not apply to bitter herbs. These were a favourite comestible with him, and a standing dish to boot. For them there was always room on his menu card. Indeed, according to one witness, he was constantly chewing them.[4] As he could not well decline the savoury meats served up at the tables of friends and benefactors, he brought supplies with him. He was once dining with a priest of Sarno,

---

[1] In Apost. no. 16, § 36.
[2] Tannoia, cap. vii.
[3] Landi.
[4] In Apost. no. 16, § 30.

the Father Stephen Liguori whom we met in the preceding chapter. He was no relation of St. Alphonsus,
though he eventually entered the Congregation. Father
Stephen's mother was at table on this occasion. Gerard
was caught surreptitiously dropping powdered bitter
herbs into his macaroni. They evidently wanted to give
him to understand that they had noticed him, for they
each took a forkful from his plate to taste it. Fearful
of untoward consequences, they did not let it go much
further than their lips. When dinner was over and
Gerard gone, a word of explanation had to be given
to the company.

But fasting and chewing nauseous herbs were the
minor items on his penitential programme. Here are
some of the major, as we learn them from Tannoia :
" All testify that the instruments with which he crucified
his flesh were dreadful-looking things. The discipline
he made such use of was furnished with twelve little
stars with steel points ; these were long and thick, and
he scourged himself pitilessly. He also scourged himself
once or twice a day with knotted cords . . . He wore
a hairshirt, and little chains furnished with sharp points
girt his arms and thighs. He also daily used other cruel
instruments for his self-martyrdom."[1]

The reader will remember the grotto at Iliceto whither
the Blessed Felix would retire to do penance. It had
already become a favourite haunt of Father Cafaro ;
it now became a favourite haunt of Gerard for the same
purpose. Here the scene in Muro cathedral would be

---

[1] Tannoia, cap. vii.

enacted over again, only with greater realism and thoroughness. He took an "executioner" with him in the person of a postulant named Andrew Longarelli who later became a Redemptorist and assured Tannoia of all that took place. Proceedings began with the tying of Gerard's hands to a post, which was to represent the Pillar of the Scourging. Then Andrew plied the wet lashes till the blood flowed freely from the bare shoulders of the victim. There followed the crowning of his head with a bundle of the asparagus plant, many of whose little thorns went deep enough to draw blood. This the "executioner" was to strike down with a rod, as centuries before it had been done to the crown on the Head of his Beloved. One day the "executioner" went further still in his realism: he fastened his victim with ropes to a large wooden cross such as are erected for Calvaries, taking care—again under orders—to pull the hands and feet, in faint resemblance to the wrenching of the hands and feet of Christ for the ploughing of the dreadful nails. In this position this new "crucified" would remain a long while meditating on the Passion of the God-Man. At last love had its fill and Gerard's yearnings to be like his Master were as fully satisfied as he could hope them to be. Naturally Andrew did not take kindly to his *rôle* of torturer and often protested, only to be silenced by Gerard's pitiful appeals for a continuance of his strange services.

At a later date, Andrew's place in the grotto was taken by one Francis Testa, a tailor by trade, whom Gerard had met in circumstances we will relate further on. At this particular time he was working in the monastery. He owed Gerard much, and the saint

demanded payment, though not in the coin Testa would
have wished. As in the case of Andrew, it often became
a tussle between Testa's good nature and Gerard's
craving for the cross. Another youth, whose name
has not come down to us and whom Landi describes
as a "*giovine mastino* . . . . a bulldog of a boy," was
also called into requisition. Muscle was evidently what
was needed. To all their protestations Gerard would
reply : "Jesus Christ wished so to do for us thankless
unmindful creatures."[1] All this went on till the Rector
intervened and put a stop to it. Gerard ceased as
willingly as he had begun.

With the sword of Christian abnegation in hand, he
pursued his lower self with a truceless pertinacity even
into the peaceful precincts of slumber. With Father
Cafaro's leave—not hard to secure from that iron ascetic
—he chose for his cell an old disused stove-room, with
neither window nor skylight, a relic of the former
Augustinian inmates, and more like a lair than a human
habitation. It was certainly more a torture-chamber
than a sleeping-apartment, and with amazing ingenuity
Gerard saw to it that sleep, even the little of it he took,
would not be the pleasant business most of us intend
it to be. The bed was a mattress stuffed with straw,
but only along the edges, as the centre was filled in
with thistles and sharp-pointed stones. Two bricks
were his pillow, and he so managed that they only half
supported his head. Around this couch he had set a
number of skulls, probably once inhabited by Augustinian
monks. The saints were not afraid to look at skulls.

---

[1] In Apost. no. 7, § 147.

They took the long view of things and made their calculations accordingly. Skulls were but a reminder. A rickety chair completed the furniture of this apartment. The superior's intervention duly evicted Gerard from it. His hours of rest were brief and again clever devices made them as unsatisfying as possible. Stones fastened to one's feet and little iron chains encircling one's head do not make for sweet repose.

When going about the country with the missionary Fathers or on other business, Gerard could not of course hawk around his penitential instruments and turn hosts' rooms upside down in order to indulge his self-denial. However, he often outwitted his circumstances. Besides wearing hairshirts and cilices, which he could easily hide, he managed to chew his beloved bitter herbs at table unseen, though he was occasionally caught. But partaking of these delicacies of an ascetic in their ordinary form did not exhaust his ingenuity. He carried about with him a small vessel containing a decoction of wormwood and other kindred herbs, of his own brewing, which he kept hidden in the sleeve of his habit ; these he would produce unnoticed for the counter-flavouring of the savoury dishes set before him which he could not well decline. He could also sleep on the floor at night, taking care to leave the sheets in a crumpled condition in the morning, so as to deceive housemaids. But housemaids and others were not always deceived, as Gerard was generally a suspect in these matters. Curiosity was quickly aroused where he was concerned and not rarely amply rewarded. When he travelled alone and did not stay with friends, his mattress was usually the earth and his coverlet the sky. At times he enlisted the services of very diminutive executioners. One day, at Caposele, the doctor jestingly remarked : " It is getting hot, Brother, and the insects are growing numerous. How are you going to get through the night with all these mosquitos ? " " Oh ! " replied Gerard, adopting an attitude towards the activities of these Lilliputian tormentors not shared by the generality of mankind, " how much I am indebted to them ! They don't let me sleep at night and so I can think continually of God."[1]

His wardrobe, need it be said ? was not overstocked. As tailor in the community, he got a great chance. He never wore anything new and made his own clothes out of old remnants. So much a thing of shreds and patches had his religious garb become that strangers had often some difficulty in recognising him for what he was. As we have seen, the *lazzaroni* of Naples made sport of his resemblance to them. Cleanliness, however, he always assiduously cultivated and was most deferential to that next-of-kin of godliness.

We will now insert that passage in the spiritual report Gerard drew up for Father Giovenale which refers to his penitential practices and which we reserved for this chapter. We are loth to abridge it even by a word. And we translate it literally.[2]

" DAILY MORTIFICATIONS. The discipline once, not to blood (*a secco*). The leg cilice one palm less three inches in width and two palms long.

" Every night and morning, that is, on retiring and rising, I make nine crosses on the floor with my tongue.

---

[1] Caione.
[2] In Apost. no. 7, § 591.

At dinner and supper I mingle centaury or wormwood with one course. On my breast a heart with iron points. I chew wormwood or centaury at least three times a day. Six *Ave Marias* prostrate on the ground in the morning and six at night.

"On Wednesdays, Fridays and Saturdays and on all vigils, I eat kneeling, and I also make nine crosses in the refectory at dinner and supper, and I abstain from fruit on all these days. I partake of two dishes only at dinner on Fridays and of one at supper. On Saturdays I fast on bread and water.

"On Wednesdays, Fridays and Saturdays I sleep with a chain round my forehead and the chain mentioned above round my leg, and I lie on another three palms long and one palm wide, which I use as a body cilice during those same days, and day and night I wear a chain round my arm. Once a week I take the discipline to blood.

"During all the novenas in honour of Jesus Christ, the Madonna and other saints, I practise the same mortifications, besides a daily discipline, not to blood (*a secco*) and another discipline to blood during the novena, together with other mortifications I will ask from your Reverence."

Now we can hardly suppose the average reader to have gone thus far in this chapter without a wince or a shrug. After all, why all this savagery towards one-self? Was it not all definitely excessive and eccentric? Were we to say so to Gerard, we can imagine him pointing questioningly to a crucifix and reminding us of a still greater excess—the love of the Crucified for sinners, and of the greatest eccentricity of all: sin.

Living in a soft and self-indulgent age, we may be too ready to set down as folly what cuts so rudely across our notions of reason and good sense in matters of this kind. " The spirit," writes von Hügel, " and even some mild amount of the actual practice of such austerities is, indeed, an integral constituent of all virile religion : the man who laughs at the plank bed and the discipline is a shallow fool. Indeed, some souls are, undoubtedly, called to more than the minimum indicated, and only find their full peace and persuasiveness in some such bodily asceticism."[1]

One thing we must say immediately : such external austerities do not constitute sanctity ; sanctity can be there without them, and to a high degree. Nay more ; the unremitting inward austerity of self-conquest, even in small things, can often call for high courage. Quoting Father Bartoli, Benedict XIV says : " Much less perfection of virtue is required for a man to subjugate and tame his body by fastings, watchings and bloody scourgings than, in every variety of accidents, to keep the affections of his mind so subject to the spirit that they never stir, never make themselves felt, or show their life, except so far as and when he pleases."[2]

Gerard excelled in every austerity. He was once asked why he punished his poor body so cruelly. Here was the answer : " I do so because I so richly deserve it, and I do so for the sake of that God Who has created me."[3] There we have it in a nutshell. " For the sake of God," he did it, and also because he " deserved it."

---

[1] *The Life of Prayer*, p. 59.
[2] *Heroic Virtue*, vol. i, p. 73.
[3] Tannoia, cap. xiii.

To be as like as might be to his God, to his Crucified God, and to undo the work of sin in himself and, as far as possible, in the world of sin about him. "This same charity," writes Berruti, " taught Gerard to make himself an expiatory victim before God for the sins of others and to move God in His mercy to grant the grace of conversion to abandoned sinners. Hence scarcely had Gerard come to know of any soul in need ... than he forthwith added other extraordinary bodily macerations to his wonted penitential severities, and thus obtained from the Divine Goodness the amendment of some sinful soul."[1] As we read in the Decree of the Heroicity of the saint's virtues, " *poenitentiae austeritate corpus suum hostiam viventem Deo jugiter exhibuit . . .* by his austere penances he continually offered his body up to God as a living sacrifice."[2] But perhaps the loving imitation of his Crucified God was the major motive of all his external austerities : the longing, yearning, hungering of his love-stricken soul to be one in all things with Jesus. We have already dwelt on this in an earlier chapter and will not repeat ourselves.[3]

There is one point, however, we must emphasise :

---

[1] Pp. 308-309.

[2] Cfr. Rom. xii, I.

[3] The spirit which inspired Gerard is not altogether dead, even in our own day—at least in Gerard's own country. In an account of a mission given in Gragnnano, a town not far from Nocera, in 1927, we are told that on the occasion of a general communion of men and youths, there was not a man, however high his station, who was ashamed to wear a knotted cord around his neck and a crown of thorns on his head in token of penance. Things went further during a mission in the parish of Sancta Maria a Toro, not far from Benevento, in 1928. On the occasion of a similar general communion of men, not only did the communicants display the same emblems of penance about their necks and heads, but they *practised* penance by scourging themselves severely ! *Analecta C.SS.R.*, Annus vii, pp. 79, 140.

to associate these lifelong murderous assaults upon himself, this pitiless stifling of nature's most reasonable and innocent aspirations, this organised rejection of every creature comfort with a dour and grim-visaged ascetic would be to read Gerard and his life utterly amiss. Were anyone to have told him that such he had expected him to be, Gerard would probably have met the remark with a laugh ; and had a stranger pityingly asked him if he were happy, Gerard might have treated him to an ecstasy, with hairshirt, cilices and all. He certainly was not amongst those whom Our Lord denounced : " When you fast, be not as the hypocrites, sad."[1] We have no hesitation in saying that he was in all probability the most exuberantly happy member of his community. According to a witness, " his fasts and bodily mortifications were accompanied with such cheerful looks as made him the admiration of all."[2] Another speaks of " his unfailing joyousness and peace."[3] And a third says : " It was only on days devoted to the consideration of the Passion of Jesus Christ . . . . and when he beheld or heard of the offences of sinners against God that he was seen to be grieved and depressed."[4] Here Chesterton is to the point : " Any extreme of Catholic asceticism is a wise, or unwise, precaution against the evil of the Fall ; it is *never* a doubt about the good of the Creation . . . . In the case of every Oriental religion, it is really true that the

---

[1] Matt. vi, 16.
[2] In Ord. no. 7, § 136.
[3] *Ibid.* no. 10, § 34.
[4] In Apost. no. II, § 66.

asceticism is pessimism ; that the ascetic tortures himself to death out of an abstract hatred of life ; that he
does not merely mean to control Nature as he should,
but to contradict Nature as much as he can . . . . in
millions of the religious populations of Asia, it is a fact
far too little realised, that the dogma of the denial of
life does really rule as a first principle on so vast a scale."[1]

Had Gerard been, even externally, what all this
sombre array of penances and privations might lead us
to think him, the Catholic world would never have taken
him to its heart as one of its best-beloved friends and
intercessors with God. As we have said, love is the
keynote of his life, even of this, humanly speaking,
harsh and forbidding aspect of it : love of God and of
his fellowmen. Any other picture of him would be
untrue and grotesque. Not that his penances became
pleasures, even when passed through the alembic of
God's love, thus defeating their own end. Hear him
addressing his own macerated body : " Suffer, body of
mine. This is not the place for pleasure ; that thou
shalt have in paradise."[2] The long view again.

A question or two will naturally be asked. To begin
with, was Gerard authorised by superiors to go to these
extremes ? This question scarcely needs an answer.
We have seen the lengths to which his obedience went
to everyone to whom he was in any way subject. In the
preceding chapter we have seen what a clean breast he
made of all his penitential rigours to his spiritual guide.
If he did go to further extremes of self-torture in that

---

[1]—*St. Thomas Aquinas*, pp. 122-123.
[2] In Apost. no. 10, § 19.

grotto at Iliceto, he ceased as readily as he began, the moment obedience spoke. Even when full allowance is made for special divine inspirations in these matters, obedience to authority always had the last word with him.

But there is a further question : In view of Gerard's poor health and the trying nature of his duties as a laybrother, how could superiors be justified in allowing him to practise such austerities ? Father Ripoli testifies as follows : " Nor did these exceptional penances render him inactive or enfeebled ; for, while he lived in the Congregation, not only did he discharge with exactness every kind of duty entrusted to him, as Longarelli, Caione and others stated, but he wanted to help his other confrères in their charges."[1] To what degree God may have added to his natural strength we have no means of knowing, and how much of his physical fitness and endurance was really miraculous we are left to guess. What we do know is that he did his work and did it well, and this in spite of his altogether extraordinary austerities.

Did Gerard thereby shorten his life ? We can draw no such conclusion. Though his days were few, we have no evidence that they were notably reduced by his way of living, since the tendency to consumption, which eventually took him off, showed itself very early. Even though his days were so reduced, we need not be alarmed by any implication. Benedict XIV asks the question whether, " without any intention of shortening his life

---

[1] In Apost. no. 7, § 151.

or hastening his death, a man may lawfully embrace a hard manner of living for a supernatural end . . . . and this although he foresees that it will, as a matter of fact, accelerate his death. And to this the true answer is given by theologians, that he may do so, not only lawfully, but meritoriously."[1] Speaking of that outstanding exponent of Christian austerity, St. Peter of Alcantara, St. Teresa writes : " I have often seen him in exceeding great glory. The first time he appeared he said : ' O happy penance, which has obtained so great a reward ! ' "[2] Surely history repeated itself when Gerard entered heaven.

The sufferings of Christ were not limited, as we know, to physical pains caused by scourge and thorn and nail. He had His Gethsemane before His Calvary, and on Calvary itself one of the most poignant moments of His agony was when His voice, gathering its remaining strength, uttered that awful cry : " My God, My God, Why hast Thou forsaken me ? "[3] It would have been strange if Gerard had nothing to suffer in his soul. His conformity with his Crucified Love would have been far from complete. His Divine Master saw to it. Moreover, he had been graced with gifts of rare splendour, and these were sure to have their counterpart in trials and tribulations of corresponding rarity and heaviness. Depth will correspond to height, the valley to the hill, the trough of the wave to the crest. The gloom of the succeeding night will deepen with the

---

[1] *Heroic Virtue*, vol. i, p. 358.
[2] *Life written by herself*, chap. xxvii.
[3] Mark, xv. 34.

brilliance of the departed day. Thabor and Gethsemane
alternate in the lives of Christ's heroic lovers. On
emerging from his vision of the third heaven, Paul
was buffetted by an angel of Satan. In one way or
another it was so with them all.

To this ruling Gerard was to be no exception. It is
more than likely that he had many a bad quarter of
an hour of spiritual distress before ever he became a
Redemptorist. That he had them after there is abundant
evidence. He tells us so himself. To a great spiritual
friend, Mother Mary of Jesus, Prioress of the Carmel
of Ripacandida, he writes : " Do not forget to recommend
me frequently to the Lord, as I am in sore need. God
alone knows my wants."[1] And again, to the same :
" I am so afflicted and disconsolate, since I am nailed
to the cross by Divine Justice as never before. Blessed
forever be the Divine Will ! But what makes me tremble
more and fills me with greater horror is the fear of not
persevering."[2]

In the very year preceding his death he wrote two
letters to the same congenial correspondent. We take
them as they are found in Benedetti's pages ; he has
evidently brought Gerard's Italian up-to-date. They
speak for themselves. The first begins : " My God,
have pity on me ! Alas ! my Mother, how can you
jest with me like that ? You know that by writing
thus you only increase the pains I am suffering for my
sins. You are in good spirits and that is why you are
always jesting with me. But what can I do ? It is

---

[1] In Ord. no. 7, § 573.
[2] Ibid., § 581.

God's pleasure, and I rejoice at your happiness. May the Lord keep you so who are so dear to Him ! That is usually the way : one rises and the other sinks. I have sunk so low that I can see no way out for me, as though my sufferings were to last forever. I do not mind if they are eternal ; *it is enough if I love God and please God in all things.* This is what tortures me : I think I am suffering without God. Woe is me, if you do not help me, my Mother, for I am utterly prostrate, in a sea of confusion, almost on the brink of despair. It seems to me that God has gone from me, that an end has been reached to His divine Mercy, and that nothing now awaits me but His Justice. Look at my unhappy state, and if the sacred pact between us still holds, now is the moment to help me and to pray hard to God for *unhappy me. Have pity on my soul, I beg of you. I no longer dare to appear before men.*"[1]

The second letter runs as follows : " JESUS ✠ MARY. Dear and venerated Sister, I am writing to you from the cross. Have pity on my distress. Did I not do violence to myself, tears would prevent me from writing this letter. My sorrows are so bitter that I seem to be passing through the agonies of death ; and just when I feel as if I were breathing my last, I come to life again to be further afflicted and grieved. I cannot express it otherwise, as I don't want you to taste of my bitterness. I know you are happy ; and your happiness gives me courage and revives me in God. May He be ever blessed for the many graces He bestows on me ! Instead of

---

[1] Benedetti, p. 244.

letting me die beneath His sanctifying blows, He strengthens me to live on and conquer. If He sends me suffering, it is only because He wants me to become a follower of my Divine Redeemer. He is my Master, I am His disciple. It is fitting that I should learn of Him and walk in His footsteps. But at this moment I am not walking at all. I am motionless with Him upon the cross, in the midst of unspeakable sufferings. I feel as if a lance were piercing me and taking away my life, and yet again the cross on which I hang with resignation does but prolong my life and my sufferings. All seem to have forsaken me. But I do not wish to go against the designs of my Divine Redeemer Who keeps me nailed to this bitter cross. I bow my head and say : This is the Will of my dear God. I accept it and rejoice to do as He bids me."[1] Yet again to the same confidant of his sorrows : " I am in the depths of affliction and nobody will believe me. God wills it so. He wishes me to die without consolation, abandoned by all ; thus I will to live and die, to give pleasure to my God."[2]

It is not easy to associate the abysmal glooms and terrors pervading these extracts with the young saint we are portraying : the ecstatic lover of his Lord, the spoilt child of Heaven, the gifted wonder-worker of his age, more angel than man by his innocence and purity. But the sufferings of the saints are of a piece with their sanctity. Everything is on the heroic plane. The sting of the penitential lash, the prick of the hair-shirt, the pang of self-imposed hunger—all these were

[1] Benedetti, pp. 244-245.
[2] Tannoia, cap. xx.

as nothing beside the anguish of mind and heart that came from titanic wrestling with forces common mortals are never called upon to meet in the battle for their souls. God: His Justice and Holiness and Love; Sin: its heinousness and ingratitude and mischief; the Soul: its splendour and destiny and danger—all were seen through eyes illumined by a faith beside which our faith is a poor thing. None but the saints themselves can understand these mysterious and tremendous trials, and even they cannot adequately describe them. They form a facet in the career and character of St. Gerard Majella which it is vital to keep well before our eyes. As Benedetti truly says: " When we hear of the miracles, the ecstasies and the mysterious communings with God with which Gerard was constantly favoured, we may perhaps imagine that his soul was always exuberantly joyful and that his life flowed along, so to speak, like a limpid stream between two flowering banks. It was quite the other way: like all contemplative souls, he had to clamber up the steep and painful path of aridity, fear and agony of soul."[1]

It is almost superfluous to add that Gerard was made conformable to the image of Him Who said: " Learn of Me, because I am meek and humble of heart."[2] Yet the humility of this wonderful man was too striking to be summarily dismissed. Humility has been well styled the virtue of the great, as it is the virtue of truly perfect souls. And Gerard's humility was in proportion to his perfection. He was the very image of humility . . . *il simbolo dell' umiltà*, as his brethren unanimously

---

[1] P. 241.
[2] Matt. xi, 29.

described him.[1] " He practised this virtue," writes
Berruti, " to such an heroic degree that contemporaries
said of him that never had there been so humble a man."[2]
" Amongst all his miracles," writes a French biographer,
" the greatest was his humility in the midst of honours"[3]
Writing of St. Hilarion St. Jerome says : " Some may
wonder at the miracles he wrought, others at his incredible
fasts . . . For my part there is nothing so astounding
as his treading under foot the honour and glory that
encompassed him."[4] That could have been written of
Gerard. We shall soon have occasion to see how great
in his case that honour and glory were. The higher
God raised Gerard up the lower Gerard cast himself
down. Though he was looked upon as a prodigy of
holiness, yet the greater he grew in the eyes of men the
smaller he grew in his own. Utter self-effacement was
his aim. One day, on arriving in a locality where he was
unknown, he fell upon his knees—unobserved, as he
thought by anybody—and was overheard thanking
God that no one knew him there. The reader will recall
his resolution to say nothing either good or bad about
himself ; he held to it whenever possible. In spite of
himself, however, he was often drawn out on the subject
of Gerard. Then he waxed eloquent. A brother who
knew him well and succeeded in extracting his thoughts
tells us that he would exhaust the dictionary's terms of
abuse and contempt. Tannoia says that sometimes he
held himself in such horror that, unable to confound
himself more, he would clasp the earth, begging it to

[1] In Apost. no. 17, § 33.
[2] P. 349.
[3] St. Omer, *Vie*, p. 70.
[4] *Vita S. Hilarionis Eremitae*, no. 29.

hide him from the eyes of men. But silence about Gerard was his principle. None knew better than he that spontaneous self-depreciation is often of inferior alloy and falls to pieces in the testing. People who will take any amount of abuse from themselves before an audience are often quick to resent it when it comes from the audience. " Please pray to the Lord," he writes again to Mother Mary of Jesus, " to remove that false esteem people have of me, so that nobody may think of speaking of or of having any intercourse with me."[1]

He was ever asking for prayers. " I find myself full of sin," he writes to another holy soul, " pray to God that He may pardon me. All are being converted, I alone remain obstinate. I beg of you to be kind enough to take the discipline for me that the Divine Majesty may pardon me."[2] And again, writing to his old friend Mother Mary of Jesus and referring to a Sister who had died, he says: " Unworthy as I am, I offered up Holy Communion on eight days for the repose of her soul; and I mean to do as much for all those who die, that they may go to heaven. Tell this to them all, so that they who survive may pray to God for me, when I shall have passed into eternity, and receive Holy Communion for me for eight days."[3] If Gerard's wishes were carried out, the treasury of the Church must have had a windfall.

In words that cut the ground from under our feet, he would say: " Man is but a worm, a nothing, if God

---

[1] In Ord. no. 7, § 575.
[2] Benedetti, p. 97.
[3] In Ord. no. 7, § 581.

does not rule and keep him by His omnipotence and providence. Therefore he should never say : ' I humble myself,' for that is as much as to say that he thinks he is something. Jesus Christ alone could say He was humbled, for, though He was the Infinite God, He became man ; and though He was Lord and Master, He became a servant."[1]

Praise of him was almost a blasphemy in his ears, and whenever possible, he cut it short. Sometimes, with more enthusiasm than prudence, admirers would tell him to his face that he was ' an angel in the flesh ' ; he would at once prostrate himself on the ground, exclaiming : " What a thing to say when I am but a great sinner ! "[2] The poor he envied as the praises of men did not often come their way. One day, on seeing a messenger arrive covered with mud and soaked with rain at the monastery door of Caposele, he exclaimed : " I should be happy if everything were wanting to me and if I were in this wretched man's state. The poor fellow ! To gain a crust of bread he must put up with neglect and contempt on the part of men, while I . . . "[3] Tears choked the rest of the sentence.

The difficulties he met with in avoiding notice and the praises of men were a real cross, perhaps as heavy a one as ever he was asked to bear. He was often heard voicing his regrets with a holy petulance. " Lord," he was heard saying when he knelt alone, as he thought, before the tabernacle, " Lord, Thou dost such great

---

[1] In Apost. no. 17, § 37.
[2] Berruti, p. 347.
[3] Tannoia, cap. xxvii.

things through me, and then Thou lettest everything
be made immediately known ! Why dost Thou not
keep them hidden ? "[1] He literally ran from honours,
and thus we shall see him dodging down by-ways,
escaping through backdoors, and resorting to all sorts
of stratagems and disguises to elude what the whole
world hunts. One day he happened to be alone in the
Redemptorist house in Naples. There was a ring at
the door. On opening it, he was confronted with a servant
in livery, who begged to inform him that the Duchess
of Maddaloni would be pleased if Brother Gerard would
call on her. Gerard took in the situation at a glance
and lost no time in exploiting it. Twisting his lips as
nearly into a sneer as he could, he said curtly : " I can't
make out why this man is being so run after. He is
a simpleton, half a fool . . . *uno scemo, mezzo pazzo ;*
and they don't know what he is here in Naples. Go
and tell that to her Grace the Duchess."[2] With these
words he abruptly dismissed the messenger. The latter
told his mistress what had happened and duly reported
the flattering remarks, adding that he had heard them
from the lips of the porter himself. Her Grace, however,
had no difficulty in seeing through such tricks. Her
little daughter was dangerously ill and she sought her
cure. Realising that it was a case of Mahomet and the
hill, she waylaid Gerard the following morning as he
was entering the church of the Holy Ghost for Mass.
Accosting him, she said : " You must obtain my
daughter's cure." Gerard, however, pointing towards

---

[1] Benedetti, p. 334.
[2] Tannoia, cap. xxiv.

the altar, replied : " He works miracles and dispenses graces and not I."[1] But the Duchess was not so easily put off and extracted a promise that he would pray for the child. This done, she went into the church to hear Mass. She was not long there before one of her servants arrived on the scene bearing the joyful news that her daughter was up and about. A little questioning showed that the cure had been wrought " at the same hour," while she was actually speaking to Gerard.

But the saint's humility was often called upon to deal, not only with the praises of men, but also with their insults, whether these were intended or not. We give an instance, and in the words of one of the chief actors in the scene. This was one Canon Bozzio, a native of Caposele, who in due course gave lengthy and detailed testimony of Gerard's virtues, but who at this particular time knew of them only by hearsay and was not inclined to believe everything Father Cafaro had been telling him on the subject. He resolved to put things to the test and see for himself. Gerard happened to be in the town of Atella where the Canon was preaching a Lenten course. One day he entered the sacristy of the parish church to find the holy brother the centre of an admiring group of priests and laymen, and discoursing with them on spiritual things. The Canon proceeds : " Seeing him thus surrounded, I suddenly began attacking him in a way that showed him what little store I set by his virtue, telling him that if that was his idea of virtue, he was greatly mistaken ; and that I for one could not bring myself to believe in it. This unexpected and unsolicited speech did not succeed

[1] Benedetti, p. 291.

in unsettling the serenity of his countenance or disturbing his interior peace ; with a gentle smile and an embrace he showed me the hidden pleasure the incident had caused him."[1] Shortly after, the Canon happened to enter the saint's room, where he found him in an ecstasy.

In the spring of 1754, there occurred in Gerard's life an incident that was to be the source of the heaviest transient disgrace and the purest abiding glory. He was calumniated, foully calumniated, and had to pass through a dark and noisome tunnel of suspicion and mistrust before emerging once again into the fresh and lucid atmosphere of the love and veneration of his brethren. In a circular letter to his spiritual sons, the holy Founder had written two years before : " I beg each of you—and that you may remember the better what I now say, I even give you an obedience—to ask of the despised Jesus Christ every day, during the meditation or thanksgiving, for the grace to bear contempt with peace and cheerfulness of spirit ; the more fervent will positively pray that He may let them be despised for His love."[2] If Gerard took this last recommendation to heart, as is more than likely, his prayer was answered, and that lavishly.

There are two versions of the story : one given by Tannoia, the other by Caione. Tannoia was in Ciorani at the time, fulfilling the duties of novice master and was evidently unable to obtain any inner first-hand knowledge of the incident. Caione was Gerard's last superior, and after the saint's death, he was commissioned

---

[1] Benedetti, p. 203.
[2] *Lettera Circolare*, 27 July, 1752.

by St. Alphonsus to investigate the matter closely and commit his account to writing. All the more recent lives we have been able to consult follow Caione's narrative, some even without referring to Tannoia. We will tell the story as Caione has told it.

Briefly and simply the painful facts are these. Amongst Gerard's unusual apostolic activities was, as we shall see, the opening of the cloister door to young girls. Now one such young girl was a certain Neria Caggiano, of Lacedonia, who was anxious to enter the convent of San Salvatore in Foggia, to which Gerard had already sent not a few. The lack of the requisite dowry stood in the way. Gerard put himself to much trouble in her behalf and at last, through the generosity of friends, succeeded in getting her accepted. After a brief stay of barely three weeks, Neria yielded to home-sickness and came out. To justify her action in the eyes of her relatives and friends, she set about defaming the nuns, evidently in no measured terms. Now Gerard was well known in Lacedonia ; to say nothing of the three years he had spent in the service of its irascible bishop, he had but a few weeks before been a consoling angel for its inhabitants during an epidemic. And so the question naturally arose : if these religious were really all Neria made them out to be, how could Gerard, who knew them so well, have allowed her to enter amongst them ? And how could he have co-operated in her so doing to the extent of procuring her a dowry ? It was a difficulty, and the girl saw it. To those who put it she would keep on repeating Gerard's name in such a way as to provoke suspicion that she was not saying all she could say. Thus Gerard's reputation for holiness and prudence stood in the way of her calumnies against the nuns being believed. Why not remove it by calumniating Gerard himself? A happy thought from hell, whose denizens had more than one score to settle with him. No sooner thought than done. In the best of lives there is so much that can be read deliberately or indeliberately amiss, and with a little evil ingenuity a criminal can be made out of a saint. For an instance we need not go beyond the Gospel.

Whenever business brought Gerard to Lacedonia, he was the welcome and honoured guest of a worthy and intimate friend: Signore Costantino Cappucci. St. Alphonsus knew the Cappucci household well and ever since his first acquaintance with them on the occasion of a mission he preached in the town in 1746, he had looked on them as a model Christian family. Now Signore Cappucci had four daughters. Two of them —Maria Antonia and Maria Teresa—acting under Gerard's advice and influence, had already entered the convent of San Salvatore, from which Neria Caggiano had just emerged. Two daughters remained at home. One of these, Nicoletta by name, was a singularly good and guileless child . . . . *onestissima e piissima donzella,* to quote Caione's words. Now in the early part of this year 1754 Gerard had stayed a whole month in the Cappucci home. There were the elements of the calumny. Neria and the devil did the rest.

With the craftiness lent her by such a master she soon trumped up an unsavoury story about Gerard and Nicoletta. But how was she to gain belief? To tell a lie is one thing and an easy thing: to have it credited is another thing and often very difficult. Neria had sense enough to know that she and her tale would be rudely flouted in Lacedonia. But the devil got an idea and passed it on to her. In Lacedonia there was a very estimable priest called Benigno Bonaventura, who was, moreover, very friendly with St. Alphonsus and had the interests of his rising institute much at heart. He happened to be Neria's confessor. Having gradually secured his confidence in her sincerity, at last she whispered her foul story about Gerard and Nicoletta into his horrified ear. There was no hinting or surmising in the telling : relentlessly she delivered herself of her concocted facts. Dates, places, circumstances, with sordid unspeakable details, were at her fingers' ends. The good priest was naturally shocked beyond words. He knew Gerard. But he also knew men ; and Gerard was a man. The best on earth was always capable of the worst, until heaven settled matters, as every confessor knows, and knows better than anyone. He had no reason for doubting his penitent, and he had to reckon with every possibility, even the worst. There were high interests at stake, and it was his duty to secure them. If Gerard were really such as Neria's alleged facts made him out to be, then the sooner he was exposed the better. He imposed upon his penitent the duty of delating Brother Gerard Majella to St. Alphonsus. Then, with her permission—in this case most willingly given—he accompanied Neria's letter with one of his own. The devil chuckled. That was that.

Alphonsus got the letters, read them and was aghast. Gerard ! the saint ! the miracle-worker ! the pride of his youthful Congregation ! Gerard to fall ! And so low ! Could he have misread ? He read again. But no ; Neria had the devil on her side and had presented her case with devilish cunning. Then Padre Bonaventura had written, not only as a friend, but as a priest and as a confessor who had made up his mind that there could be no reasonable doubt about Gerard's guilt. No ; unfortunately Alphonsus had not misunderstood and had read the accusing documents aright. What were his reactions ? Alphonsus had been a great lawyer, was already a great saint, and would one day be looked upon as the prince of moral theologians. Alphonsus, too, knew men. None better. For nearly thirty years now he had been dealing with them—with all sorts and conditions of men—and the incalculable possibilities of evil were well known to him. Looking at matters objectively, and leaving entirely out of account any special inspirations he may have been favoured with on the occasion—and none are recorded—we must suppose that the slanderous story had the same effect upon him as it would normally have upon any normal man. After all, a lie, unless very clumsily clothed, does make its appearance in the garb of truth and, as such, holds possession for the time being. No matter how extravagant and fantastic it may seem, if what it sets forth is barely possible, then that bare possibility must be reckoned with and may not be ruled off-hand out of court. And it was here that the deadly power of Neria's calumny came in : by alleging evil it called attention to the possibility of evil, while the good that had so far been taken for granted had now to be proved, or the evil admitted. As a French biographer puts it, " this involuntary prejudice, so difficult to overcome,

is the first effect of calumny, even though this takes
the shape of a mere insinuation : in spite of ourselves,
we begin to doubt the innocence of the accused."[1]
Gerard's guilt in a certain concrete case was possible,
and that possibility had to be reckoned with.
Alphonsus knew Gerard by repute and up to this had
revered him as a saint. He knew how estimable the
Cappucci family were. But he also knew that St.
Augustine had said he had seen men fall whose virtue
seemed as secure as that of St. Jerome and St. Ambrose.[2]
He knew that impeccability is not of this world ; and
of fallen cedars of Lebanon he had himself already seen
more than one. Of course there can be no question
of Alphonsus having been instantaneously and absolutely convinced of Gerard's guilt. Had he been so,
he would not have been Alphonsus de'Liguori, the
outstanding lawyer and moralist, to say nothing of the
saint ; though, if he had been so convinced, he would
have ruthlessly expelled him from the Institute. All
the same, Alphonsus was shaken, naturally shaken by
the calumny.

Gerard's biographers are not at all at one on this
point. Landi writes : " Hell, enraged at all the good
Gerard was doing in the house and out of it, set about
hatching as horrible a plot as can well be conceived
in order to bar the way to his going out and so avoid
further losses. It brought about an attack on his good
name on the part of individuals in a certain town, who
wrote a cunning and defamatory letter against him to
the Rector Major, who, *without giving credit to the*

[1] Dunoyer, p. 282.
[2] Cf. *Selva*, II, iii, 12.

imposture, ordered him to present himself at Pagani. This he did *to test his spirit*."[1] (Italics ours). Father Ripoli states in his deposition : " Even though the suspicion of his guilt rested on a light foundation . . . . St. Alphonsus would have sent him home. He considered him to be certainly innocent, and if he inflicted punishment on him, it was not because he was convinced of his guilt, but merely to test him."[2] On the other hand, both Caione and Tannoia assert that Alphonsus did entertain a positive doubt on the subject of Gerard's culpability. " If our holy Father did not at once believe it implicitly," writes Tannoia, " he was at least in doubt about it."[3]

Anyhow, his first step was to commission Father Andrew Villani, one of the general consultors of the Congregation and a trusted friend and director, to proceed at once to Lacedonia, where the Cappucci family lived, and thence to Iliceto, to make prudent inquiries. The Father interviewed Neria Caggiano, who maintained her charges. He interviewed Padre Bonaventura, who maintained his conviction of Gerard's guilt. Though Villani could glean nothing further that was positively prejudicial to the accused, still the information he gathered did not warrant his complete justification. Forthwith Alphonsus summoned Gerard to Nocera.

It is not certain if Gerard had been aware of the object of this summons. According to Caione, Villani made his investigations chiefly if not solely in Lace-

---

[1] *Istoria della Congregazione del SSmo. Redentore.*
[2] In Apost. no. 7, § 160.
[3] Cap. xxiii.

donia, and as his case was still pending, it is not likely.
At the same time, he seems to be hinting darkly at
coming trouble when, on the eve of his departure, he
writes in a letter to a friend in Caposele[1]: " I am leaving
for Pagani, where my Superior has summoned me.
I beg of you to pray constantly for me. I am in sore
need of it." He left Iliceto, where he had spent the
first five years of his brief religious life, never to see
it more.[2] One thing we do know : in that sudden
summons he heard the voice of God, and that was
enough. The angels went with him.

On arrival Gerard presented himself before Alphonsus.
It was the first time they had ever met, and the meeting
was sad and strange. The father Gerard had revered
and loved from afar as his God on earth he now faced
as his judge. The laybrother whose fame was on all
men's lips and whose reputation for sanctity had thrilled
the holy Founder with the purest joy, Alphonsus now
beheld as a possible hypocrite and seducer. It was a
tragic meeting between these two men, either of whom
would have died rather than sully their soul with one
deliberate venial sin, and each of whom would one
day be canonised. Alphonsus read the accusing letters
and waited for Gerard to speak. Gerard did not speak.
Like the Great Accused in Pilate's hall, he " was silent."

---

[1] Padre Gaetano Santorelli. Benedetti, p. 250.

[2] Though the house of Iliceto will be mentioned more than once
in subsequent chapters, as the plan of our biography will demand,
we just mention here that as it disappeared from Gerard's life on this
particular occasion, so it was destined to disappear entirely from
the annals of the Congregation in 1866, being suppressed by a hostile
government, together with a dozen other Neapolitan foundations.
After its suppression, it became a reformatory for boys. To-day
it is in great part a ruin.

" He remained as though frozen," says Tannoia, " and uttered never a word to exculpate himself."[1]

What had happened ? We can imagine—or perhaps we cannot imagine—the horrible shock received even by his disciplined and heroic soul by the impact of such an accusation, and an accusation, too, which, if not disproved, would carry with it his expulsion from the bosom of that religious family which it cost him so much to enter and which was dearer to him than life. Not that he thought for one moment that, left to himself and his own unaided frailty, he was less capable of sin than any other man. These words of his on this occasion have been recorded : " If God had not kept His hand over me, I should have done worse than that."[2] We remember his fifth resolution :— " Amongst all the virtues that are dear to Thee, my God, what I love best is purity and spotlessness in God's sight. O Infinite Purity, I trust in Thee to keep me from every impure thought, even the least, which I in my wretchedness might conceive in this world." And now here was this foul, foul accusation ! In an instant his smitten heart was loud with the clamour of contending voices. Nature, recoiling from the blow, called imperiously for an immediate and vigorous disavowal of the loathesome charge. But long since nature had been getting short shrift from Gerard. He now gave it a deaf ear and listened to other speakers. There was his Rule—never of course meant to apply to such a case—forbidding him to excuse himself when accused. There was his vow, his special vow always to do what

---

[1] Cap. xxiii.
[2] In Apost. no. 17, § 9.

he thought to be the most perfect thing. Above all, there was his love, that love for his crucified and humiliated God and his own life-long yearning to be like Him. He remembered how *He* " was silent." Swiftly and irrevocably he decided. With bowed head he listened and said nothing. His confessor would hear of his innocence : the proof of it he left to God.

This attitude, however heroic for Gerard, did not help matters for Alphonsus. The accused had not indeed admitted his guilt. But neither had he denied it ; and in such cases silence is suspicious and compromising. Whatever Alphonsus thought of it, he now took drastic action and, short of expulsion, inflicted every penalty that would have suited the case had the accused been found guilty. He was forbidden to hold any intercourse whatever with the outside world, even by letter. He was forbidden to receive Holy Communion. The first privation was for his contemplative soul in many ways a relief ; what the second involved could be described only by himself.

It was not long before the penances inflicted on Gerard, especially the deprivation of Holy Communion, laid him open to suspicion on the part of the community of Pagani ; and though the nature of the accusation was of course withheld from all except those fathers who were officially charged to investigate it, still the conclusion was inevitable that it was something very grave. Meanwhile the attitude of his brethren was most sympathetic. They simply could not bring themselves to believe in his guilt, and those who knew him most intimately kept urging him to justify himself. He was grateful but adamant. To all his comforters and well-

wishers he would say : " If God wishes me to be mortified, why should I strive to withdraw myself from His
Will ? And if it is His Will that my innocence be brought
to light, who can do it better than He ? . . . . Let God,
then, do as He pleases, for I wish only what God
wishes."[1] To his Divine Master his prayer was : " My
cause is Thy cause ; if Thou willest my humiliation,
I cheerfully submit to it as Thou didst, for Thou didst
tread that path Thyself."[2] One day he was urged to
beg Alphonsus' leave to receive Holy Communion. For
a moment he hesitated. The stakes were high. Then
he said, with renewed emphasis and decision, energetically
striking the balustrade as he spoke : " We must die
under the winepress of God's Will."[3] Against that
same Father Alphonsus, now his judge as well, he bore
not a trace of bitterness. Passing him in the corridor
one day, shortly after that first painful interview, Gerard
gazed lovingly at him, saying : " My Father, you have
the face of an angel. The mere sight of you fills me
with consolation."[4] And so he let things be, remembering
the words : " Commit thy way to the Lord, and trust
in him : and he will do it. And he will bring forth thy
justice as the light, and thy judgment as the noon-
day."[5] His days and nights went in prayer, and all
his leisure was given to communing with his sacramental Lord.

The prohibition to receive his Jesus was the penalty
that lay heaviest on Gerard's heart. When we recall

---

[1] In Apost. no. 7, § 266.
[2] Tannoia, cap. xxiii.
[3] *Ibid.*
[4] Landi.
[5] Ps. xxxvi, 5-6.

the favoured child of Capotignano, the weeping boy
walking sadly back from the rails where he was considered too young to receive, the angelic protégé
of St. Michael being miraculously given the Bread of
angels, the sacristan of later years hovering lovingly
around the tabernacle—it is indeed pathetic to think
of him now debarred from partaking of that Blessed
Food for which he was ever hungering and of which
he stood in such sore need. And when we remember,
too, who it was who had imposed that painful penance
on him—that it was another saint of the Eucharist,
the author of the *Visits to the Blessed Sacrament*, the
Apostle of Frequent Communion—do we not seem to
see an angel with a flaming sword before the " paradise
of pleasure " barring the way, as it was barred long
ago, to the Tree of Life. If ever Gerard's human efforts
to make the Will of God his own were called upon to
rise to heroic heights, it was surely now. One morning
a certain Father asked him to serve Mass. " Let me
alone, let me alone," was the answer ; " do not tempt
me ; I might snatch the Host out of your hand . . . .
che vi strapperai l'Ostia dalle mani."[1]   But no remission,
no mitigation of the dread sentence would he seek.
" It is enough to have Him in my heart," he would say ;
" the Lord wishes to punish me for my little love for
Him and is flying from me ; but I will never lose Him
from my heart."[2] All the while he redoubled his
penances and prayers, taking comfort from the thought
that the more he suffered the more conformable he
became to the great Sufferer of Gethsemane and Calvary.

[1] Landi.—Cfr. Tannoia, cap. xxiii.
[2] In Apost. no. 15, § 32.

His one real grief was the sinful state of her who had so cruelly calumniated him, and he gladly bore his penance to purchase grace for her soul.

His sudden disappearance from public had already caused painful surprise, and it was impossible to keep it from being noised abroad that he was under a cloud. Within the Congregation, as we have said, sympathy was deep and general, though no doubt many found it hard enough to explain his persistent silence satisfactorily.

Gerard had one very great and holy friend in Father Francesco Margotta. This saintly man—a man after Gerard's own heart—had been in turn lawyer, the governor of towns, and the president of the seminary in the diocese of Conza before he became a Redemptorist. His worth was soon appreciated by Alphonsus. He helped in the foundation at Caposele and became rector there in 1749. He was for many years procurator-general of the Institute, and in that capacity spent much of his time in Naples, where he had Gerard as companion during the two visits the latter made there. For many years he went through an inner martyrdom of aridity and scruple. He died of famine fever at Naples, in 1764. Gerard had informed this beloved confidant of everything, and his letter drew the following reply:

"My dear Gerard, Your letter has given me a two-fold pleasure: you tell me you remember me in your prayers; and you assure me of your conformity to God's Will in your present trial. I wish you everything that is good and pray that you may ever make greater progress in the service of God. I wish to confirm you in your good dispositions, so that you may act out of

obedience and live solely to do God's Will by the most
perfect submission to superiors. I keep you in my
unworthy prayers to our Lord and our Mother, that
you may be given the necessary strength to become
in all things conformable to the Will of God and that
you may fulfil all the holy aspirations of your heart."[1]

Gerard was still silent. Alphonsus himself seems to
have been perplexed ; so much so indeed that he thought
it well to send the brother to another house, where he
could enjoy greater freedom of conscience, if perchance
that conscience of his were really burdened. Who was
more painfully and sympathetically alive to the ever
possible needs of the individual conscience than the
great missionary and theologian ? Accordingly, he sent
Gerard to the novitiate house in Ciorani, enjoining on
its Rector Father Rossi and the novice master, Father
Tannoia himself, to keep him under close observation.
At the end of ten or twelve days he was recalled to
Pagani. " Our most minute observation," writes
Tannoia, " failed to discover anything blameworthy
in him."[2] He added that what struck them most was
that he never spoke a word to anyone about his trouble,
contenting himself with giving his confidence to his
dear Lord and his Mother Mary.

Benedetti relates a touching incident that occurred
during his stay in Ciorani.[3] Holy Communion was being
brought to the room of an invalid in the house. As
the sacred particle was being borne on the paten, it
had fallen unnoticed to the ground. On reaching the

---

[1] Tannoia, cap. xxiii.
[2] *Ibid.*
[3] P. 256.

sick room, the officiating Father, as well as all who were accompanying him, were in consternation at the discovery. The whole company left the room immediately to search for It. Gerard, who was evidently in the procession, left also. So lively was his faith and so ardent his love for his sacramental Lord, Whom he had not been allowed to receive for over a month, that he became out of himself and, running over to the other brothers, with outstretched arms, he began looking for his Jesus with the troubled ardour that reminds us forcibly of the Magdalen after the resurrection. He was the first to find Him. Great was his jubilation, though it died away with a sigh at being unable to house Him in his heart.

Gerard's second stay in Pagani did not last long. Father Giovenale was going to Caposele to take over the superiorship temporarily from the Rector, Father Mazzini, who was ill, and Alphonsus sent Gerard with him. Tannoia's excellent report, Gerard's uncomplaining silence, and the arresting fact that miracles and ecstasies were being laid to the credit of the alleged criminal had all combined to bring about a change in the attitude of Alphonsus. It was during his first stay in Pagani that Gerard suddenly appeared before Alphonsus in the refectory in answer to a mental summons from the holy Founder. And who knows ? perhaps Heaven itself had spoken to one saint in favour of another. At any rate, Alphonsus had begun to look on the accused with a kindlier eye. Before the travellers left for Caposele, he did something that made a world of difference to Gerard : he allowed him to receive Holy Communion on Sundays, enjoining on Father Giovenale at the same time to mortify him well and, above all, to see that he held no intercourse with outsiders. The saint was evidently not yet quite convinced of his innocence and was taking no chances.

They reached Caposele towards the end of June. A few days later a letter reached Alphonsus. It was from Neria Caggiano. She had been taken seriously ill, the fear of God's judgments had brought her to her senses, and she had been going through a hell on earth. She confessed her calumny to Padre Bonaventura, who laid upon her the obligation of formally retracting it. She did so in the letter Alphonsus now received, stating that her former letter had been written at the instigation of the devil and was but a tissue of lies. If that former letter was surely one of the saddest he had ever got, this letter must have been one of the most welcome. There was universal rejoicing throughout the Congregation. Gerard himself was the least affected by the news. To quote Tannoia : " As he had not been cast down by the calumny, so he showed no elation when he saw that his character was cleared."[1] He took everything— sweets and bitters—from the hands of God, from those hands which, as he put it in his first resolution, " shower down on me the precious gems of the divine Will."

Alphonsus sent for him at once, this time to take him to a father's heart. When the holy Founder asked him why he had not said a single word in his defence, he replied : " How could I, my Father ? Does not the rule forbid me to excuse myself and to bear in silence whatever mortifications are imposed by the Superior ? "

---

[1] Tannoia, cap. xxiii.

To face p. 207

" Very good, very good, my son," rejoined Alphonsus, with difficulty mastering his emotion, " go now and God bless you."[1] As we read in the *Positio super Virtutibus*, " It is well to note here that the rule in question is undoubtedly to be understood of excusing oneself where breaches of regular observance are concerned, and not where there is question of enormities so unworthy of a religious. Anybody else, no matter how obedient, would have thus interpreted that rule. When Gerard in his great humility and utter heroism did not do so, he won the admiration of all his brethren, not excepting the holy Founder himself." The room that was the scene of this incident is still pointed out to Redemptorists who go on pilgrimage to Pagani in their comings and goings across the world.[2]

On another occasion, Alphonsus remarked to Gerard that he must have been distressed at being deprived of Holy Communion. " Never," came the answer, " Jesus Christ did not wish to come to me, and I could not resent it."[3] Thus with ruthless logic did he practise his great devotion to the Will of God. Henceforth Alphonsus knew Gerard and appreciated him for what he was. As the saint one day remarked to Father Margotta, " I now know this Brother's virtue, and had he given me no other proof of it, this last would have been enough for me."[4]

Thus ended this painful episode. According to

---

[1] In Apost. no. 7, § 222.
[2] It has been thrown on to canvas in a well-known painting by Gagliardi, the artist mentioned in the preceding chapter. Cf. page 143, note.
[3] Tannoia, cap. xxiii. [4] In Apost. no. 7, § 159.

Tannoia, it lasted about two months ; Caione speaks of
" a few months." A question or two will naturally come
to the mind. If St. Alphonsus was not convinced of
Gerard's guilt, why did he treat him with such harshness ? We think that the best explanation is that the
measures he took against him were more precautionary
than penal. The very nature of the crime laid to the
Brother's charge demanded a cessation of all further
intercourse with the outside world, until he should
be cleared of it ; then, with all the great missioner's
experience and knowledge of the consciences of men,
he would forestall the possible further crime of sacrilege
by debarring the accused from the altar rails. Other
difficulties present themselves not at all so easy of
solution. Since Alphonsus must have known the reputation Gerard enjoyed in the Congregation for blind unquestioning obedience to every point of rule, why did
he not suspect that the protracted silence of the accused
would be due to this obedience ? Why did he let two
months go by without asking Gerard himself for an
explanation of his silence and demand a categorical
reply in the name of obedience ? Surely the first interview with the accused was not the last ; though none
other is recorded. Why did not those Fathers and brothers
in the Congregation who knew Gerard well approach the
holy Founder on this subject of self-defence and at least
suggest to him that perhaps the long persistent silence
might be due to blind obedience to rule ? If they did,
we are told nothing about it. We have no answer to
offer to these questions, except to say that perhaps God
took charge of the whole unpleasant business from start
to finish and inspired the chief actors in it so to think

and do as to make the occurrence the source of ultimate glory for His servant.

As we look back upon it now and see it through the halo of his canonised sanctity, we are inclined to fix our gaze rather on its ultimate triumphant issue than on the preceding trial, rather on the righting of a cruel wrong than on the bitterness of that wrong itself. But, humanly speaking, with all Gerard's love and patience and resignation, this incident in his life must have been bitter indeed. He loved his religious brethren with the heart of a saint, and by them he was beloved and revered. And now ! We can scarcely believe that he was now looked upon in the same light by every member of the Congregation as he was still looked upon by his many holy and intimate friends. He was under a cloud ; and judging from the nature and severity of the penalties imposed, many must have suspected the worst. Perhaps there were some who, angered at the bare possibility of being duped by bogus sanctity, had already begun to think of removing him from the pedestal of their veneration and turning him out of the temple of their hearts. Perhaps even his miracles were already being attributed to Beelzebub. Gerard must have realised it all. He must have caught many a furtive glance of painful curiosity levelled at him ; he must have surprised many a whispering group and noticed the sudden drop in the conversation at his approach ; he must have sensed the ill-concealed effort to seem at ease in his presence and the atmosphere of awkwardness and strain his presence brought with it. The long and silent endurance of all this, so easily forgotten in the glory of his eventual rehabilitation, must have been a martyrdom for his heart calling for a martyr's heroism.

One day, during the course of the trial, Gerard was asked how he could live without Holy Communion. He replied : " I recreate myself in the immensity of my God."[1] The infinite attributes of God were his mental food during those days of tribulation. He re-doubled his austerities, slept little, passed his days in prayer in the church, and when night came, would spend hours contemplating the heavens and in them reading the greatness of their Maker. He would then take a little rest lying in a coffin that once held the remains of another saintly Redemptorist, the Venerable Cesare Sportelli, who had died four years previously in the odour of sanctity. Let us close this chapter with this sublime and touching picture. We see Gerard casting himself and his trials into the ocean of God's immensity ; gazing, a mere speck on this planet of ours, into the infinity of wheeling worlds above him, and then taking his brief repose in that grim reminder of the fleeting years and the emptiness of human things. Standing between a coffin and the sky—symbols of an end and a beginning—he saw himself and his sufferings in their true perspective. He was scarcely twenty-eight. In some sixteen months, his chaste and mortified body would lie in a coffin of its own, while his soul would speed more swiftly than the rushing meteor to the bosom of his God, leaving this universe immeasurably beneath him and with the burning splendour of his sainthood quenching the cold radiance of its stars.

---

[1] Tannoia, cap. xxiii.

CHAPTER VII

GOD'S WIZARD

SO far, here and there in our pages, miraculous happenings of one or another kind have already appeared. But now the miraculous forms so large and striking an element in St. Gerard's life—being indeed the very warp and woof of it—that to treat of it as something incidental would be less than justice. It would be like writing a biography of Napoleon or Shakespeare and mentioning incidentally that the former won battles and the latter wrote plays. Not without reason has St. Gerard Majella been called the wonder-worker of the eighteenth century. Some of these wonders we are going to record in detail in this chapter.

Now we are quite aware that the miraculous in the lives of the saints is not to everybody's liking. In a curious way it gets on many people's nerves. Some there are who have no time for miracle-working saints, because in them they see nothing attractive, nothing imitable, nothing that can claim affinity with their own poor human clay; and so they simply do not admit them into the circle of their heavenly acquaintances and friends. We would remind such people of certain things: the working of miracles and other similar gifts are in no way essential to holiness, though where they do accompany virtue, they testify eloquently to it;

many of the saints worked few miracles in life, and some of them—including St. John the Baptist and the " Little Flower "—worked none at all ; the Sacred Congregation of Rites never begins the discussion of any miracles alleged to have been wrought by a servant of God until it has been satisfactorily established that he practised the virtues in an heroic degree. St. Teresa of Avila would have willingly forgone the greatest of her ecstasies to perform a single act of ordinary virtue, and on her deathbed what consoled her most was the simple elementary fact that she was dying a daughter of the Church. The saints who worked most miracles in life were not saints because they worked miracles ; they worked miracles because they were saints. The sanctity came first, the miracles second and, as we have seen, in some cases they did not come at all till after death. Imitation, not admiration alone, the Church has ever in view in canonising her children ; and the greatest wonder-worker amongst them is imitable, not in his miracles but in his virtues.

Others there are, not necessarily outside the household of the Faith, who look askance at all miraculous lives and dismiss them airily with a shrug. They seem to shrink instinctively from what they cannot account for or what they cannot themselves achieve, and they seem to look on miracles as a reflection on their own deficiencies and an undesirable reminder of their human limitations. They would almost give one the impression that they are jealous of the Almighty and of His favoured servants ! We have a faint suspicion, too, that at times this sceptical attitude is just a pose. Perhaps the nearest thing to the nursery literature of childhood are the

miracles presented to us in the stories of God's holy
ones. Now some people dread appearing to relapse
into the credulity of those far-off days and think it a
sign of strength and independence of thought to question
what the many believe. Accordingly, the more a saint
can be shorn of his miracles by scholars and historians
and the nearer he can be brought to the proportions
of the man in the street the better they like it. As we
remarked in an earlier chapter, we cannot be too grateful
to scholarship and research for their achievements in
the matter of hagiography; but the pendulum may
swing too far the other way, and a censorious attitude
towards the subject is sometimes taken up by those
who should know better. As the postulator in St.
Gerard's cause exclaimed during the discussion of an
incident in his life:" Surely we are not rationalists
and naturalists who hate the word 'miracle' as the
victims of hydrophobia hate water! "[1] We know that
many alleged miracles have been disproved; but, says
Newman, "it as little derogates from the supernatural
gift residing in the Church that miracles should have
been fabricated or exaggerated, as it prejudices her
holiness that within her pale good men are mixed wlth
bad. Fiction and pretence follow truth as its shadows."[2]

And now what is a miracle? It is an event or fact
that can be known by the senses, transcending the usual
order of created things, and due solely to a special intervention on the part of God. In Newman's words, " a

---

[1] *Resp. ad Nov Animadv.*, § 62.

[2] *Essays on Miracles*, p. 238.

miracle . . . . displays the Deity in action."[1]

And, to begin with, *can* miracles happen ? For the Catholic (for whom the fact that they can is an article of faith), for the Christian, for the believer in a personal God the question answers itself. " Surely," says St. Augustine, " God is called almighty for no other reason than because He can do what He wills."[2] If God can create, He can surely do with His creation what He chooses. To effect any change in what already exists is surely, in human speech, a lesser achievement than to bring it into existence out of nothing. He who can do the lesser thing can do the greater. Whether He effects this change through the instrumentality of another or no is all one. Living as we do in the atmosphere of our human disabilities and hourly at grips with difficulties, we find it hard to grasp the idea of omnipotence, and we questioningly shrink from any alleged display of it. " God can do more than man can understand," says the author of the Imitation.[3] We creatures are beset with limitations on all sides ; we think in terms of them ; the mere idea of the unlimited gives us a jolt, upsets all our modes of thought and makes us almost resent what we fail to understand. " What men are accustomed to behold," says St. Augustine again, " they

---

[1] *Ibid*, p. ii. It must be noted that we are speaking throughout of miracles in the strict and technical sense of the word and as just defined. We have not at all in mind the *ordinary* display of God's providence, which is often really far more wonderful than anything we read of in the lives of His saints. " The ruling of the whole world," writes St. Augustine, " is a greater miracle than the feeding of five thousand people with five loaves : and still no one wonders at it : men wonder at the latter, not because it is greater, but because it is rare."—*In Joan. Evangel.* Tractat. XXIV, i.

[2] *De Civitate Dei*, lib. xxi, cap. vii.

[3] Bk. iv. 18..

believe in ; what they are not accustomed to behold, they do not believe in. When God works miracles, He does unaccustomed things, because He is God." And again : " If you understand how, it is no longer a miracle."[1] Miracles are a reminder of the feeble creatures that we are and of the almightiness of our Maker. By them God lets us see unmistakably that He is not bound by our laws or hemmed in by our created confines.

But what about the Laws of Nature ? (We concede the capitals this once). In spite of many poets and some scientists, and in spite of the capitals, nature is neither a god nor a goddess, but God's creation governed by laws which He has fixed for it—that is, if the rules that control blind unreasoning forces can be called " laws." Now surely God is not to be the only legislator who is not free to break or suspend or abrogate His own laws whenever He thinks fit, if a higher purpose calls for it. Sticklers for these " laws of nature " must be reminded that these laws are the laws of the God of nature and, as far as He is concerned, are in no way the laws of the Medes and Persians. Surely the Lord may do in His universe what a bishop may do in his diocese and what any legislative body in the world may do within the limits of its jurisdiction : He may override and repeal His own legislation at will. Surely it is not true that in God's case alone the law is above the lawgiver.

But now these so-called " laws of nature," so sacrosanct in the eyes of those who look with disfavour on the miraculous, are merely the normal tendencies of natural forces. The *actual* order of things we see in

---

[1] *Serm. de tempore*, 147 ; 247.

created nature is not an absolutely necessary order; it is but hypothetically necessary, that is, *because God has willed it so.* But God could have willed it otherwise and could will it otherwise even now. He is free to change, combine, annihilate all or any part of His creation, as well as the rules He has imposed on it, should it so please Him. If Omnipotence does not mean this it means nothing. " I believe in God the Father Almighty " we often say; we must believe ungrudgingly in all the implications of this tremendous attribute.

Of course once the possibility of miracles is admitted, neither their nature nor their number need worry us. All miracles are equally impossible to man and equally possible to God. The least of them calls for the exercise of divine power, and a thousand come as easy to God as one. Once we enter the domain of omnipotence, there is no question of one miracle being more miraculous than another. It may be rarer and more spectacular and may be a greater challenge to our acceptance; but as far as miracles are miracles they are all essentially the same. To admit one miracle and laugh another out of court as being *too* extraordinary, *too miraculous* is not logic. " To declare with a smile that such and such a miracle is of course beyond the limit," writes the late Henri Ghéon, " is to set a limit to the power of God which has no limit. You can accept the possibility of miracle or reject it. What you cannot do is to cry: ' Halt ! just so much miracle and no more.' For that is simply to accept miracle while denying its very essence. The more difficult miracles are to swallow the more likely they are to be true—since, if they *are* true, they most powerfully attest the power of God : which is what miracles are for, and that is their very *raison d'être*."[1] It will be well to bear all this in mind in view of the multitude of Gerard's miracles and the extraordinary nature of many of them.

Miracles, then, *can* happen. But are they *likely* to happen ? And *do* they happen ? " Miracles," writes Newman, " are not only not unlikely, they are positively likely ; and this for the simple reason, because, for the most part, when God begins He goes on. We conceive that when He first did a miracle, He began a series ; what He commenced, He continued : what has been, will be. Surely this is good and clear reasoning. To my own mind, certainly, it is incomparably more difficult to believe that the Divine Being should do one miracle and no more, than that He should do a thousand ; that He should do one great miracle only, than that He should do a multitude of less beside . . . . you believe the Apostolic miracles, therefore be inclined beforehand to believe later ones."[2] This likelihood of miracles occurring becomes a certainty in the light of Christ's words : " Amen, amen, I say to you, he that believeth in me, the works that I do, he also shall do : and greater than these shall he do."[3] The truth is that were there no miracles forthcoming in the lives of the saints—of those holy men and women who believed and prayed as they did, we should be looking for them. Moreover, the Apostle has a word of warning for those who would irreverently probe and pry into the hidden

---

[1] *St. Vincent Ferrer :* Introd. xiii.
[2] *Present Position of Catholics in England*, vii, 7, pp. 306-307.
[3] John. xiv, 12.

purposes of a divine intelligence : " Who hath known the mind of the Lord ? Or who hath been his counsellor ? "[1]

We read of a miracle—perhaps a highly spectacular one—wrought in a most drab and commonplace setting and for a seemingly trivial purpose. There seems to be no proportion between the prodigy and its humdrum circumstances, no reason for the stupendous intervention of Omnipotence which the least miracle connotes. Infinite Wisdom, however, and infinite Love may see reasons and purposes that lie hid from us. Besides testifying to the truth of the Christian religion, they testify to the sanctity of God's servants, to His love for them and to their power with Him ; they stamp the act of a particular virtue with the divine approval ; they show to what lengths divine commiseration can go in relieving human difficulties and distress.

But, as a matter of fact, *do* miracles really happen ? And can they be verified ? We are of course speaking only of miracles recorded in the lives of the saints, for of these alone may we as Catholics ask the question. Now, though we are not bound to believe in any miracle not recorded in Holy Scripture, since it rests on merely human testimony, still to question what hundreds of human eyes have seen and to reject evidence that has been sifted by the soberest and slowest tribunal on earth is neither intelligent nor fair. Writing of the caution and thoroughness with which the Sacred Congregation of Rites proceeds in its investigations into the virtues and miracles of prospective saints, Father

---

[1] Rom., xi., 34.

Faber says : " Putting out of view all idea of divine assistance, and looking at the matter simply as a question of evidence, it is hardly possible to conceive any process for sifting human testimony more complete, more ingenious, or more rigid than the one scrupulously adhered to by the Congregation of Rites in this respect. Much depends upon the decision, and there is no necessity for coming to a decision at all : these two things are continually before the eyes of the judges and render the ordeal one of almost incredible strictness . . . a fact only requires the appearance of being supernatural to awaken against it every suspicion ; every method of surprise and detection is at once arrayed against it ; it is allowed no mercy, no advantage of a doubt, and anything rather than the benefit of the clergy."[1] And Benedict XIV, the great master in these matters, records his own experiences : " We ourselves, who for the space of so many years discharged the duties of promoter of the faith, have seen with our own eyes, as we may say, the Divine Spirit assisting the Roman Pontiff in defining the causes of canonisation ; for in some of them, which had advanced so far most prosperously, sudden difficulties never known before have all at once started up, retarding their hitherto successful career ; whereas in others, on the contrary, difficulties which seemed insuperable have been removed and silenced with a strange facility by means of things that have un-expectedly come to light, and thus the causes reached their desired end."[2]

---

[1] *An Essay on Beatification and Canonization*, p. 63.
[2] De Can. 1. 44, 4.

Even liars have an object in their lying, and unless we are prepared to admit the likelihood of mass perjury in the processes of canonisation, we must take seriously the findings of a body of men who take so seriously their own work and are so well equipped for it from the human point of view, to say nothing of the supernatural. With regard to Gerard's own case, the members of the tribunal wrote thus of the witnesses : " We have met with absolutely nothing in the witnesses that could warrant the withholding of our trust in their statements. They were either priests or religious, or at least persons so conspicuous for their piety and religion that, as far as we can make out, they are one and all beyond all exception. With regard to their depositions we have been able to discover no grounds for suspecting either that they came forward for their examination after having been previously given information, or that they had been induced to state what was false or to with-hold what was true through any motive of friendship or enmity. We are satisfied that they stated whatever came to their knowledge with sincerity, consistency and assurance. Consequently, we consider them to be worthy of complete trust."[1]

One brief final word about a well-known and specious objection : new discoveries are coming to light every day ; may it not happen that to-morrow's newly-discovered force in nature will work today's " miracle " and explode it ? Now no man in his senses will believe that any future discovery will raise dead men to life, make men born blind see all of a sudden, instantaneously

---

[1] *Resp. ad Nov. Animadv.*, § 16.

work cures of all sorts for which time is absolutely essential. Is it not a curious thing that all the far-reaching and revolutionary discoveries of recent years have not been able to explain or reproduce the miracles we read of in the Holy Scriptures or the lives of the saints ? To those who carp at miracles and persist in searching for a human explanation of a superhuman fact we suggest the close and honest reading of the cure of the blind man as told by St. John in the ninth chapter of his Gospel. It should be a tonic. Let us now return to Gerard.

Tannoia speaks of him as one who " has been justly styled the *wonder-worker of our Congregation* and the glory of his country." His life of the saint ends thus : " Many volumes would scarcely suffice were I to record all his heroic deeds and reckon up the prodigies he worked and continues to work daily. I will therefore conclude this sketch with the words of St. John the Beloved Disciple : ' Many other signs also did he . . . . which are not written in this book.' "[1] And speaking of the " incredible prodigies " wrought by Gerard in the course of his journeys, he writes : " We never took pains to collect them, and such as came to our knowledge were heard as it were by chance from priests who came to our house."[2] Gerard's holy contemporary and confessor Father Cafaro spoke of his life as a continuous miracle. It was indeed a glittering chain of wonders. Now in a book of this size all we can do is to select instances that best embody and show forth the various

---

[1] English Edit., p. 453.
[2] *Ibid.* p. 423.

types of miracle. We shall begin with Gerard's supernatural power over God's inanimate creation. More
than one case of this has already been given in preceding chapters.

When our Lord changed water into wine at the
marriage feast, the Evangelist speaks of the event as
the " beginning of miracles."[1] We will begin with a
miracle in which sour wine was changed into sweet,
not because it was the first miracle Gerard worked,
but because he said something on the occasion that is
worth noting. A certain widow in Melfi, named Vittoria
Bruno, mentioned in a former chapter, had sold her
vintage. On the purchaser coming to take it away,
a whole cask was found to have gone sour. He refused
it. This meant a substantial loss to the poor lady and
she was much distressed. As she was grieving over the
mishap, Gerard happened to be in the house. On hearing
of the calamity, he used the words that so often heralded
a miracle : " *Non è niente, non è niente* . . . it is nothing,
it is nothing." Now little slips of paper bearing the
name of the Immaculate Conception were much in
favour amongst the pious in those days ; and probably
to shift the credit of what he was about to do from
himself to our Blessed Lady, he told Donna Vittoria
to throw one of these into the offending cask, assuring
her that its contents would be set right. Much as she
venerated Gerard, she hesitated. Noticing this the
latter said : " Is it you who have to make the wine
become good again ? No, but it is God ; and so do as
I told you."[2] She did as Gerard told her, and the sour

[1] John, ii, II.
[2] Caione.

wine was at once made sweet. Gerard proved himself, not a juggler but just a human instrument in the hands of a divine power. This is an instance where our sense of proportion may be shocked : a miracle worked for such a comparative triviality as the saving of a cask of wine. Our Lord evidently did not look at things in that light when, to save the faces of a bridal party at a wedding breakfast, He made good wine, not out of bad wine, but out of water. The case is peculiarly valuable as it gives us the saint's own testimony to the miraculous nature of the occurrence.

The miraculous multiplication of food is of course nothing new in the lives of the saints. It is particularly interesting, as it is usually so palpable and undeniable. The man amongst the five thousand in the desert who, after having partaken of the multiplied bread and fishes, would have refused credence to the miracle would, we think, have met with a poor reception. After all, without being professional bursars or cooks, most of us have a fair idea how far the products of the kitchen can go ; and if we saw them going definitely a great deal farther than we thought possible, we should either have to doubt our own senses (which few of us would be willing to do) or admit the intervention of a higher power. Now, that Gerard was frequently the instrument of this higher power in this particular way there is abundant evidence. Tannoia writes : " It was the firm belief in Caposele—and our community was given many proofs of it—that bread was visibly multiplied in his hands."[1]

---

[1] Cap. xxvi.

On one occasion, when the brother baker went to fetch his loaves for the community supper, he found not a crumb, though an entire ovenful had been baked that day. Gerard was porter at the time. There was a famine in the land, many hungry mouths clamoured at the monastery gate, and it was his duty to feed them. He had been given a free hand and freely he used it. Moreover, he knew by conviction and by experience that Providence would provide. The baker, however, thought differently ; much ruffled he went to the rector and with a wealth of appropriate gesture let him know how matters stood. Gerard was sent for and in the presence of the angry baker rated for his imprudence. The worst of it was that it was too late to buy bread in Caposele. He bowed his head under the rebuke and then quietly remarked : " Your Reverence need not worry ; God will provide." And turning to the baker : " Brother, let us look more closely ; there may be bread there." " Not a crust," snapped the baker, " but since you insist, come along with me and see." Gerard followed the brother's rapid strides to the cupboard. " Now," said the baker triumphantly, as he flung it open, " see for yourself if there is as much as a crumb there." The cupboard was full ! " Oh ! blessed for ever be God ! " Gerard exclaimed, as he hurried off to the oratory to give thanks.[1] Meantime the rector had come upon the scene and asked the baker to explain matters. The latter did so, admitting belatedly that nobody could have done it but God. And the rector agreed with him.

---

[1] In Apost. no. 12, § 70.

There were times, too, when food not only multiplied but was evidently brought him by unseen hands or actually created, so to say, in his own. During the famine just alluded to, a certain workman in Caposele, unable to support his two young daughters and fearing the worst if they were not looked after, had commended them in a special way to the charity of the saint. One day, the girls arrived late for the distribution of bread. The very last loaf had been given away. Gerard had a moment's distress. Then he suddenly darted into the house, reappearing almost instantly, beaming with satisfaction and carrying two white piping hot loaves in his hands. The girls had kept their eyes upon him. He had been seen to go to no cupboard, and the loaves differed suspiciously in shape from those baked in the monastery. He gave them to the girls, who brought them home and lost no time in spreading abroad the news of the prodigy.

A man who had seen better days and was naturally loth to queue up with the poor was favoured in a similar way. He had hung back in a corner of the hall until the crowd had gone. Now it was no rare thing for people of rank and means to assist out of curiosity at this distribution of food by the holy laybrother. At times they would even send their children to mingle with the crowd and thus surreptitiously procure some of the bread, which they would keep religiously as a relic. Thus it happened that, though Gerard had seen this man, he had taken no notice of him, thinking him to be a mere onlooker. His attention was now drawn to him and his case explained. It was more than enough to stir the saint's kind and sympathetic heart. " Oh !

why did he come so late ? " he exclaimed, " I have given all away."[1] There was a similar momentary anxiety, a similar darting in and coming out, and drawing from the folds of his habit a small white loaf still smoking, he joyfully gave it to the astonished and hungry man. This loaf, too, was unusual in shape. Moreover, the oven was just then empty and cold ; and, adds Landi, " it was not the time for baking, as it was very late, and our community did not make bread of that shape." The man was allowed, evidently at his own request, to enter the monastery and examine the oven and the kitchen. Not a trace of fresh bread could he find anywhere. Furthermore he questioned the cook, the baker and others, who assured him that the last baking had taken place on the morning of the preceding day. Both the distance and the weather ruled out all possibility of its having come from the town. All held that the bread Gerard had given the man was miraculous.

This frail young man, preyed upon for a lifetime by his self-inflicted penances, with his slender physical resources already being eaten up by tuberculosis, displayed at times a strength that clearly came from above. Two memorable instances are recorded by all his biographers. One of them occurred in the latter half of July, 1755, the very year of his death. Rising from a sick bed at the bidding of his rector in a state of comparative health, he started on a collecting tour. The first place in which he stayed was the district of Senerchia. Here the building of a new parochial church was nearing completion, and for the roofing several

---

[1] Landi.

large chestnut trees had been felled in a wood that
crowned a neighbouring mountain. These were now
awaiting transportation. The builders had seemingly
miscalculated the weight of the trees, as all their efforts
to move them proved fruitless. They defied man and
beast. Gerard heard of the predicament and met the
men. "It is God's church," he said to them, "and
God will see to it that it is completed."[1] He then asked
to be conducted to the wood. There he fell upon his
knees and prayed. On rising again, he fastened a rope
(a handkerchief, according to Berruti) to one of the
largest of the chestnuts. Then in solemn words that
explain all miracles and sum up theology concerning
them, he cried out : "Creature of God ! I command
thee in the name of the Most Holy Trinity to follow me."
And in the sight of the assembled workmen he drew
the huge tree to the building as if it had been a straw.
Mindful of his Master's words, he did not "stagger in
his heart,"[2] and if he did not move a mountain, he
moved a tree. That was not all. He bade the workmen
do as he himself had done, and miraculously sharing
his own miraculous strength, they, too, drew the trees
through almost impassible ways to their allotted places
with incredible ease, "as though they had been so many
sticks,"[3] to use Tannoia's phrase.

The second instance is one of Gerard's most celebrated
and spectacular prodigies. It occurred during the saint's
first stay in Naples, in 1754. It was a day in autumn
and it was blowing hard. Gerard was out and his business

---

[1] In Ord. no. 7. § 471.
[2] Mark, xi, 23.
[3] English Edit., p. 416.

brought him near the storm-tossed shore. As he made
his way along the beach, near the spot called *La Pietra
del Pesce*, his attention was drawn to a crowd of people
in the distance looking seaward and gesticulating wildly.
Cries of terror and dismay soon broke upon his ears.
Glancing out over Naples' famous bay, whose blue
serenity was now lashed into a dark tumult of waters,
he descried a boat in distress, full of people, and driven
helplessly out to sea.[1] The storm was growing in fury,
and the stricken craft seemed doomed. The thought
of the hapless passengers and crew, the sight of that
crowd wringing their hands in futile sympathy, was
too much for Gerard's heart. Flinging his cloak over
his left shoulder, he blessed himself and in a moment
was seen treading the foaming welter, as long ago his
Divine Master trod the tempest-tossed waters of Galilee.
The astonished onlookers on the shore held their breath.
The despairing occupants of the boat could not believe
their eyes. We are told that when the disciples saw
Jesus walking on the sea, " they were troubled, saying :
It is an apparition. And they cried out for fear."[2] On
this occasion, darkness did not lend its terrors to the
scene ; but the sight of this gaunt human form speeding
fearless and erect across the waves must have made
them realise that help from a more than human source
was at hand. And now, above the scream of the storm

---

[1] It is not easy to discover the size or nature of the vessel. Landi
speaks of it as " una barchetta con varie persone " ; one witness
as " una barca mercantile " ; other witnesses as simply " una barca " ;
and Berruti as " una barca di pescatori." It matters little. We know
what an unmanageable thing the smallest craft can be in rough seas,
and from the circumstances it is clear that this was no mere pleasure-
boat.

[2] Matt., xiv, 26.

and the roar of angry waters, a voice rang out : " In the name of the Most Holy Trinity, come hither ! "[1] At once the boat stood still. Gerard approached it, caught the prow with his hand and drew it ashore as though it had been a cork. His clothes were quite dry. For some moments the crowd could scarcely realise what had happened ; but when they saw their dear ones safe and saw how their rescue had been effected, they at length found tongue in frantic cries of *"Miracolo! miracolo!* . . . a miracle ! a miracle ! " Before they could surge around him, however, the miracle-worker was running down a by-street, his pursuers hot on his heels, exclaiming : " *Il Santo! il Santo!* . . . the Saint ! the Saint ! " But the saint succeeded in giving them the slip and found shelter till nightfall in a friend's shop. He ran from that crowd for all the world like a thief from justice, only that in this case Gerard ran from being made a thief, a thief of that glory which—none knew better than he—belonged to God.

This evident miracle, witnessed by a large number of people, made a great noise in the capital, and Gerard could not show himself out of doors without drawing the unwelcome attentions of the passers-by. On the following day, a friend of his, Canon Camillo Bozzio, mentioned in the preceding chapter, arrived in the city on business and called on the saint to take him out. On their way an ecclesiastic came against them. As he passed, he pointed out Gerard to his companion as the man who had saved the boat the day before. In a moment Gerard had broken away from the Canon and

---

[1] Landi.

was off at a quick pace. The latter, who knew nothing of the incident, could not keep up and called after Gerard to take it easy and wait for him. But faster and faster went Gerard. He was soon noticed by two *lazzaroni*, who now joined in the chase, crying after the fugitive the hated words : " The Saint ! The Saint ! "[1] While the now breathless canon had stopped to hear from one of the two what it all might mean, the runaway made good his escape. On returning to Caposele Gerard was asked by Father Caione to explain the incident. With a naive smile he replied : " I caught it with two fingers and drew it ashore." That was all. Quite a simple matter when behind the two fingers was the hand of God. " You threw yourself into the sea, because you were so warm no doubt," chimed in the community doctor Santorelli jocularly, alluding to Gerard's ecstatic state on that occasion. " In the state in which I then was," he said, " I could have flown through the air."[2] When requested by Father Margotta to explain things, he replied with the obvious platitude : " O my Father, when God wishes it, everything is possible."[3] But then God is not always prayed to by a saint.

We have seen Gerard emerging from the water with dry clothes. It was not the only instance of that creature of God respecting the garments of the saint. One day, Father Caione had sent him to Caposele on business. He had not gone far when he was overtaken by a violent thunderstorm accompanied by torrential rain. The rector, knowing Gerard, despatched a messenger after

---

[1] In Apost. no. 17, § 48.
[2] Tannoia, cap. xxv.
[3] In Apost. no. 7, § 271.

him to bid him return. He caught up with the saint whom he found walking quietly along the flooded road. He was dumbfounded on noticing that not a drop of rain had fallen on the brother's clothes and that he was *" asciutto come un osso . . .* as dry as a bone,"[1] as the witness phrased it. When they got back, everybody in the monastery saw plainly that Gerard's clothes were dry, while those of the messenger were wet through.

Amongst the endowments forfeited by Adam with his innocence was his dominion over the animal world ; and the attitude of that world towards man ever since is a painful reminder of what happened. However, many of God's saints, particularly those whose lives show least the taint of original guilt, seem to have in some measure re-captured Adam's lost sway over this province of God's creation. Now in the soul of Gerard we have indeed to look hard to find traces of the Fall and its accompanying disabilities ; and it will therefore come as no surprise to see him exercising a lordship over the dumb animals that once belonged so fully to mankind.

Gerard did much of his journeying on horseback. Now one day he called at a forge to have his mount shod. The operation was well and duly done, but the smith, hoping to exploit the charity and simplicity of a saint, demanded an exorbitant price. Gerard had not the smallest intention of putting a premium on profiteering. Besides, he had his vow of poverty to look to. Angered at the glaring dishonesty of the man, he commanded the horse to cast off the shoes. With a leap and a vigorous kick the animal instantly obeyed. Its rider then mounted

---

[1] In Apost, no. 18, § 116.

and rode off. The blacksmith, realising that his little game was up, called after him to stop. Without even turning his head Gerard rode on. If the saints were simple, they were no simpletons, and charity never winks at injustice.

Sometimes it was the animals themselves that got the worst of his miraculous powers. Once, when riding to Corato, in the province of Bari, he came across the steward of an estate looking disconsolately at a field. The saint dismounted, went over and asked him what was the trouble. " Ah ! Father," said the man, taking him for a priest, " even though you knew, you could do nothing to comfort me." " But, my good man," retorted Gerard, " cannot God help you ? "[1] Then the steward told him how field-mice had been playing havoc with the crops and how he did not know what was going to become of his wife and child. Thereupon Gerard asked him whether he would prefer the mice to die or go elsewhere. Taking no chances, the steward un-hesitatingly declared for the death sentence. Thereupon the servant of God, turning towards the devastated field, made a sign of the cross over it. It was at once strewn with dead and dying mice. The astonished steward was profuse in his thanks. Reminding him that it was God he should thank, Gerard rode away. Meanwhile, the steward began walking through the land ; everywhere it was the same : all over it his diminutive but destructive foes had been laid low. Recovering from his amazement, he pursued his deliverer, calling out : " Wait for me, man of God, wait for me ! " But there

---

[1] In Ord. no. 18, § 42.

was something the man of God feared more than the
steward feared the mice, and putting spurs to his horse,
he was soon out of sight. The former, however, evidently
taking another way, had reached the town before him
and lost no time in telling all whom he met upon the
road what manner of man was coming amongst them.
The result of the growing crowd was that Gerard found
himself the central figure of a triumphal procession on
entering the town. And no man liked that less.

For Gerard all creation was the language of its Creator,
and at times it spoke so eloquently to his enamoured
soul as to call forth his supernatural powers. His kinship
with the Poor Man of Assisi is seen especially in his
remarkable ascendency over birds. Standing one day
on the balcony of a house in which he was staying in
Caposele, he noticed in the distance a turkey-cock
strutting proudly up the road in all his befeathered
majesty. There was something about this little lord
of the poultry-yard that reminded this childlike and
holy man of the Lord of creation Himself ; and he cried
out ecstatically : " Come here, come here, creature of
God ! "[1] Half running and half flying the bird was at
his feet in a moment, where it was made the recipient
of unwonted fondling. Whatever about rapacious and
hungry robins, we are not aware that turkey-cocks
respond so readily to human endearments. Tannoia,
who records the incident, says that on that occasion
Gerard fell into an ecstasy lasting about half an hour.

A little boy had been given a present of a pretty bird,
to which he was much attached. One day he showed

---

[1] Tannoia, cap. xxvi.

it to Gerard, who, after caressing it for some time, un-reflectingly set it free. Tears and lamentations at once ensued, bringing the whole household around. Realising that he was the unwitting cause of a catastrophe, Gerard went to the verandah from which the bird had flown and cried out : " My pretty one, come back ! The boy is crying and does not wish you to be free."[1] Like a penitent prisoner who had broken gaol, back came the little creature to the saint, who restored it to its delighted owner. The storm at once subsided. The company were astounded, adds the witness.[2]

His own fellowmen were of course the chief object of Gerard's extraordinary endowments. The most commonplace type of miracle (if the miraculous may ever be spoken of as commonplace) to be met with in the lives of the saints is, we suppose, the sudden curing of the thousand ills that human flesh is heir to. Such miracles, however, are usually spectacular and the best appreciated, at least by those in whose favour they are worked. As we know, the Gospel pages are studded with them ; and so are the pages of Gerard's short life. His special circumstances brought him into contact with all sorts and conditions of men, and like his Divine Master he " went about . . . . healing all manner of sickness and every infirmity amongst the people."[3] Nothing like all his miraculous healings have been recorded. Speaking of a visit Gerard paid to one district alone, Tannoia writes : " I must pass over in

---

[1] Benedetti, p. 377.
[2] *Ibid.*
[3] Matt. iv, 23.

silence the numerous instantaneous cures he wrought."[1]
Nor in a book of this compass can we find room even
for anything like all those cases that have been set
down. Indeed in recording miracles of this type there
could be a certain monotony of detail that might prove
wearisome. We will restrict ourselves, therefore, to a
few of the more interesting.

A youth lay dying of tuberculosis in Iliceto. Humanly
speaking he was doomed, and the doctor told his family
as much, remarking that in order to cure his patient
he would have to provide him with new lungs. However,
neither the patient nor his family would acknowledge
themselves beaten. They knew of Gerard, of his sanctity
and his miracles, and they asked his rector to allow him
visit them. He duly arrived, to find the doctor in the
house before him. He comforted the boy and encouraged
him to trust in God, in Whose hands, he reminded him,
are the destinies of men and by Whom he would be
quickly cured. This rather nettled the doctor, who read
into it a reflection on his own professional skill. He there
and then repeated his verdict in the patient's room and
in presence of the whole family, blurting out that the
case was hopeless, as the lungs were too far gone. Then
Gerard spoke again : " What do you think, doctor,
cannot God, the Creator of all things, make new ones,
or restore the sick man's diseased lungs to their former
state ? May God be pleased to work this miracle in
order to increase the confidence of the faithful and
encourage them henceforth to put all their trust in Him
alone." He then rose to go, promising to pray for

---

[1] English Edit., p. 319.

the dying youth. From that moment the boy's condition began to improve, and in a few days he was himself again. The "doubting Thomas" was convinced and was the first to admit that nothing short of a miracle could have effected such a cure.

When travelling through the archdiocese of Conza, Gerard was brought to a house in Auletta where a poor girl was pointed out to him so crippled from birth that she could stir neither hand nor foot and was incapable of any work. Using a variation of his familiar formula, he said : " There's nothing wrong with this girl ; she is all right."[1] He then called her over to him. To the amazement of everybody in the room, including the accompanying priest, the crippled girl sprang out of bed, hurried over to Gerard and gratefully kissed his hand. When the news of what had occurred got about, a crowd quickly gathered and cries of : " A miracle, a miracle ! " went up on all sides. Gerard fled to the presbytery. The crowd pursued him, yelling : " The Saint, the Saint ! " In great distress the saint managed to escape to a neighbouring district by a backdoor and got out of earshot of what was more intolerable to him than the worst abuse. The cure was complete and lasting, and years afterwards Gerard's *miraculée* was pointed out to visitors.

Here we must find room for an instance of healing which is scarcely more miraculous than the heroic self-conquest that attended it. A young man was suffering greatly from a cancer in the leg and was, moreover, much distressed at not being able to work. Hearing

---

[1] Landi.

of the wonderful things done by the Servant of God, he asked his parents to bring him to Iliceto. They did so at the cost of no small inconvenience. On arrival they found that Gerard was out. When he returned and saw what was amiss, he was greatly moved. Thereupon he bent down, undid the bandages and, without a moment's hesitation, sucked the horrible sore, saying, " have confidence in God, He can certainly heal you."[1] The pain ceased immediately. The party left Iliceto heaping blessings on their deliverer. Next day, on removing the fresh white bandage Gerard had wrapped about the leg, the young man found it completely healed.

We read in the Fourth Book of Kings that when Eliseus struck the waters of the Jordan with the mantle of Elias, they were divided and he passed over.[2] We remember ,too, that touching page in the Gospel wherein we are told how a woman with an issue of blood touched the hem of Christ's garment and was healed of her infirmity. She had said within herself : " If I shall touch only his garment, I shall be healed."[3] And healed she was. We read, too, that " God wrought by the hand of Paul more than common miracles. So that even there were brought from his body to the sick, handkerchiefs and aprons : and the diseases departed from them : and the wicked spirits went out of them."[4] And the same Acts of the Apostles tell us that " they brought forth the sick into the streets and laid them on beds and couches that, when Peter came, his shadow at the

---

[1] In Apost. no. 7, § 404.
[2] II, 14.
[3] Matt. ix, 21.
[4] Acts. xix, 11-12.

least might overshadow any of them and they might be
delivered from their infirmities."[1]

With these sacred and venerable precedents before us,
and bearing in mind the assurance of Christ, " Greater
than these shall ye do," it need not be a matter for
surprise or incredulous smiling if we are told that not
only Gerard himself, but the most homely things
associated with him were the agents used by God to
display His own almighty power and testify to the
holiness of His servant.

In 1755, when on his way for the second time to
Naples, in company with Father Margotta, he stopped
some days in Calitri, the latter's native town, where
the Father had some business to attend to. The Archpriest Berilli gave them hospitality. One day a lady
called Arcangela Rinaldi happened to visit the house.
While there she was seized with a splitting headache.
As she wandered about half-demented, her eyes fell on
Gerard's old hat lying in a corner of the room. She had
heard much about his doings in Calitri, and half in jest
half in earnest she took the hat and put it on her head,
saying : " I want to see if this brother is really a saint."[2]
Instantaneously the headache left her. The members
of the Berilli household were quick to realise their
opportunities and tried to secure anything their holy
guest had used. His shoes looked decidedly the worse
of wear. They agreed that he would be the better of a
new pair and accordingly had a new pair made. No
doubt they had to play some pious trick on Gerard
to secure the old. These soon proved their worth. A

---

[1] *Ibid.*, v. 15.
[2] In Apost. no. 18, § 45.

servant boy in the household was one day suffering from violent internal pains which nothing seemed able to relieve. Gerard's shoes were produced, and at their touch the pains vanished immediately. After a few days they returned with even greater violence. The boy called for the shoes; they were again produced, with the same result. We have it on the testimony of the archpriest that the shoes became quite famous in Calitri, where they went the rounds and were instrumental in the working of many cures.

Not only did Gerard cure people miraculously himself, but at times he passed on his miraculous powers to others. Here is an instance of this vicarious healing. A good woman called Emmanuela Vetromile in his native Muro, whom he loved as a mother and to whom he had given much of his youthful confidence, had a niece in her house to whom she was much attached. Ursula—such was the girl's name—had fallen victim to a chronic disease which the doctor pronounced incurable and which he said would soon prove fatal. She was given up as a hopeless case. Ursula's days were obviously numbered. Signora Vetromile was greatly distressed at the thought of losing her and was on her way to enlist the good offices of St. Anthony of Padua in the church of the Conventual Fathers, when she met Gerard. He told her to go back home and make the sign of the cross three times on the dying girl's breast and three times on her forehead, assuring her that Ursula would be cured. The woman believed and did as Gerard bade her. To the amazement of the doctor she was cured immediately. All Muro rang with it.

Gerard did not cure every patient presented to him.

None knew better than he that God's Will is not always ours and that His Will is infinitely more in keeping with our best interests than is our own. An unhealthy body is not rarely the price we are asked to pay for health of soul, and illness properly borne has opened heaven to many a one who else might have never gone there. The saint knew all this well and on occasion could be cruelly kind.

A gentleman with whom he was staying in Castelgrande had a little daughter named Judith who, as a result of small-pox, had been left blind. Her mother was particularly put about and earnestly sought Gerard's aid. He promised to pray for the child and told her to do likewise. Shortly after, however, he assured her that if little Judith recovered her sight it would be the ruin of her and urged her to be resigned to the Will of God. At the same time he promised her that God would make it up to the little girl by enabling her to do much better than others the sort of work usually done by women. Judith remained blind, but displayed extraordinary skill in all kinds of household work and actually helped much in the education of her younger sisters.

There is one sort of physical suffering in the relief of which Gerard exhibited his supernatural power more than once during his lifetime and in which he has exhibited it times innumerable since his death. An instance or two will, we think, be of special interest. In Senerchia, where he miraculously drew the trees for the roofing of a church, a poor woman was dying in child-birth. Gerard's prayers were sought and obtained, and mother and baby lived. This case finds a place in both the ordinary and apostolic processes and was evidently regarded as miraculous.

The saint had been paying a farewell visit to the Pirofalo family in Oliveto, some miles from Caposele. When taking his departure he left his handkerchief on a chair where he had been sitting. A young girl drew his attention to it. " Keep it," Gerard replied, " it may be useful to you one day."[1] Years passed. The girl eventually married and was brought to death's door at her first confinement. She invoked one after another of her patrons, but all to no purpose. Then she remembered the handkerchief, which she had devoutly treasured, and had it brought to her. No sooner had it touched her than her troubles were over and baby was happily born. The witness (her grandson) who has recorded this fact concludes his statement as follows : " My grandmother jealously preserved this miraculous handkerchief. Eventually it became my heritage ; but now I have but a shred of it, as the rest has been cut up into small pieces for his clients." And ever since, the same Gerard Majella has been busy the world over shepherding thousands of little ones to their mother's first caress and hovering like an angel of light and gladness round thousands of cradles. So closely indeed has he identified himself with the relief of this particular sort of suffering that to-day there is a movement afoot to have him constituted patron of expectant mothers.

More than once was Gerard appealed to in favour of those who in many ways are the most helpless and piteous sufferers of all, viz., the insane ; and more than

---

[1] In Apost. no. 7, § 341.

once he showed how he could minister to a mind diseased.
There was a young girl in Lacedonia, by name Lella
Cocchia, whom her mother's recent death had left in-
consolable. She was particularly worried about her
mother's soul. Gerard set her mind at rest on that score
in a supernatural way ; but some time later, whatever
was the cause, the poor girl completely lost her reason
and remained in that state for many months. She
became a violent and rather terrifying case, and in her
bad moments would break out into blasphemous and
obscene language. Everybody pitied her. When Gerard
visited Lacedonia in 1754, he was told about her and
was greatly grieved. He went to her house, approached
her and made the sign of the cross on her forehead.
Lella was instantaneously and radically cured, and
began at once to sing the praises of God and His holy
Mother in hymns she had never been known to sing before.

A particularly sad and striking incident was that of
a priest of Oliveto, named Dominic Sassi. As a result
of protracted scruples, he had fallen into melancholy
and finally become a definitely mental case. The poor
priest now spent most of his days shut up in his room,
lying on his bed, howling and blaspheming in dark
despair, though he had led a blameless life. For seven
years he had been like this, unable to say Mass or receive
the sacraments. His family and friends had left no
stone unturned to effect his cure ; all human means
had been exhausted. Time and again he had been taken
to Our Lady's most famous shrines. He had been
brought to Caposele that the saintly Father Cafaro
might pray over him. All in vain. Heaven seemed deaf.
Now when Gerard was in Oliveto on his last journey

to Caposele, in 1755, the archpriest Don Angelo Salvatore, with whom he was staying, one day alluded to this poor sufferer and asked the saint to help him. "What can I do in the matter?"[1] was the rather cold and disconcerting answer, in which we seem to catch an echo of Christ's answer to His Mother at the marriage feast of Cana. Anyhow, he promised his prayers. Without informing his host of his intentions he went to Sassi's house the following morning and walked unannounced into his room. He was met with a torrent of yells and imprecations. Unperturbed by these he approached the demented priest and quietly made the sign of the cross on his head. Instantaneously the sufferer became reasonable and calm. Gerard noticed a harpsichord in the room and he asked the priest to play. The latter at once complied and together they sang Our Lady's litany. The music quickly brought the whole household trooping into the room. They could not believe their eyes or their ears. Great was the rejoicing. So complete was the cure that Don Sassi could have said Mass the following day; but Gerard thought it better that he should just receive Holy Communion in the church for the first two mornings. On the eve of the third morning, when at dinner with the archpriest, Gerard remarked: "Don Domenico is to celebrate to-morrow and I should like you all to receive Holy Communion at his Mass."[2] Next morning, the feast of St. Augustine, Don Sassi said his first Mass for seven years. It was a great occasion, and the whole parish rose to it. All his relations and friends accom-

---

[1] Tannoia, English Edit., p. 418.
[2] Benedetti, p. 375.

panied the celebrant to the church. Everything was
ready, everybody was there—except Gerard. Now they
knew he intended communicating at the Mass and so
they sent for him. They went upstairs, knocked at his
door, and receiving no answer, went in. They found
him kneeling before his bed, in an ecstasy, clasping a
crucifix in one hand and holding the other to his breast,
his face pale as death and turned heavenwards, his eyes
closed, insensible to the world about him. The archpriest, his brother the doctor and the whole household
were summoned to the scene. Not daring to disturb
him, they silently withdrew. Returning in about half
an hour, they found him just emerging from the ecstasy.
They asked him how he had spent the night. Suspecting
he had been seen in the ecstatic state, he remarked
quietly : " I slept but little last night, and this morning
I fell fast asleep."[1] Thereupon he followed them to the
church where, together with the archpriest, he served
Don Sassi's Mass. Not only did the latter celebrate
with much devotion, but, in spite of the long seven
years' interval, he observed the rubrics most minutely.
His cure was permanent and he continued to celebrate
regularly. Whenever the bell for his Mass would ring
the people would say : " Let us go and see Brother
Gerard's miracle."[2] And an outstanding miracle it was
Concerning it Tannoia has these words : " The fame of
this prodigy was spread far and wide, Father Caione
wrote to me, and that not only in the neighbourhood
but even in far distant places."[3]

---

[1] Benedetti, p. 376.
[2] Tannoia, English Edit. p. 419.
[3] *Ibid*.

Thus the heart of this man, who was so pitiless towards his own innocent self, melted with pity at the sight of human suffering of any kind. On assumed suffering, however, and trickery of all kinds he had no mercy. Near the house in Naples where he and Father Margotta were staying a certain impostor was turning many a dishonest penny by sporting a pair of crutches and bandaged legs. Whether by supernatural or natural means Gerard knew all about it and had repeatedly warned the fellow to give over his roguery and turn to honest work. But it was all to no purpose. Meeting him one day plying his nefarious trade, Gerard went up to him, told him roundly what he thought of him, threatened him with damnation for his dishonesty, and there and then whipped the bandages from his legs. Without any miracle at all the crutches dropped at once and their owner ran off as fast as two sound legs could carry him.

Besides possessing the power of working miracles in the usual and popular acceptance of the term, Gerard Majella was enriched with other supernatural gifts to an extraordinary degree. One of his French biographers writes of him : " Few saints have been so favoured with such wonderful supernatural endowments. Intellectual illuminations, divine locutions, heavenly apparitions, combats with the demons, ecstasies, raptures, prophecy, the discernment of spirits, bilocation, ecstatic flight, the privilege of invisibility—in a word, almost all the phenomena of the mystical order are summed up in Gerard as in a living picture."[1] Let us speak in this

---

[1] Dunoyer, *Vie*, p. 294.

chapter of some of these gifts, reserving others for a later one.

It almost goes without saying that Gerard prophesied. This supernatural knowing and foretelling of a future that God alone could know has already been recorded in our pages ; but some further instances will be of interest. One day he called to see a fellow-townsman in Muro named Carmine Petrone. His eyes suddenly became fixed on Petrone's son, a child of three, who was playing about the house. Turning to his father he encouraged him to be resigned to the Will of God, for Antoniuccio (such was the little fellow's name) would be taken from him in a few days and would die with a musical instrument in his hands. Shortly after, the child was taken seriously ill and grew rapidly worse. One day he asked for a guitar that was in the house. They gave it to him to please him, and as his little hands fingered its strings after the manner of children, he went to God.

Another little boy was the object of a prophecy of quite another kind. His name was Michelangelo Innelli, and he lived in Oliveto. When questing in the town, Gerard one day saw him playing in front of a house. Pointing him out and looking at him intently and with a troubled countenance, he exclaimed : " Oh ! God, what a monster is growing up in Oliveto ! "[1] The words made a great impression on the bystanders, but they could make nothing of them. Michelangelo belied his name and grew up more of a devil than an angel. When a lad of fifteen he was found out in an act of horrible

---

[1] In Apost. no. 18, § 117.

and unnatural immorality, and when rebuked by his father, he seized a gun and threatened the latter's life. The father seized another and in self-defence shot his son dead.

In the following instance we see the saint reading the hidden present as well as the hidden future. A youth named Nicolò Benincasa was one day in Gerard's company. While secretly admiring his virtue, he said within himself apropos of an illness from which he was suffering : " This Brother Gerard works so many miracles for others and he does not pray for me that this pain in my chest may go away." He had scarcely formulated these thoughts when the saint turned and said : " What did you say just now ? You said I was not praying for you. That's not true, but God does not wish you to be well. My son, you are not for this world."[1] And so indeed it was. The boy died shortly after.

Gerard was once holding holy converse with a community of nuns in Foggia, when he suddenly paused and turning to one of them asked her if she went frequently to confession. On hearing that she did, he begged her to keep constantly united to God, as the day of her death was not far off. Whatever she thought of this remark about her confession, she—and the community with her—took what he said about her death as a joke, as she was quite young and in perfect health. But Gerard met her later and reminded her that the most perfect health can fail in the twinkling of an eye. Solemnly he repeated his warning to remain constantly united to God, as the Lord would come and call her

---

[1] Benedetti, p. 327.

within eight days. The Sister, knowing Gerard for what he was, took no chances and followed his advice. Within eight days she was dead.

His prophecies were not all of death. In Melfi was a youth of eighteen named Michele Di-Michele, who had to interrupt his studies for the priesthood through ill-health and return home. Thinking him cured, the doctor allowed him back to the seminary after two months. But a relapse sent him home again. Now Gerard was an old family friend and on the occasion of his visit to Melfi mentioned before to look after the three invalid Fathers, he called to see him. Feeling his pulse, he said to the boy : "What fever? what fever? You are well." The fever had indeed vanished, as the doctor had to admit. Meeting the youth some days later, he said with emphasis looking tenderly on him : " One day you will be one of us."[1] " Yes," retorted Michele, " when I touch the sky with my hand," thus indicating the impossible. As a matter of fact he had not the faintest idea of becoming a religious of any sort, let alone a Redemptorist. As Tannoia tells us, " he almost held the very name in horror, and he particularly disliked our Congregation."[2] But five months had not passed when a religious and a Redemptorist he became. As he said to Tannoia himself, " For six months my mind was torn with a thousand contradictory things, until finally—I do not know how—I decided on entering the Congregation."[3] He lived in it holily

---

[1] Tannoia, cap. xviii.
[2] English Edit. p. 324.
[3] Cap. xviii.

for nearly forty years, dying in Caposele in 1795.

What is called the discernment of spirits—the gift of reading the secrets of the heart—was also Gerard's to a striking degree, and he probed consciences with a sureness that terrified the guilty and brought comfort to the distressed. Of this former power we shall soon have much more to say ; of his power as a comforter in this respect we give one instance. Father Giovenale, to whom Gerard one day went to confession, was much worried himself as to how he stood with God. After receiving absolution, the penitent, with a curious change of *rôle*, said to the confessor : " Be of good cheer, my Father, you are in God's grace. It is the devil who is causing this trouble." The confessor looked at him in amazement and then, strangely enough, said tartly : " You are a fool and don't know what you are talking about."[1] And bidding him make five crosses on the floor with his tongue, he dismissed him. But the confessor knew what he was doing ; and so did the penitent.

We have already alluded to one mystical phenomenon in Gerard's life, viz., that of ecstasy. It is quite common of course in the history of the saints, especially of those in whom the mystical life was more pronounced. What the word " ecstasy " conveys to the mind of the average Catholic layman who meets it in the life of a saint we are not quite sure. " The etymological meaning of the word," writes Farges, " ecstasy, ekstasis, extra stare, sufficiently denotes it. There is *alienation* of all sensitive life, or life of relation, as though the soul were no longer in the body. Nevertheless this total suspension of the

---

[1] *Annotazioni di un antico manoscritto.*—Cfr. Benedetti, p. 272, note.

sensitive life does not altogether carry with it that of
the vegetative life. The functions of nutrition, breathing,
circulation of the blood and so on, although enfeebled,
continue without consciousness. If, however, the senses
fade away, the human understanding, on the contrary,
upheld and transformed by divine grace, must be completely awake for this sublime contemplation. As a
special degree of contemplative or mystical prayer, it
consists essentially in so luminous a vision of the presence
of God and so vivid a sense of the union of the soul
with the divinity that there results from them not only
the total suspension of the interior powers of the soul
. . . but also complete anæsthesia of the outward senses."[1]
Speaking of the extraordinary form of ecstasy called
"rapture," the same author writes : " The soul seems
to separate itself from the body and to take its flight
towards its blessed home ; even the body at times follows
the movement of the mind and finds itself raised from
the earth by means of a divine attraction acting contrary
to the laws of gravity. This is the marvellous phenomenon
of levitation. It is the outward and visible sign of what
happens inwardly when the soul is raised by God to
those heights which approach so closely to the Beatific
Vision."[2] So when we read of Gerard being raised in
the air, as we have already done and as we shall do
again, we need not be shocked or puzzled. Whether
at such moments his body was miraculously raised from
below or miraculously drawn up from above without
losing its weight, or whether it miraculously lost its
weight and became lighter than air is open to debate.

---

[1] *Mystical Phenomena*, Part I, chap. iii, § 4, pp. 163-164.
[2] *Ibid.*, p. 169.

That true ecstasy has nothing whatever to do with mere natural swooning or hysteria the Catholic at any rate need not be told. To quote Farges once again : " Natural or pathological swooning is a phenomenon of lethargy and death, undermining the health, emptying the understanding and the heart . . . . Ecstatic and divine swooning is an expansion of the life of God, hidden beneath the appearance of death, in no way producing ill effects on the health ; illuminating the mind and inflaming the heart, for the greater glory of God and the salvation of souls . . . Ecstasy is like a lovely day in springtide, flooded with light and heavenly joy ; the hysterical crisis is a night of terror and frightful nightmare. The divine phenomenon is peaceful and coherent, even in transport ; beneficent and fruitful like all that is well ordered ; the hysterical phenomenon is pathological disturbance, incoherent, more or less indecent, injurious, fatiguing and barren."[1]

Now with St. Gerard ecstasy was so frequent as almost to cease to be a phenomenon. There were few saints whose ecstasies were so continuous ; indeed he might almost be said to have lived in an ecstatic element. We have seen how the mere sight of a holy picture or the words of a hymn would throw him into these raptures. Most of them must have occurred in the privacy of his cell, with the angels only to witness them. However, as we have already recorded, they were often seen by whole households, by entire communities and by crowds.

While in Oliveto, on his last questing tour, he was the guest of the archpriest Angelo Salvatore. On the day

---

[1] *Mystical Phenomena*, Part 1, chap. iii, § 173 ; Part II, chap. ii, § 5, p. 474.

of his arrival, the guest did not appear at the dinner table. His host went upstairs to fetch him, but instead of entering the room he looked through the keyhole. Such a breach of etiquette was surely justified with a guest like Gerard from whom anything in the supernatural order might be expected. Salvatore's pious curiosity was amply rewarded. He saw the saint in ecstasy and raised three palms from the ground. He withdrew immediately to call the household to witness the wonderful sight. Nobody thought any further about dining, and they left Gerard as they found him. At last he appeared, face aflame, in the dining-room, apologised for being late and expressed the hope that he would not be a burden on the family or upset their domestic arrangements. Afterwards the archpriest marked on the opposite wall of the room the exact height to which they had seen the saint raised in the air during the ecstasy.

At least on two occasions in Gerard's life there occurred that most spectacular display of supernatural power known in mystical theology as the ecstatic flight. The first instance happened when he was a novice. Tannoia thus records it : " One day, as Gerard was returning to Iliceto in company with two peasant youths, who were employed in the house, he came to a country church dedicated to Our Lady. He began to discourse on the mysteries of the Blessed Virgin. In a moment he became transfigured before their eyes, to their great amazement then, seizing a pencil and writing something on a piece of paper, he made a leap as if he were throwing a letter into the air. This was followed not only by a rapture but by a flight. In an instant the peasants saw him borne away before their eyes for more than half a mil in the direction of our house ; that is to say, from the church where he had been to a district called *il Francese*. The two old peasants who died recently[1] never ceased, as Canon Stramiello testified to me, speaking of the amazing thing they had seen.[2]

Amazing it certainly was, perhaps too amazing for some people to swallow. However, when all is said and done, to overcome the laws of gravitation by rising in the air an inch or a mile, to remain suspended in it (a phenomenon witnessed by thousands) or rush through it are all one, because all equally miraculous. As we have said before, it is all a question merely of degree not of kind. Whether a saint's ecstasy entails a horizontal or a vertical movement is really beside the point. We might as well differentiate between the movements of an angel. As Benedict XIV writes :[3] " Ecstasy is a participation, though imperfect, in the beatific vision of the elect in heaven, and levitation is a participation in the gift of agility, which the bodies of these blessed ones possess in glory."[4]

There is a further miraculous phenomenon, comparatively rare even in the lives of the saints, but frequently met with in Gerard's, particularly at its

---

[1] Tannoia, cap. ix.

[2] Tannoia wrote these words in 1804.

[3] *Heroic Virtue*, vol. 3, p. 242.

[4] This most rare phenomenon of the mystical life was displayed in by far the greatest abundance by St. Joseph Cupertino (1603-1663). The account of his raptures and ecstatic flights makes truly amazing reading. On one occasion he was raised from the ground and remained suspended in the air before the eyes of Pope Urban VIII, who declared that if Joseph were to die during his pontificate, he would bear witness to what he had seen. And it is interesting to recall that Urban VIII is the Pope whose familiar decree at the head of the lives of so many holy people waves a deterrent finger against those who would rashly anticipate the judgment of the Church on the holiness of her children.

close. When we are unreasonably hustled in getting about, we sometimes say testily to people : " You know I can't be in two places at once." It may come as a surprise to some of us to hear that we can. It is not likely that we ever shall be, but we can. And the saints could and many of them were. It is an obviously supernatural gift ; but Gerard possessed it. It is called " bilocation." There is unimpeachable evidence to prove that on many occasions he was seen in different and distant places at the same time. Bilocation—at first sight almost a contradiction in terms—is merely another divine intervening in the natural order of created things. How precisely it does happen and where the miraculous precisely comes in is another matter, on which great theologians and thinkers are far from unanimity. " Examples of bilocation, when proved, are usually explained," writes Father Thurston, " either by the imagination of the beholder being impressed miraculously by the image of a person not physically present, or by the production by God of a real external image of an absent person, or by the person being seen through all the intervening space as though he were present."[1]

We have said that Gerard possessed this rare and astounding endowment. " A heavenly favour," writes Benedetti, " which had never been granted him (at least as far as we know) in the whole course of his life, was vouchsafed him in abundance as the day of his departure from this world drew near. Like St. Alphonsus, he was seen, and seen very often in two places at one and the same time : as if Our Lord had wished to

---

[1] *Butler's Lives of the Saints*, vol. x, p. 233, note.

make him share (as He had done in the case of others of His servants who were great lovers of the Blessed Eucharist) in that prerogative of His sacramental life by which He is present simultaneously in a thousand places on earth."[1] A few instances should be of interest.

A servant in the De-Gregorio family in Lacedonia lay dangerously ill and in great pain. As Gerard had already worked a striking miracle in this house, the sick man was encouraged to invoke him now. One evening, in the height of his sufferings, he cried out : " O Brother Gerard ! where are you ? Why don't you come and help me ? " He had scarcely uttered the words when there was a knock at the door and Gerard entered. Approaching the bed he said : " You are calling me. I have come to help you. Have you a lively faith in God ? Have it and you will be cured."[2] He forthwith made the sign of the cross on the man's forehead and without more ado left the room. The servant was perfectly cured ; his pains had disappeared, and he got up and dressed. His first impulse was to thank his deliverer. But Gerard was nowhere to be found. On inquiry it was ascertained that outside the De-Gregorio house no one else had seen him that day in Lacedonia.

One day Gerard had a long talk in his monastery in Caposele with a certain young man named Theodore Cleffi, a very great friend and a very charitable man. Before leaving, Theodore undertook to bring the saint a list of the most deserving cases in Caposele. On his way home he called in to see a man who was lying ill and in great poverty. On being asked what he stood

---

[1] Pp. 321-322.
[2] In Ord. no. 18, § 138.

most in need of, he replied quite cheerfully : " I need nothing, as Brother Gerard has just been visiting me and left me all I want."[1] Cleffi could not believe his ears. He told the man that that could not possibly be true, as he himself had just left Brother Gerard in the monastery. The sick man, however, stoutly repeated his assertion that Brother Gerard had but just gone, and to prove it, produced the good things the saint had brought him. With Gerard's antecedents bilocation was the only reasonable explanation.

Tannoia assures us that the saint made frequent use of this truly extraordinary gift. " How often," he writes, " was he not seen visiting the sick at Caposele without ever having left the house ! "[2] Doctor Santorelli, the medical attendant of the community and a great friend of Gerard, stated that one day, while he was going his rounds, the latter appeared beside him the whole time more clearly and surely than if he had been seen with bodily eyes. When his rounds were over and he returned to the convent, the doctor met the Brother and said to him : " What did you want with me ? I could not get away from you the whole day." " What did I want with you ? " came the answer, " don't you know that I am going away tomorrow and that I wanted to pay a farewell visit to my dear sick people ? "[3]

Here is the same incident as related by a witness in the process : " It is well known that Doctor Nicholas Santorelli, the doctor of that community (of Caposele),

---

[1] In Apost. no. 12, §. 97.
[2] English Edit., p. 384.
[3] Landi.

one day found him (Gerard) in every patient's house ;
and asking him how he could spend so much time with
them, as if he had nothing else to do, the Servant of
God replied : ' Hush, hush ! for nobody but yourself
sees me here.' As a matter of fact, beyond the doctor,
who was his confidant, nobody else saw him that day
in the homes of the poor, while at the same time he
was not missing from the monastery."[1]

One day Gerard was waiting to hear from Muro about
some urgent business in which the glory of God was
concerned. As no word was forthcoming, he said : " I
must go there myself tomorrow."[2] And Lorenzo di Maio,
a man worthy of all credence, affirms that he saw the
saint in Muro the following day, while it is likewise
affirmed that he never left his monastery in Caposele.
" Isn't it wonderful ? " Father Margotta remarked to
Santorelli on another occasion, " Gerard has been in
his room all the night, and yet he has been seen at the
same time in an ecstasy before the Blessed Sacrament
in the Franciscan choir by the whole community ! "[3]

In the following instance Gerard himself throws
some light on the nature of these appearances. It
occurred in Santorelli's own house. The Servant of
God had been visiting there one day and when taking
his leave said that he would be back again in the evening.
The doctor smiled, as he knew that Gerard's rules forbade
him to be out of doors after the *Angelus* without
necessity. Then the saint said : " No, no, I am not

---

[1] In Apost. no. 18, § III.
[2] Tannoia, cap. xxvii.
[3] *Ibid.*

joking ; I will return, not in the body, but in the spirit."[1]
That night the doctor's sister Monica distinctly saw the
Brother fixing a searching gaze upon her. She declared
that she was quite ready to state on oath if needs be
that she had really seen him.

There have not been wanting saints who were endowed
with the truly breath-taking gift of becoming invisible
to actual eyes. With all that goes before in mind, it
will not be such a tax on our credulity to hear that
Gerard was one of these. After all, from being seen in
two places at the same time to not being seen at all,
though present, is a short step enough in wonderland.
And we readily admit that in exhibiting this side of
our saint's career we are in truth conducting our readers
through a wonderland. But wonders are not necessarily
impossibilities. According to the testimony of witnesses,
Gerard displayed this power several times in Iliceto.
Father Ripoli testifies as follows : " It was a matter
of common knowledge in the Congregation when I
entered it, especially amongst the older members who
were contemporaries of the Servant of God, that many
times and in various circumstances he made himself
invisible."[2] We will record one famous instance that
occurred in Caposele.

The clouds of the great calumny that had darkened
the good name were lifting. It was a Saturday, and on
his following morning Gerard was to receive Holy Communion for the first time for many long and lonely
weeks. It was a great occasion for his heart, and he had
asked Father Giovenale's leave to spend the intervening

---

[1] Landi.
[2] In Apost. no. 18, § 43.

hours in strict seclusion. The leave was readily granted. When Sunday morning came, the same Father happened to need Gerard's services and accordingly sent for him to his room. He was not found there. They looked for him in the church, in the choir, but in vain. Then the house was searched from attic to basement. All to no purpose. Meanwhile Doctor Santorelli appeared on the scene and was told what all the pother was about. The doctor wagered he was under the bed. Again they went to his room, taking care this time to look there. No Gerard! Then the doctor, who knew Gerard as well as anyone, got an idea: let them wait till the moment for receiving Communion came and he would surely emerge from his hiding-place. The doctor was right. When that moment came, the communicant duly appeared. After his thanksgiving, Father Giovenale sent for him and asked him where he had been all the morning. "In my room," was the unhesitating answer. "How in your room?" pursued the Father, "when I sent all the brothers hunting for you, and they could not find you either in your room or anywhere else. Make ten crosses with your tongue on the ground." Which Gerard promptly did. But more was to come. "I wish you to go without Communion for a month and to fast on bread and water for a month," the Father added. The culprit evidently did not take him seriously, as he laughingly replied: "Make me do so, Father, for the love of Jesus Christ."[1] We wonder which was the more tempting penitential morsel in Gerard's eyes—a month on bread and water or a month without Communion.

---

[1] Landi.

Anyhow, as Father Giovenale insisted on knowing the whole truth, he was told it in these words : " I asked your Reverence's leave to remain recollected with God in my own room, and that I might be able to enjoy my Jesus to my heart's content, I asked Him to make me invisible so as not to be disturbed, and He heard my prayer."[1] The saint added that this grace of invisibility had been granted him through the intercession of Our Lady.[2] " What's all this mystery about ? " retorted the Father roughly ; " I forgive you this time, but mind you make no more requests like that."[3] The doctor would not leave matters there. Meeting Gerard in the church, the latter told him how he had received Holy Communion. Drawing the Servant of God into the sacristy he began to question him : " Gerard, tell me the truth, where were you ? The Lord make a saint of you ! How can you say you were in your room, when I looked everywhere around it with Brother Nicholas and could not find you ? " Then Gerard took the doctor by the hand, led him to his room and showed him where he had been sitting all the time on a little straw stool near the door. " But," said the doctor, " we searched here carefully and could not find you." " You did not see me," Gerard replied, " because sometimes I make myself very small . . . . *mi faccio piccirillo.*" Tannoia adds : " Gerard's room was but twelve palms square, and as it contained only a small bed and table, there was nothing in it that could conceal anyone. We must therefore exclaim with the Royal Prophet : ' God is

---

[1] Benedetti, p. 259.
[2] In Ord. no. 7, § 108.
[3] Tannoia, cap. xxvi.

wonderful in His saints' and can refuse nothing to their prayers."[1] "This incident," Santorelli's nephew —a priest—testified in his deposition, "made such an impression on us children that whenever we would play the game usually called hide-and-seek . . . *accovarella*, in which one boy hides and the rest have to find him out, we used to say : *Facciamo fratel Gerardo* . . . . let us play at *Brother Gerard*." This gift of becoming invisible is truly very wonderful and very useful ; though invisible laybrothers could prove a liability in a house, even though they were saints !

Gerard's supernatural sway was not restricted to this world : it extended even to the other, especially to the world of demons. His outstanding humility and obedience, his tremendous love for his Incarnate God and his amazing influence over souls are four things that would lead us to expect this. A Gerard Majella could scarcely pass amongst men without arousing the animosity of Hell. And so indeed it was. We know what a long and fearful war it waged openly on a saint nearer our own times— St. John Baptist Vianney, the Curé of Ars—and we know why. Now Gerard snatched many a soul from the jaws of Hell, as we shall soon see in some detail, and Hell was not going to take it lying down. Let us hear Tannoia : " He became the butt of the demons, who gave him no peace and left no stone unturned to dissuade and subdue him. Many a time at night there appeared before him not one but several demons threatening and tormenting him that he might stop robbing them of souls. His confessors declare that he

---

[1] English Edit., p. 368.

was also dragged through the corridors of the house. 'You won't stop,' a demon said one night to him, 'and I'll not stop till I have taken you out of this world.' Sometimes they would seize him and hold him so tightly that he thought he would die. Finding him one day in the kitchen, several devils tried to throw him into the fire. At other times they would rush on him like furious dogs and threaten to tear him to pieces with their fangs . . . . These encounters took place more often on Friday nights."[1] No wonder these evil spirits were particularly noisy and turbulent on those nights when the saint used to give himself up to penitential practices for the atonement of sin and the conversion of sinners.

A certain Father Martuscelli, who became Rector of Caposele, thus gave his testimony at the process : " The demons so tormented him that an old brother in Caposele, by name Carminiello, used to tell me that he heard from Brother Stephen Sperduto, Gerard's contemporary, how the former often showed Sperduto the bruises on his body from blows inflicted by the demons ; these he would put to flight by means of holy water, and with it also he would heal his bruises."[2]

Landi tells us that towards the close of 1754, ten months before his death, when sitting round the fire with the community of Caposele at the evening recreation, Gerard once entertained his brethren with an account of his adventures with the spirits of evil.[3]

The undaunted St. Teresa of Avila had often to measure swords with such adversaries. She tells us

---

[1] Cap. xv.
[2] In Ord. no. 9, § 150.
[3] Benedetti, p. 38.

how she acted : " I would take the crucifix in my hand and thus address them : ' Now come on all of you ! Since I am God's servant I want to see what you can do.' "[1] Gerard did likewise. " You can bark away," he would say to these infernal dogs, " you can bark away ; but with my Mother Mary (*Mamma Maria*) and my Jesus with me, you cannot bite."[2] The sign of the cross and holy water were his two great weapons. Constant practice in the use of the former weapon made him familiar with it, and when his infernal foes came upon the scene, he wielded it with unfailing success. As with Teresa so with Gerard holy water was also a powerful instrument of defence. Its application was invariably followed by a rout. And with the same Teresa Gerard could say : " Far from inspiring me with fear, the devil seems rather to be afraid of me. Through the goodness of my sovereign Master, I hold such a sway over the devils that I look on them as so many flies."[3]

But Gerard did more than bravely bear all the demons did against him. He went over to the offensive. He saw through every disguise and flung them from many a stronghold. One Sunday morning word was brought to him that two young men were behaving in a suspicious way in front of the monastery church at Iliceto. Nobody knew who they were or whence they came. The Fathers eyed their movements with curiosity. Gerard came upon the scene and recognised them at once. Approaching them, he said in a commanding

---

[1] Life, chap. xxv.
[2] Tannoia, cap. xv.
[3] Life, chap. xxxi.

tone : " What are you doing here ? This is not your place." He thereupon commanded them in the name of God to go back to hell. The two mysterious strangers instantly vanished and were never seen again. " The fact is incontestable," adds Tannoia when recording this incident, " as several of our community witnessed it."[1]

As the saint was praying in the church in Castelgrande, a piercing cry made him look round. Two women had entered, each leading by the hand her daughter who was possessed by the devil. The words they uttered were : " Who is that person who is persecuting us every-where ? "[2] The evil spirits spoke through the mouths of their hapless victims as long ago they spoke when they came within the presence of Jesus. Gerard arose and went over and encouraged the poor mothers to trust in God. Then, undoing his cincture, he charged them to put it round the two girls on their return home, assuring them of their speedy deliverance. He told them to bear in mind the goodness and omnipotence of God. The women did as he had bade them, and all fell out as he had foretold.

But Gerard did even more than foil the machinations of the demons on innumerable occasions : he actually pressed them into his service. The following is a famous and striking instance. Our readers will remember how, in 1752, the Bishop of Melfi had asked the saint's superior to allow the wonderful laybrother stay with him for some days. The last day of his visit came. Late in the evening he made ready to ride home to Iliceto. Obedience had spoken and nothing could stop him, He set out

---

[1] Cap. xv.
[2] In Apost. no. 18, § 54.

in a thick blanket of fog, which soon almost blotted
out the road. The traveller lost all sense of direction.
He now found himself in the thick woods that lined
the banks of the river Ofanto. The night was upon him
and heavy rain was falling. Ravines were everywhere
and the recent floods made the going very uncertain
and very dangerous. The river had left its banks, so
that he no longer knew which was level ground and
which was precipice. Recent war *communiqués* have
given us a fair idea of what swollen Italian rivers can
be like.[1] Suddenly out of the mist and gloom emerged
a figure, human in shape, barring the way. Nearer
it came and close to him came a face evil and sinister,
whose eyes glowed darkly with a hatred kindled in
another world. Gerard knew him. The saint recognised
the fiend. We will let one of Gerard's friends, Don
Costantino Capucci, tell the rest of the story.

"About four o'clock in the morning," he writes in
an account that has been handed down to us,[2] " I heard
a knock at the door and, on my asking who was there,
I was surprised to hear it was Brother Gerard. I got
up and opened. Seeing him wet through, I said : ' What
brought you at this hour and in such weather ? ' ' God's

---

[1] The *Ofanto*, the principal river of Apulia and traversing almost
the whole breadth of the peninsula, was the ancient *Aufidus* of classical
fame. Its unruly behaviour was well-known to Horace :—
       " Sic tauriformis volvitur Aufidus
    Qui regna Dauni praefluit Apuli,
       Cum saevit, horrendamque cultis
          Diluviem meditatur agris."
                Carm. lib. iv, 25.
On the south bank of the Ofanto, about six miles from its mouth,
are the ruins of the small but famous town of Cannae, where Hannibal
annihilated the Romans in B.C. 216.
   [2] Landi ; Tannoia, cap. xv.

Will be done,' he replied with his wonted simplicity,
' I have come from Melfi ; but night came on with fog
and rain, which blotted out the road. I found myself
in the midst of such ravines along the Ofanto that,
only for God's assistance, I should have lost my life.
When on the brink of one of these, a man, or rather a
demon, came against me and said : ' Here is my hour
and my man. There is no hope for you, since you have
disobeyed your superior and God will not forgive you.'
At first I was taken by surprise ; but I recommended
myself to Jesus Christ and knew that this was no man
but a demon. I said to him : ' Unclean beast ! I command thee in the name of the Most Holy Trinity to
take my horse's bridle and without doing me any hurt
to lead me straight to Lacedonia ; thus I came in safety
with a devil as a companion ; I should otherwise have
lost my life there to-night, or I should have had to
remain amongst the dark intricate paths along the
Ofanto. When the enemy of God reached the church
of the Trinity, he said : ' This is Lacedonia ' and with
these words he vanished . . . *s'è squagliato.*' " On
returning home, Gerard, who had no secrets from his
superiors, told the whole story to Father Fiocchi.
Perhaps most of us would have preferred remaining
in the woods all night and taken our chances rather
than avail of the services of such a guide. But then
most of us are not saints.

The evil spirits, however, were not the only superhuman beings he enlisted in his service. At times he
seems to have won over even the angels. On one particular day in Caposele Gerard had been given the office
of cook. After Holy Communion that morning, he

withdrew to make his thanksgiving before a large crucifix
to which he was especially devoted. An ecstasy followed.
Kitchen and cooking and dining were soon quite forgotten, and his dear suffering Lord filled all his thoughts.
Hours passed. Dinner hour came. Then it was discovered that there was no cook to be found and that
the kitchen was locked ! There was an immediate search.
At last another laybrother found the missing cook just
emerging from his retreat, with face aglow and beaming
with joy. " Brother Gerard," exclaimed his confrère,
" what have you done ? The bell is going to ring for
dinner and the kitchen is locked." " Do you think the
angels will not help me ? " came the reply ; " you'll
see that they will."[1] The good brother had not in truth
been expecting such a solution of a domestic problem
and had not been associating angels with such a homely
performance as the cooking of a dinner. He did not
know what answer to give to this challenge. Anyhow,
the community proceeded in due course to the refectory,
where, to their utter amazement, they found a repast
spread for them the like of which they had never tasted.
Similar instances of angelic intervention in the common
doings of men are to be met with in the lives of other
saints. There is the well-known case of St. Isidore
Agricola, in whose life we read how angels took his
place in the fields and guided a yoke of oxen at the
plough while the saint was at his prayers in the church.
After all, the angels are not merely idle ornaments in
the scheme of human things. They are intensely active
in all sorts of ways for the good of men—as the devils
are for their undoing—but their activities are for the

[1] In Ord. no. 7, § 500.

most part hidden, and only on rare occasions are they seen at work. We need scarcely add that the holy absentmindedness displayed by Gerard in this instance is for admiration, not for imitation, as we may not always count on the angels in such matters.

If this chapter reads more like a page from a book of fairy tales then sober history, we would remind our readers that truth is admittedly very often stranger than fiction, and nowhere more so than in the lives of the saints. Some of the great truths of our holy faith to which we willingly give our adhesion involve a greater miracle—if we may so put it—than any we read of in the lives of the saints and really prepare the way for our acceptance of the truth of these. " I firmly believe," writes Newman, " that saints in their lifetime have before now raised the dead to life, crossed the sea without vessels, multiplied grain and bread, cured incurable diseases, and superseded the operations of the laws of the universe in a multitude of ways. Many men, when they hear an educated man so speak, will at once impute the avowal to insanity, or to idiosyncrasy, or to imbecility of mind, or to decreptitude of powers, or to fanaticism, or to hypocrisy. They have a right to say so, if they will ; and we have a right to ask them why they do not say it of those who bow down before the Mystery of mysteries, the Divine Incarnation. If they do not believe this, they are not yet Protestants ; if they do, let them grant that He who has done the greater may do the less."[1]

Gerard was in truth a wizard, but his wizardry came from God. God alone of course can adequately tell

[1] *Present Position of Catholics in England*, vii, 8, p. 313.

why some saints have been more gifted with miraculous powers than others. The times in which they lived, the special purposes God had in view in sending them amongst men, the distinctive nature of their sanctity have surely had much to say to the distribution of His endowments. In the case of St. Gerard Majella one explanation of God's generosity suggests itself : no saint has ever surpassed him in absolute, unquestioning and heroic devotion to the carrying out of the Will of God ; could it be that God rewarded this by doing the will of Gerard, often for apparently trifling reasons, even when doing it involved the working of a miracle ? And seemingly Gerard was not shy about exercising his power over the heart of God. Do we not see the daring of a spoilt child of Heaven in the following ? Writing to Sister Mary of Jesus Christ to urge her to pray for the recovery of another Sister, he says : " I do not want her to die, and say as much to my dear God, for I want her to become more holy and to die in old age, so that she may have the joy of having spent many years in the service of God. Come, wrestle with the Power of God, and this time let God do as we wish. In the name of God I give you an obedience not to let her die, and I wish to begin a novena to the Power of God for the health of this religious."[1] The Sister lived.

We can readily imagine the sway exercised over men by Gerard adorned as he was with such virtues and girt with such powers. We are going to look at it more closely ; but before doing so, we are going to make a pilgrimage with God's wizard.

---

[1] Tannoia, cap. xx. The English translation of this letter is particularly unhappy and completely misses the spirit of the original.

CHAPTER VIII

A PILGRIMAGE WITH GERARD

IN the second nocturn for the feast of St. Michael
the Archangel, the 8th May, we read as follows :—
" During the pontificate of Gelasius the First (A.D. 494
or 540), in Apulia, on the summit of Monte Gargano,
at the foot of which dwell the inhabitants of Sipontum,
a celebrated apparition of the Archangel Michael took
place. It happened that a bull broke loose from a herd
of cattle belonging to a certain Garganus. After a long
search, it was discovered at the mouth of a cave. When
an arrow had been shot at the bull, the arrow was turned
back on the archer. The occurrence so terrified those
who witnessed it and, subsequently, everybody else,
that no one dared to approach the cave. The people
of Sipontum consulted the bishop, who ordered a three
days' fast and prayer and said that the matter should
be referred to God. After three days, the Archangel
Michael warned the bishop that he had taken that spot
under his protection and had thus shown that it was
his will that God should be worshipped there, to commemorate himself and the angels. Accordingly, the
bishop and the people proceeded to the cave. On discovering that it was shaped like a church, they began
to use that spot for divine worship. It subsequently
became famous for many miracles." So far the Roman
Breviary.

This venerable summit rises in a steep slope to a height of five thousand feet above the waters of the Adriatic and forms what is known as the spur of the heel of Italy. Near its crest is the world-famous sanctuary of the Archangel. Down along the succeeding centuries Monte Gargano had drawn multitudes of pilgrims, and it did so still in Gerard's day.

Now in the autumn of 1753, probably during the September holidays, the young men who were studying dogmatic theology at Iliceto under the guidance of Father Alexander De Meo, a scholar of prodigious erudition, were very anxious to go on pilgrimage to the famous shrine.[1] The felicitous combination of spiritual and temporal advantages which such an outing involved had its peculiar appeal no doubt for the piety of exuberant youth. They laid the matter before the rector, Father Fiocchi. He gladly approved of the idea, but on the condition that Brother Gerard should take charge of the party. The students lost no time in organising the holy outing. As the distance from Iliceto to Monte Gargano was over forty miles, and as neither motor cars, nor trains nor even bicycles had yet been thought of, it was a serious affair enough. The journey

---

[1] When Alexander de Meo was scarcely seventeen, he was already studying theology in the seminary and outshone, not only his classmates, but the professor himself. St. Alphonsus, who gave him the chair of dogmatic theology at the age of twenty-five, looked on him with something like awe. " Father de Meo's genius," he would say, " helps to give me some idea of the wisdom of God." No small praise from a future Doctor of the Church. The greatest savants spoke of de Meo as ' a walking library.' But he had something better than learning : his humility was correspondingly profound. He was a *Servus Dei*, and in the inscription on a painting of him we read the words : *Altissimam scientiam cum pari animi modestia conjunxit.*

had evidently to be done chiefly on foot. According to
Tannoia's account, the party consisted of a dozen
persons ; according to Landi, of ten. Amongst them
was the professor, Father De Meo himself, as well as
a hermit—one Fra Angelo di San Girolomo—who took
charge of two hired donkeys for the conveyance of
luggage and possible casualties. They based their
calculations on an absence of ten days. For the whole
undertaking the rector handed Gerard thirty carlins—
about twelve shillings ! It was scarcely enough to cover
the expenses of two of the pilgrims. It was not stinginess
on his part but stark necessity : the house could afford
no more. After all, it was a holy luxury as well as a holy
enterprise. However, Father Fiocchi knew what he was
about when he put Gerard in charge. Wizards can be
very useful people, especially when they are of the right
sort. Moreover, he felt he could reckon on the hospitality
of friends.

Needless to say, Gerard was jubilant. And he had
good reason to be. Friendship with the great Archangel
had not been an afterthought in his life ; it was of long
standing, and Gerard owed him much. How could he
ever forget that first miraculous Communion he had
received from him in early childhood ? As we have
seen, St. Michael came first in the lengthy list of his
heavenly intercessors and friends, and his devotion to
him was marked with enthusiastic loyalty. To be told
to lead a pilgrimage to his sanctuary was, then, an easy
and a sweet obedience : he could ask for nothing better.

Gerard accepted his thirty carlins with the most
disconcerting indifference. Had they been three instead
of thirty, it would have been the same. Not so the

students. They had no intention of living solely on pious exhilaration, and with eyes on the commissariat, they no doubt visualised the demands that were likely to be made on this meagre pittance and the possibly resulting short commons. They at once voiced their alarm. " *Dio provvederà* . . . God will provide "[1] was the only answer they got from their imperturbable guide, and with that they had to be content. Anyhow, all set out in high spirits.

Foggia—some sixteen miles away—was the first halting-place ; and here we must halt with them. There is not a Redemptorist in the world who has not heard of Foggia. To-day it may be said that there is not a person in the world who reads his daily paper and listens in to his wireless who has not heard of it. Foggia, the ancient capital of Apulia and seated in the midst of the great plain, was no mean city. In past ages it had been known as the granary of Apulia, and its commerce with the Adriatic coast had resulted in its taking on quite a cosmopolitan complexion. With all its ancient and Christian lineage it was an evil city, so corrupt that out of a population of thirty thousand there were no less than a thousand women of dissolute life. Foggia was ripe for the chastising hand of God, and in 1731 a dreadful earthquake had almost wiped it away. When our pilgrims visited it, it was barely rising from its ruins and had nothing to show but long streets of low-built houses and a fragment of the imperial palace to testify to its vanished splendour.

Foggia figured much in the life of St. Alphonsus,

---

[1] Tannoia, cap. x.

especially in connection with one celebrated incident. On the 30th November, 1745, fourteen of his missionary sons, with he himself at their head, opened the spiritual exercises in the city. The mission was not to close till the eve of the following Epiphany. It was nothing less than a general offensive against the powers of Hell. Now one evening towards Christmas, the saint was preaching on Our Lady. In the church of S. Maria Maggiore was a celebrated miraculous image of the Madonna venerated under the title of *Our Lady of the Seven Veils*. Suddenly the eyes of the vast congregation went swiftly from the preacher to the picture and back again from the picture to the preacher. Mary's face had become fresh and living, while a ray of dazzling light was seen to shoot from it and rest on the countenance of Alphonsus. The thousand people that composed his audience then saw the saint in an ecstasy. His biographers tell us that so great were the cries of enthusiasm that they brought the good nuns of the neighbouring convent to their windows to see if a riot had broken out.[1] No wonder that Foggia deserved more

---

[1] The Cathedral Chapter of Foggia, desiring to procure from Rome the solemn crowning of the miraculous picture, asked St. Alphonsus to testify to the miracle. He replied as follows :—

"Nocera, 3rd October, 1777.

"We, Alphonsus Maria de'Liguori, bishop of St. Agatha of the Goths and Rector Major of the Congregation of the Most Holy Redeemer, affirm and testify, even on oath, to all who will read this letter the truth of the following fact :

"When in Foggia in the year 1732, we were preaching a course of sermons to the people in the church of St. John the Baptist. At the time this church possessed a large picture called the *ancient picture*, in the centre of which was an opening oval in shape and covered with a black veil. Now, on different days and on different occasions, we saw the face of the most holy Virgin Mary appear outside this opening. It was like that of a young girl of thirteen or fourteen ; it was veiled

than a passing glance from the pilgrims.

They reached the city by nightfall. It was indeed a joy for Gerard to visit the miraculous picture, and he had to tear himself away. However, with his holiness and his gifts, he was no stranger in Foggia and it would have more of him than a passing glance. No sooner had his presence become known than at once it made quite a flutter in the town, especially in clerical circles, where ecclesiastics vied with one another for the honour of being his host. He soon found himself the centre of a piously inquisitive group of clergy and gentry, who plied him with questions in theology and the ascetic life. And as in the case of the Child Christ in the temple, "all that heard him were astonished at his wisdom and his answers."[1]

Of course the good Sisters had to share in the holy feast. This was easily and adroitly managed : a member of the community of the convent of the Annunziata sent for him. There were some little matters of conscience she would like to talk over. The good-hearted Brother, who never refused a favour he could possibly

in white, and turned from right to left. We were filled with the most tender devotion and the greatest joy, and we could not restrain our tears when we saw that this august countenance no longer resembled a painting, but a living face in full relief, flesh-coloured, and like that of a young person who was turning right and left. Moreover, we were not alone in contemplating it ; the whole congregation assembled for the sermon looked at it also and prayed with great fervour to the holy Mother of God in the midst of exclamations and sobs.

In faith of which we have affixed our seal to this testimony.

Given at Nocera dei Pagani, on this 10th day of October, 1777.

Alphonsus Maria de' Liguori, Bishop,

Fr. Antonio Romito, secretary."

Corrispond. General. Lettera DCCCLXXVI.

[1] Luke, ii, 47.

grant, accordingly went. The little matters of conscience were satisfactorily talked over. The poor Sister, however, got more than she bargained for : before leaving, Gerard told her to make ready for an early death. She was quite young, in the best of health and in excellent spirits at the time. But in four months she was dead. After this, we are not told if any of the other good Sisters expressed a wish to talk over little matters of conscience with Gerard.

It is not recorded how Gerard managed to pay hotel expenses at Foggia. But when morning came, a new problem presented itself. Though continental religious think nothing of excursions afoot that would appal their brethren in these latitudes, still there was a limit to endurance, and some of his young men were not in sufficiently good fettle, after the march of the previous day, for the further twenty-four miles of bleak monotonous country that lay between them and Monte Gargano. Merciless ascetic as Gerard was where his own poor self was concerned, he was mercy personified towards others and was never one of those who think it a part of asceticism to mortify their neighbour. Accordingly, he hired a two-horse conveyance of some sort that would take the whole party to Manfredonia, the town that lay at the foot of the mountain. Now we must not forget that he started out with some twelve shillings. The students did not let him forget it, and on hearing of this new venture, chorused despondently " But how can we pay for it ? "[1] They were evidently bent on taking no chances. Quietly came the same

---

[1] Tannoia, cap. x.

uncompromising answer: "God will provide." And sincerely hoping that He would, they all climbed into the vehicle and drove on.

In the meantime the two donkeys were giving trouble. The poor beasts were not overfed, they were not used to outings of this sort and naturally did not share the holy enthusiasm of their masters. Their indifferent trot gradually dropped into a hopeless crawl, with the result that they and their hermit driver were soon lost sight of by the main body.

When the vehicle reached a wayside tavern at the sign of the *Ponte di Candela*, Gerard halted to order refreshments and also to give Fra Angelo and his donkeys time to catch up. They were now about eight miles from Manfredonia. In due course the hermit was seen approaching, puffing and panting and covered with dust and perspiration. The donkeys were spent. Gerard at once brought their driver into the tavern and procured him the refreshments he so sorely needed. These, however, were no sooner disposed of than the saint, to the hermit's dismay, gave the signal to proceed. This was too much, and in spite of the refreshments, the hermit struck. After all, as he argued reasonably enough, the donkeys were not his own, and if they died on the way, as they might very well do, he would be responsible. Perhaps the good man did not know with whom he had to deal—with one who could brush argument and obstacle miraculously aside. He was soon to discover. "The donkeys must come," said Gerard, "and I mean to make them go."[1] Suiting the action to the word,

---

[1] Benedetti, p. 173.

he thereupon harnessed the recalcitrant asses to the waggon in front of the horses. He then bade the grumbling hermit mount one of them and the son of the owner of the conveyance the other. Fra Angelo had evidently acquired sufficient spirituality in his hermitage to obey. Finally, Gerard himself took his seat on the box, and giving the donkeys a vigorous cut of the whip, cried out : " In the name of the Most Holy Trinity I command you to gallop."[1] And gallop they forthwith did, " like two racehorses,"[2] to use Tannoia's expression, covering without slack or halt the remaining eight miles to Manfredonia. The thrill the students got out of this miraculous drive—for such in truth it was—can be imagined. Poor Fra Angelo's feelings as he clung for bare life to the galloping asses, with two galloping horses and a car full of people immediately behind him, are not recorded. Perhaps his safety was miraculous, too.

On reaching Manfredonia towards evening, they parted company with their vehicle and almost with the entire remainder of their resources. When the owner was paid off, there was about ninepence in the treasury ! And though they had completed the second stage of their journey, they had not yet reached their destination ! Once more, with an anxious eye to the future, the students gave vent to their alarm, though surely this time, bearing in mind all that had so far happened, with less insistence. Gerard, however, made no change in his re-assuring formula : " God will provide." And God seemed to be providing very effectively indeed.

---

[1] Landi.
[2] Cap. x.

Gerard was fully alive to the state of their finances; but he was still more alive to God's goodness towards those who trust implicitly in Him. He now performed a daring act of holy bribery. When leading his pilgrims to the church to pay their respects to the Blessed Sacrament, he stopped on the way to buy a beautiful bunch of pinks with all that was left of his money. They then entered a church which was attached to a thirteenth century castle. After a brief prayer, Gerard arose, mounted the altar steps bouquet in hand, and having laid it in front of the tabernacle, was heard to say: "Lord! I have thought of Thee. It is now Thy turn to think of my family."[1] The bribe worked immediately. The castle chaplain happened to be in the church at the moment; unobserved he saw Gerard's act and heard his words. Drawing closer to the visitors, he recognised the Redemptorist habit. He called the saint aside and gave him and his party a cordial invitation to be his guests for the night in his house adjoining the church. Gerard was most grateful, but pointed to their number. The chaplain, however, waived that consideration aside and insisted on putting up the whole party. His one regret was that owing to his mother being ill for the past two months, he could not entertain them as he would like. To his great wonderment Gerard there and then tided him over that difficulty by telling him to make the sign of the cross on his mother's forehead and assuring him that she would be well. The priest lost no time in doing so, and on their arrival at the house, they found the good lady waiting to welcome them at

---

[1] In Apost. no. 7. § 248.

the door and showering a thousand blessings on the holy brother. Like St. Peter's mother-in-law of old, she " arose and ministered to them."[1]

But that bunch of pinks was to purchase more from Our Lord than bed and board for the pilgrims : it bought a new thurible for Iliceto. Another priest in Manfredonia, who already knew Gerard by repute, had heard of the incident in the church and was so touched by it that he called on the saint and offered him a most beautiful silver thurible for his own church in Iliceto. He was as good as his word : a silver thurible worth sixty ducats duly arrived at the monastery. " The gift was most acceptable," writes Tannoia, " as the thurible we had was only a silver-plated brass one."

After having supped heartily and slept well, the pilgrims arose filled with a new buoyancy at the now undoubted providence attending their pilgrimage. God was certainly " providing," as their guide had so repeatedly assured them He would. When soul and body had been refreshed, they began the ascent of the five thousand foot summit of Monte Gargano. There are few things more exhilarating than the opening stages of an early morning mountain climb. For the first thrilling hours, as foot after foot of rising ground is devoured with a swinging step, in the strength of the young day, with its fresh breezes allying themselves with the enterprise and whispering encouragement into the ear, the towering summit is looked upon as nothing but a glorious and challenging objective, hiding its

---

[1] Matt., viii, 15.

difficulties and dangers behind the resplendent veil of coming triumph and achievement. And thus it was with our pilgrims now. For a time it was all sheer poetry. But in due course the prose inevitably appeared, and dry prose at that. As the morning lost its invigorating newness and the Italian sun took control, with never a sheltering tree to be seen, one student after another surrendered. Luckily the two donkeys were the better of the night's rest and a good breakfast, and thus the young men requisitioned their services in turn. Gerard alone climbed the whole way on foot. Though his feet ached and faltered, his thoughts were in heaven. Besides, there was further holy bribery to be done, and he wanted many things from the great Archangel whose shrine he was approaching.

At long last they topped the sacred summit of Monte Gargano. They went straight to the famous sanctuary, where each one gave himself to his devotion as he listed. But the long climb had done its work, and the voice of the inner man was now breaking in on their piety. When the students had given what they considered a reasonably long time to the Archangel, they approached their holy guide to remind him that they would all be the better of a dinner. They found Gerard motionless, with his eyes open and turned heavenwards. His breathing was scarcely audible. They called him, but got no reply. Fearing some mishap, they drew closer and shook him gently by the arm. But he gave no sign of life. Finally, they put their arms about him and lifted him bodily up. Then his ecstasy ended—for it had been an ecstasy —and he came quietly to himself. Looking round and seeing their worried glances, he remarked : " It is nothing,

it is nothing. Let us go now and replenish our strength."[1]
Their kind host in Manfredonia had had an eye to their
future as well as to their present needs and had not
sent Gerard on his way without giving him something
towards meeting expenses on Monte Gargano itself.
Thanks to this generosity and foresight, they were
enabled to dine well and pass the night in an inn not
far from the sanctuary.

On the following morning they revisited the holy
place and fell again to their prayers. This time, however, Gerard kept his feet firmly on the earth and made
sure that his company had a substantial meal. The
day wore on pleasantly and at last dinner-hour came.
They were all assembled round Father De Meo in a
room in the inn. Gerard had gone out, and the students
were wondering how he would be able to provide a
dinner. One of them, Ricciardi by name, was prepared
to swear that on the previous day there were not more
than four grains (about 2d.) in the purse. After some
time Gerard came in and told them to sit down to table.
Then, taking twenty-four grains from the purse (about
a shilling), he handed them to the hermit, commissioning
him to buy bread. When he noticed his company smiling
dubiously at one another, he said, echoing the words of
his Master on many a similar occasion : " Men of little
faith, is it thus you obey ? Come ! sit down to table."[2]
It happened to be a day of abstinence ; and down they
sat to a table piled high with all sorts of excellent fish.
They could scarcely believe their eyes. Father De Meo

---

[1] Benedetti, p. 176.
[2] *Ibid.*

—who, by the way, for all his learning seems to have been completely in the background on this expedition— quietly drew the hermit aside on his return and asked him who had been responsible for such a menu. Fra Angelo assured him that he had purchased nothing but the bread he had been sent out to buy. Wherever the fish came from, the money that bought it clearly came from an unusual source. Then the hermit remembered something that threw light on matters. What the student Ricciardi had asserted about the state of the purse the day before was indeed true : it contained only four grains. But in the evening, as Gerard was praying before the altar, a stranger had gone over to him and put a sum of money in his hands which was enough and to spare for the rest of the pilgrimage. Whether this stranger was an angel or a man the angels alone could tell. In Gerard's case it could just as likely have been the one as the other.

At last the hour came to take their leave of Monte Gargano. Gerard asked the innkeeper for his bill. He saw at a glance that he had been outrageously over-charged. Perhaps the man thought that a client who could order such abundant fare and pay for it would not notice even an obvious and substantial discrepancy in the account, or at least that he would not haggle over it. Or perhaps, as in the case of the dishonest blacksmith narrated in the preceding chapter, he looked upon a saint as fair game. Whether he had heard of Gerard before or not, it is more than likely that some members of the party had been telling him what manner of man he had under his roof and that the wonderful happenings on the way and in the sanctuary itself had reached his ears. What did a man like Gerard care about money? Anyhow, a man whose thoughts were more in heaven than on earth would not notice the little fraud. Thus, maybe, the innkeeper argued when he prepared his bill. He did not know that nobody sees the earth so well as those who keep their heads in heaven, and that they who fancy that the saints are easy dupes in things temporal run the risk of being fooled by their own folly. The innkeeper was speedily brought to book. However, though his palpable dishonesty was pointed out to him, he refused to climb down. Then Gerard took drastic and dramatic action. "If you do not keep to what is just," he told the man, "you will pay for it by seeing your mules die."[1] He had scarcely spoken when the innkeeper's son came rushing excitedly into the room, crying out: "Come quick! I don't know what's wrong with the mules. They are rolling about on the ground in an alarming way. Quick, quick!"[2] This news brought the swindler at once to his senses. He now realised that he had to do with a saint, and a very dangerous one to trifle with. He fell on his knees and implored Gerard's pardon. The pardon was gladly given, but with it went a stern reminder that God is with His poor, and a warning against any further dishonesty. The pendulum now swung the other way: the disillusioned innkeeper did not now want to accept payment at all. But the saint left a fair price on the table, and so doing, departed with his little band. We do not know if there were any such things as visitors' books in the inns of those days.

[1] Benedetti, p. 177.
[2] Ibid.

This time it could have given rise to an awkward situation. As Gerard passed the suffering mules on his way out, he made the sign of the cross over them and at once they became normal. Later the innkeeper made honourable amends by becoming a benefactor of the house of Iliceto.

After a farewell visit to the sanctuary, the pilgrims began the descent. The descent of a mountain can be even a more trying performance than its climb. Apart from physical reasons, the objective has been achieved and the stimulus of challenge and enthusiasm is no longer felt. When the travellers had reached the foot of Monte Gargano and had gone a good stretch on the road, they were thoroughly tired and excessively thirsty. Gerard cheered them on, assuring them that they would shortly reach a well. Once again, however, he had to deal with that strange hardness of heart so repellent to his own burning charity. Now there happened to be a prolonged drought in the country ; water was scarce, and in order to deprive others of the use of it the owner of this particular well had removed the cords by which the buckets were lowered. Gerard asked the man to lend them. He was met with a blank refusal. Appeal and argument proved useless. Then the saint spoke as only the saints can speak who have been endowed by God with power to drive home what they say with deeds. " You refuse water to your neighbour whom you are bound to love as yourself ; and the well will refuse it to you."[1] And so saying he proceeded on his way. The

---

[1] In Apost. no. 7, § 255.

party had gone about half a mile when they heard some-one calling after them. It was the owner imploring Gerard to return and informing him disconsolately that the water had left the well and that it was the only one in the district from which the poor people could draw. Moreover, he now promised to give the water not only to themselves but also to their animals. Thus in his own distress the poor had a new interest for him. It was the old story of the sick devil turning saint. At all events, they all retraced their steps to see the well. Though a short time before they had been looking longingly down at the unattainable water, they now saw that sure enough the well had completely dried up. This man, too, had been taught his lesson. The sight of his penitent tears as well as of the thirsty students was too much for Gerard. Another sign of the cross and the delicious water came gurgling up afresh. They drank in plenty. Even the two donkeys now came in for their share of the beverage. In concluding his account of this incident Tannoia observes dryly : " What is still more remarkable is that he (the owner) never refused water to anyone again."[1] Henceforth the cords were always in readiness for all comers. He had evidently taken to heart Gerard's parting words : " For charity's sake, my brother, do not refuse to your neighbour water which belongs to everybody. Otherwise God will refuse it to you. Has not Jesus Christ commanded us to love one another as brothers ? Oh ! be charitable, if you want God to show mercy to you."[2]

---

[1] Cap. x.
[2] In Apost. no. 7., § 257.

They now resumed their journey to Manfredonia, where they passed the night, most probably under the same hospitable roof of the castle chaplain. On the following morning, they set out to cover the distance to Foggia on foot. It was now quite another story. This time they had no vehicle of any sort, and the weaker members of the party had to enlist in turn the services of the two donkeys. No doubt they had been amply refreshed both in body and soul; but they had now to face a walk of twenty miles, and though the chronicles of the time do not tell us if they walked them all the one day, still this long trudge under the Italian sun must have been a trying business. Moreover, as they were soon to prove, there was all the difference in the world between going to Monte Gargano and returning from it. This time it was their holy guide who suffered most. We must remember that the poor brother was within two years of his death from tuberculosis, and hæmorrhages from the lungs were already no rare occurrence with him. He had not the physical stamina of the young men in his charge, and all his heroic charity and self-denial were unequal to the strain on his broken and mortified frame. Yet not a murmuring word did he utter on the way, as he dragged himself painfully along. Nothing could induce him to take his turn on the donkeys, and it was only when he was discovered more than once actually spitting blood that they realised what those twenty miles meant for him.

In due course the pilgrims were very hungry, and Gerard had nothing now but a few pence. But if his body was weak, his heart was stout and his soul as strong in trust as ever. When they reached an unnamed village according to one biographer ; when they reached Foggia itself according to another, Gerard had once again recourse to the holy bribery that had worked so well in replenishing their depleted stores in Manfredonia. With his few remaining coins he purchased another bouquet of flowers and then led his little band to the church. This bouquet he likewise deposited before the tabernacle, with a similar childlike remainder to his Divine Friend within to do His part. That Friend did not fail him now either. On leaving the church, they were met by two young girls who presented Gerard with two basketfuls of good things. Who and what these girls were the angels alone again could tell. The travellers spent the night in Foggia.

Seven miles from Foggia, in the midst of a lonely wood of oaks, stands yet another of those venerable sanctuaries of Mary with which Italy abounds. Here she was invoked under the title of the *Incoronata*. Now Gerard knew all about this shrine and had already made more than one pilgrimage to it. He could not resist its attraction now. He naturally had to reckon with the views and capabilities of his young men. By this time they had done their share of walking, and indeed their share of praying, too. However, they had had a good night's rest and were ready for anything he suggested. Besides, they knew what pleasure this little détour would give him, and they felt that after all the wonderful things he had done in their behalf on the way, they owed him this much. So they all went to Our Lady's sanctuary. Gerard had scarcely set foot within the chapel when once again they were treated to the sight of a saint in ecstasy. By this time, how ever, they knew more or less what to expect, and there were no further violent efforts on their part to bring their guide to earth. But this did not prevent one of the younger members of the party from asking the saint quietly what had happened him. "Nothing," came the answer. "it is a weakness to which I am subject."[1]

But their minor pilgrimages were not yet at an end. Wherever a sanctuary of Jesus or Mary beckoned, Gerard had to go. This time it was his Crucified Lord that called him. Yet another détour brought them to the town of Troia, nearly fifteen miles from Foggia, which boasted of a miraculous and wonderfully sculptured crucifix. The work had been executed by order of the Bishop of Troia, Monsignore Cavalieri, who, besides being a very holy man, was the maternal uncle of St. Alphonsus. The countenance of the Crucified was so expressive that nobody could look on it unmoved. The effect it had on Gerard can be imagined. He was quickly in a rapture.

At last the multiple pilgrimage came to an end. Before the pilgrims reached home, however, their leader crowned its accompanying wonders with a prophecy. Among the students was a youth called Peter Paul Blasucci. He was the brother of that student Dominic Blasucci of whom we said something in an earlier chapter, and who, seven months previously, had died in the odour of sanctity. Now one day in the course of the pilgrimage Gerard turned to Peter Paul Blasucci and told him he would one day become Superior-General of the Con-

---

[1] Tannoia, cap. x.   T.

gregation. Forty years later the prophecy was fulfilled, when, on the 24th April, 1793, he was elected to that post. He governed the Institute till his death, which occurred on the 13th June, 1817. He had been a bare month professed when this prophecy was uttered, and we know that youthful religious who have but just emerged from their novitiate do not usually display qualities foreshadowing a capacity for such high office.

The pilgrimage to Monte Gargano lasted nine days. Gerard brought back to his rector, not only all his company in safety, but a far heavier purse than the one with which he had set out. As he handed it to his superior, he said : "God provided."[1]

---

[1] In Apost. no. 7, § 232.

CHAPTER IX

IN THE VINEYARD

THE title of this chapter may surprise. St. Gerard Majella, for all his outstanding holiness and endowments, was no priest. He could not say Mass, he could not absolve from sin, he could not administer the sacraments, he could not preach, except in the most informal way and of course by the silent but splendid eloquence of example. He was a layman, a laybrother first and last, and never for one moment did he forget it. As such he became pre-eminently the model for all Redemptorist laybrothers to come ; he shone brilliantly with all the virtues that should characterise them ; he observed to perfection their own particular rules and constitutions, and no laybrother was ever less tempted to step into a sphere not his own or take in hand any work, however excellent or useful, to which God and obedience had not called him. None grasped more fully the nature and implications of his specific calling. As we have shown in an earlier chapter, the Redemptorist laybrother is called, not to work in the vineyard of the Master as his priestly confrères work, but by working assiduously in lowlier spheres—in the garden, the kitchen, the refectory, the tailor's shop— to release those who are called to work in that vineyard, and in a particular manner to pray for their success.

Moreover, the preceding chapters should, we think, have amply shown what a worker Gerard proved himself to be in the various departments of a laybrother's little world. Thus, besides the apostolate of prayer and example, none other seemed open to Brother Gerard, and so, we say, the title of this chapter may surprise.

But there are exceptions to every rule, and if God thought well in Gerard's case of overriding the laws of nature so frequently by enabling him to work miracles, it is no matter for wonder if, for a higher purpose, He inspired superiors to override certain rulings of the Institute, that His servant might put his extraordinary gifts and virtues to a fuller and more fruitful use. A love for God and souls such as burned in the fiery furnace of Gerard's heart was not destined to be imprisoned within the walls of his cloistered home, but was meant to leap out in devouring tongues upon the surrounding world of men and inflame every heart it could reach. The light of Gerard's sanctity was not destined to lie hid under any bushel, but was to be " a spectacle to the world and to angels and to men."[1] In any case, certain circumstances to which we will return presently made his outdoor life and all his comings and goings less a departure from the normal than they would be today.

We need hardly say that Gerard had not waited till he was a Redemptorist before sharing in the apostolate. We have seen how even as a child he would gather children about him and lead them in prayer and hymn. In his school-boy days his ascendency over his school-mates and his unusual aptitude for imparting religious

---

[1] I Cor., iv. 9.

knowledge were not lost upon his master. As a youth he would bring the little ones of Christ to his " dear Prisoner " in the tabernacle. He would teach them their prayers, fill them with a horror of sin, and fascinate them with truths about God and divine things drawn from the abundance of his own fascinated heart. With his miraculous childhood in mind, he could in a wonderfully literal sense address his little audience in the words of St. John : " That which was from the beginning, which we have heard, which we have seen with our eyes, which we have looked upon and our hands have handled, of the word of life . . . we declare unto you."[1]

Nor had Gerard overlooked a field of apostolic action that lay nearer to hand. His holiness was a leaven in the bosom of his own family, and this spoilt child of his Eucharist Lord infused not a little of his own ardour for Holy Communion into the hearts of his mother and sisters. Nor did he stop at good example. Though the Benjamin of the Majella household, he did not fear to plead his Master's cause and in his own sweet way made bold at times to chide where chiding was called for. One of the three girls—we are not told which—had evidently more than her share of Eve's vanity, particularly where dress was concerned. One day he found her eyeing some articles of feminine adornment with what he considered undue complacency. Foreseeing dangerous possibilities, he called bluntly for a sacrifice and asked her to throw the pretty trifles into the fire. How she responded to the invitation biographers do not say.

---

[1] I John, I, 1-2.

On entering the Congregation, Gerard found himself a member of an institute whose specific purpose in the Church was the direct and active apostolate of saving and sanctifying souls. Nothing could have been dearer to his heart. We remember the words he penned when concluding the long list of his resolutions : " O my God ! would that I might convert as many sinners as there are grains of sand in the sea and on the land, as there are leaves on the trees, blades of grass in the fields, atoms in the air, stars in the sky, rays in the sun and moon, creatures in the whole earth." And this was no mere poetic effusion. The love of God, particularly of God Incarnate and Crucified for the love of men, was the master passion of his heart. It meant loving what He loved and hating what He hated. He could in all truth say with the Psalmist : " I beheld the transgressors, and I pined away ; because they kept not Thy word."[1] The nearer the saints approached God's own sinlessness the more they sickened at the sight of sin. Thus it was with Gerard : he sickened at the sight of sin. At the mere thought of sin renewing the Passion of Jesus Christ he would at times fall fainting to the ground. In the words of a witness, " in his eyes an offence against God was a disaster."[2] " Whenever he witnessed a transgression of the divine law . . . .," states another, " he was so distressed that he would often break out into lamentations, declaring that he would gladly give his life a thousand times that God might not be outraged and that His divine law might be perfectly fulfilled."[3] The remem-

---

[1] Ps. 118, 158.
[2] In Apost. no. 9, § 102.
[3] *Ibid*, § 108.

brance of the world's coldness towards its God was a dagger-thrust to his flaming heart. Normally he was cheerful with more than the wonted cheerfulness of the children of light, but when dark and heavy tidings of man's iniquity fell upon his ears, his sunshine underwent a visible eclipse ; then silence and dejected looks, with sometimes sighs and tears, revealed his sorrowing heart. All he could do by penance and prayer to bring sinners back to grace was done with the uncalculating lavishness and heroism that we know. But now it was given to Gerard to take a more direct and personal hand in this great and holy work. He was to step into the very Vineyard itself and in company with the Master's official and anointed gatherers, pluck fruits of surpassing richness and abundance.

Before speaking of Gerard's apostolic activities abroad, we must speak of the souls he won for Christ within the precincts of his own monastery. None knew better than St. Alphonsus what a harvest could be reaped from enclosed retreats conducted in the houses of his Congregation. He had made many a one himself before he left the world, and it was in the course of one of them that he took the great decision, which was to mean so much for the Church, to give himself entirely to God and the saving of souls. Accordingly, he saw to it that the giving of such retreats should be inserted in his rule. Ecclesiastics and laymen (as many as sixty of these latter would at times come from the same locality), the man of means and the toiler—all got their turn. They withdrew for a few days from the turbulent world into a quiet solitude where a preacher spoke to their ears and God to their hearts about the things that really mattered and mattered eternally, and emerged from it better, wiser, stronger, braver men, to fight the battle of their own soul and draw others to do likewise.

Here Gerard got his chance and took it. During these retreats he wielded mightily the weapons of prayer and penance and example that were within the grasp of every other laybrother in his community. But God had put into his hands another weapon and endowed him with another gift with which not even the anointed preacher or confessor had been endowed, *viz.*, the discernment of spirits, or the reading of the consciences of men. Here was something quite special to Gerard and one of the greatest wonders of his wonderful life. It is also, we do not hesitate to say, the gift that has gained for him, perhaps more than any other, an ever-growing multitude of grateful clients down even to our own day. Certainly one of the best known and most popular aspects of his life was—and is still—his unofficial but most effective relationship with the confessional. Gerard solved cases, read consciences, disposed penitents—did everything in short but give absolution. The reading of consciences came as easy to him as the reading of an open book, and many a page made very unsavoury reading. He was fully alive to the crime and the tragedy of a sacrilegious confession by which, through false shame or an unfounded fear, the sinner, by withholding from God's minister what he has a right to know and what God already knows, turns a remedy into poison, piles fresh guilt on that from which he seeks to unburden himself, and forges new fetters for his hapless soul while striving to shake off the old. Gerard saw fully and felt deeply the pity of it all, and so he freely exercised his astounding powers in behalf of this foolish and unhappy class of sinner. He was naturally given more scope for this in the course of his journeyings up and down the land ; but he got many a chance during the enclosed retreats, and he was not the man to let such chances slip.

A certain professional man, who had been giving public scandal for many years, found himself, through circumstances not of his own making, taking an unwilling part in a retreat preached in the monastery of Iliceto. He went through the exercises with sufficient external seriousness to save his face, but without any intention of changing his heart. He had already added sacrilege to hypocrisy by a bad confession ; he was now about to add one sacrilege to another by a bad Communion. Gerard met him on his way, stopped him, and looking into the whited sepulchre, voiced his horror and indignation at the intended enormity. Detailing the sins he had concealed, he bade the wretched man make a good confession, if he did not want to lose his soul. The sinner did so and returned home after the retreat a fervent penitent. Unhappily he did not walk for long on the road of virtue. He went back to his evil ways and in the course of some months was worse than ever. Again a retreat came round and through human respect he made it. Again his making of it was a sham. Gerard, however, was still in Iliceto and for a second time was to be reckoned with. On meeting the man the saint asked him how he was faring spiritually. The retreatant was happy to inform him that all was well. But Gerard knew better : he knew that the man had lied. He knew, moreover, that his was a desperate case that called for drastic measures to meet it. Armed with a crucifix, he entered the retreatant's room, closed the door and the windows, and faced him. In no mincing words he tore off the mask of his hyprocrisy, laid bare the wickedness of his ways and drove home his ingratitude to God. " Look ! " he cried, " who has inflicted these wounds on Jesus Christ ? Who has shed that blood ? " And lo ! as he spoke, blood was seen to flow from the crucified Figure in Gerard's hands ! The saint went on with his apostrophising of the sinner : " And what wrong has this God done you ? "[1] he asked, as he detailed in flaming words the events of Christmas night. And lo ! as he spoke, there was a vision of the Babe of Bethlehem lying in Gerard's hands ! But he would leave nothing to chance. This time it was to be an all-out offensive against a most formidable stronghold of evil. And so, after hearing the pleading of Bethlehem and Calvary, the sinner was now confronted with the terrors of Hell. Reminding him with mounting earnestness that God is not mocked in vain, Gerard showed the now trembling man the doom awaiting him if he did not give over his evil doings. Conjuring up the vision of a demon in the name of his offended Lord, he shot his last bolt. No more was needed. The sinner stood before him frozen with terror. On seeing that his work was at last accomplished, the saint bade the vision disappear. More dead than alive the now thoroughly repentant man hastened to confession. This time his conversion was complete and lasting. The convert was the first to tell of all that happened and

---

[1] Benedetti, pp. 94-95.

gave his confessor leave to publish the whole story.
It is recorded, as we have told it, by Gerard's two contemporary biographers Landi and Tannoia and is to be
found in the acts of the apostolic process.

This was not the only occasion on which the saint
made use of his powers of presenting a terrifying vision
from the other world to the eyes of an obstinate sinner.
He once took a retreatant aside who was about to receive
sacrilegiously. After reminding him that there was a
grievous sin on his soul which he had deliberately concealed, he went on : " Do you not know what a great
crime it is to commit a sacrilege ? I want you to see
the hideousness of a sacrilegious soul."[1] And there and
then the man was given to see the horrible vision of
a lost soul. It was more than enough to fill him with
terror and repentance. He at once undid the guilty
past, and the memory of what he had seen remained
with him as an abiding and salutary reminder.

A number of laymen from Castelgrande were making
a retreat in the monastery of Caposele when Gerard
was there. Amongst them was a pleasant fellow named
Francis Mugnone. Meeting Francis strolling in the
grounds one day, Gerard went up to him, gave him a
kindly but serious look, and then asked him without
further ceremony if he had made a good confession.
Francis replied that he had. " That's not true," came
the retort, " look behind you."[2] Francis looked behind
him and beheld a diabolical apparition. He lost no
time in returning to his confessor.

During another of these retreats a man had confessed

[1] In Ord. no. 7, § 502.
[2] *Ibid*. no. 18, § 32.

sacrilegiously and was about to make matters worse by receiving unworthily at the general Communion. In fact he had already gone to the church for the purpose. Gerard was praying in the tribune. He at once went down, took the man aside and opened his eyes to the horrible nature of his intended crime. He, too, sought out a confessor immediately and put things right. In the urge of his new-found sorrow he now went to the other extreme : returning to the church, he fell upon his knees and told the assembled retreatants what Gerard had done for him, adding that it was now his intention to bear the shame of confessing his sins before them all. Fortunately one of the Fathers was there in time to stop him.

Amongst the retreatants on one occasion was a certain gentleman of means. His conscience needed much righting, but he meant to right it and with the best will in the world began the exercises. Unhappily, whatever the preacher said in the opening lecture or however he said it, the poor man lost all heart and there and then made up his mind to go home. Using the devil's logic, he had probably drawn wrong conclusions from indisputable premises and had practically fallen into despair. Naturally he had kept his mind to himself. But Gerard knew it. He lost no time in taking action. There was a knock at the retreatant's door. The saint entered and without any preamble said : " What's wrong with you, Signore ? Banish this hellish distrust, for God and most holy Mary must help you."[1] The sinner was amazed ; and grace did the rest.

---

[1] Tannoia, cap. xiv.

It was not necessarily retreatants whose path Gerard thus dramatically crossed. At times a chance visitor to the monastery who was not what he should be came within the sweep of his enlightened gaze and had to take the consequences. There is a celebrated instance of this recorded by all his biographers. When Gerard was in Caposele, it so happened that the Archbishop of Conza, Monsignor Giuseppe Nicolai, came there to spend a few days with the community. He was a great benefactor of the house. In his suite came his secretary, a layman and a Roman by birth.[1] Now his Grace thought a great deal of his secretary, for he was no ordinary man. Besides possessing first-rate capacity for business, he was exceptionally good company wherever he went, was an excellent *raconteur*, had an inexhaustible fund of wit, and in fact was an altogether charming fellow. This time he charmed the community. He charmed Gerard—at least so it seemed. Indeed Gerard had apparently fallen completely under his spell. He laughed heartily at the secretary's witticisms, showed much nimbleness and grace in repartee, had many a free and easy chat with him and marked him out for quite an exuberant display of affection. It was all with a purpose. The sad truth was that the poor secretary's bubbling good spirits was a mask hiding a very unhappy man. His laughter found no echo in a heart long untenanted by God. In more senses than one the secretary was leading a double life. Gerard saw it all, and his pity was immense. He did not tear off the mask as he tore off the bandages of the posturing cripple. He

---

[1] Father Ripoli states that he actually posed as a priest, taking in the bishop and everybody.—In Apost. no. 7, § 164.

rather peeped behind it and gazed sadly but kindlily
into its wearer's eyes, and then gently removed it. One
day he met the secretary in one of his most jovial moods
and, like a good Italian, threw his arms affectionately
about him. Virtue went out from that embrace and
awoke within the poor man's heart the first blessed
stirrings of remorse. As Benedetti puts it, " the unhappy
man found no rest after that embrace and had become
like a wounded beast bearing about with it the hunter's
shaft that had entered its vitals."[1] But that clasp of
a saint's arms had done more than wound : it won the
sinner's confidence in the holy Brother, whose company
he now deliberately sought out. As soon as Gerard
saw that the fruit was ripe for plucking, he plucked it.
On the third day after the secretary's arrival, he called
him into a quiet corner and fell weeping at his feet.
" My friend," he then began, " I cannot understand
how you can be so cheerful when you are living at
enmity with God. You cannot deny you are a married
man and have a wife in Rome. How can you pretend
to be free and live like a profligate with a dissolute
woman ? "[2] Then solemnly and sorrowfully he detailed
the circumstances of his disorders, mentioning the
precise number of years he had been thus living without
a thought of God or of his own soul. There was no
denunciation, no threats, no terrifying visions needed
here. There was a shortlived show of bewilderment
and hesitation on the part of the secretary. Then
realising that the game was up, he too knelt and wept
Humbly and unreservedly he pleaded guilty to every

---

[1] P. 354.
[2] Tannoia, cap. xxvi.

count in the indictment and begged his accuser to help him with his counsel and his prayers. Both were lavishly bestowed. It was now the moment to preach God's mercy, and Gerard preached it. Father Fiocchi—in whom he seems to have had great faith as a confessor for such cases—happened to be in Caposele at the time for the purpose of meeting the archbishop, and Gerard sent him this new capture. " Only God or the devil," the convert afterwards remarked, " could have made my state known to him ; but it could not have been the devil, as I am filled with heartfelt contrition."[1] He had not yet done with the saint's revealing glance. As he was on his way to receive Holy Communion the following morning, he was accosted by him and reminded of a certain sin he had forgotten in his confession. " Go and confess it," said Gerard, " and then you can go and receive Jesus Christ in peace."[2]

The swift and basic change in the secretary's moral life could not but effect his external demeanour. The entertainer and the wit grew serious and reserved. Not rarely now were his eyes full of tears, but the tears were not of laughter. It was soon clear to all observers that his Grace's secretary was an altered man. Like everybody else his Grace was puzzled. He first questioned others and then finally sent for his secretary and asked him to explain. The reply was a burst of weeping, as the poor man repeated the words of the Samaritan woman : " Come, and see a man who has told me all things whatsoever I have done."[3] And then and there

---

[1] Tannoia, cap. xxvi.
[2] Benedetti, p. 355.
[3] John, iv, 29.

the archbishop heard the whole sad tale. When he and his suite returned home, the change wrought in the secretary soon became the subject of general comment. One day the latter met the president of the seminary, who at once asked him what had come over him and where had all his fun and liveliness gone to. And then and there the president also was made the recipient of his story. In fact this truly grateful and humble man kept telling everybody he met of all that happened in Caposele. His master obviously could no longer keep him in his service. However, he sent him back to Rome with a letter of recommendation to a certain Monsignor Casoni, a near relative of his own. In Rome, as elsewhere, he told his new master what had occurred and fired the prelate with something of his own enthusiasm for Gerard. A certain cardinal heard all about it and wrote to Monsignor Nicolai to send Gerard to Rome. On the arrival of his letter, the saint was dead. For the few remaining months of his life he kept up a correspondence with his famous penitent. Unfortunately none of it has come down to us.

But St. Gerard Majella was destined to do more than lay at the feet of his Master an occasional soul plucked from the jaws of hell as he went about his lowly and specific tasks of a laybrother in his monastery. He was, as we have said, actually to enter the Vineyard side by side with the missionary Fathers of his community, sometimes even preceding them in their sacred work and making ready the fruit for the gathering, and sometimes, too, following the harvesters and seeing to it that their harvesting was permanent and secure. To judge from the numerous place-names mentioned as scenes of his virtues and miracles, he must have spent much of his short life as a Redemptorist away from his convent home. And this was in fact the case. No bushel was to hide his light, nor were monastic walls to hem in the sphere of his activities. Providence brought it all about.

The Neapolitan Fathers of Gerard's day were wont to take a laybrother about with them on their apostolic journeys who would give a hand in domestic work and help to look after their material wants in the houses in which they stayed. The length of the missions and the unusual number of the missioners called for some arrangement like this, as community life was lived practically as at home. We can imagine how the kind and thoughtful hostesses and housekeepers in the presbyteries and private homes to which Redemptorists in these lands are accustomed to-day would frown on such an intruder into the business of their hospitality —unless of course he were a miracle-working Gerard.

Again, the times of which we write were hard times, and as the community and the missioners did not live on air, a Brother was often needed to do a little " quest-ing," if the community found itself in straits, as it frequently did in those days, or if the parochial larder were to meet the requirements of the missioners. The house of Iliceto in particular, where Gerard spent most of his short life, was often in sore distress. In the early days of this foundation St. Alphonsus had written to Father Rossi : " Let us be comforted, dear Father ; without belonging to any mendicant Order at all, we shall have to do a little begging here."[1] As a matter

---

[1] Cfr. Lettera 19 Dec., 1744.

of fact, no Redemptorist foundation had such slender resources to fall back upon as Iliceto. So there was no way out of it ; if the community were to survive, friends and benefactors had to be approached and the sources of charity in the various parishes where the Fathers worked, openly if reluctantly tapped.

Furthermore, transport and correspondence in Gerard's day must have been very makeshift and uncertain, when the steam-engine and the telegraph had not yet revolutionised both and when the motor 'bus and telephone were still undreamt of things. And yet business had to be done and communication established between country and town and between one community and another, and the laybrother's walking and riding powers were frequently called into requisition. All this naturally meant more protracted absences than would be necessary to-day.[1]

But there was another reason, too, more personal to Gerard, for all this going abroad and holding intercourse with men. Men soon knew Gerard to be what he was, and they were calling out for him. They knew that within those monastery walls of Iliceto and Caposele was a saint of the first order and a wonder-worker to boot ; and they wanted him. It was not for nothing that visitors and retreatants of all conditions—clerical and lay, the well-to-do and the lowly—spent some days

---

[1] Writing as late as 1915, Edward Hutton says : " Indeed the only thing the traveller need fear in the South is distance : the distances between the greater places . . . . are enormous ; and this fact alone makes walking for the most part impossible. Nowhere else except in Spain is distance, I think, so overwhelmingly impressed upon the traveller."—*Naples and Southern Italy*, p. 139.

under the same roof with this extraordinary man of God. They brought back the good tidings to their dioceses and towns and homes that a saint—a real saint—was walking in their midst, at no great distance at all, and a saint, moreover, who seemed to have been endowed with something of the omnipotence of God. And so bishops, priests and laymen of influence and distinction clamoured for him, that they might be edified by his example and enlightened by his wisdom and aided by his superhuman powers. Superiors, however, were wisely slow in yielding to such appeals. Gerard was a laybrother, and the sphere of his activity was not where he was now being called. He was a man, and the dangers inherent in such a departure from his normal life were obvious. And so for long Gerard's rectors—particularly Fathers Cafaro and Fiocchi—held out in their refusal to let him go ; until they were at length convinced that special obligations towards individuals and the belief that the glory of God and the good of souls were really calling for his services induced them to give way.

And thus it came about that Gerard Majella, that half-angelic being, whose conversation was so eminently in heaven and who found his dearest delight in intercourse with God, saw his lot cast amongst the noisy haunts of men and was called upon to look sin and sinners in the face. Indeed had Gerard never set foot outside his monastery, it would have been no easy task for him to hide his holiness. There is nothing so telltale, for the good odour of Christ has a way of permeating every atmosphere and is stronger than stones. And so, especially during the last three years of his life,

Gerard went up and down the land, sometimes alone and sometimes in company with others, visiting innumerable villages and towns and bringing with him as he went his unearthly holiness, his tremendous spiritual powers, and a reputation that grew with his days.

Perhaps some of our readers will have already asked themselves what did Gerard look like. And perhaps this is the place best suited for the answer to that question. We fear we are unable to satisfy their curiosity on the point as fully as they would wish. We know he was a tall and lean man whose bones could be numbered. His head was unusually large, a fact that was the source of much merriment to the companions of his childhood: *Gerardo capo grosso*, they would call him. He had a high forehead, elongated features, and cheeks dug deeply into by penance. His face was usually pale, but flushed swiftly when he was in ecstasy, or when he spoke on holy things, or when he received Communion and assisted at Mass, or when he strove to break through the stone of a sinner's heart. Then that face at times seemed literally on fire. It was normally lit up with an extraordinary serenity and joy. Beyond these authentic details is guess-work. Apart from a painting made from a waxen cast taken after death, we know of no contemporary portrait. To sit for one would have been, we should imagine, one of the most difficult obediences ever given the saint. There are many pictures of him with which we are familiar, differing much in the degree to which they flatter. They cannot all be authentic. Perhaps the phrases used by a witness: *volto di paradiso* . . . a heavenly face, *faccia di un angelo in carne* . . . the face of an angel in the flesh,[1] best sum up for us what that face was really like. A floodlit building, apart altogether from its architectural merits or demerits, can always be a thing of beauty. And, we think, the face of a great saint like Gerard Majella, lit up with the glow of his tremendous love for God, must have been beautiful with a beauty altogether independent of outline and complexion. "A man of outstanding virtue and intelligence," writes La Bruyère, "who passes for such, is not ugly, even when his features are misshapen; or, if he is ugly, his ugliness makes no impression."[2] Surely those eyes that gazed so often on divine things and were fixed more on heaven than on earth, must have been luminous with a light that drew and fascinated men. Sinners shrank from them, until sinners they ceased to be; holy souls could not look at them enough.

Let us now see St. Gerard in the Vineyard. It will be of interest to hear some contemporary comment. One witness tells us that he collaborated unremittingly with the Fathers on the missions, especially by his zeal in instructing the people. He eagerly sought out those who had strayed from the path of duty, had private talks with them, and thus led them back to the path of virtue. His particularly pleasant and engaging ways ensured him complete success. The Fathers used to say that the labours and example of Gerard did more good than a thousand missions and sermons."[3] "Where-ever he accompanied the missionary Fathers," adds

---

[1] In Apost. no. 14, § 124 ; In Ord. no. 14, § 142.
[2] *Caractères*, p. 416.
[3] In Apost. no. 7, § 345.

Father Ripoli, " he alone did more spiritual good than all the Fathers together would have done."[1] Tannoia is very explicit on the subject. Speaking of a visit the saint paid to Cedagna, he writes : " He could well be called ' the hunter of souls ' ; at home and abroad he was all eyes to catch them and bring them back to God . . . . The good Brother had not a moment to himself. Countless people, who might almost be styled his ' penitents ', were around him even at night, that they might hear his edifying words. Priests and gentlemen were to be seen amongst them . . . .[2] His voice was the voice of virtue. He did not speak, he thundered and wielded such a sway over hearts that stones became wax in his hands. When he reproved amendment followed, when he spoke of sin it was held in abhorrence ; a mere wish of Brother Gerard was a command for all. An eminent prelate once remarked : ' God speaks through his lips. We may not gainsay him, or rather, I should say, we must obey him.' I am not enlarging on the numerous conversions of abandoned souls won back for Jesus Christ by this holy Brother, and led to penance. Their number is too great. Fathers Margotta and Caione asserted that a hundred missioners could not have done what his zeal and insight into the hearts of men enabled him to do. There is not a district in the neighbourhood of Iliceto, Caposele or elsewhere that could not relate its prodigies of conversion wrought by him . . . "[3] Speaking of a mission in Calitri, he writes : " Prophecies, conversions, the reading of hearts

---

[1] In Apost. no. 12, § 50.
[2] English Edit., p. 329.
[3] Cap. xiv.

were things of daily occurrence, and the other Fathers had nothing to do but see that sinners already contrite were fit for sacramental absolution."[1] " Our Fathers were unanimous in saying," writes Berruti, " that Brother Gerard did more good by his zeal, his reading of hearts, and much more by the example of his own life, than many missioners would have done by a long course of exhausting missions."[2] Speaking of his stay in Naples, Tannoia writes as follows : " Crowds came to our house every day to see him : some to consult him, others to enkindle their fervour by listening to his holy conversation, others again to lay bare the sad state of their consciences and prepare for a good confession. Some came to recommend themselves to his prayers ; some, finally, to implore graces and heavenly favours in their temporal needs . . . . Even distinguished members of the secular and regular clergy were amongst his callers."[3]

He was in all truth what he had been called : a " hunter of souls." To vary the metaphor slightly, he was what Christ said He would make of His two disciples Peter and Andrew—" fishers of men " (Matt. iv, 19). And many a great fish Gerard landed for his Master. " I present you with this big fish," he once said as he handed over one of his catches to a confessor, " you'll find it nice."[4] Sometimes, under one pretext or another, he would seek out sinners in their own homes ; sometimes he would accost them in the middle of the

---

[1] Cap. xxix.
[2] P. 98.
[3] Cap. xxv.
[4] Berruti, p. 93.

street and work his way into their heart, thus gaining
a right of entry to their conscience. When he had
succeeded in touching them he would follow them home,
draw a vivid picture of the wretched state of their soul,
and finally win them over to God. It was generally
said that he had but to cast his eyes on a sinner to
dispose him and work his will with him. But when
gentleness failed, he could be stern and terrible. With
the obstinate he would argue, plead, insist, often on
his knees and with streaming eyes. When he spoke
of hell, sinners seemed to see it opened beneath their
feet ; when he spoke of God and His love, his face was
aflame and his hearers felt driven to renounce all this
world could give for the sake of heaven. He had the
all-compelling power of great sanctity and shook and
swayed men's hearts with a force they could not with-
stand. We are told that whenever a sinner turned a
deaf ear to the exhortations of the missioners (who
counted so many men of outstanding holiness amongst
them) he was turned over to Brother Gerard, who soon
led him back a sincere and willing penitent to the feet
of the confessor.

The following letter to Gerard's Rector at Iliceto,
Father Fiocchi, from a certain Father Scoppa tells us
what he saw at Corato :—

[1] " Very Reverend Father Rector,

" Divine Providence sent Brother Gerard to Corato
unexpectedly, or rather through a miraculous ruling,
for the saving of souls so dear to Him ; for his example

---

[1] Benedetti, pp. 147-149.

has stirred up the devotion of the whole population and wrought wonderful conversions. The well-to-do classes —both men and women—followed him about in crowds, and a single word from him about the things of God was enough to awaken wonder and compunction in their hearts. Words would fail me, Father, were I to write details on the subject. Your Reverence cannot conceive the multitude of his followers in the city. They never left him and carried him around as if he were a saint just come down from heaven. Then, not satisfied with having conversed with him throughout the day, innumerable gentry and ecclesiastics thronged the house of Signore Felice Papaleo, which they would not leave till six or seven in the evening, urging him the whole time to tell them something about God. And it was wonderful how every word that came from Gerard's lips pierced the hearts of all his hearers. At the mere mention of anything about God by him silence fell upon them and deep sighs could be heard, for with a few words he softened and terrified the hardest hearts. Aroused by the example of his sanctity, the gentry not only want a mission in Corato, but from fifteen to twenty of them want to go (to the monastery of Iliceto) to make a retreat, and many, moreover, are urged to leave the world. Honestly I am beside myself.

"And all this is little compared to what I have yet to tell you ; for not only has the love of God been enkindled by means of this Brother in the hearts of the faithful in general, but a certain community of nuns who were very relaxed has been reformed by one appearance of the Brother in their midst, and one single talk from him was so effective that it induced them to turn aside from all sorts of vanities and yield submission to the Mother Superior, which previously could not be brought about. Now they obey her promptly . . . . Father, I can give you no idea of all that God has wrought through this Brother. All good men want him back here again when the mission takes place. And I humbly beg of you, for the love of Jesus Christ, to send him, as it is a question of God's greater glory.

" I should like to write at greater length, but were I to write all I could time would fail me. I hope to go and speak with you in person, D.V., when I will tell you many wonderful things.

I remain, etc . . . . "

It can well be imagined how eagerly the missionary Fathers of the community sought to enlist Gerard's services when going on their apostolic journeys. With him on their staff success was assured. Nor was it only when in company with his missionary confrères that he achieved wonders of conversion. Bishops, priests, townspeople would appeal to his superiors for Gerard whenever there was serious trouble to be dealt with. As we have seen, superiors did not jump at such invitations; however, there was no way out of it at times, and results soon justified their acquiescing.

In the year 1753, there was trouble in Castelgrande. In the street along whose cobble-stones Gerard had once been cruelly dragged by a band of mischievous boys stood the house of the Carusi family. It was in front of it that he had risen bruised and bleeding, but rejoicing that he was accounted worthy to suffer something for the name of Jesus. In this same house Gerard was now

badly wanted, for within its walls was deadly and undying hatred. Many years previously Don Marco Carusi's
son Francesco, a lad of twenty, had quarrelled with a
notary—one Martino Carusi—from the same district and
perhaps a relative, had fought a duel with him and in
it had lost his life. The young man's parents had
never forgiven. Never would they forgive. Relatives of
the guilty man had left no stone unturned to heal the
wound, but to no purpose. The injured father and
mother were adamant and had entrenched themselves
within that most formidable of fortresses, a hating heart.
It became a blood-feud in deadly earnest. The evil
thing spread. Rival sympathies stood arrayed in rival
parties, and there was an ever-present danger of a clash.
So things stood when somebody thought of Gerard. Yes,
what about Brother Gerard ? If, as seemed likely enough,
a miracle of grace were needed to effect a reconciliation,
surely Brother Gerard was the man to work it. He had
ever been an angel of peace wherever he went, and his
power over the heart of God and man was immense.
No sooner said than done. A few representative towns-
people called one day on Father Fiocchi, the rector, at
Iliceto and asked him to allow Brother Gerard to go to
Castelgrande and see what he could do towards removing
the scandal and re-establishing peace. For his own good
reasons Father Fiocchi was slow to comply with the
request. Castelgrande was some twenty-five miles away
—a long distance in those days—and after all, though
a saint, Gerard was but a laybrother and this sort of
thing was not his specific work. However, a letter from
Father Cafaro, who was giving a mission in an adjoining parish and who had thus an opportunity of making

himself acquainted with all the bearings of the case, decided the rector, who forthwith told Gerard to go. With him went Brother Francis Fiore. Brother Francis used to ride a little ahead of Gerard. He was thus often taken for the latter, and the country-folk would leave their work in the fields and run for his blessing. Whereupon Brother Francis would cry out in words that remind us of the Baptist's disclaimer : " I am not the saint ; there he is coming."[1]

It was anything but a pleasure trip. Those twenty-five miles had to be covered under a June sky, and they had but one mount between them. To add to the natural difficulties and discomforts of the way the powers of evil, scenting their overthrow in Castelgrande, took a hand in the business by trying to terrorise God's messenger of peace. What shape these terrors took is not recorded, but his challenging words have been : " By means of obedience I will carry out the command of God," he cried, " and do thou, firebrand of hell, rage and cast thyself into the abyss." [2] One curious incident of the journey has been handed down. As the day was falling, the travellers reached the foot of a mountain they had to cross. As Gerard had insisted on his companion riding, while he went on foot himself, he now felt very tired. Suddenly he beheld a grey horse approaching. Who owned it or whence it came—whether it was sent by God or the devil—was never known. The sequel seems to point to the latter source. Anyhow, Gerard mounted it and rode on with his companion. The mystery horse,

---

[1] Landi.
[2] Tannoia, Cap. xvii.

however, soon left the main road that led to Castelgrande and brought its rider close to a very dangerous ravine known by the name of *Di Fauce*. In stern words Gerard bade it change its course and bring him on to the main road again. Which it immediately did. Bearing in mind what we have already recorded of the saint's empire over demons and animals, we shall see nothing unusually hard of belief in the incident. It was but one of many signs Hell gave him on his way that it did not want him to go to Castelgrande. But Castelgrande was reached that evening about eight o'clock. The travellers were given hospitality by the mayor, Dr. Cajetan Frederici, a great friend of the Congregation. Now Gerard was well known in Castelgrande ; the holy tailor of Muro was not forgotten by its people, and they had witnessed many of his miracles ; and so, when it got about the following morning that he was in their midst, the whole town was in commotion, and Frederici's house became the rendezvous for every section of the population. They came for comfort and advice, and both were lavishly dispensed.

Gerard, however, did not lose sight of the object of his coming, and he lost no time in setting to work. He called on Signore Carusi. It was a saying of his that before speaking about God, we should first speak to Him. Not satisfied with doing this himself, he told Brother Francis to keep praying before the Blessed Sacrament while he was accomplishing his delicate and difficult mission. He was under no delusions as to what was before him. He knew his hot-blooded countrymen well. He knew it was no mere matter of human argument and persuasion he had undertaken. He was well re-

ceived by Signore Carusi, so well indeed that before
the interview ended, he ventured to suggest a reconciliation. However, though the man was softened and the
old bitterness had been seemingly allayed, this first
suggestion was definitely rejected. Gerard left, disappointed but hopeful. His hopes were well-founded.
As a result of a second interview the father gave way
completely and declared his willingness to forgive and
forget. Unfortunately, before the reconciliation could
actually take place, Gerard received an urgent letter
demanding his presence in Muro. As Muro was but a
mile and a quarter away, he went, requesting his host
Frederici to busy himself in the meantime in arranging
for a meeting between the two opposing parties on his
return. During his absence, however, the powers of
evil had likewise been busying themselves undoing the
good already effected in Castelgrande. On his return
a few days after, Gerard found that the pitch had been
queered.

Don Marco Carusi had indeed been won over, but
Gerard had evidently reckoned without Donna Teresa,
Don Marco's wife. A mother's love for her murdered
boy was now the measure of her mother's hatred for
his murderer, and her husband's declaration of his
willingness to bring about a reconciliation blew the
ever smouldering embers of her longing for revenge
into a fury of flame. She stopped her ears to all argument and appeal. She did something else. Opening a
drawer, she took from it a ghastly heirloom : the blood-
stained clothes of her slaughtered child. Holding them
close to her husband's face, while her daughters, steeped
in their mother's bitterness, looked on, she screamed :

" Look, look at these clothes and then go, if you can, and be reconciled ! This blood of your son cries for undying enmity against his murderer, and are you going to embrace him ! But the cries of a despairing mother will find someone to avenge my boy."[1] Then, flinging the garments dramatically at Don Marco's feet, she rushed like a fury from the room. It was more than the father could bear. The unholy fire of her own unrelenting hatred caught the tinder of his heart, and it flamed with hers. No, there would be no reconciliation. It was into this charged atmosphere that Gerard stepped on his return. When told of what had taken place in his absence, he merely remarked : " No, no, the devil will not win. God must be victorious."[2] He went immediately to Carusi's house. He renewed his appeals, this time before both parents. But he soon realised that he was addressing two stones. Then he too did something else ; he too could be dramatic ; he too had a blood-stained heirloom to appeal to. Going on his knees, he drew forth his crucifix, laid it at their feet, and thrice asked them to tread upon it. They grew pale and recoiled. But his ruthless logic pursued them : they must either forgive, as Christ had bidden them do, or by their mortal hatred crucify that Christ again and tread Him under foot. They could not have it both ways. He confronted them pitilessly with the frightful inconsistency of refusing to tread on a crucifix while outraging the Crucified. The appeal and the argument, the face and the voice of him who was using

[1] Benedetti, pp. 156-157.

[2] *Ibid.*, p. 157.

both shook the citadel of their hardened hearts, but did not bring it down. Solemnly he then addressed them : " Know that when I first came here, I came at the request of others ; now it is God Himself Who sends me. Your son is in Purgatory and will remain there as long as you persist in your obstinacy. If you want to deliver him quickly, forgive quickly, and then have five Masses said for his soul. If you will not do this, expect a severe but just chastisement. What the chastisement will be I do not tell you, so as not to terrify you more ; but it will certainly fall on you."[1] And so saying he turned to go. The fortress fell. They stopped him, fell on their knees before the crucifix and declared their readiness to forgive. It was not a gracious yielding. Anyhow, the reconciliation did take place, and lasting peace descended on the community. As a gesture of finality and completeness, the garments that had so dramatically intervened in Gerard's holy work were washed clean of their accusing stains. About three hundred people followed the peacemaker for more than a mile out of the town on his departure, heaping blessings on his holy head. After that, many of the townspeople of Castelgrande travelled from six to seven miles to Caposele every Saturday to get confession and receive Holy Communion on the Sunday morning, though it meant spending the night away from their homes and sometimes sleeping in the open air. Father Cafaro had good reason for saying on hearing of his expedition to Castelgrande, " Wherever that man goes, he puts

---

[1] Benedetti, p. 157.

the whole countryside in a ferment."[1]

More than once Gerard was made the mouthpiece of God's wrath when dealing with hardened sinners. A sin unfortunately but too common amongst his countrymen, and one that must have sent a peculiarly sharp pang through his loving heart, was blasphemy. If anything could lash his gentle soul into a holy anger it was to hear his God and Lord affronted in this revoltingly personal way. On one occasion, when crossing the Piazza di San Marco in Muro in company with the president of the seminary, he met a man uttering dreadful blasphemies against the Blessed Trinity. Addressing the blasphemer, he said : " You will not stop ? Then God will stop you."[2] Three days later, the man was shot dead on the same square.

If Gerard let men see that God was not to be trifled with, God let men see that His servant was not to be trifled with either. The following incident occurred during his second visit to Naples, some months before his death. In order to avoid the notoriety that was his lot everywhere he went in the capital, he shunned the main thoroughfares as much as possible and usually kept to the secluded bystreets. Now during this first visit to the city, while passing through one such alley, two prostitutes had accosted him and thrown ridicule on his modest and prayerful demeanour. On that occasion, he had succeeded in shaking them off without saying a word. On his return to the metropolis, however, the same two wretched women met him again

---

[1] Tannoia, cap. xvii.
[2] In Ord. no. 9, § 30.

as he was about to enter the same street. This time they were more aggressive and unabashed. It was the carnival season, when licentiousness and revelry were abroad. One of the pair had a tambourine in her hand, the second another musical instrument hung about her neck. Impudently barring the way, they began to play their instruments and dance lewdly in front of him, accompanying the performance with loud laughter and obscene words and gestures. Gerard's eyes flamed with holy indignation. He stood still, his hands on his hips, and then, raising his voice, said solemnly : " So you won't stop ? and you wish to witness a great chastisement of God ? "[1] Scarcely had he spoken when one of the women, probably the bolder of the two, fell to the ground, exclaiming : " *Madonna mia, muoio, Madonna mia, muoio* . . . I am dying, I am dying." She was dead. Four men who had seen her fall ran over and carried her into the house. Her companion fled in terror. Let us hope that that last cry of a wayward child, uttered even in that moment of swift retribution, reached her Mother in heaven and did not go unheard.[2]

With impostors of all kinds, as we have seen, Gerard

---

[1] Benedetti, p. 342.

[2] What really happened the unfortunate woman is not described with uniform precision by all biographers. Berruti has it thus : " Come se fosse stata colpita da un fulmine, cadde a terra per subitanea apoplesia." (p. 166) According to the first French life (p. 427), " elle tomba comme foudroyée en disant : ' O Madone, je meurs.' Elle resta sans mouvement, et quatre hommes, accourus au bruit de sa chute, la transportèrent dans sa demeure." Benedetti (p. 342) says almost identically the same thing : " cadde tramortita a terra." He refers us to Landi, Tannoia and the Acts of the process, but quotes from none of them. In the English edition of Tannoia (p. 365) we read : " one of them fell down half dead and had to be carried home."

stood on no ceremony. The following case has the peculiar merit that it was the express desire of the individual concerned that, in the event of the saint's life being written, her story should be told. There is a species of person—and the species is not extinct—who display their piety much as they would display their talents or their wealth and seek to move in circles where they hope such things will be seen to the best advantage. Such a person was Teresa Moronti of Melfi. Teresa sought to move in saintly circles and to rub shoulders with people who enjoyed a reputation for sanctity. With these she would talk sanctity with remarkable fluency and gusto. A certain Father Martino, an Augustinian and the most renowned confessor in Melfi, was of course Teresa's spiritual physician. Naturally she would be seen giving her custom to none but the best. Now, probably towards the close of October, 1753, Father Fiocchi, the Rector of Iliceto, came to Melfi to preach a novena in preparation for the feast of St. Theodore, November 9th. At the express wish of the bishop, Gerard accompanied him. As a result never had there been such a novena. Gerard was lionized. Everybody—lay and ecclesiastical—wanted to see the saint. Naturally Teresa Moronti wanted to see him. Perhaps she wanted still more to be seen by him. Gerard would appreciate Teresa Moronti. Accordingly, one day she met him as he was leaving the bishop's palace and

---

Now in the Acts we read (no. 7, § 276) as follows : " La più petulante cadde *morta* sul suolo." Certainly a sudden death seems to be more in proportion to the ' gran castigo di Dio ' which the saint threatened than a mere fainting fit or even an apoplectic stroke which had not a fatal ending. And it does not necessarily rule out the final act of mercy on the part of God.

lost no time in introducing herself and incidentally displaying her spiritual finery. Without a word or a wince Gerard heard her out. Then with great earnestness he thus addressed her : " My daughter, why are you trying to palm off your stories on me ? You have been making sacrilegious confessions and communions these many years, and now you want to pass for a saint ! Go and make a good confession if you do not want to be damned."[1] To give her her due, the poor lady did not want to be damned. She went at once in a great state to Padre Martino. Without mentioning any specific sin, she merely told him she was anxious to make a general confession, as Brother Gerard had advised her to do so. The confessor, naturally enough, saw no reason why this very pious penitent of his should be so disturbed by the remark of a laybrother. After all, holy as Gerard was, he was not a priest. So good Padre Martino told Teresa bluntly enough to have sense. Teresa, however, persisted in her request, assuring him of her conviction that her conscience was in a bad way and that Brother Gerard, evidently enlightened from above, had truly enlightened her. The poor priest now quite unnecessarily and rather unwisely lost his temper and said some uncomplimentary things about this Brother Gerard. Which, of course, did not mend matters. Teresa had no peace of mind until she went to another confessor—a Canon Leonardo Rossi—and told him plainly the ugly truth that for the past ten years she had been concealing a sin through shame and communicating sacrilegiously. This priest she now allowed

---

[1] Tannoia, cap. xviii.

to tell her whole story to Padre Martino and, as we have said, to all future generations, if Gerard's life ever came to be written. Meantime Teresa made good, and the whited sepulchre was changed into a shining temple of God.

Another incident of this kind occurred during the saint's stay in Naples. One day he entered a shop in company with a priest to buy some beads and medals. The shopkeeper began to display his own piety with even greater alacrity than his pious wares. Gerard listened and said nothing. Seizing the first chance he got, he drew the man aside and unceremoniously unmasked him by telling him amongst other things of a sin he had never confessed and which God and himself could alone have known. Gerard then went out, leaving the shopkeeper dumbfounded and thoroughly alarmed. So alarmed was he that he told the priest, who had remained behind, all that happened. Fortunately he lost no time in telling a confessor also.

On another occasion he drove home with dramatic force a lesson sorely needed by those who seem to lose all sense of proportion and set an undue value on objects of piety while neglecting to put the house of their soul in order. In Vietri a lady whose life was far from being what it ought to be once asked Gerard for a picture of the Blessed Virgin. As he handed it to her, he said: "There is the picture for you, but think of what may happen you and recommend yourself to most holy Mary, for your days are few."[1] Though she was still young and in perfect health, she had scarcely reached her home

---

[1] Berruti, p. 220.

when she was seized with a high fever. Recalling the saint's words, and wisely fearing the worst, she sent in all haste for a confessor, made a sincere confession and died within three days.

Gerard's prophetic warnings, always fulfilled, were a powerful weapon in his hands when dealing with sinners. On the occasion of his visit to Muro, during his stay in Castelgrande of which we have just spoken, he was the guest of a certain Alexander Piccolo. Now it so happened that Alexander's wife Catherine had these many years been living in sacrilege through her unwillingness to confess a certain sin. Gerard mentioned the sin to herself and warned her to make a good confession, as she was soon to appear before God. He furthermore reminded her to invoke the holy names of Jesus and Mary that thus she might die a good death. At the moment Catherine was in the best of health. However, in a few short months, she fell ill and died so unexpectedly that she could not receive the last sacraments. Meeting her husband the saint said : " Your wife had the good fortune to die with the names of Jesus and Mary on her lips ; I offered my communion for her soul."[1]

When passing through Calitri, on his way to Naples for the second time, Gerard was told of a certain well-to-do man named Berilli whose sole concern seemed to be to have a good time in this world, leaving his chance of a good eternity in the next to take care of itself. Gerard called on him, spoke seriously of the things that matter and tried to induce him to make a

---

[1] Landi.

retreat that was soon to be given in Caposele. Berilli was quite courteous, heard his visitor out, but produced the whole armoury of arguments used by such men against making a retreat. Holding the wrong end of the stick, he urged the press of business and the like. All his arguments, however, broke helplessly against Gerard's reasoning. Thereupon Berilli took final refuge in the cowardly compromise so familiar in such cases : he deferred doing what he admitted had to be done. He promised to go to Caposele in the following October. " But you will not see October," came the solemn rejoinder.[1] He did not see it. Though in excellent health at the time, he took suddenly ill in August and died in a few days, apparently impenitent, according to one witness.

Strange as it may sound, the confessional was actually the greatest and perhaps the most striking sphere of Gerard's apostolic activities. His liturgical title in the Church is that of *confessor*. Now every intelligent Catholic knows that by *confessor* here is meant, not a priest who sits in the confessional, but a follower of Christ, an outstanding exponent of Christianity. Yet perhaps no lay confessor of Christ ever went as near being a confessor in the sacramental sense as did St. Gerard Majella. As we have said, he did everything but give absolution. About his theological lore we shall have a word to say later on. We have mentioned his reading of consciences ; as Tannoia puts it, " he had almost a more intimate knowledge of the consciences of others than of his own."[2]

---

[1] Tannoia, cap. xxix.
[2] English Edit., p. 301.

We have seen him use this gift when dealing with souls that came his way in the course of retreats given in his own monastery. We have seen him use it no less strikingly when he went abroad on his many journeys. We hope we shall be serving a useful purpose by giving still further instances. Not without reason has Gerard won for himself the title of Patron of a Good Confession. There will always be call for his patronage in this respect.

A certain notary in Muro, named Pietrangelo de Rubertis, had a particularly fine cherry tree in his vineyard. One night he spied a marauder paying it his attentions. He succeeded in capturing the fellow, but dismissed him with a warning as a first offender. However, the cherries had evidently proved stronger than the warning, and he returned for a second helping. The owner caught him a second time, but, though very angry, gave him a second chance. On the thief returning for a third helping, the notary shot him dead and buried the body in the vineyard. The crime was committed at night and far from any inhabited locality. Thus the missing man was never traced, his slayer never caught. He concealed the deed, even from his wife, and, worse still, concealed it in confession and lived in sacrilege for many years. On the occasion of Gerard's first visit to Muro after his profession, God sent him across the notary's path. The saint looked at him, and then, without further ceremony, thus addressed him : "Signore, when confessing to your spiritual father you did not disclose your murder of that man who stole your cherries and whom you buried in your vineyard."[1]

---

[1] In Ord. no. 7, § 97.

The notary was dumbfounded. He lost no time in making a good confession, the first for long years.

When passing through Rochetta, on his way to Iliceto, Gerard was informed that a certain workingman from Calabria was living in concubinage to the great scandal of the town. Gerard sent for him and he came. He so laid bare the secrets of the sinner's conscience that the man became thoroughly frightened and repentant. He burst into tears, promised to amend, and kept his word.

While crossing the piazza in Auletta on one occasion, he accosted a man who was a perfect stranger to him, drew him aside, and asked him how he could live in peace. He then mentioned a particular sin he had never confessed and told him to recover God's grace at once. The man fell on his knees, admitted everything and followed his advice.

Father Giovenale was one day hearing the confession of a man. Gerard passed, casting a displeased and troubled glance at the confessional. He approached the Father as he emerged, told him that the man's confession was not valid and implored of him to get him back. The Father knew Gerard too well to demur and called his penitent back.

A young girl was leaving our church in Caposele one morning after having been to confession. Gerard happened to be there at the time. Calling her aside, he began : " What brought you here ? " " To go to confession," was the reply. " I know," returned Gerard, " but you have not made a good one."[1] He then told the terrified girl a sin she had just concealed through

---

[1] Tannoia, (English Edit.), p. 379.

shame. She went back to the confessor.

We give the following instance in Father Landi's own words.[1] " Amongst these conversions we wish especially to relate that of a young woman whom matters of business often brought to our monastery. For many years she had scoffed at the anxious care of which she had been made the object on the part of some of our most prudent and zealous Fathers. All they got for their untiring efforts to bring her back to the right path was to hear from her that no scruple worried her and that her conscience accused her of no sin. In fact, as far as externals went, she had all the appearance of being a spiritual person ; but her soul was stained with a thousand sins and had long since been sullied with the foulest enormities. Gerard, supernaturally enlightened on her pitiful state, accosted her one day and got into chat with her, as he was wont to do in the case of souls whom he knew to be in need. The result was that he forced her to admit everything she had been concealing from so many confessors. Then, having awakened contrition in her in a wonderful way by his glowing words, he sent her to the rector of the house of Iliceto, Father Fiocchi, who was passing through *Materdomini*, in order that she might make a general confession. She made it with such sorrow and with so many tears, and with so strong and constant a purpose of amendment, that she has been ever since a model for her companions. She now dresses in black. She has been thus for many years and now more than ever she continues to edify everyone by her way of life entered

---

[1] Landi.

upon with so much fervour. Whenever she recalls Gerard, it is never without tears, convinced as she is that he was for her a true angel of God sent to help her to escape hell."

It is well to note that in all such instances there was never any attempt at denying the charges brought against these sinners by the saint. Besides, saints are not easily bluffed. The sudden impact of the unexpected truth simply smothered any notion the accused may have had of denial or resistance ; there was always immediate and complete surrender.

Indeed, apart from the confessional altogether, it was never a wise thing to come into Gerard's company with a burdened conscience. One could have no guarantee that he did not know all about it. He was once chatting familiarly in S. Gregorio with the archpriest Robertazzi whose guest he happened to be. A gentleman called in and joined in the conversation. All of a sudden Gerard changed the subject and, looking grave, put a case of moral theology to his host. " Signor Arciprete," he began, " suppose a man had made up his mind to commit a grave sin, but, touched by grace, retracted his guilty intention, would he be obliged to tell this in confession, even though he repented before committing the act ?"[1] The archpriest was surprised at the seeming irrelevancy of the question. However, he answered it according to accepted principles and said nothing. We may be sure that Gerard was too charitable to look at the newcomer while he propounded his difficulty. Anyhow, whether the fact that the latter's conscience was " caught "

---

[1] Landi.

like the conscience of the guilty king in *Hamlet* hastened
his departure or no, he very soon rose to go. Before
leaving the presbytery, he drew the priest into another
room, told him he had a saint under his roof and humbly
admitted that the question proposed by Gerard answered
his situation only too well. He made a clean breast of
everything to his own shame and Gerard's glory. The
reader will no doubt have remarked how well in keeping
with their racial characteristics is the frequency and
readiness with which so many of Gerard's converts
switched from concealing sin from confessors to
generously divulging it amongst strangers.

Nor was it the consciences of those alone who did
not tell enough in confession that Gerard read: he
likewise read the consciences of those troubled ones
who tried to tell too much. To the scrupulous he came
as a boon and a blessing. "Religious and priests,"
writes Tannoia, "confessors and spiritual directors
persons of distinction applied to Gerard to have their
doubts cleared up and to be freed from their worries
Even several of the principal members of our own Con
gregation, though learned and enlightened men, found
peace only in having recourse to him . . . . Father D
Francesco Garzilli, a former canon in Foggia and a
theologian and wise and experienced director of souls
though more than a septuagenarian, in all his spiritual
troubles would consult him with the utmost humility."
The following letter from the laybrother to the priest
would almost make us believe that there had been an
accidental interchange of signatures :—" May the grace

---

[1] Tannoia, (English Edit.), p. 394.

of God fill the heart of Your Reverence and may the most Holy Mary preserve it for you. My dear Father, I am much consoled and rejoice greatly at the game the Divine Majesty is playing with you, and I hope He will grant you a complete victory. Come now! no more fears, but be of good cheer, for God is with Your Reverence and will not abandon you. Your Reverence has doubts about your confessions. This is just a slight mortification that God wishes to send you, by thus keeping you worried. You say you are the cause of it yourself. Necessarily you must think so ; otherwise you would not be worried. It is thus His Divine Majesty deals with His favourites, allowing them to be troubled through not seeing that it all comes from Him. If Your Reverence knew that it all came from Him, where would the trial come in ? Everything would then be heaven on earth. Trust and hope in God, my dear Father, and for charity's sake recommend me to Jesus Christ and to most Holy Mary, that they may bless us both." [1] And in a letter to a priest who was unduly anxious about his own state as well as about his work for others he writes : " With regard to the scruples about your past life, your conscience has been well examined, as I know, more than once ; so your Reverence must not think any more about it. Your worries and doubts are all the wiles of the infernal foe, whose aim is to make you lose that beautiful peace of conscience. Therefore pay no further heed to such suggestions and drive them away as real temptations. Be careful to preserve true interior peace, so that you may be able to make all the more progress in holy per-

[1] In Ord. no. 7, § 565.

fection. Concerning the rule of conduct, I am sending it to you in accordance with your Reverence's wishes ; follow the first I gave you and no other . . . . As for your persistent scruples about the confessional, I tell you that this trouble of yours is truly a temptation to induce you to abandon God's work, which has been destined for you from eternity for your greatest spiritual profit. I tell you in God's name never to yield to such a temptation, for if your Reverence were to abandon the confessional, it would be to the great detriment of your spiritual life ; if you gave that up, God would not give you the great reward He has in store for you . . . . With regard to your knowledge, God has given you as much as you need for your work . . . . I thank you for the affection you bear me altogether beyond my deserts . . . I beg of you to pray always for me, as I need it sorely . . . kissing your sacred hands, etc. . . ."

There was a poor distressed nun who was a prey to scruples that no confessor seemed able to settle satisfactorily. A single interview with Gerard—who began by telling her what her troubles precisely were (not a bad beginning !)—laid them to rest forever.

In Calitri a lady of high social standing was a prey to certain worries of conscience which she could not bring herself to reveal to any body. She heard about Gerard and called on him. However, at the last moment her courage failed her and she became tongue-tied in his presence. Seeing her embarrassment, he said : " Well, since you wont do the talking, I will."[1] He there and

---

[1] Landi.

then took up her hidden anxieties one after the other and gave each the requisite solution. She afterwards declared that nobody could have known by any natural means what Gerard had spoken about.

In the light of all these instances we can easily understand how immensely popular this strange unofficial "confessor" became. No wonder he had busy days. We are told that the house in which he stayed in Lacedonia was like a public meeting-place where there was a ceaseless come-and-go of people. He had scarcely a moment he could call his own and was kept at his truly wonderful work till far into the night. As we have said, he was called a "hunter of souls." And hunt them he did. He would go from house to house in his hunting, armed with his mighty weapons. There he would lay siege to the citadel of their heart with a boldness that shrank from nothing and a patience that never flagged, and capture it for Christ. "The conversions he wrought in the neighbourhood of Caposele," writes Tannoia, "were innumerable. He never left the monastery without returning with some new labour of love, so that he was soon surrounded by as large a crowd of his dear penitents (if we may so call them) in Caposele as he had been in Iliceto, who followed him about wherever he went."[1]

At times his prey were driven supernaturally into his net. The reader will remember one Francis Testa, whose services as torturer Gerard had enlisted in the grotto at Iliceto. This is how they first met. Though Gerard was still but a novice, his superiors sometimes

[1] Cap. xxviii.

sent him out alone on one errand or another. Indeed
one motive they had in this was deliberately to distract
him from a state of recollection which they deemed
excessive. One day, when he was on his way to Sant'
Agata di Puglia, he came to a crossroads. An inner
voice said to him : " Stop ! a great sinner will soon be
here."[1] Gerard stopped and waited. He soon saw a
man coming against him. As he drew near, a face with
the melancholy and despair of sin told him he had his
man. Gerard stood his ground. The man glanced at
him furtively and quickened his pace, as though he
meant to pass him out. Gerard at once accosted him
and asked in the friendliest way where he was going.
He was told with a growl to mind his own business.
It was of course the very thing Gerard intended doing.
He was after his Father's business. He meant to be his
brother's keeper. He repeated his query kindlily,
suggesting that perhaps he could be of service to him.
" I am going about my business, let me pass, Friar,"
came the ungracious and uncompromising retort. The
man then tried to rush past, but this time Gerard held
him fast. Looking into those dour and angry eyes, he
said quietly : " I know you are in despair and are about
to give your soul to the devil. *Or via ; non è niente* . . .
Come, it is nothing ! God has sent me here especially
for you. Don't doubt it." These words were light and
fire for him. The clouds broke from his mind, his heart
melted into blessed and assuaging tears. At once, there
on that roadside, the poor fellow placed himself like
clay in Gerard's hands and made a clean breast of every-

[1] Landi.

thing. The saint gave him comfort and counsel and sent him to confession to Father Fiocchi in Iliceto. " Tell him," he said, " that I sent you. Make a grand confession and have no fear." So thorough was his repentance that he begged to be given work as a tailor in the monastery. He became a man of great prayer and penance and gave a great example to the community. In the circumstances we already know he made himself the very unwilling instrument of the saint's own penitential rigours. After many years, he went to Naples and there devoted himself to nursing the sick in a hospital till his death.

Sometimes it was the sinner himself who accosted Gerard and unwittingly fell into his toils. One day he was on his way home to Iliceto. When within a few miles of the monastery, near Monte Miglione, he met a youthful tramp on the road. Gerard's appearance at once aroused the latter's curiosity. And not without reason. His hat was probably the least shapely in the community, where the best was poor. An old much-patched cloak over an old much-patched habit hung loosely on his tall gaunt frame. His shoes had seen many much better days and had but little of their original leather left. We may take it for granted that he was not meticulously shaved. As he walked along lost in prayer, he must have looked unusually strange in the eyes of the young vagrant, who found it hard to make him fit into any of the categories of men in the world he knew. Indeed he was rather like a gipsy. Could he be a gipsy? The young man had enough religion left to believe in the devil (if that can be called religion), and if he had any interest at all in another world, it was chiefly in the lower one. The young man was thinking in terms of money. He associated gipsies with fortune-telling, and perhaps . . . perhaps . . . this odd-looking personage . . . . At the same time, the devil might have a hand in it, and he was not too anxious for many reasons to meet the devil just yet. At all events, the prospect of possible hidden treasure emboldened him to take risks. He stopped Gerard on the road and asked him if by any chance he might be a sorcerer. Supernaturally enlightened, Gerard saw at a glance with whom he had to do. For a moment he was taken aback by the nature of the question. However, he quickly jumped to the possible implications of his reply. Accordingly, he gave some sort of evasive answer. Yes, possibly he might be a sorcerer. Thus encouraged, the youth, judging that such a person was very possibly in quest of hidden treasure, offered his services. He would be in a position to cry halves. Gerard asked for nothing better. But he first made it clear that his enterprise called for skill and courage. Oh ! there was no doubt about the skill and courage ; if that was all that was needed, he was Gerard's man. And as they went along together, the youth began to regale the saint with vivid details of his misdeeds. Among the other feats of courage which, he thought, should qualify him for the adventure was the fact that he had been an absentee from the sacraments for six years. Gerard listened with feigned approval and delight, thinking hard the while and maturing his plans for the capture of the sinner's soul. Promising the youth that they would share the treasure, they walked along. At last they came to a dense wood. Gerard struck into it,

followed by his companion, with visions of the objective
glittering before the eyes of his mind. In the very thick
of it the saint halted. He evidently knew the exact
spot where the buried treasure was. Then Gerard
removed his cloak and slowly spread it on the ground.
This done, he rose silently and beckoned to his companion to approach. The latter obeyed. He bade him
kneel and join his hands. But by this time the youth
was thoroughly frightened. What did all this mean ?
What was going to happen ? Who or what was this
long lean weird-looking man now standing over him
in the depths of this silent solemn wood ? Did these
dark encompassing trees hide something sinister which
he was now about to see ? Was that patch of ground
covered by that old cloak about to open beneath him ?
Was hell about to come up ? He trembled as he knelt,
guessing fearfully at the unknown. Then Gerard, casting
a look to heaven and praying secretly, faced his companion and thus solemnly began : " I promised to find
you a treasure ; I am keeping my promise. But the
treasure I speak of is not of this world ; it is the treasure
of treasures, the treasure of paradise. If you wish to
see it, here it is."[1] He thereupon drew forth a crucifix
and held it to the young man's upturned face, bidding
him look well at the treasure he had long since cast
away for the vile and worthless vanities of sin. Then
for one half hour, as Landi tells us, in the gloom and
stillness of the forest, in fiery words that burned as
they fell, the preacher drove home the enormity and
folly of sin and the frightful havoc it had wrought in

---

[1] Landi.

the sinner's soul. As the young man listened—for he had to listen—to the detailing of his misdeeds, his whole being sagged and swayed and fell beneath the fiery torrent. All his sinful braggadocio was at an end. The swaggerer had crumpled up, and there was now at his feet nothing but a poor sobbing boy shaken with terror and remorse. "Save me, Father," he cried, taking Gerard for a priest. Then the preacher stopped. Raising the lad gently from his knees, he threw his arms about him and induced him to accompany him to Iliceto. There in a good confession he found the treasure he had been seeking all along, though not where it was to be had. After a few days of peace and prayer, he left the monastery, thanking God and blessing His servant.

There was nothing Gerard would not do—no pain or humiliation he would not undergo, no danger he would not face—if he could thereby win a soul to Christ. On such occasions Gerard Majella ceased to count. Martyrdom in such a cause would have been a delight as well as a glory. It did not come his way. But suffering did. We give the following striking instance related by Tannoia and Landi.

Between Foggia and Iliceto was a large tract of arable land, the property of the Duke of Bovino. The people had cut a wide path through it into Foggia, which gave them a shorter and easier way than that which led over the neighbouring hill. As a result, this land had suffered considerably, and with a view to asserting his rights, the Duke had hired men to keep trespassers away. He had evidently not been too happy in his choice, as some of these fellows took the law very much into their own hands and dealt summarily with offenders.

Their methods were more than rough-and-ready. Indeed Tannoia goes so far as to say that there had been " many fatal incidents."[1]

Now Gerard had been sent on some business to Foggia, and was riding home again alone along the forbidden path utterly unconscious of the prohibition of the Duke to use it. He was soon made painfully aware of it by a fellow rushing at him savagely and dealing him a blow with the butt-end of his musket, which severely injured a rib and brought the rider stunned from his horse. Even when his victim was down and completely at his mercy, the ruffian continued to use the vilest language, and pointing the musket at his heart, told him he had long been waiting to get his own back on a monk and that the opportunity had now been given him. As soon as Gerard had recovered himself, he knelt before the infuriated man and humbly apologised for his mistake. The apology was received with a fresh shower of blows. Then Gerard, bringing all his love for his Crucified Lord and all his hatred for what he considered to be his own sinful self to bear on the situation, clasped his hands submissively and said : " Strike, my brother, strike, you have good reason to do so[2]." This reaction to a brutal assault was something quite new in the experience of his assailant, and if ever a mild answer broke wrath, it broke it now. Gerard had dealt a shattering blow at the man's heart and conscience. Flinging away his musket and striking his forehead with both hands, he turned his reproaches on

---

[1] English Edit., p. 278.
[2] *Ibid.*p. 279.

himself. What had he done? What had he done? He had killed a saint? He had forsooth come very near it. He begged Gerard's forgiveness on his knees. Needless to say, it was to be had for the asking. The saint embraced him and apologised anew for his mistake. What alone concerned him now was the man's soul. As he had been definitely injured by the blow, he asked his assailant to help him to remount and then to get up himself behind and support him till they reached the monastery. During the remainder of the journey never a word passed Gerard's lips about what had happened. All the talk was indeed on Gerard's side, but it was all of the injury the man was doing his own soul and of the urgency of looking after it. On reaching the monastery, it was found that the saint was in a bad way. When questioned as to what had occurred, he said he had fallen from his horse! Moreover, he asked the rector to give something to the good man who had so kindly accompanied him home. It was certainly quite another view of the situation, which, without departing from the truth, adroitly changed a brutal aggressor into a generous and helpful friend. When seeing him off, Gerard just gave him a word of warning not to deal with others as he had dealt with him, as he might be the worse of it. Everything argued well. The man made no secret of the incident and actually returned to Iliceto to make a general confession. Indeed for some time he frequented the monastery much to the good of his soul. Alas! for habits of sin. Not so very long after, while he was again doing duty as a guard for the Duke, another laybrother—this time a Franciscan—came riding along the forbidden path, likewise wholly ignorant of regulations. There was a similar savage rush at this new trespasser. The Franciscan, seeing himself assailed, jumped from his horse and pleaded for mercy in the name of St. Francis and St. Anthony. But realising that he pleaded in vain and recognising that he was a match for his assailant, this stalwart son of *Il Poverello* wrenched the musket from him and dealt him a blow that in one way brought him to his senses and in another took them half away. When the good brother judged he had had enough, he smashed up the musket and rode straight to the Duke, who was then in residence at his country-seat. Displaying shoulders that bore witness to the violence of which he had been made the victim, he demanded that an end be forthwith put to the man's activities. The fellow was accordingly dismissed and the road left open. One would have thought that the offender would have had the wisdom to take such a lesson to heart. Far from it. He was shot dead some time later while involved in another quarrel and, according to one witness, on the very spot where he had maltreated Gerard. The latter wept bitterly on hearing of it. These tears of a saint were probably the only tears the ruffian got. To the very end Gerard never forgot him in his prayers. He had good reason to remember him, as he bore about with him a perpetual reminder of the incident in the shape of an injured chest, which brought on frequent hæmorrhages and no doubt hastened his death. We may hope that Gerard's prayers—to which, we may be sure, Gerard's penances were joined—won for that unhappy man the momentary flash of light and the momentary stirring of the heart in love and sorrow that could save his soul. Can even a pistol shot be quick enough to intercept that final grace coming from a world where time does not count?

Did Gerard ever fail to convert a sinner? There is at least one recorded case, and it is as well to remember it. An unhappy man who had been deceiving the world by a show of sanctity lay dying of a horrible disease. So foul was the odour that came from the sick room that none but the most essential callers ever entered it. But Gerard entered it, and not only showed the sufferer the tenderest charity, but brought all the eloquence of a saint to bear upon the sinner and make him turn to God. But he died the death of a reprobate. The saint's prayers followed him into eternity, until the miserable soul appeared to him and told him to desist, as by a just judgment of God he was lost. Gerard never thought of this without a shudder. There is a limit to the abuse of grace, even when a saint pleads.

And what about the little ones of Christ's flock? What about the children? Would Saint Gerard have been all we know and love in him if he had not drawn the children? Did he not draw the Child of Mary when a child himself? And so the children could not resist him, no more than they could resist his Divine Master long ago. Here is the testimony of a centenarian given at the process of beatification in 1843, ninety years after he had seen Gerard in Melfi :—" When Brother Gerard came to Melfi, I was about ten years old and I often spoke with him. To all the young people who were around him he would speak of the holy love of God and of fidelity to the duties of our holy religion. *Cosa date voi a Dio* . . . What are you giving to God?'

he would say. Then he would make the sign of the cross on our forehead and distribute pictures of the Mother of Sorrows amongst us. He was very fond of mortifying himself. I myself noticed that he wore a hairshirt. He was particularly charitable towards the poor and gave away his own food to them. One day, when leaving school, I saw him practise this act of virtue towards them. On another occasion I saw him call over a poor man, and after having brought him as far as the bishop's palace, he took off his shoes and presented them to him. What was most remarkable in him was his zeal for everything pertaining to the salvation of souls and the conversion of sinners."[1] There was evidently not much lost on that little fellow, even to the wearing of the cilices.

[1] Benedetti, p. 183.

CHAPTER X

GERARD AND THE NUNS

PERHAPS we should have to be a saint like Gerard, believing as he believed and loving as he loved, to realise with what recoiling horror, with what a searing of the soul he looked on the sins of men thrust beneath his eyes in all their brutal nakedness, as he came and went amongst them. For the sinner he had indeed his divine Master's commiseration ; but to meet so many, as he did, estranged from that God whose love was the overruling passion of his own life must have wrung his heart with infinite perplexity and distress. And so, when he came across souls who shared his own lofty ideals and enthusiasms ; when he met them on the higher altitudes of Christian holiness which he walked himself, breasting the same steeps, breathing the same unpolluted air and allured by the same towering splendours,—then Gerard was another man, rejoicing with an exceeding great joy.

The saints, however, were always givers of their own good things, and Gerard was not content with gazing admiringly at those whom he chanced to meet on the slopes of Christian perfection : it became his ambition to set the feet of as many as possible on that mountain-side and urge them upwards. And thus it came about that one of the strangest activities to which Providence called this extraordinary laybrother was the recruiting of young women for the cloister and what was nothing less than the spiritual direction of nuns. This " secondary vocation," as Benedetti calls it, deserves a chapter.

St. Gerard Majella may lay no slender claim to the title of Patron of Postulants. By his untiring efforts to garner them for Christ, by the pains he took to smooth their road to the cloister and open its door, and by the great number who owed their admittance to his inspiration and encouragement, he made a name for himself in life that should urge young people whose thoughts are on their future to invoke him to-day. Postulants he found in plenty—amongst his own kindred, in the various households into which his many journeys to town and countryside brought him on the business of his community,—above all in his Master's Vineyard itself, where, in his own wonderful way, he worked side by side with his missionary confrères. Had he never broached the subject of religious life, he was a living and most eloquent exponent of it for those whose leanings were ever so little in that direction. If they saw in him at their harshest the harsher things of it—its detachment and surrender, its crucifixion of the flesh and of the will, its unremitting demands upon self-interest and self-love —they likewise saw in him in its most attractive guise its brighter side : the peace and freedom that spring from total sacrifice. But Gerard spoke, and the eloquence that could, when occasion called for it, shake the terrors of divine justice in the face of the unrepenting sinner and point to a yawning hell, enchanted youthful and aspiring souls with visions of the hundredfold and pointed ecstatically upwards to the waiting throne. " It was the general belief," writes Berruti, " that any young girl who listened to the holy discourses of the Servant of God and saw the glowing fervour with which he portrayed the beauty of a soul that loves the Lord, the nothingness of the fleeting goods of this life, the dangers of losing one's soul eternally that abound in the world, soon made up her mind to bid good-bye to relatives and to all the delights of sense in order to become the spouse of Jesus Crucified."[1] His winning ways were irresistible, and hesitant souls quickly cast the die with an unwavering hand. Neither could reluctant parents long hold out against him, as tactfully but decisively he tore to shreds the reasoning of human prudence and the arguments of false affection. Once he detected a true vocation in a girl, both she and her parents were powerless against his words.

He had often to cope with difficulties of a material kind in the interests of his postulants. In his day, as in our own, many a young girl, with every qualification for the religious life, was brought to a standstill at the convent gate, amid the shattered dreams of her girl-hood, through lack of means. But Gerard was not one to be baffled in his holy enterprises by obstacles of this sort. Though we read of no miraculous dowry, dowries he managed to provide by every means by which he could scrape them together. Hat in hand he went round amongst his wealthy friends—and these were many— and amongst his influential confrères who had wealthy friends of their own. He was not shy and was not easily put off. Rebuffs meant nothing to him—his soul had

---

[1] Pp. 134-135.

battened on such things—and they certainly did not mean that his friends had seen the last of him. There was visit upon visit, letter upon letter until the requisite ducats were forthcoming, if only "because of his importunity." But indeed it must be said that Gerard's friends gave generously and thus enabled him to open the convent door to numbers of impecunious postulants.

He pulled strings to perfection. A certain nun of the Carmelite convent of Ripacandida—Sister Mary Joseph —had a sister with a Carmelite vocation but without a Carmelite dowry. Gerard lost no time in getting things going. Don Antonio Caracciolo, the Prince of Torella, was worth winning over; and so was his friend and agent Signor Benedetto Grazioli. Now Gerard was aware how greatly the saintly ex-prioress Mother Mary of Jesus was revered by Grazioli and his wife Donna Nuncia. Mother Mary of Jesus had therefore to be approached. But her successor in office, Mother Mary Michael, had first to be reckoned with. So this string had first to be pulled. Gerard pulled it by the following letter :—" Get Sister Maria to write to Don Benedetto and ask him for a big contribution for the sister of Sister Maria Giuseppa, and he in turn can apply to the Prince of Torella. We shall be satisfied if the Prince's contribution together with his own amount to two hundred ducats. I should have a scruple in doing all I should like ; but if Father Fiocchi allows me, we will see the undertaking through. I have written also to Sister Mary Francesca in Muro asking her to get a contribution from her brother."[1]

---

[1] Tannoia, cap. xx.

As no reply was forthcoming, he wrote again :—

" Most Reverend Sister, I am writing from Foggia and am writing in haste. I wonder what's going on over there. I have no idea, as I have got no reply to any of my letters. I think you must be out of notepaper. If that's so, please let me know, and I'll send you a quire, so that you can write to me. Enough about that. By God's grace I have got another contribution for that affair. But you are keeping me in suspense. For the love of God let Mother Mary of Jesus write to Donna Nuncia, that she may get a good contribution for the business from her also ; but her husband must know nothing about it, and it must be done at once and with all speed. Let her know that contributions from other quarters have come in, so that she may help too. Let me know if my letters have reached you. I am not well. Kind wishes to everybody. Your unworthy servant and brother in J.C.   GERARD MAJELLA."[1]

At last a reply came, and it was a disappointing one. As the prioress evidently thought it impossible to procure the dowry in question, she gave Gerard to understand that the admission of the girl would present great difficulties.   Gerard replied :—

" My dear Mother Prioress, the contents of your esteemed letter have pained me. God's Will be done. I have been given three sequins for you by a person who wishes to remain anonymous. I am keeping them for the present. If God wishes the enterprise to succeed I will forward them to you."[2]

---

[1] Benedetti, p. 230.
[2] *Ibid.* A sequin (zecchino) was a gold coin valued about 9/4.

A further letter from the prioress made the saint question the Carmelite vocation of the young girl, and so he sought to open another door elsewhere. His choice fell on a convent in Foggia founded in 1700 by the Bishop of Troia, Emilio Giacomo Cavalieri, a maternal uncle of St. Alphonsus, which housed a flourishing and fervent community. The girl readily accepted the proposal, though here, too, there arose the menacing spectre of a dowry. Gerard thereupon wrote as follows to Father Margotta :—

"Father, Sister Mary Joseph has been asking me for the past three years to get her sister into Ripacandida. I am not a free agent in the matter myself, but now the Lord is urging me to help her. Father Fiocchi is also most anxious about it. He is willing to give me a contribution and wishes me to approach others. I had scarcely opened my lips before I got fifty ducats. The Lord has opened doors widely to me. I intended sending her to Foggia, and the prioress agreed to admit her for 300 ducats. Come ! Father, find this sum wherever you can without any human respect. I am trying to get it together myself unblushingly. Try the Berilli family and others. You can do everything if you will."[1]

But, for all his unblushing efforts to find money for his protégées, he had a keen sense of justice in these matters and was not slow to impress it on others when the need arose. He had suggested tapping a certain source in behalf of a would-be postulant. The Mother Superior, referring to the possible contribution, said that if the sum realised did not suffice to get the girl

---

[1] Tannoia, cap. xx.

into a convent, it might help to get her married. Gerard
wrote :—" What's that you say, Mother ? Neither I
nor anybody else may do such a thing, without bringing
discredit on our Congregation. Whatever help I procure
is to make a nun of the girl, not to get her married.
If this can't be done, then all the money must go back
to the donors."[1]

Dowries were not the only difficulty Gerard had to
contend with. Besides misplaced affection on the part
of certain parents, a more obvious form of self-interest
presented itself, at least on one occasion. It came to
his ears that a young man of the Santorelli family,
Girolamo by name, had been trying to wean one of
his young protégées from her vocation. He went about
it crudely enough by sending her gifts, adroitly adapting
some of them to her situation by making them take
the form of objects of devotion. The young gentleman,
however, reckoned without Gerard. He received the
following letter, in which we see this youthful knight of
God chivalrously breaking a lance in defence of Christ's
fiancée.

" *Riveritissimo Signor D. Girolamo,*" he begins with
disarming politeness, " I should have written long ago
to you, but such was not God's Will. I am writing now
to tell you that I never thought you could have done
such an amazing thing, or that you would be so weak.
You were foolish enough to send Caterina love-knots
and rosaries through the medium of that respectable
person. What madness ! I really couldn't believe it.
I tell you that she is under God's protection and mine.

---

[1] In Ord. no. 7, § 564.

Why do you want to challenge God's power ? Mind what you are doing and remember that such conduct is unworthy of an honourable man. I may be far away from you, but nothing is impossible to God. Mind what I am saying. What is more, you have actually dared to curse the death of her confessor and of him who put the postulant's dress upon her.

" You know that I wish you well, and yet you go to this length. However, I forgive you, as you were carried away by youthful impulse. Such people think little of hell and of the infinite loss of God."[1] Tannoia tells us that Gerard wrote a great many letters of this kind, which have not come down to us.

The miraculous enters so abundantly into the whole of Gerard's life that it would be strange if it were entirely absent from this particular sphere of it. Every activity of his we have so far described has had upon it the divine approval of a miracle. His work for postulants was to be no exception. At least one miraculous happening is recorded.

The reader will remember the Capucci family of Lacedonia. The youngest girl—poor innocent Nicoletta —had, it will be recalled, been foully made the unconscious instrument of Gerard's great trial. Two of her sisters were his postulants. The saint himself, as well as their father, accompanied the girls to the convent in Foggia. On reaching the river Cervaro, the travellers found it so swollen by the recent rains as to be altogether unfordable. Then what happened at the Red Sea and at the Jordan long ago happened again. At the saint's

---

[1] Tannoia, cap. xxviii.

bidding the rushing waters stood, rose up like two walls
on either side, and opened a way for them. Signor
Capucci, a shrewd and well-educated man, bore testimony
to this in his old age and would often speak of having
witnessed a great miracle.

Speaking of rivers recalls an incident of another kind.
Amongst Gerard's innumerable postulants was a niece
of his own. He was keenly interested in her vocation,
encouraged it in every way and succeeded in getting
her admitted as a lay postulant into the same convent
of Foggia. He accompanied her there himself from Muro.
While on the way, he could speak of nothing else but
the duty of aiming at perfection. She was to become a
saint, mind ! a great saint. Did she understand that ?
He had been worked up to a high pitch of enthusiasm
on the subject, when they reached the banks of the
Ofanto. Pointing to the river, he suddenly turned and
said to her with a hint of threat in his voice : " Do you
mean to become a saint ? If you don't, I will throw you
straightway into the river."[1]   The poor girl must have
vowed eminent sanctity on the spot ! Gerard's words
need not detain us : it was just his way of putting things.

Though Gerard himself had never looked back when
once he had put his hand to the plough, yet he well
understood the difficulties of those who did and with
an eager and an eloquent pen flew to the rescue of the
tempted novice. We do not feel justified in shortening
even by a word a letter he wrote to one such at Ripacandida who could not avert her eyes from the beckoning world.[2]

---

[1] Tannoia, cap. xx.
[2] *Ibid.*, cap. xxviii.

" My dear Sister in Jesus Christ, I tell you on the part of God to abide in a steadfast and holy peace. All this is the work of the devil, who wants to drive you from this holy place.

" Take care, my daughter, for the wicked impostor is full of guile and cunning and is laying snares for you ; he is angry at your being where you are, for he would like to prevent you from becoming a saint.

" We have all to suffer temptations against our vocation, and these God sends in order to test our fidelity. Keep up your heart and give yourself unreservedly to God ; He will then help you.

" And how is it possible that you can have forgotten those beautiful resolutions you so often made when you offered yourself to Jesus Christ and requested to become His spouse ? If you then longed for this, why do you now wish to renounce it ?

" O my dear Sister, who but God can give you peace ? Has the world ever yet satisfied the heart of man ? or the heart of a princess, of a queen, of an empress ? It has been nobody's experience, we read of it in no book. What we do know is that it sows thorns and thistles in the hearts of its votaries, and the more of its wealth and honours were theirs and the more of its pleasures they enjoyed, the greater was their anguish of mind. Who are you who are speaking ? Would I could let you speak with the happiest worldling, that you might see how false appearances are. But take my word for it. I have experienced it abundantly : life in the world is a sorry business. May God protect you from it, my dear Sister !

" God has your interests at heart, and so He has

allowed temptation to come upon you in order to test
your loyalty. Have courage, then ! Overcome, yes,
generously overcome every temptation by proclaiming
yourself at all times the spouse of our most noble Lord
Jesus Christ.

" It is a beautiful thing to be the spouse of Jesus
Christ. In Him is perfect happiness, perfect peace,
every satisfaction, every good. What is the fleeting
show of this world beside the heavenly and enduring
happiness enjoyed in heaven by a soul espoused to Jesus
Christ ? I do not say that she who lives in the world
cannot save her soul ; but I do say that such a one is
in constant danger of perishing and that she cannot
sanctify herself as easily as in the cloister.

" Reflect, I beg of you, on the shortness of time, the
length of eternity, and consider how everything comes
to an end. Everything comes to an end for those who
live in the world, as if they had never been in the world.
Why then lean on what cannot give support ? Alas !
everything that does not lead us to God avails us nought
for eternity and is vanity. Unhappy the soul that trusts
in the world and not in God !

" I beg of you, my dear Sister, to go for a short while
to your cemetery where lie the bones of so many nuns
of your monastery, and there consider what it would
have availed them had they been the greatest ladies
in the land. Oh ! all they have gained by living poor,
mortified, humble and secluded lives in that little
convent ! It may be that they had to suffer much, but
what peace was theirs at death on realising that they
were dying in the house of God ! At the hour of death
everyone wishes to become a saint ; but then it is no

longer possible. What we have done for God is alone ours.

" Should the storm not yet have passed over, I have the greatest trust and hope in the Most Blessed Trinity and in most holy Mary that you will yet become a saint. You must not belie me. Crush the head of that great infernal beast who is trying to drive you from that holy place. Despise him ; tell him you are the spouse of Jesus Christ and make him tremble.

" Have courage ! Love God with your whole heart. Give yourself to Him always without reserve, and thus let the devil be crushed . . . *crepi e muoia*. Pray for me, as I always do for you."

It would have been strange if such a letter fell short of its purpose. It is a summary of all the reasoning that made Gerard what he was. It is a saint's apologia. The disillusioned novice became an excellent religious.

The precise number of postulants Gerard has to his account is nowhere stated ; but we know that they were very many, and many a Reverend Mother must have blessed him. Thus we read how, on one single occasion, he personally conducted seven young girls to the convent of Saragnano. Not only did he send two girls of the Capucci family to the monastery of Foggia, as we have already seen, but, moreover, he placed no fewer than twelve other cousins of one degree or another of the same family in the same holy house. Speaking of this convent and that of Ripacandida, Tannoia says that he did everything he could to keep them " well-filled."[1] The humble brother did not think what a tribute he

---

[1] English Edit., p. 336.

was paying to these communities.

But we have now to speak of something still more unusual in the life of a laybrother, however holy and supernaturally gifted, than the filling of convents with prospective nuns. Gerard actually directed professed nuns—scores of them—in the higher walks of the spiritual life. Even though he could have brought every qualification, except priestly ordination, to such a high and delicate task, he himself would have been the last in the world to admit his fitness and the last to exploit it. As we said in the preceding chapter, none better than he knew his place in the Church and in his Congregation ; and had he not been convinced beyond all yea or nay that it was God's will that he should undertake this work so strangely out of keeping with everything a Redemptorist laybrother is called upon to do, no power on earth could have driven him to do it. As he writes in a letter to a nun (we presume the italics are own), " *My will is entirely in the hands of my superiors . . . let them do what they like with me and I am satisfied.*"[1] On the other hand, once he saw the finger of God beckoning unmistakably in that direction, then no power on earth could have deterred him from following it. In the long history of God's Church and in the working out of the innumerable divine schemes for God's glory and man's salvation nothing leaps more readily to the eye than the fact so eloquently chronicled by St. Paul : " The foolish things of the world hath God chosen, that he may confound the wise : and the weak things of the world hath God chosen, that he may confound

---

[1] In Ord. no. 7, § 577.

the strong. And the base things of the world and the things that are contemptible, hath God chosen : and things that are not, that he might bring to nought things that are : that no flesh should glory in his sight." [1] We see God casting aside or ignoring instruments seemingly fitted for His work and picking up others seemingly worthless and with His omnipotent hand behind them accomplishing marvels. Gerard Majella is a further illustration of this truth.

It must be said at once that the work he now entered upon was congenial. This he admits and tells us simply and beautifully why. " Do not be surprised," he writes to the Prioress of the Carmelite convent of Ripacandida, " if I write to you with such affection, as my one and only reason for doing so is that I have come to look on you as the true and beloved spouses of Jesus Christ. This thought fills me with a longing to converse continually with you. There is another thought also that goes straight to my heart : you, the spouses of Jesus Christ, remind me of and represent the Mother of God." [2]

Nor did Gerard's commission for this holy work come originally from his own religious superiors. His superiors —Fathers Fiocchi, Cafaro and Margotta—and above all, his holy Founder himself were far too prudent to suggest any such departure from the normal life of a laybrother, even though his name was Gerard Majella and even though they knew him to be a saint. Even when persons of distinction appealed to them to send Gerard amongst the people that they might profit by

---

[1] I Cor., i, 27-29.
[2] Benedetti, p. 209.

his sanctity and his gifts, they persisted long in their refusal. No, the call did not come to him from within his own community. It came from another quarter—from episcopal palaces, when learned and holy bishops, recognising the saintly Brother's outstanding qualifications, read in them the expression of a divine purpose that he should undertake the task. They had seen the miraculous blessings that had followed on his apostolate amongst the people ; they had good reason for believing that similar blessings would follow on his work amongst religious. After due consideration, his superiors therefore gave their sanction to the proposal. When all is said and done, the whole business is but another instance of that derogation from the ordinary ruling of Providence which is so conspicuous at every stage of Gerard's life and which we must admit if his life is to be understood. The spiritual direction of nuns was simply his vocation, " a vocation within a vocation,"[1] as his French biographer calls it, one of those vocations, strange indeed but none the less authentic, which have filled some of the most glorious and delightful pages in the story of the Church. We need but add that Gerard's supreme success vindicated the decisions of bishops and superiors alike and amply fulfilled the highest hopes. Before speaking of this success, we are going to make a slight digression and dwell briefly on one particular qualification Gerard brought to his new work : his supernatural knowledge of divine things.

In every saint this knowledge is to be looked for. In a saint whose humility and self-denial are so striking

---

[1] *Vie*, par un Père Rédemptoriste, p. 211.

it is to be looked for and is found in striking abundance. Sanctity is the only short cut to theology, but a short cut it is. " The soul of a holy man discovereth sometimes true things : more than seven watchmen that sit in a high place to watch."[1] So *Ecclesiasticus* tells us, and his words are pregnant and profound. " As for theology," writes the Blessed De la Colombière in a letter to a young Jesuit scholastic, " I confess that if it were to be done over again, I should always meditate twice as much as I studied."[2]

Gerard's theological lore was very wonderful. We feel sure that he never opened a text-book of dogmatic or moral theology in his life ; but for all that he was a first-class theologian, with the Holy Ghost Himself as his professor, and the wonderment of those who heard him speak must have often made them put the question put by the wondering Jews as they listened to Christ : " How doth this man know letters, having never learned ? "[3] He was in truth looked upon as an oracle of divine knowledge. Tannoia writes : " I will not enlarge on his knowledge of all the mysteries. It is enough to say that it made him most famous both in his Congregation and out of it. He was everywhere regarded as a great theologian."[4] The various bishops with whom he was brought into contact were not slow to discover this, and they made no secret of it. The reader will recall how, while yet a novice, Gerard was allowed to spend some days with Mgr. Basta, the Bishop

---

[1] xxxvii, 18.
[2] *Life* by Margaret Yeo, p. 60.
[3] John, vii, 15.
[4] English Edit., p. 301.

of Melfi, at his Lordship's own request. Though a man
of great erudition, he considered it no loss of time to
have daily talks with his humble guest on all branches
of theology. Not only did he consult him on diocesan
affairs and submit to all his decisions, but he discussed
with him the loftiest truths of religion. Nor did the
bishop keep all the good things to himself. Members of
his household jumped at the opportunity of listening
to God's theologian and hearing him speak with such
sublimity and depth, especially of the mystery of the
Incarnation, and in their enthusiasm they would liken
him to an Augustine or a Jerome.

In his Congregation this gift did not long remain
hidden. " One day," a witness states, " during the
customary scientific discussion the rector of Iliceto was
holding with the students and other Fathers of the
community Gerard happened to be present. When the
discussion came to a close, the rector, half in jest, asked
Gerard for his opinion. The latter gave it in such a
skilful and masterly way that the whole company was
dumbfounded."[1]

His Lordship of Lacedonia—Mgr. Amato—whom
Tannoia speaks of as " the flower of the bishops of his
day," practically made Gerard his spiritual director.
He never let him pass through without having a lengthy
talk with him on diocesan affairs or about his own soul.
" To talk spirituality and theology with Brother Gerard",
he would say, " is to declare oneself his disciple ; and
to become his disciple means to come away from him
a theologian, so great will be the light received."[2]

[1] In Apost. no. 7, § 237.
[2] Tannoia, cap. xix.

Mgr. Vito Mujo, Bishop of Muro, and an excellent theologian himself, remarked after Gerard's death : " I could not cease admiring the masterly way in which he expounded questions in theology." [1] As another witness puts it, " he discoursed with great depth and sublimity on the mysteries of our holy religion . . . . as if he had been a great theologian who had given many long years to their study."[2]

Priests and others had similar experiences. The archpriest Domenico Capucci, a very distinguished ecclesiastic, never wearied of discussing his own spiritual problems with Gerard. Though he was under Father Cafaro's direction, it took the humble laybrother to assure him peace of soul. On one essential point the saint took him to task : though an excellent priest in many ways, he let his zeal for the souls of others outpace his own spiritual life and had not given mental prayer its due place in his scheme of things. Gerard saw how matters stood and told him so. Prayer came into its own once more and, after a holy life, Capucci died a holy death. " The most obscure mysteries," writes Canon Bozzio, " became clear on Gerard's lips, and when, in a transport of divine love, he sounded their depths, no theologian or savant could keep pace with him."[3]

Doctor Santorelli is equally emphatic : " When Brother Gerard began to speak of divine mysteries, he seemed out of himself. On his lips the most difficult questions became easy and matters the most obscure were made clear and intelligible. Conversing with him left me

---

[1] Benedetti, p. 123.
[2] In Apost. no. 9, § 18.
[3] Tannoia, cap. xxvii.

dumbfounded, when I realised how a poor unlettered laybrother could penetrate so profoundly into such depths and expound them intelligibly."[1] The same Canon Bozzio tells us that when, on one occasion, he and Gerard were conversing alone, the latter asked him the meaning of certain verses of the seventeenth Psalm, particularly of the tenth verse : " He bowed the heavens, and came down : and darkness was under his feet."[2] The Canon did his best, only to find that Gerard could do much better.

A witness in the apostolic process tell us that Gerard was asked by Canon Pianese, president of the seminary in Muro, to give a commentary before the students on the opening words of St. John's Gospel : " In the beginning was the Word, etc." Thereupon the saint spoke on the eternal generation of the Son of God with a loftiness and precision that amazed his audience.

He was equally at home in moral theology. " Some of the ablest confessors," writes Tannoia, " both of the secular and regular clergy, would call on him to draw on his supernatural wisdom for the solution of their difficulties in the guidance of souls. Gerard would discuss the most intricate questions in ascetic and moral theology like a master. He solved doubts with the wisdom of a doctor ; so that some would leave him repeating in their wonder : " I confess to thee, O Father, Lord of heaven and earth, because thou hast hid these things from the wise and prudent and hast revealed them to little ones."[3] While a guest in the Franciscan convent

---

[1] Tannoia, Cap. xxvii.
[2] Ps., xvii, 10.
[3] Matt. xi, 25.

of his native Muro, his cell became a consulting-room
for the confessors of the place.

When Gerard's theological attainments became known
in Naples, he was soon the talk of the capital. He had
many callers who were curious to put these attainments
to the test. Father Celestino de Robertis, a member of
the Congregation, thus describes the discomfiture of one
of these : " One day, when I was in Naples, a certain
priest entered into discussion with him on the mystery
of the Most Holy Trinity, a subject he then happened
to be studying. Various points arose out of the subject,
such as the generation of the Word, the co-eternity of
the Father and the Son, and the procession of the Holy
Ghost from both. Brother Gerard replied to every
question better than any theologian. I was amazed at
the way he approached the subject and at the precision
and lucidity of his exposition. Not only was he not
worsted, but it was as much as the priest could do to
avoid his own confusion."[1]

Challengers were usually worsted. A young priest
from Muro, who rather fancied himself in the domain of
theology, went one day to Caposele expressly to measure
swords with this laybrother. Gerard pressed him so
closely in argument that he was literally reduced to
silence. Then, smiling sweetly on his prostrate antagonist
and fellow-townsman, the Servant of God said : " *Paesano*,
you have studied theology, but you are no theologian.
That science is acquired only by humility and prayer."[2]
Caione tells us that another priest, who really was a good

---

[1] Tannoia, cap. xxv.
[2] *Ibid.*, cap. xxvii.

theologian, one day began to talk theology with Gerard.
He soon discovered, however, that he had met more
than his match. On being asked by the Brother to explain
the words : " In the beginning was the Word : and the
Word was with God : and the Word was God,"[1] he set
about it with much hesitancy. Thereupon Gerard took
up the text and dismissed the subject in a few crystal
words.

That Gerard should be a theologian himself was
wonderful enough ; more wonderful still was it that he
could make theologians of others. There were occasions
when he actually passed on his knowledge miraculously.
Landi tells us that a priest of Muro, Don Donato Spicci,
was making a retreat in Caposele in the Lent of 1755.
Gerard had leave to talk to him during his free moments.
Don Donato noticed a book lying on the table in the
tailor's shop. It was the life of the Venerable Sister
Maria Crocifissa, to whom the saint had a great devotion.
The priest took it up and opened it at the twelfth chapter
which dealt with the interior solitude of Christ on Calvary.
" These matters," said Gerard, " are not for you,"
adding with a smile, " You are a theologian, and yet
you cannot understand the meaning of these words."
The priest read on. Frowns and wrinkles soon showed
him to be in difficulties. However, he tackled it again,
remarking : " but it isn't French or Hebrew, and anybody with any wit should make it out." " Very good,"
replied Gerard, " read a passage for me very slowly
and thoughtfully and then explain what the Servant of
God means." Don Donato read on but could not make

---

[1] John, I, i.

head or tail of it. Gerard's friend Santorelli, who happened to be present, was unable to refrain from laughing at the poor priest's discomfiture. The poor priest did not like this. " Don't be annoyed, *O mio Don Donato*," Gerard went on, " come over." He thereupon made the sign of the cross on the priest's forehead, saying good-humouredly : " Read now and you will be able to understand and explain everything." And so it happened.

Another priest could not see his way through certain passages in the work of Bishop Palafox entitled *Pastore Della Buona Notte*. He brought his difficulties to the saint. Him, too, Gerard signed, saying : " In the Name of the Most Holy Trinity read now."[1] He also read and saw and made others see as well.

During his stay in Naples, Gerard became the intimate friend and, we may almost say, the fellow-worker of a learned and holy Jesuit, Father Francis Pepe. This busy man did not think he was wasting his time spending hours on end talking spirituality with the humble lay-brother. Now Father Pepe had obtained from the Pope —and from no less a Pope than Benedict XIV—the most extensive powers over the Church's treasury of indulgences. On applying to him through Father Margotta, Gerard " was given a goodly number of plenary indulgences (we are quoting Tannoia) to be dispensed to whom he would, to those who went frequently to Communion and made a daily visit to Jesus in the Blessed Sacrament ; to such also as honoured the Blessed Virgin with a special devotion by visiting her image and fasting on Saturdays.

---

[1] Tannoia, cap. xxvii.

He also obtained the faculty of granting the privileged altar to worthy and devout priests."[1]

Nor were the good nuns forgotten in his largesse. The following letter from a laybrother to a Mother Superior must surely be unique of its kind. We insert it for the edification of the canonists.[2]

" To the Very Reverend Mother Maria Celeste of the Most Holy Saviour, Prioress of the Monastery of the Most Holy Saviour in Foggia. Jesus X Maria. May the divine grace and consolation of the Holy Spirit always be in the soul of your Reverence and of all your daughters, and may our most holy Mother (*Mamma*) Mary keep it therein. Amen. Amen.

" My dear and most venerable Mother, as a result of urgent appeals on my part to the Very Reverend Father Francis Pepe of the Society of Jesus, who, as you are aware, has full authority granted him by the Sovereign Pontiff to impart every indulgence, I have already obtained, thanks to our dear God and most holy Mary, the following indulgences, which will be applicable for all your daughters, as well as for the boarders, both for such as are with you now and such as will come hereafter, in perpetuity, under the one condition of receiving Communion ; they are : 1. a plenary indulgence on the feast of the Most Holy Trinity ; 2. a plenary indulgence on all the feasts of Jesus Christ ; 3. a plenary indulgence on all the feasts of most holy Mary (*Mamma*) ; 4. a plenary indulgence on all the feasts of the holy Apostles ; 5. a plenary indulgence

---

[1] Cap. xxv.
[2] In Ord. no. 7, § 554-555.

on the feast of St. John the Baptist ; 6. a plenary indulgence on the feast of St. Ann ; 7. a plenary indulgence on the feast of St. Joseph ; 8. a plenary indulgence on the feast of St. Michael the Archangel ; 9. a
plenary indulgence on the feast of St. Joachim ;
10. a plenary indulgence on the feast of St. Elizabeth.
I would just ask you to have this letter kept, so that
those who come after may be able to avail of the aforesaid indulgences and may bear in mind, moreover,
that they are all obliged to pray to the Lord for me,
and to apply to me whatever indulgences they can by
way of suffrages for my soul after my death. The same
recommendation holds good for all future prioresses,
and I likewise beg of them to have some Communions
applied to me, and in particular I remind the prioress
who will be in office immediately after my death to
see to it that whatever indulgences all the Sisters may
gain during the subsequent eight days are applied to me.
On my part, I will remember to pray for them to the
Lord God, that He may make saints of them. Amen.
Be kind enough, Reverend Mother, to remember me to
all my Sisters, and let them all pray to God for me, as
they have so often promised me to do. Do this, Reverend
Mother, out of obedience. I remain, Yours in Jesus
Christ. Naples, 8th March, 1755. Let our Sisters be
reminded that, to gain the aforesaid indulgences, it is
necessary that they form the intention on the morning
or before receiving Communion, in order to gain the
said indulgences. All good wishes to D. Nicola. I commend myself earnestly to his holy prayers, as I pray
for him. Your Reverence's unworthy servant and
brother in Christ, GERARD MAJELLA, of the Most Holy

Redeemer."[1] [2]

Gerard had certainly no intention of being the loser by this pious transaction. The indulgences he never needed must have been another windfall for the Church's treasury. This letter is surely a monument to the humility of a saint. It shows us unmistakably what Gerard must have thought of himself.

Such was the spiritual director that bishops and superiors sent to nuns. Small wonder is it that the nuns welcomed him more as an angel than as a man. Small wonder is it that they hung on the lips of this pupil of the Holy Ghost Himself and laid bare without reserve the secrets of their soul. His first apostolic journey was to his native town, in the autumn of 1752, shortly after his religious profession, and the first convent to share the good things he brought was that of the Poor Clares of Muro. The noise of his virtues and miracles had penetrated the grim doors and grille that shut out the boisterous world, and the Sisters longed

---

[1] The anonymous French biographer writes : " In accordance with the wishes of the writer, this precious manuscript was preserved religiously in the monastery archives. Many a time since the Brother's death this relic of him was made use of in favour of the sick. The following instance occurred about 1840. A Sister named Raphael suffered much from her eyes. On applying the holy Brother's letter to them, she was instantaneously cured."—*Vie*, par un Père Rédemptoriste, p. 429.)

[2] A witness states that after Gerard's death he met Father Pepe and asked him about the faculties he had granted to the Servant of God for dispensing indulgences. The Father replied : " Yes, he was a great servant of God, and as I had the faculties for doing so, I thought him worthy of being empowered to dispense them, all the more so as he was endowed with the gift of reading hearts ; and so I felt certain that he would make a more fruitful use of this faculty than I should myself."—In Apost. no. 7, § 294.)

to see the saint. Indeed they had a special claim on his services. Was it not in their little chapel but a dozen years before that Gerard had received the sacrament of Confirmation ? Surely many a Sister in such a community—whose members seem to possess the secret of longevity—would remember the little boy as he turned his cheek to receive the bishop's gentle stroke (what harder strokes it was after to receive !). What a giant of Christian strength, what a battle-scarred soldier of Christ he had since become ! And so they appealed for him now, many times. But his prudence and humility would not let him go. Who or what was he ? What authority had he, an unworthy laybrother, to speak to them ? What could he do for them ? However, they soon found the chink in his armour : he had a marked and well-known weakness for obedience. Accordingly, the bishop, Mgr. Mujo, was appealed to and not in vain. He was a wise and learned prelate, who knew Gerard well. He jumped at the suggestion and forthwith sent him to the good Sisters, having previously written to them that " a chat with Brother Gerard is worth more than a whole course of Lenten sermons."[1]

The saint went and went often. The result may be imagined. Each visit meant a brief discourse, and each discourse gave his audience " a very foretaste of heaven,"[2] as Tannoia phrases it. They could not get enough of him. Nor must it be thought that the preacher's words were an unvarying rapturous outpouring on the love of God and kindred subjects. The saints never lost contact

---

[1] Tannoia, cap. xxx.
[2] English Edit. p. 403.

with the realities of earth, and the dazzling atmosphere in which their own souls dwelt never blinded them to all sorts of unexpected and undesirable possibilities in the souls of others. And so, with a sure unerring hand, Gerard pointed out the dangers to their sublime ideals that arose from a world on which they had indeed turned their backs, but which had never turned its back on them. They were cloistered nuns, and boldly and earnestly he preached the cloister. " It is in the silence of the cell," he went on, " that God speaks to the heart of the faithful soul. It is there that she finds true consolation in pouring out her heart's affections to Our Lord Jesus Christ and her most sweet Mother Mary."[1] " My Sister, let us become saints,"[2] were words that were ever on his lips.

The good seed did not fall on stony ground. Abuses which, as long as human nature is what it is, will find their insidious way into the best of religious families and which, in the case of this particular community, had baffled the efforts of every confessor, disappeared. Under the fiery breath of this human seraph the love of God flamed up anew in these virgin hearts.

As an instance of what this unofficial reformer was able to effect, we tell the following. A certain Sister in the above community—one of those who, after cutting cables that bound them to the world, allow themselves at times to be tied by threads in the cloister—had become unduly attached to an *ex-voto*, a little heart made of gold. She loved her little golden heart with something of a miser's love, wore it always, and in spite of the advice

[1] Cap. xxx.
[2] In Apost. no. 13, § 66.

of various confessors, could not bring herself to surrender
it. One talk with Gerard and the little golden heart
disappeared, setting free her own infinitely more precious
heart to resume its flight Godward. Gerard was long
remembered by the Poor Clares of Muro.

Yielding to the requests of certain priests and laymen
of Corato who had been making a retreat at Iliceto,
Father Fiocchi allowed Gerard to spend some days in
their midst. In Corato there were two convents of nuns
calling out for his services. In the Dominican convent
things were not at all what they should be or what they
had once been. The salt of the earth had lost its savour
and common life had gone by the board. The world
found itself far too much at home within its walls.
Gerard lost no time in grappling with the situation and
succeeded where scores of others had failed. The ties
of undue intercourse with outsiders were gradually
broken, the ties of community life within drawn gradually
closer, and the Sisters lived anew the life to which they
had dedicated themselves. A few talks with Gerard
was enough.

That He was with His servant in his holy work God
sometimes showed. In this convent a low window looking out on the street gave room for much irregularity.
Gerard asked to have it walled up. Fastening a large
crucifix to it, he reminded them that nuns who want
to save their souls should look only on Jesus Christ.
But the hint was not taken. One fine morning, soon
afterwards, they found the offending window walled up.
By whom we can but guess. In Gerard's case the guessing may be bold. Anyhow, workmen could scarcely
have got in and done the job unnoticed. And no work-

men had been noticed. Whoever were the masons, their masonry made a great impression on the Sisters and helped matters considerably. To commemorate the incident it was given the name of " Gerard's window."

Before leaving the Dominican nuns, Gerard one day favoured them with an ecstasy while discoursing on the love of Our Lord. As a reward and as a spur for the future he also left them a postulant ; it was the best proof he could give that he was pleased with them. Her name was Vincenza Palmieri. Vincenza was an only daughter and the heiress of a wealthy family. She had been to school in this convent at an early age. Her education was now nearing completion, and she was counting the days till her mother would come to fetch her home. She felt no attraction for the religious life. Perhaps she had seen more than one thing in this particular community that was not calculated to edify ; and young girls, even the most worldly-minded of them, can have very high ideals in these matters, ideals which it will take little to shatter. Anyhow, Vincenza thought she would never see the last of the place. Gerard heard all about her from the nuns and sent for her. She naturally guessed what she was wanted for and no doubt devoutly wished that people would mind their own business. However, she went. She evidently meant to bring matters to a head at once, for, on meeting Gerard, she blurted out that she hated the place and was dying to leave it. She does not seem to have been one of those young ladies who, when the convent is suggested to them, " protest too much " that they will have none of it and whose emphatic " No " is often changed into just as an emphatic " Yes." Vincenza meant what she

said ; she could never stand the keeping silence and
being housed within monastic walls. Besides, her family
had other plans for her. The saint let her run on at
will and then said quietly : " You will change your mind ;
you will be a nun and will be a model for the rest."[1]
Vincenza re-asserted her purpose. Gerard re-asserted
his prophecy, adding that she would live long and holily
in the convent. Vincenza withdrew determined. Thank
God that was over ! But saints and prophets are not so
lightly disposed of. Soon afterwards her mother came
to bring her home. But Vincenza would not go and
earnestly requested to be allowed to enter the novitiate.
In due course she made her vows, lived a most holy life
and died almost a centenarian. It is stated in the process
that she had a vision of St. Joseph at her death. We
wonder if Gerard, who was long since in heaven, was
looking at his protégée over the holy Patriarch's shoulder.

The second religious community in Corato to which
Gerard preached—if we may use the word—was that
of the Benedictine nuns. He paid them many visits.
The Mother Abbess Azzariti was a particularly holy
soul, who took her position so seriously that she longed
to be relieved of her burden and gave Gerard no peace
till he promised to join with her in prayer for this intention. " You will be heard," he said at last, " but you
will be burdened with a heavier cross."[2] He prophesied :
her resignation was accepted, but she soon fell victim
to a cancer which afflicted her cruelly for years before
her death.

---

[1] In Apost. no. 7, § 368.
[2] Cfr. In Ord. no. 7, § 494.

In this convent, too, there was an ecstasy as well as
a prophecy. It was Good Friday evening, 20th April,
1753. According to custom, a very appealing picture of
Christ Crucified had been carried in procession through
the city and had now been borne into the church of the
Benedictine nuns. Gerard, who had been spending the
day in prayer there, looked at it and at once, as if drawn
upwards by some higher force towards the sacred image,
was raised visibly in the air in the sight of a vast crowd,
" several palms from the ground,"[1] as an eye-witness
has testified.

Corato was not the only place where he brought
blessings to the daughters of St. Benedict. Fathers
Fiocchi and Margotta had done much to revive fervour
in the Benedictine community of Atella. Mgr. Basta
of Melfi now asked him to consolidate the good work.
The saint did so by interviews and letters. The Sisters
showed such docility in following his direction that he
sent them several estimable postulants.

There is a fragrant page in the chronicles of this
community. Speaking of the vocation of Sister Maria
Cianci, it tells us that in the year 1752 or 1753, Gerard
visited her native place when questing for the house
of Iliceto and was the guest of her parents. Maria was
but four or five years old at the time. One day, when
dinner-hour came, Gerard took the little girl by the
hand and lead her into the dining-room, saying : " I
am going to dine near this little child, for she will be
a nun one day."[2] A nun she eventually became. After

---

[1] In Ord. no. 7, § 496.
[2] Benedetti, p. 240.

Gerard's death, she entered the Benedictine convent of Atella, where she lived holily and died an octogenarian. Her niece, Sister Maria Carmela, a member of the same community, tells us in her deposition how her aunt would often recall with pride that she had dined with a saint. The scene is one of those delightful cameos that suddenly and unexpectedly appear in the pages of the lives of God's heroes. It is like the song of a little bird suddenly alighting near us in a grandiose and austere setting. It is like a violet wafting its fragrance upwards in a grove of stately trees. Side by side the tall gaunt ascetic and the little girl sat and ate : two children of God, in many ways so alike because both so near and dear to Him. We can sweetly picture Gerard making the little one at home and so much at home with her himself, and Maria stealing shy glances upwards at her holy friend—she had a long way to look !—and wondering.

Yet another Benedictine community—that of Calitri—must be mentioned. Here, too, the Sisters were calling out for the saint. Father Margotta urged him to go and he went. Speaking of his relations with these nuns Tannoia writes : " Gerard was a sort of extraordinary confessor to them, and they all wanted to discuss their spiritual needs with him."[1] One of the Sisters had been feeling a marked repugnance to convent life and had made up her mind to return to the world. She made no secret of her intention when speaking with Gerard. He, however, spoke with such warmth and power about the blessings of the religious state that she was changed at once and henceforth had no desire but to sanctify

[1] English Edit. p. 398.

herself in the cloister. When taking the accounts of
conscience of the community—we really can describe
these interviews in no other way—he met a poor Sister
so worried by scruples that nothing and nobody could
bring her peace. On this occasion it was Gerard who
spoke first, detailing her troubles to herself and telling
her how to act in future emergencies.

In two convents whose names have more than once
appeared in our pages, and whose inmates reaped the
benefit of Gerard's zeal, were two eminently holy nuns.
Both held the office of superior. We must give them
more than a passing mention. The first of these convents
was that of the Most Holy Saviour at Foggia. We must
go back for a moment to an historic date in the annals
of the Congregation of the Most Holy Redeemer, *viz.*,
October 3rd, 1731. On that day, a certain Sister Maria
Celeste Crostarosa, a very saintly nun in the convent
of the Holy Saviour at Scala saw in vision a priest leading
a band of apostolic men through cities and towns. She
heard a voice saying : " This is he whom I have chosen
to be the head of a work that is to promote My glory."[1]
She recognised Alphonsus de Liguori. She communicated the vision to him and thus became linked up with
the founding of the Institute. Maria Celeste was led
by a chain of events which do not concern us here to
reform the monastery of the Most Holy Saviour in
Foggia in 1738 and died in the odour of sanctity in
1755. Now one day Sister Maria Celeste read these
words in a letter from Gerard to a member of her com-

---

[1] Tannoia, *Della Vita ed Istituto di S. Alfonso Maria de'Liguori*.
lib. I, cap. xvii.

munity : " I desire to love God, I desire to remain always with God, I desire to do everything for God."[1] Deep called unto deep. In this compressed but all-embracing programme of the holy Brother she saw the replica of her own ideals. An interview followed. Each recognised the saint in the other. Henceforth, if at all possible, a visit to Foggia meant for Gerard a visit to the holy Mother Superior of San Salvatore. It was Teresa of Avila with Peter of Alcantara and John of the Cross over again.

On September 14, 1755, a month before his own death, Gerard, when in the company of his brethren at Caposele, remarked : " In Foggia to-day the beautiful soul of Mother Maria Celeste took its flight to heaven."[2] Subsequent inquiry showed that he had spoken truly, though about a hundred miles separated him from Foggia. The cause of this holy nun was introduced in 1901.

But the Mother Superior had no intention of monopolising the holy laybrother. In any case, Mgr. Faccoli, the Bishop of Troia, and his successor Marco de Simone, in whose jurisdiction the monastery was, saw to it that her community shared in the good things. It was indeed a labour of love for Gerard. The ground was well prepared ; the community was an exceptionally fervent one, and his words fell into receptive hearts. " His words," says one who heard them, " made us sigh after the goods of heaven. He often treated of the attributes of God, of His wisdom and infinite goodness ; moreover,

---

[1] In Apost. no. II, § 8.
[2] *Ibid*. no. 18, § 47.

he spoke frequently of Jesus Christ and the Madonna. When he spoke, his heart may be described as a volcano of divine love, and his glowing countenance was like the face of an angel come down from heaven to speak with men."[1]

This holy community was given to witness one of the most noteworthy of his ecstasies. It was the eve of Trinity Sunday, probably in the year 1753. He was just leaving the cell of an invalid Sister whom he had been asked to visit, when the strains of the first vespers of the feast issuing from the choir fell upon his ears.[2] The thought of the Triune God, after Whom his heart panted and in Whose Name he wrought so many prodigies, was too much for him. Under the influence of his rapture, Gerard sped with amazing swiftness through the cloister, repeating aloud the words of the liturgy : " *O altitudo divitiarum sapientiæ et scientiæ Dei! quam incomprehensibilia sunt judicia ejus . . .* O the depths of the riches of the wisdom and of the knowledge of God ! How incomprehensible are his judgments, and how unsearchable his ways ! "[3] Meantime the Office came to an end. The Sisters came filing out of the chapel, and there they saw him transfigured before their eyes. Realising that he was seen, he wrestled in vain against the power that held him : " O my Sisters," he cried out, " let us love God !."[4]   For an instant he was

---

[1] Benedetti, p. 235.

[2] It was surely no mean tribute to Gerard's sanctity and prudence that he had been given leave to enter the cloister in this way, that sick nuns might be able to avail themselves of his holy counsels.

[3] Rom., xi, 33.

[4] In Apost. no. II, § 112.

motionless, his eyes glowing and turned heavenwards.
Then, suddenly and swiftly, he rose from the ground
to a considerable height. After a few moments he came
to earth again and to himself. The ecstasy was over.
A pale drawn face told the onlookers what mysterious
violence he had been subjected to. What we stained
and lowly mortals look forward to as an unending
experience in heaven Gerard had foretasted momentarily
on earth. In a great saint like him everything is of a
piece : sanctity, suffering, miracles, endowments,
experiences. Once we recognise his spiritual stature,
nothing need surprise.

Perched upon a rock, in the neighbourhood and in
the diocese of Melfi, is the town of Ripacandida. It
contained a monastery of Carmelite nuns founded in
1735 by a holy priest named John Baptist Rossi. We
have often mentioned it. St. Teresa would have loved
her daughters in Ripacandida, so well did they pray,
so fervently did they keep their rule. Even St. Alphonsus
was amazed. At the close of a retreat he gave the Sisters
he exclaimed : " I did not think I should find such a
nosegay on this rock."[1] Indeed he had to lay a restraining hand on their austerities. He loved this community ;
it was after his own heart. " Tell me," he writes to the
Prioress, Mother Mary of Jesus, " what I can do to be
of service to that community, which I love so much."[2]
His saintly sons Fathers Fiocchi and Margotta tasted
the same joys in its service and gave it the same love.
Early in his religious life Gerard had been brought
into contact with the Sisters, and particularly with

---

[1] Berthe, *Saint Alphonse De Liguori*, vol. 1, p. 432.
[2] *Corrispond. General*, vol. 1, p. 180.

this same Mother Mary of Jesus. This holy woman herself was gifted with such a spirit of prayer that, as we gather from the correspondence of St. Alphonsus, she was another Teresa. She had done much to revive the spirit of the holy Foundress in her community, and in Gerard she discovered a valuable adviser and assistant. Here, too, it was a case of mutual recognition and identity of aim. Tannoia thus picturesquely phrases it : " When they met, they were like two mutually reflecting and enkindling fires, like two seraphs of love."[1] It was in the presence of this community of Ripacandida that Gerard had the ecstasy described in an earlier chapter in which he bent the bars of the grille.

As we have remarked more than once, Gerard Majella was first and foremost a laybrother, with all the lowly duties such a word connotes ; and his monastery was his home. The looking after its manifold material needs in his own allotted sphere was his official daily work. Personal visits to convents and interviews with their inmates could be, after all, no more than occasional things and more often than not incidental to primary undertakings. However, if he could not say in person all that was on his burning heart, he could write it. He had his pen, and he used it well. Here, too, it must be remembered, this obedient man never acted on his own initiative : the approval, not only of confessors and directors, but also of the local Ordinaries blessed his efforts in this direction. " We cannot read Gerard's letters without amazement," writes Father Cafaro, " when we bear in mind that Gerard was but a lay-

---

[1] Cap. xx.

GERARD AND THE NUNS

brother who had barely learned to read and write."[1]
He wrote a great number. Speaking of his correspondence
with the community of Ripacandida Landi says :
" Scarcely a week passed without Gerard writing to the
Carmelites there on spiritual matters or receiving letters
from them." " There was not a nun in the convents
of Foggia and Ripacandida," writes Tannoia, " who
did not correspond with him on the state of her soul"[2]
According to the same biographer, his correspondence
with Mother Celeste Crostarosa has not come down
to us. Fortunately many letters to religious have survived. Two of these we feel we must give the reader
in their entirety before we conclude this chapter.

A new prioress, Mother Mary Michael, had been elected
in the monastery of Ripacandida. Realising that she
could not go to a better source, she wrote to Gerard for
counsel. He replied as follows :—[3]

" My dear Mother Prioress, excuse me for the love
of Jesus Christ and most holy Mary for not having sent
you on at once the directions you asked me for. My
habitual sloth is to blame. God's Will be done ! And
now if I write in haste, kindly excuse me also.

" To begin with, as the Mother Prioress takes the
place of God, she must discharge the duties of her office
with the utmost conscientiousness, if she wants to please
Almighty God Who has set her in His place. She should
have the greatest prudence, if she is always to act
according to the dictates of the spirit of Jesus Christ.
She should excel in virtue and in giving good example

[1] Tannoia, cap. xx.
[2] English Edit. p. 334.
[3] Benedetti, pp. 221-223

and she should never give the slightest scandal to her daughters. Her heart should be a pure vessel filled with holy virtues, and every virtue should emanate from her and be thus communicated to her daughters, so that they all may advance in the same virtues as their mother.

" The Superior should never lose sight of her own unworthiness, bearing in mind that of herself she can do only what is evil and that God has placed her in office out of sheer kindness, as there are many others who could fill it and please Him better. In view of her imperfections, she should humble herself and excuse the faults of others. She should discharge the duties of her office in the spirit of God's love and not shrink from it as from something God had not put upon her, and she should realise that God has destined this office for her from all eternity. Therefore she should fulfil its duties with angelic perfection and adhere closely to the divine Will, while remaining in her position with utter indifference and without being attached to it.

" When in doubt and unable to decide for herself, she should take counsel with one who is enlightened by God. But, having once decided on her course of action, she should have the glory of God alone in view, carry out her decision without heeding others, and for God's sake be ready to give her blood and her life, because it is God's cause.

" For the love of the same God she should despise self-esteem in a special way, as if it did not exist. She should bear in mind only that she is the superior and say to herself: God wills that I should fill this post, and so I must do His Will in all things and watch over everything and fulfil my duty in everything. The best of everything I must give to others and keep the worst for myself, that thus I may please God. Finally, I must suffer in all things, that I may find my joy in following the holy example of my beloved Spouse Jesus Christ.

" The thoughts of a superior should be like a wheel continually in motion, revolving incessantly around the needs of her daughters. Her daughters she should love in God with a pure love and without distinction of persons. Bearing in mind rightly that her daughters can procure what they need only by obedience, she should have no thought for herself and bestow all her thoughts on them. Should eatables, articles of clothing or other things come in from outside, she should not help herself until she has supplied others.

" She should endeavour to instil confidence into all, especially if she notices a lack of it in anyone towards herself. In this case she should summon up all her strength and prudence to win her affection. Even though she does not feel any inclination to do so, she should show her kindness and do violence to herself for the love of God. If she does not do so, if she does not show her a mother's tenderness, her daughter's distress will grow. She will lose heart and become desperate, or at least she will not advance in the love of God, because there will always be a thorn in her heart. This is very likely to happen with women.

" She must be firm and gentle. As God's representative she must exact obedience from those who will not hear the voice of God, and she must chastise them with prudence.

" Correction must first be given with mildness. If this is done, a certain peace will remain which will induce the culprit to recognise her wrongdoing. The correction might, for instance, be given in this way : Your unworthy behaviour can no longer be borne either by me or by so many holy souls who witness it. What am I to do with one so imperfect ? Don't you realise, my daughter, that your bad example is the cause of scandal to all these holy souls ? It would have been better had you remained in the world and given your place to another who would have become a saint. I am telling you this, and I must tell it to you, because I am your mother. God knows how much I love you and wish you well and how much I desire your sanctification. Make up your mind, my daughter, to sanctify yourself and promise God to get rid of your imperfections. Do this, and if there is anything I can do to help you, come to me with childlike confidence.

" If correction is given in this way, then, believe me, the daughter will approach her mother, while the mother, by showing her trust in her daughter, will succeed in removing false impressions, when occasion offers, and will induce her to walk in the true way of perfection. More is gained by mildness than by severity. Severity breeds trouble, temptation, darkness and apathy. Mildness brings peace and encourages your daughters to love God. If all superiors would act in this way, all their subjects would sanctify themselves. The many miseries we see in some religious have their source in a want of prudence. Where there is trouble there the devil is to be found ; and where the devil is God is not."

The remainder of this precious document is, most unfortunately, lost. However, we agree with Gerard's Italian biographer when he writes : " The least experienced in ruling others will readily acknowledge the wisdom of the author."[1]

The second letter is of quite another nature. Even the lay reader must realise how unusual and delicate was the work of spiritual direction to which Providence had called this lowly laybrother. It demanded extraordinary prudence, and Gerard was paid an extraordinary compliment by men like Cafaro and Fiocchi—to say nothing of Alphonsus himself—when they allowed him to undertake it. Two outstanding virtues of the saint, however, with which we are acquainted assured security and success where there was such ample room for peril and disaster. Gerard's humility took him by the one hand and Gerard's obedience by the other and led him safely and triumphantly through. Earlier in our story we have given passages from his correspondence with nuns which reveal his thoughts about himself. We now give a letter in which we hear the authentic voice of the obedient religious.

Gerard had been corresponding with Ripacandida for many months when suddenly, for reasons we can do no more than guess at, the Bishop of Melfi, Mgr. Basta, forbade the nuns all correspondence on matters of conscience with anyone but the ordinary confessor of the community.[2] As Gerard was not expressly excepted, he came under the ban. Now as most of the community had been unreservedly following his direction, to their own untold spiritual benefit, we can easily imagine

---

[1] Benedetti, p. 221.

[2] "Perhaps," writes Benedetti, " at the suggestion of the Neapolitan Carmelites, who wanted to introduce into the monastery certain mitigations of the primitive rule of St. Teresa."—p. 214. (Cfr. Corrispond. di S. Alfonso. vol. i, p. 193, 211).

how upset many of the good Sisters were by this bolt from the blue. Nor were they slow to voice their annoyance and displeasure. As the prioress herself was involved in the prohibition, she let Gerard know through the medium of a priest both what had happened and its reactions on her community. The prohibition was evidently restricted to the writing of spiritual letters, not to the receiving of them ; and accordingly the prioress received the following from Gerard :—[1]

" Very Rev. Mother, if the dear bishop has forbidden you to write, he has done well ; such is the will of our dear God, and I rejoice greatly that thus Our dear Lord has relieved you of many worries. All this is a sign that He loves you greatly and wishes you to be closely united to Himself. Be of good heart ! Have courage ! These happenings must not upset you. They should rather be a source of joy. When there is question of doing God's Will, everything must give way. You, Reverend Mother, know this better than I do, or anybody else.

" What would you have me say ? I have already told you, and I tell it to you now in all confidence, though you could teach me yourself in the matter. I cannot understand how a soul consecrated to God can find anything bitter in this world and can feel anything but joy in the fact that His holy Will is accomplished in all things.

" The Will of God is the only stay of our soul. Accursed be that self-love which robs souls of so immense a treasure, of a heaven on earth, of God Himself ! Oh ! how wretched

---

[1] Tannoia, cap. xxii.

s human ignorance that makes us indifferent to such
a great possession ! Perhaps it is not the great God
Who rules all things who has allowed this to happen ?
Perhaps what He wishes on this occasion is not His
sacred Will, as it does not seem to be ? Perhaps there
s another line of conduct better calculated to lead us
to salvation ? O God ! what other and better way
of salvation have we ? And what else can we find to
give Him greater pleasure than to do His divine Will
always and in everything ? And what else does He wish
of us but that this His divine Will be done always
perfectly, *as He wills, where He wills, when He wills,*
so as to be always ready to obey His slightest command.

"Let us, then, be indifferent to everything, so that
we may carry out the divine Will with that highest
purity of intention that God asks of us. What a great
good is the Will of God ! O what a hidden and inestim-
able treasure ! Ah ! if I understand Thee aright, Thou
are worth as much as my God Himself. Who can understand Thee but my dear God ? I assure you, Reverend
Mother, it affords me great consolation to know that
you are one of those souls who feed on the beautiful
Will of my dear God alone, for I am well aware of your
heroism in this matter. Keep on, then, being transformed
into and becoming identified with the beautiful Will
of God. And what the angels are doing in heaven let
us wish to do on earth.

"Let everybody read these few lines. I believe and
have believed that his Lordship's prohibition to write
to others extends, not only to yourself, but to all the
sisters. He did right, and I beg of you not to let it
distress you, for that would be to murmur against God.

May His most holy Will be always done ! And I now declare to you that I am quite satisfied that you no longer write to me ; and I say the same to all the Sisters. And if you should detect the slightest shadow of disobedience in their sending me their regards, for the love of God please let them not do so. I am quite satisfied. It is enough if you recommend me to the Lord. This, then, is my wish, for I know well the mind of this holy prelate, who wants you all to be closely united to Jesus. If I go over there, I will refrain from asking leave to speak with you ; hence there is no use in writing, and if my superior sends me there at any time, there is no use in my seeing you, as we shall see each other in paradise. While we are on earth, let us sanctify ourselves by doing the will of others, not our own, for the will of others is the Will of God.—GERARD of the Most Holy Redeemer."

It would not have spoken well for Gerard's spiritual direction of the Carmelites of Ripacandida had such a letter failed in its purpose. No wonder it was given an honourable place in the archives of the monastery. After some time, his Lordship withdrew the prohibition at least as far as Gerard was concerned, whom he had never really aimed at and whose spiritual guidance he had expressly wished the whole community should follow.

What the bishop thought of Gerard as a spiritual guide is easily seen. As we have said, the Prioress of Ripacandida was an exceptionally holy woman and was called by God to walk the higher ways of prayer. However, in her humility, she feared delusions, and there were not wanting those about her who suggested grounds for such fears. At last, shortly after the incident just recorded, the bishop went in person to Ripacandida to subject her spiritual state to a close investigation. Besides himself and Father Fiocchi, he insisted on another taking his seat on the board of examiners; and that other was Brother Gerard.

CHAPTER XI

A SAINT is essentially a lover, first of God, and then, for God's sake, of all that God loves ; and the more purely and intensely he loves, the more of a saint is he. All the saints were great, for they all loved greatly ; but not in all did this love show with the same brilliancy and warmth. Supernatural endowments, temperament (for grace builds on nature), personal environment, individual career—all these things have much to do with the greater or lesser flaming forth of their charity.

Now amongst those saints whose love for God and their fellowmen is a marked and visible characteristic, bursting from their heart in a thousand ways, assuming at times spectacular forms and leaping to the eye on every page of their story, is assuredly St. Gerard Majella. We have seen how he loved God. Times innumerable that love rose to transcendent heights in ecstasy and rapture, and rose higher still in his complete and unconditional capitulation to God's Will, particularly when that Will meant suffering and humiliation for himself. We are not going to repeat ourselves on this subject. But before we describe Gerard's passing from this world, we must speak in some detail of certain aspects of his love for God and man which we have reserved for this chapter.

The tremendous truth that God became man for love of man—for love of Gerard Majella—swept Gerard's heart. We have just seen how deeply he could peer into this mystery of unfathomable love and with what lucidity and precision he could discourse on it. But the deeper he saw the more ardently he loved, and knowing what we do of him, we shall not be surprised to learn that devotion to the Divine Infancy was especially dear. How could the child of Muro ever forget the Child of Bethlehem? Gerard had scarcely stepped from the cradle when these two children—Mary's Son and Benedetta's—met and loved. How could he ever forget Capotignano and his Divine Playmate and the little white loaves? Though he left the days and ways of childhood behind, shedding everything but their innocence and charm, yet to the very end the Infant Jesus—the *Gesù Bambino* of his own sweet Italian— never lost His place in his heart, which had never ceased to be the heart of a child. According to Tannoia and others who knew him well, this devotion was a source of particularly pure angelic joy for him. Christmas Day was in its fullest sense a gala day for his soul. Its preparatory novena was made in his usual fashion, except that he threw into it a weight of prayer in the church and penance in his cell commensurate with the occasion. And when the great morning dawned, his heart tuned in with the chorusing angels. When he was sacristan, the Christmas crib got of his best, and all that love and skill could do to body forth the divine events of Bethlehem was done. He would bend ecstatically over the inanimate images of that Mother and Child, as he realised all they meant for the world and for himself. We read that when David was bringing the Ark into Jerusalem he "danced with all his might before the Lord,"[1] and we read in Berruti's pages that Gerard gave vent in a similar way to the exuberance of his joy before the crib. All the good things of Christmas— its gifts and toys, its freedom and merriment, its colour and music and warmth—its atmosphere half of heaven and half of earth—that make of Christmas the great festival for children had all their counterpart in the spiritual world in which this child of God lived and moved and loved.

But his love for Jesus drank from another source besides the crib: it drank from the tabernacle which enclosed no lifeless image but the substantial and abiding presence of his Lord. Gerard's devotion to the Blessed Sacrament was too special, too striking, too beautiful to be dismissed with a word. Literally it can be said that he and his sacramental Lord were lifelong friends. From the moment Gerard heard at Benedetta's knee that Jesus was *really* in the church, in the tabernacle, in the ciborium, in the consecrated Host, he drew the logical conclusion with all its practical implications: he should strive to get as near that Presence as possible and remain in It as long as he might.

We have see how as a child, and later as a youth in the world, all the time that had not to go to other things went to visiting Jesus. It was nothing for Gerard to spend hours on end with Him, for the hours in that company were minutes. When the day was not long enough, he borrowed largely from the night; and we

[1] 2 Kings, vi, 14.

have not forgotten how he would coax the sacristan of Muro's cathedral to entrust him with its keys. Then he would lock himself in, and while the world slumbered, hold untiring and loving converse with Him whom he would call: *Carcerato mio Dio.*[1]

However, it was when the saint entered religion and became a permanent dweller under the same roof as Jesus that his devotion found its greatest scope and took on its loveliest aspect. We are sure that if his vocation to the cloister had meant nothing else than this, he would have put it before all the world could offer. Jesus and Gerard were now literally living in the same house : it was a fact as true and plain and simple to him as that Gerard was living in the same house with anyone of his confrères. He needed no reminder of it. When he opened the oratory door and entered, there was no striving to recall the truth that he was entering that Presence. The consciousness of It at once descended upon him and possessed him as truly and fully as would the consciousness of any human presence into which he had suddenly come. There was the same instantaneous realisation of entering the presence of Jesus when he entered the chapel as there was of entering the presence of his superior when he entered his superior's room. There was no preliminary adjusting of his thoughts. We can hardly imagine him beginning his visit to the Blessed Sacrament with an act of faith ; if he made one, it must have been very brief and rather formal.

---

[1] This was a favourite idea of his. When writing to his holy friend Mother Mary of Jesus in Ripacandida he speaks of the tabernacle as a prison of love . . . *carcere di amore*, and addresses the prioress as *prima carceriera*, head gaoleress. In Ord. no. 7, § 573.

After all, the making of such an act does suppose the formal deprecating of a doubt. And for Gerard the veil between Him and his Lord must have been very thin.

And so Gerard made the most of Jesus. He had his laybrother's duties to perform, many of them menial and seemingly trivial, and nobody ever had more orthodox views on duty and its incontestable and inalienable claims. But when duty left him free, people knew where to find him. As a religious, too, he had leave to steal from sleep. He always spent some hours of the night in the church and, as Tannoia tells us, " he was to be found in the morning in the very spot where he had placed himself the night before."[1] The siesta or afternoon nap provided for by his rule and so necessary for an Italian, went the same way. When outside his monastery he made instinctively for the Real Presence, wherever he could find It, and gave It all the time it was possible to give.

A witness tells us that he would " speak to Jesus with an intensity of love and faith, like a passionate lover, like a friend having a heart-to-heart talk with a friend ; and as he knelt in adoration, his countenance aglow (" like a live coal " says another), his overcharged heart heaving sighs of love, his eyes ever fixed on the tabernacle, he seemed to have been transformed into a seraph."[2] He surely experienced the truth of his holy Founder's words : " It is sweet for everyone to be in the company of a dear friend ; and shall we not

---

[1] English Edit. p. 261.
[2] In Apost. no. 9, § 106.

find it sweet, in this valley of tears, to remain in the
company of the best Friend we have, and who can do
us every kind of good ; who loves us with the most
tender affection and therefore dwells always with us ?"[1]
" He would frequently be heard asking and answering
questions, as if he were speaking face to face with
Jesus,"[2] yet another witness records. He was once
overheard uttering these words : " Thou callest me a
fool ? And have I not learnt my folly from Thee Who,
though an Infinite God, remainest imprisoned here
for my sake ? "[3] These exhibitions of a saint's holy
ardours were often surreptitiously enjoyed by members
of the community who would slip into the oratory for
the purpose and take up their position in quiet corners.

During his stay in Naples he had a good deal of time
on hands and the city's numerous sanctuaries saw much
of him, as he went about seeking for his Beloved. It
was no rare thing for him to spend half a day in one
of them hidden away in some corner and stretched
in prayer upon the floor. As the devotion of the Forty
Hours went on continuously in the capital all the year
round, he knew where to go. He writes to Mother Mary
of Jesus : " I am staying here in Naples, and now more
than ever I regale myself—*me la scialo* . . . with my
dear God."[4]

As sacristan he got a great chance, and no sacristan
ever made more of his chances. Though the house of
Iliceto was a poor one, Gerard's love made him rich
in expedient when there was question of beautifying

---

[1] *Visits to the Most Blessed Sacrament*, xix.
[2] In Ord. no. 9, § 142.
[3] In Apost. no. 11, § 94.
[4] Cfr. Tannoia, cap. xxiii.

the habitation of his Lord. The feast of Corpus Christi and its octave was a wonderful time for him. He walked on air and for eight full days his soul held high revelry. It was a holy riot of joy and love.

At Iliceto visitors were many, especially during the enclosed retreats, and it sometimes happened that there were not rooms enough to go round. Thus, not infrequently, when Gerard returned from one of his many outings, he would find his cell occupied. There were no 'phones, no " wires " in those days, and letters were slow travellers, being often outstripped by their writers. On such occasions the floor of the church became his couch, and he did not ask a better. He found another resting-place also. The high altar was a hollow structure ; it could be entered from the back by a little door, and there it gave space enough to lie in. Gerard often spent his night there praying. Great saints, however, as well as great poets sometimes nod, and once, after a long vigil of love in this recess, poor Gerard nodded and slept the sleep of the just. He was not sacristan at the time. Whatever was left of the early morning hours passed by. Suddenly the slumbering saint awoke. What was that ? It was the bell at the altar above him heralding the consecration at the first public Mass ! He was in a dilemma. Were he to emerge from his hiding-place, the people would see him and the cat of his nightly vigils would be out of the bag of his humility. Accordingly, he remained where he was ; another Mass followed, and it was not until it was over that Our Lord's fellow-prisoner was able to effect his escape.

In one way no one ever found less difficulty than

Gerard in leaving God for God, in leaving Him in the oratory, when it was not his duty to be there, to find Him in the kitchen or the garden or his tailor's work-room, whither obedience had summoned him. And yet there were times when he had to fight against his other self and literally tear himself away from the magnetic influence of the Real Presence. Tannoia describes a truly extraordinary scene of which he him-self was an eyewitness :—" It was a touching sight," he writes, " to see the struggle that sometimes went on within him as a result of his love for Jesus and his spirit of obedience. Obedience, however, always triumphed. One day, when I happened to be in the church, but in a place where he could not see me, he passed and genuflected before the tabernacle. He then struggled to rise ; but finding himself unable to do so, he exclaimed aloud : ' Let me go, for I have something to do.' Whereupon he hastily withdrew, as though he were tearing himself away by main force from the presence of his beloved Lord."[1] " Surely one of the most moving stories in the whole of hagiography,"[2] writes the late Father Thurston in his short sketch of the saint's life.

" Whenever he had to pass through the church and cross the sanctuary," the same Tannoia writes, " he did so like lightning. Doctor Santorelli once asked him why he went with such haste. ' What else can I do ? ' Gerard replied, ' more than once He has taken me un-awares and I must make haste, as I am afraid He may play some trick on me.' And he was fully justified by

---

[1] English Edit. p. 269.
[2] *Butler's Lives of the Saints*, vol. x, 232.

the following occurrence. One morning the doctor, having left the house by the sacristy door, went ahead while Gerard went and prostrated himself before the altar of the Blessed Sacrament. Now, just as the doctor was leaving the church, he heard the Brother utter a loud cry, and on going over to see what had happened, he found him extended on the floor in a state of ecstasy. When he came to himself and saw the doctor and several others around him, he bent his head in silence and confusion and ran off. Next day the doctor met him in the house and began to laugh. Gerard guessed the reason and remarked : ' Did I not tell you that there is no jesting with Him ? Don't you see what surprises He springs on me ? ' "[1] Tannoia adds : " Time would fail me were I to relate all the miraculous occurrences of this sort that took place in this house (Caposele)." He finds room, however, for the following.

" At times Gerard would break into sighs to the surprise of his company. One day, having been taken to task by Father Caione for this, he took the Father's hand and placed it over his heart. Father Caione had to admit that it was beating at an alarming rate and that he could not understand how Gerard could bear its violence. On another occasion, he said to Doctor Santorelli : ' If I were alone on a mountain, I should love to set the world on fire with my sighs.' And when he placed the doctor's hand over his heart, Santorelli felt it throb so violently that it seemed as if it would leave his breast."[2]

But relations with his Eucharistic Lord were not

---

[1] Cap. xxvi.
[2] *Ibid.*

restricted to ecstacies and rapturous sighing. He drew
help for others from that divine treasury which he knew
so well how to open, and this at times even in material
difficulties. One of the last duties he ever had to perform
as a laybrother was to act as clerk of the works while
an addition was being built to the house of Caposele.
Now one day, during the course of these operations,
he was summoned to the rector's room. The latter told
him frankly that he was in difficulties. Funds were so
low that he feared he could not proceed with the building.
" Father," said Gerard, " draw up a petition to Jesus
Christ in the Blessed Sacrament."[1] The rector had no
objection to this, merely stipulating that Gerard himself should present it. The latter was only too pleased.
When the petition was duly drawn up, he proceeded
with it at once to the church, followed no doubt by the
superior, laid it on the altar, and then, knocking at the
tabernacle door, was heard to say with the simple daring
of a spoilt child : " Lord, here is our petition ; it is for
You now to answer it." He then returned to his work.
It was Thursday. The following night he spent in prayer
before the altar. At daybreak on Saturday he knocked
again at the little door behind which dwelt the Father
of the poor. Scarcely had he descended the steps of
the altar when he heard the door-bell ring. He ran to
open. Two bags filled with money were lying there.
He hurried off with them in triumph to the rector's
room. The priest Donato Spicci already mentioned,
who happened to be present, asked to be given two
pieces of this money, which he never ceased to treasure.

---

[1] Benedetti, p. 351.

If Gerard's heart flamed and grew ecstatic before the tabernacle, it suffered and bled at the thought of those who could be there and were not. The sight of empty churches and crowded city squares stuck daggers in it. And so, wherever he went, in town and countryside, he told men of their forgotten Friend. Wherever he could find worshippers in the highways and by-ways of his own little world, he would plead with them to keep vigil with his " dear Prisoner." Writing long years after his death, Tannoia tells us that " it was to him that the populations of many districts are indebted for their assiduity in visiting the Blessed Sacrament."[1]

No one understood better than Gerard that the tabernacle is only the lodging-house of Jesus on earth and that His home is the heart of man. Now what a tabernacle, however beautiful and rich, is to a human heart, a visit to the Blessed Sacrament—however close and loving—is to the sacramental embrace of Communion. We have already seen what Communion meant for Gerard. Every stage of his life, almost from infancy to death, was illumined by some wonderful and lovely incident in connection with his devotion to the Sacrament of sacraments. No reader of his life can easily forget the mystic loaves that this child of grace received from his Divine Friend ; or the bitter tears of the boy of eight, as he walked back dejected from the altar rails where his Lord had been denied him ; or that wondrous First Communion given him by angelic hands. No reader can easily forget those sadly sweet occurrences during the dark days of calumny and suspicion, when he could

---

[1] English Edit. p. 269.

not trust himself to serve Mass lest he should snatch the Host from the hands of the priest to feed his ravenous heart ; when he hung lovingly over the recovered particle, which he dared not consume ; when, after the trial had ended and he was free once more to receive his Lord, it was only when the moment came to do so that he emerged from his mysterious invisibility.

We remember his thirty-sixth resolution : " My thanksgiving shall last until after midday, and my preparation for next day from midday until six o'clock in the evening." Six hours for the one and six hours for the other ! It is quite clear that by preparation and thanksgiving he means something particular and specific, and not merely the practice of God's presence and the spirit of prayer which he cultivated so intensely even while discharging his duties with such promptitude and thoroughness. The resolution needs no comment. The Eucharistic embrace of his Jesus was the supreme moment, the essential act of his day ; everything else led up to it and flowed from it. To miss it meant starvation for his soul.

Canon Bozzio relates the following incident. "I noticed that his soul was under the stress of supernatural emotion. On my asking if he had received Holy Communion, he replied that he had not done so owing to some obstacle or other which his humility had placed in his way. When he called on me after dinner the same day, I saw at once that his hunger for the Eucharistic Bread, which a sense of his own unworthiness had kept under in the morning, had revived and had given rise to a vehement inward yearning for his sacramental Lord. The Servant of God tried to divert his mind and heart by taking a walk in the country and singing the *Lamentations* of Jeremias. But all to no purpose. I then brought him to the parish church. We locked the door and together sang the hymn beginning with the words : *Fiori felici* . . . O happy flowers . . . while he accompanied on the organ, which he played fairly well.[1] My own voice resembled that of the organ, issuing as it did from a cold unfeeling heart, while his gave expression to a soul wounded with love for Jesus."[2]

Two names—Jesus and Mary—are ever linked together in the thoughts and affections of every child of the Church and follow swiftly and easily on each other from his lips. If the love we give the Son is ever, and of necessity must be, infinitely beyond the love we give His Mother, it is still true to say that the love that Mother claims from us is, and should be something immeasurably greater than any which the highest and dearest saint in heaven may receive.

Gerard knew it well, and this special love Mary got from him in abundance from the first to the last of his life. She was early in the field of his young heart. He could never afterwards recall Capotignano without recalling her. Mary's many shrines in the various districts in which he passed his days were so many

---

[1] Tannoia relates the following : " As he was afterwards going into the choir (of the convent of the Most Holy Saviour in Foggia), he was asked to play the organ. He declined, saying that he did not know how ; but as they continued to press him, he at last consented and executed a most beautiful pastorale in the most masterly manner." (English Edit. p. 336). Bearing in mind Gerard's shrinking from even the shadow of an untruth, we wonder if the Holy Ghost was his music master as well as his professor in theology.—Cfr. Appendix I.

[2] In Ord. no. 7, § 542.

magnets that drew him sweetly but irresistibly towards her. She and Gerard had held mysterious converse at Caposele long before he lived there as a Redemptorist. Iliceto, his first home in the Congregation, held an added charm for him when he was told that it was one of Mary's sanctuaries.

Gerard's attitude to Mary alternates delightfully between that of a lover and that of a child. He readily understood why St. Bernard spoke of her as the " *Raptrix cordium* . . . the Ravisher of hearts," and when asked why he clung so long to her images and shrines, he replied : " The Madonna has ravished my heart, and I have given it to her."[1] It is probable that even in his twelfth year he vowed his virginal love to Mary. As he grew to manhood, people would sometimes tease him by asking him if he ever intended marrying. They would get this cryptic reply : " I will choose a beautiful lady for my spouse."[2] According to Tannoia, he would say plainly : " I am already married. I am wedded to the Madonna."[3]

On one famous occasion he let people see his meaning. He was twenty-one at the time. It was the third Sunday in May, 1747. Now on this particular Sunday it was customary to celebrate a feast in honour of the Immaculate Conception in the cathedral of Muro. It was preceded by a novena and no splendour was spared. The crowds were very great. Everything was ready for the procession in which Our Lady's statue was to be carried round. Gerard was kneeling in prayer.

---

[1] Benedetti, p. 38.
[2] In Apost. no. 6, § 13.
[3] English Edit. p. 252.

Suddenly he arose and was seen elbowing his way
through the vast congregation, till he reached the
statue. All looks were now directed towards him and
there was an expectant hush. His eyes shone with an
unwonted light. His face was aflame. Standing before
the statue, he took a ring from his finger and placed it
reverentially on one of the fingers of Mary's image,
crying aloud as he did so, in a transport of love and
joy : " Behold ! I am wedded to the Madonna ! "[1]   As
he afterwards beautifully put it, he there and then
ratified before the world what he called the espousals
of his own purity with the purity of the Virgins of virgins.
Berruti states that on that occasion he at least renewed
a vow of chastity. The Virgin of virgins looked after
him well : he passed amongst men more like an angel
than a child of earth. " An angel of purity . . . a mirror
of purity . . . an angel clad in mortal flesh "[2]: such are
some of the expressions on the lips of witnesses in the
process. Father Celestino de Robertis, who was his
confessor for some weeks towards the close of Gerard's
life, used to say that he felt ashamed as he saw him
kneeling at his feet, as innocent and unsullied as one
of the Lord's own angels.

These wonderful espousals were to remain no dead-
letter. Caione tells us how on one occasion the saint
was commissioned to accompany two young students
from Iliceto to Ciorani. It meant staying overnight
in an inn. So extraordinary was his charm that the
innkeeper's daughter fell in love with him, and reversing
the *rôle* usually played by young ladies in these matters,

---

[1] Benedetti, p. 39.
[2] In Process. *passim*.

she proposed to him. Courteously but decisively Gerard told her he was consecrated to the Madonna. The Italian maiden understood.

Tannoia speaks of this love of his for Mary as " truly extraordinary."[1] Caione tells us that the mere mention of her name was enough to send him into a rapture.[2] Mary's feasts were events in his life, prepared for by intensive prayer and multiplied austerities, and celebrated with lyrical enthusiasm. His joy on these days was likened to that of a son on meeting his mother after a long absence. When superiors allowed him he spent a great part of the preceding night in the church. Even as a boy in the world he would sing her praises on such occasions as he went along the street and would literally dance for joy, utterly oblivious of the passers-by. Mary's picture was at times enough to send him into an ecstasy. Whenever he visited Melfi, he used to be the guest of a family named Scoppa. Now one day the lady of the house, Donna Anna, chanced to draw the attention of her guest to a particularly beautiful picture of the Blessed Virgin hanging on the wall eight palms from the ground. Exclaiming : " O Donna Anna, what a beautiful thing you have ! "[3] he rose like a feather to the height of the picture, which he grasped rapturously with both hands. It was a new experience for the good lady, and she promptly fainted. The reader will not have forgotten the wonderful ecstatic flight of Gerard when he discoursed on Mary's dignity as Mother of God.

---

[1] English Edit. p. 251.
[2] *Ibid.*, p. 374.
[3] In Ord. no. 7, § 92.

This dignity of hers awed him and made him particularly eloquent.

Indeed unless one were prepared to witness such supernatural displays, it was not wise to bring Gerard into such surroundings. Many were the callers at the house of Signor Capucci in Lacedonia, where the saint often stayed, and many were the prodigies they witnessed. One day the master of the house was showing Gerard and his visitors through a room which contained a number of religious paintings. Amongst them was one of Our Lady. Gerard had scarcely looked at it when, turning to the company, he exclaimed : " Isn't she beautiful ! Look ! isn't she beautiful ! "[1] Then, suiting the action to the word, in the sight of the whole group, which consisted of priests and gentry, he rose in the air to the height of the picture repeating the words he uttered a moment before. He then kissed it rapturously.

In a Congregation founded by the author of the *Glories of Mary*, and in which devotion to Mary has such a high place, this lover of the Virgin Mother felt at home. He lovingly embraced every traditional practice in her honour. He loved her under every aspect ; but her Immaculate Conception, her divine Motherhood and her Sorrows chiefly absorbed his thoughts. Though the dogma of the Immaculate Conception had not yet been promulgated, the Fathers of the Institute, following the example of their blessed Founder, bound themselves by vow to defend it. It was not customary for the laybrothers to do this, but Gerard had asked and obtained leave for it. It is said that most of the

---

[1] In Ord. no. 7, § 523.

miraculous medals of the Immaculate Conception which
Father Pepe, S.J. distributed amongst the faithful in
Naples passed through Gerard's holy hands. Indeed he
seems to have had an inexhaustible supply of rosaries
and scapulars for distribution, and wherever he went
he was always trying to win new clients for Mary. He
revelled in beautifying her shrine and in organising
processions in her honour with all the colourful and
melodious ritual so dear to her Italian children.

Gerard's love for Mary his mother was the love of a
very little child. She was in his eyes the real mother
of his soul, his "*Mamma Maria*," as he loved to call
her in his letters. One day Santorelli asked him if he
loved the Madonna. " Doctor," he replied, " you really
torture me ! Do you hear what he asks me ! "[1] And
so saying he hurried away to hide his emotions.

There was a certain Father Andrew Strina in the
community with Gerard at one time. Now Father
Andrew was a very simple holy soul who had a particular
devotion to the Divine Infancy. On one occasion, the
Father and the Brother met at recreation. This time
it was Gerard who began the teasing. Going over to
Father Andrew, he said in mock reproach : " You don't
love the Infant Jesus ! "[2] He quickly got a Roland for
his Oliver. "And you don't love the Madonna," retorted Father Andrew. On the very verge of an ecstasy
Gerard clasped good Father Andrew in his arms.

Mary's answering love for her child was more than
once spectacular. We have it on the testimony of Fathers
Giovenale and Caione that one night she appeared to

---

[1] Tannoia, cap. xxvi.
[2] *Ibid.*

him in the church in Iliceto and flooded him with
heavenly joy. And they were to meet at the supreme
moment of Gerard's death.

The third great love of Gerard's heart was his neighbour. After all, it was the great touchstone of his
sanctity, and for the very simple reason that it was the
great touchstone of his love for God. The theory of
Christian charity a child can understand : only spiritual
giants carry it out to the full. To love one's neighbour
as oneself, to do as we would be done by, to see Christ
in one's neighbour, no matter how faint and blurred
and distorted and even repulsive be the image, and to
treat him accordingly—what doctrine could be plainer,
more outspoken and at the same time more beautiful ?
Yet, as we all know too well, what doctrine is more
difficult in practice, when a particularly unlovable and
unChristlike neighbour crosses our path, not in the
abstract but in the concrete ? Hypothetical unpleasant
people it is easy enough to love and put up with ; when
they appear in the flesh it is another question. What
Gospel teaching calls for a more radical and ruthless
re-adjusting of our attitude towards those who people
our own immediate world ? Few indeed are they who
carry it out to all its logical conclusions. All the saints
did so, and because they did so they were saints. And
the saints are few. Obviously, however, not all the
saints were given equal opportunities for the display
of this love, since they were not all brought into the
same close and constant relationship with others. While
many of them—the greater number indeed, at least in
modern times—spent themselves directly in one way or
another in the service of their fellowmen, others there

were whose activities in their behalf were restricted to solitary prayer and penance and the distant example of a holy life.

Now in his own lowly sphere of a Redemptorist lay-brother St. Gerard Majella belonged to the former class. He lived his comparatively brief life amongst men, and before ever he entered the cloister, and particularly after having done so, he went about, like his divine Master, " doing good." " I would give my life a thousand times for my neighbour," he would say, " if I could get it back again a thousand times to sacrifice it for his sake."[1] As one witness puts it, " he wanted everyone to be holy and happy."[2] He was milk and honey for others, gall and wormwood for himself. It may be said of him that he loved all men, except Gerard Majella.

Perhaps the most constant demands on our charity are made when we are called upon to help others, to do them a service when they are in difficulties. Its exercise can range from the trivial to the sublime. Our failing to help others can at times make us merely rude ; at times our helping them may make us heroes. Before Gerard ever became a Redemptorist, he had what almost amounted to a holy passion for helping others. And divine Omnipotence seemed to be at the back and call of His servant, for what after all were Gerard's countless miracles but countless instances of God helping him to help others when, humanly speaking, he was powerless ?

However, it was when he became a member of a religious community that opportunities abounded for

---

[1] Benedetti, p. 80.
[2] In Apost. no. 12, § 99.

gratifying this holy longing for doing good to his neighbour. We refer the reader to that very ordinary but very comprehensive and most exacting body of resolutions he drew up for himself, which were to govern his relations with others. To help others at all costs and in all circumstances, where help was possible, was one plank in his platform. He literally jumped at every chance and helped with such obvious gusto that it was a joy to ask his help and to receive it. The sight of anyone in difficulties of any sort grieved him and stirred him to action. The cost was never counted. Thus, according to the custom of his day, his journeying was usually done on horseback, and if ever he came up with a man carrying a heavy load, he insisted on rider and man changing places.

Once, when on his way to Sant'Agata di Puglia, not far from Iliceto, he saw a poor woman struggling up the rugged hill on which the town stood and carrying on her head a heavy basket of clothes she had just been washing in a neighbouring stream. He went over at once, insisted on taking the basket on his own head, and in spite of much natural repugnance, bore it through the public square, not leaving it down till he had reached the door of the woman's home.

On another occasion, when accompanying a number of candidates for ordination from Melfi to Atella, he came across a party of labourers who were evidently in difficulties. A stream that lay between them and their work was in flood and they feared to venture over. Gerard and his company were on the other side. He was on horseback. He at once took each of the men in turn up behind him and thus carried them all safely across.

It was no fun, and he was warned of his danger. "Love for my neighbour urges me," was the reply, as he spurred on his mount with the words, "Come, horse of mine, let us give pleasure to our God!"[1] Forthwith he went boldly ahead.

In the various spheres in which he was employed as a laybrother Gerard had endless opportunities for practising that small heroism of charity in community life known so well to religious as choosing the worst things for self. He never did anything else. His tailor's shop in particular gave him great scope, and without much danger of display. Thus, for instance, it was discovered that during one excessively severe winter in Iliceto he had gone without an undervest in order to give it to another Brother. His own poor body, already marked out for an early death, was covered with nothing but a shirt and a threadbare habit. He had written: "I will leave the best and most convenient place to others, taking for myself what God may leave me. Thus others will be pleased, and myself as well." Never was resolution better kept.

This branch of Gerard's charity once rose to a great height. His friend, poor Father Margotta, *il suo caro Padre*, as he loved to call him, was a prey to much anguish of soul. Now in such cases Gerard could prove a great comforter. According to a witness, he consoled the afflicted *con faccia di paradiso*,[2] as he puts it, urging them to trust in God and to bear their trials patiently in order to reach heaven and give pleasure to Jesus Christ Who has borne so much for love of us. Common-

---

[1] Benedetti, p. 80.
[2] Cfr. *Ibid*. p. 133.

place motives enough for Christian forbearance, which anyone of us no doubt would suggest to the distressed ; but when they were suggested by a saint *con faccia di paradiso* it was quite another matter. Now at this particular time Gerard was away from his friend, who was in Naples. But he prayed for that friend. He did more : imitating his Lord also in this who " carried our sorrows," he asked God to relieve Father Margotta of his cross and lay it on his own shoulders. He was taken at his word. Santorelli one day entered his room and found him writing a letter. " What are you doing there ?" inquired the doctor with the boldness of an intimate friend. Gerard told him : he was writing to Father Margotta to inform him that henceforth he would be free from his sufferings and to let him know the joy it gave his correspondent. Letters from Naples proved that Father Margotta's sufferings ceased that day. That same day, too, a change came over Gerard which showed that his brave offer had been accepted by Heaven : his wonted cheerfulness had given way to a strange depression ; the gleam had gone out in his eyes, the smile had faded from his face. He seemed to be another man. Struck by his altered countenance, Father Caione, as his rector, demanded an explanation. It came in these words : " I had not the heart to see Father Margotta suffering any longer, and so I offered myself to Jesus Christ to suffer in his stead."[1]

Few things call for more delicate, understanding, and not rarely unrequited charity than illness. Gerard loved the sick, or rather he loved his suffering Lord in these

---

[1] Tannoia, cap. xxvii.

His suffering members. This ascetic man, so fierce and implacable where his own innocent body was concerned,—this pursuer of the cross, who hunted after pain as men hunt after pleasure, was a mother to the sick. Naturally his chances of doing them service grew vastly in frequency and scope when he entered religion. The sick, moreover, found a place in his resolutions. Brother Pasquale, whom Gerard had tenderly nursed, spoke thus of him to Father Caione : " How kind that Brother is to the sick ! How ready he is to render them every service ! What a comfort his holy conversation was to me ! Happy the patient who has him for a nurse ! "[1] Tannoia tells us that visiting the sick was Gerard's " favourite occupation."[2] And he did it daily ; it was his resolution to do it several times a day. But his visits meant more than holy discourses. He anticipated a patient's every want and did everything his heart could suggest to alleviate pain.

While he was in Caposele, some of the students were studying philosophy in the house. Amongst them was Pietro Picone who shortly after his profession had fallen into consumption. He was so won over by Gerard's kindness that he could not do without him. One night he asked Brother Nicolas the infirmarian to fetch him. As it was midnight, the Brother thought it better not to do so. What was his surprise on seeing the saint coming to offer his services to the sick youth ! Pietro died a few days later in Gerard's arms.

It was all one whether the sufferer was a confrère or a guest. He saw Christ equally in each, each got of

[1] Caione.
[2] English Edit. p. 297.

his best, and it is hard to see how Christ in person could have received more sympathy and care. A certain Canon Francis Anthony Sabbatelli of Melfi had been taken seriously ill while staying in our house at Iliceto. Now Gerard and this priest were perfect strangers to each other. The good Brother, however, scarcely left the patient's bedside day or night. The Canon, not realising the gravity of his illness, saw no need of a night nurse and so never suspected Gerard's presence in the room, till one night he woke up suddenly to find him standing at the foot of the bed scanning his face as an anxious mother would scan the face of her sick child. And he had gone without his night's rest to be there.

A glimpse he once got of the interior of the Home for Incurables—the *Casa degl' Incurabili*—in Naples awoke all the tenderness of his heart. He was lavish of the time he spent there. As often as hospital rules allowed him, he would be seen going from bed to bed, doing every service he was free to do, dispensing the balm of his holy and instructive words, and in particular, with that skill of which he was a master, smoothing for the dying the dread passage to eternity. [1]

There was a large mental home in the capital whose inmates had a very special attraction for Gerard. His heart went out to them. As he thought of their condition, his thoughts went back to that dreadful night in the court of Herod when his Lord, with a fool's vesture on, was treated in mockery as one of these. He gathered

---

[1] It was while performing similar acts of charity in the same institution that his holy Founder, a score of years previously, had heard the voice saying : " Leave the world and give thyself to Me."

them about him, spoke to them of God in a way that
their poor darkened intellects could grasp, and with the
subduing power of sanctity soothed and cheered their
troubled souls. Whenever he could do so, he would
never fail to bring them little dainties. They loved his
visits, they would run joyfully to meet him, and words
like these would break from them as he left : " You
comfort us, Father. We'd love to have you always.
Don't leave us. We don't want you to go, because
you tell us things the others don't. Your lips are
heavenly lips . . . *bocca di paradiso*."[1] One day their
affection took a dangerously exuberant turn. As he
was bidding them good-bye, two of the patients rushed
at him and seizing each an arm, held him fast. " No,
no," they cried, " we don't want you to leave. Nobody
consoles us as you do. The others don't tell us what
you do. You have heavenly lips." And they hugged
the poor Brother to the point of suffocation. A third
inmate, sizing up the situation in a lucid interval,
intervened, shouting : " Hallo there ! You musn't make
so free with the fools' confessor." And with a few
vigorous thumps Gerard was saved from his friends.
In his individual chats with them he no doubt paved
the way for the real confessor, and perhaps he shared
more secrets even than he.

If it can be said that the great heart of Gerard had
any reserved and particularly warm corner in it,
perhaps that corner was for the poor. Deservedly was
he called " the father of the poor,"[2] and in the enthusiastic words of one witness : " never was there seen such

---

[1] Tannoia, cap. xxiii.
[2] In Ord. no. 12, § 117.

a lover of the poor of Jesus Christ."[1] In " these least brethren "[2] of his Master he recognised and loved that Master in a most special way. He literally identified the poor with Christ, as Christ had identified them with Himself. The amazing words of Our Lord as recorded in the Gospel was the secret of all his heroic charity towards them. Had Christ in person come to Gerard to be nursed or fed or clothed or given an alms, He would not have got a better welcome or more tender and generous treatment.

The poor had been one of his early loves. Even in his child's heart they had had their place, and he could have made the words of Job his own : " From my infancy mercy grew up with me : and it came out with me from my mother's womb."[3] Giving an alms, especially to poor children, had been a hobby of his childhood and a hobby he indulged in, not merely when it meant giving what he could spare, but when it meant making serious inroads on his own frugal meals. We have seen how faithful he was to this practice as a bishop's boy and later on when earning his livelihood as a tailor in Muro.

However, as with the sick, so with his beloved poor, it was as a Redemptorist that he was given his great opportunity of befriending them. As we have seen, many of his most spectacular miracles were wrought to fill hungry mouths ; and indeed we must believe that his display of supernatural power on such occasions served him well as a passport to the community larder.

---

[1] In Ord. no. 21, § 76.
[2] Matt. xxv, 40.
[3] xxxi, 18.

For he gave rectors and ministers no peace where the interests of his dear poor were in question. And where could they draw the line when dealing with one who so obviously had God on his side ? Cooks and refectorians might protest laudably enough against what seemed to them indiscreet generosity : only too often they had to eat their own words on beholding a miracle. And so they let him alone.

We have already given more than one instance of this when speaking specifically of him as a wonder-worker. We venture to give another. It occurred in Naples. One morning, in the absence of the superior, Father Margotta, Brother Francis Tartaglione gave two carlins (about 6d !) to Gerard to purchase something for the midday meal. On his way to the city he was accosted by a poor fellow who was clearly trying to keep body and soul together by selling what was then the equivalent of our matches, *viz.*, flint-stones and tinder. The look he gave Gerard was enough. The dinner was forgotten —or perhaps we should say, God's poor and God's power were remembered ; and with the two carlins the man's whole stock-in-trade was bought out. On meeting Brother Francis, the former asked him for the provisions. " Let us not mind these things. God alone and nothing else," was the rather disconcerting reply. " That's all very well," retorted the Brother, who, though a very holy man, took a practical view of things, " but we have to eat." Then noticing the flint-stones and tinder lying on the table, he naturally asked what all these were for. Gerard blurted out the whole story. Poor Brother Francis had sufficient virtue to smother his feelings and hope for the best. At this juncture the superior came in. Gerard told him likewise all that had happened, adding of course that he had presumed leave to act as he did. Father Margotta, in whom, it must be said, Gerard had an ally in such proceedings, smiled, but asked where the dinner was to come from. " God will see to us," was the answer, which had become almost a formula with Gerard by this time for the ushering in of a miracle. Miracle or no miracle, a witness in the apostolic process tells us what happened : " When midday struck, as they were both discoursing on heavenly things, and were inebriated with the love of God, the door-bell rang. They ran to open. There they saw a basket of cooked food sent by some unknown benefactor."[1]

Ten months before his death, Gerard was sent to Caposele, where, soon after his arrival, he was given the office of porter. If ever he coveted a particular employment in the community, it was that of porter, perhaps after that of sacristan. On receiving the keys, he remarked : " This key must open the gate of paradise to me."[2] But before paradise came at all for himself, they were to open other doors. Let us hear Tannoia : " Our house was at times besieged with poor people. Large numbers came daily ; but no mother showed such tenderness to her little child as Gerard showed to his dear poor. He sent all away satisfied ; nor did he ever show any annoyance at their tricks and rudeness. Many surreptitiously presented themselves for relief twice over, but although he saw through this, he was only delighted to be taken in and would say : ' These

---

[1] In Apost. no. 7, § 207-208.
[2] *Ibid*, § 62.

thieves are dear to Jesus Christ ! ' At times he would add with a smile : ' Sure Jesus Christ Himself stole hearts.' What was particularly admirable was his tenderness for the sick poor who were unable to come personally to the convent. These would send their children or other relatives with vessels for food, and he left no stone unturned to see that their wants were supplied. He would have gladly gone fasting himself to feed the poor and the sick."[1] He would say : ' The sick poor are Jesus Christ visible, and the Blessed Sacrament is Jesus Christ invisible.' "[2] His friend Santorelli once ventured to take him to task for his lavish giving, which he really considered excessive : Gerard should discriminate and give only to such as were in genuine need. But such reasoning did not in the least convince the porter : since they all asked him in Christ's name, they must all receive. That was his answer and that was his logic.

" His charity towards the poor," writes Tannoia again, " was very far from being confined to what he gave at the door. He gave relief to many respectable but needy families who would have been ashamed to come and beg at the door. How many poor widows and married women got help from him in all their needs ! How many girls were saved from temptation to sin by his zealous efforts to provide for them and find them situations ! And how promptly did he not hasten to the assistance of those who appealed to him ! And Providence never failed to second his holy wishes."[3]

---

[1] Cap. xxvi.
[2] *Ibid.*
[3] *Ibid.*

One would imagine that cooks and kitchen staffs should by this have known Gerard's powers and ungrudgingly given him a free hand. Yet this does not always seem to have been the case. The cook at Caposele, for instance, looked with no kindly eye on all this wholesale giving. He kept one eye on Gerard and another on the dishes. One day the porter began helping himself to the contents of the kitchen in the interests of his " dear poor " with seeming indiscrimination. It was the last straw. " What are you doing there ? " came the angry query; " there will be nothing left for the community."[1] " God will provide," came back the usual answer. The cook was none too sure of that and went off muttering doleful prophecies. Of course God did provide, and so amply that there was a substantial remainder for the poor."

The winter of 1754-'55 was an exceptionally severe one. The previous harvest had been a failure. The cold was intense, and the protracted frost and snow hindered work in the fields. Naturally the mountainous districts got the brunt of it and Caposele was hard hit. The poor suffered cruelly, and, as Tannoia tells us, up to two hundred of them—men, women and children —clamoured every morning for food at the monastery gate. The Rector, Father Caione, rose to the occasion and handled the situation in no indefinite or grudging way. He entrusted it to Gerard and gave him an absolutely free hand. Here are his words as Tannoia records them : " You must take full charge. If these people are not relieved, they will starve. I place no

---

[1] Tannoia, Cap. xxvi.

restrictions on you and give you full authority to dispose of everything in the house . . ."[1] The position was evidently extremely grave.

This occasion was a windfall for Gerard's charitable heart. He did not wait to be told twice what to do. He set to work at once with all the energy that was his in such a cause. Nothing is more ingenious, nothing richer in expedient than love, and his love for these pitiable creatures was very great. Heating, clothing, food were at once searched out wherever they could possibly be found. A large fire was kept going in front of the house for those who were awaiting their turn outside. Braziers were kept going in the hall for those within. Many were wretchedly clad. Armed with the rector's words—which he had no difficulty in interpreting literally—Gerard rummaged every nook and corner of the community wardrobe and, in the words of Tannoia, " took out all the old clothes he could find and handed them over to the tailor to be made up for the poor."[2] Never before was there such a mending and patching and darning and turning and altering as went on during that winter in Caposele. We must not forget that the porter had once been the tailor of Muro and knew well what a needle and thread and a pair of scissors could do, and wonders of tailoring were performed. We need not add that he drew generously on his own meagre stock.

The feeding of the poor was taken in hand by him in the same lavish way. Naturally the good rector had to see that his own religious family did not starve, and

---

[1] Cap. xxx.
[2] *Ibid.*

so one day, in spite of the generous permission he had given Gerard, he thought it well to set some reasonable bounds to his charity. Accordingly, he renewed his leave to give everything away that the poor really needed, but on the condition that the community should not lack the necessaries of life. However, his Reverence was humbly and quietly told not to worry, and it was during this trying period of distress that the amazing multiplication of food took place which we have already recorded. Indeed without a miracle the feeding of so many starving people would have been impossible. Money, too, came in strange ways. " Three or four times," Caione writes, " Gerard himself brought me a considerable sum in silver, telling me he had found it wrapped in paper and stuck in the keyhole of the front door. How it came there was known only to God and Gerard."[1] Nor did the apostle in him forget to feed and strengthen the often starving and sickly souls of the poor. The example of a suffering Christ, the teaching of His Gospel, the hope of an eternal heaven, together with the need of keeping their consciences in order—all these Christian truths were driven home with the persuasiveness a saint alone commands.

No wonder Gerard was never forgotten by the poor. No wonder they spoke of him as their father and honoured and loved him as the great saint he was. No wonder he was commonly spoken of as a miracle of charity. No wonder that when the news of his death was noised abroad, a multitude of sobbing poor made their way to the monastery of Caposele bewailing as

---

[1] Tannoia, cap. xxx.

they went the loss of their father and friend.

The children were the special object of his pitying love. These small victims of cold and hunger tore his heart. At the sight of the children shivering in the cold, he would burst into tears and say : " It is we who have sinned, while these poor little ones, though innocent, have to bear the punishment."[1] He would then take their little frozen hands and warm them in his own. Here we have a beautiful and moving picture of the true Christian ascetic : not dried and hardened by penitential rigours, emptied of all love for his fellows, a sort of spiritual highbrow gazing with cold aloofness and a half-averted face on common human suffering, but rather one who has directed the full stream of the love of his chastened heart away from himself towards all that suffer, recognising in them, whoever they may be, the tortured members of Christ. We love this great saint whose story we are telling, as we see him rapt in ecstasy and toying prodigiously with the forces of nature ; we love him as we watch in awe his amazing familiarities with his sacramental Lord ; but perhaps we love him most of all when we see him in the hall of Caposele, his own innocent flesh girt with penitential chains and tortured with a hairshirt, taking the numbed hands of the little ones of Christ into his own, and with his eyes full of tears, gently chafing them to warmth. What we read in the office of St. Fidelis of Sigmaringen might be written of St. Gerard : " While waging a salutary war against himself by fastings and watchings and

---

[1] Tannoia, cap. xxx.

scourgings, towards others he showed the love of a mother for her children."

One hundred and seventy-five years after Gerard's death, on Sept. 2nd, 1929, a moving scene took place. At the conclusion of a series of wonderful festivities in connection with the first jubilee of the saint's canonisation, in the very place where he had so often and so lovingly fed his dear poor, and where he had risen in ecstasy on hearing the blind flutist play St. Alphonsus' hymn, the poor of Caposele were given a sumptuous meal. The Fathers of the community and other visiting priests were their waiters, and amongst them, a linen apron hiding his purple, was the Redemptorist Archbishop Cesarano of Conza. The sight must have added to Gerard's heaven.

CHAPTER XII

THE PASSING OF A SAINT

WHEN speaking of Gerard's love for his sacramental Lord and of the practical use he made of it, we referred to certain building operations that were in progress in Caposele. It was a question of additions and repairs. The original monastery was old and far from adequate to the growing needs of the community. Now during this period Mgr. Nicolai, the Archbishop of Conza, happened to be spending four or five days in the house as a guest. In him the Fathers had a true and generous friend. His Grace had this new undertaking much at heart, as it insured an increase in the number of missioners in his diocese and would afford facilities for enclosed retreats for the clergy and laity two or three times a year. It was on the occasion of this visit that the remarkable conversion of the archiepiscopal secretary took place which we have recorded in an earlier chapter.

But Mgr. Nicolai's interest in the work was not restricted to pious desires and bland encouragement. In a special circular letter he urged his flock to contribute generously to the undertaking and headed the list himself with a handsome subscription of three hundred ducats. He did more : in order not to leave things to chance, he suggested that members of the community should make the round of his archdiocese and collect. The Rector, Father Caione, gladly and gratefully fell in with the proposal. He naturally thought of Gerard : Gerard should at any rate be of the number. He was a practised hand ; the gatherer of alms at Iliceto had been an outstanding success. He battened on the humiliations and rebuffs incidental to such an occupation. Besides, a miracle-working saint was sure to open the purse-strings, and the money was vital.

But there was one serious obstacle : the precarious state of Gerard's health. As we know, he had never been robust. His physical frailty had indeed been the one great drawback to his entering religion at all and had very nearly proved fatal to its success. And his health had never improved. The gaunt and sickly boy who presented himself at Iliceto six years before had merely grown into the gaunt and sickly man. And we remember those ominous hæmorrhages that occurred on the pilgrimage to Monte Gargano. They had now become frequent and were often copious. A collecting-tour would mean moving incessantly about in the summer heats and visiting many unwholesome districts ; and Gerard was not one to spare himself or do things by halves. His superior knew well that if he told him to go, he would be off without a thought or a word, even though he knew he was going to his death.

Against all this there was the fact that the Brother had always been able for his work and, as it had been put, actually did the work of four. Besides, his brief career in the Institute had been already so packed with miracles and supernatural endowments of all sorts that it was obvious that Heaven had a special hand over him and was ruling him with a special providence. And so, superiors thought, risks might be taken in his case that would scarcely be justified in the case of another.

One evening Father Rector sent for Gerard. He questioned him closely about his health and told him plainly of the business with which he had a mind to entrust him. With equal candour and sincerity Gerard gave a full account of himself, assuring Father Caione of his perfect readiness to undertake it. Thereupon the superior placed his hand on the Brother's head, saying mentally : " In the Name of the Most Holy Trinity I wish you to be well and to go questing." Gerard smiled. On being asked why, he replied : " Your Reverence does not speak and does speak. You wish me to be well and to go questing. I wish to obey. I wish to be well and to go questing."[1] With this auspicious beginning the rector now felt sure that the Will of God was being done in the matter. Accordingly, without further misgiving, he commissioned the Brother to undertake the work. Another Brother—Francis Fiore—was to go with him and share the archdiocese with Gerard. The saint set out on his last journey. It was destined to be a long series of wonders, many of which we have anticipated and chronicled in other chapters.

About the middle of July, 1755, he began his tour in Senerchia, going successively from there to Oliveto, Auletta, Vietri, and reaching San Gregorio most likely on the vigil of the feast of the Assumption. During his stay in this place as the guest of the archpriest Robert-tazzi, death knocked rudely at the door : while praying

---

[1] Caione.

in the church, he was seized with a copious hæmorrhage and with fever. But the knock struck listening ears. Already in the previous June, he had told Brother Januarius Rendina, the old Brother who was so dear to him on account of his exemplary life, that his death was certainly approaching and that he had asked Our Lord that he might die of consumption and forsaken.[1] And a few days later, meeting his other friend Doctor Santorelli, he said : " Doctor, don't you know that I shall die this year and die of consumption ? " " How do you know that ? " inquired the doctor. " I have asked this grace of Jesus Christ," replied Gerard, " and he has promised to grant it to me." " But why of consumption ? " pursued the doctor. " Because," returned Gerard, " if I die of that I shall be forsaken to a certain extent, for while every charity is shown the sick in our community, still with that disease one can't expect the same attention on account of infection."[2]

On this occasion, however, the local doctor in San Gregorio did not see any great and pressing danger, and adopting the panacea of the day, he bled the poor patient. This medical verdict was enough for Gerard. However plainly he read the future, obedience always guided him in the immediate present. Accordingly, he resumed his journeying and proceeded to Buccino. It was August 22nd. On the evening of his arrival, there was another hæmorrhage. Two doctors were hastily called in and another bleeding inflicted. He was further-more given doctor's orders to return to the milder climate

---

[1] Landi tells us that consumption was the common malady of those early days.

[2] Tannoia, cap. xxxiv and Caione.

of Oliveto. He did so at once, though considerably weakened with the loss of blood and though it meant a walk of six or seven miles along wretched roads. When he got there in the evening, he was a very sick and tired man. On hearing of his state, the archpriest Salvatore and his brother the doctor invited him to stay with them. Next day, August 23rd, as the hæmorrhages were increasing and as he did not know whether he should proceed to Caposele or remain where he was, he sat down and wrote the following letter to his rector :—

"I must tell Your Reverence that I got a hæmorrhage as I was kneeling in the church in San Gregorio. I saw a doctor privately and told him what had happened. He assured me over and over again that the blood did not come from the lungs, but from the throat, saying I had neither fever nor headache, and declaring over and over again that it was nothing. He bled me in the head ; this caused me no discomfort.

"I reached Buccino last evening, and as I was getting into bed, the cough and hæmorrhage returned as before. Two doctors were called in, and they prescribed certain medicines and bled me again, this time in the foot. The second hæmorrhage, too, was unaccompanied by any pains in the chest and caused me no trouble. They also told me it did not come from the lungs. However, they told me to leave at once next morning, that is, this morning, and advised me to go to Oliveto, partly for the sake of the climate and partly in order to consult Doctor Giuseppe Salvatore, who is an eminent physician. He was not at home on my arrival, but his brother the archpriest told me he would be back this evening.

"I am telling Your Reverence all this that I may

know what I am to do. If you wish me to continue the questing, I will do so without any trouble, for I feel better than when I was at home, as far as my chest goes. The coughing has stopped.

" So send me an emphatic command, come what may. It grieves me to distress Your Reverence. It is nothing, my dear Father. Recommend me to God, that He may always grant me the grace to do His divine Will and divine pleasure. Oliveto, 23rd August, 1755."[1]

This letter brought by special courier was handed to Father Caione in Caposele that same evening. It gave him and the community a painful shock, and at once he realised its import. He sent word to Gerard by its bearer to remain with the Salvatore family for the present, appealing to their charity to keep the patient till he was fit to travel home. They asked for nothing better ; it was on them the favour was being conferred. As the customary Saturday evening devotions were taking place in the church at Caposele at the time, the rector asked the prayers of the congregation for Brother Gerard. He also sent word to Brother Francis Fiore, who was in the neighbourhood of Oliveto, to proceed there at once and nurse his confrère.

Whatever happened, whether it was due to the excessive heat or to the fact that he had overdone his travelling, the would-be nurse collapsed on arrival and had to go straight to bed in a room downstairs in a state of high fever. There could be no question of his going upstairs where his patient lay. The archpriest's medical brother saw the new invalid without delay and

---

[1] Benedetti, p. 372.

then both went to report to Gerard. After a moment's pause the latter said : " Will you please tell Brother Francis from me to be obedient ; he is to drive away that fever and come up, as I cannot be looking after a sick man."[1] It was an amazing message for one sick man to send another. The doctor smiled incredulously and demurred. But Gerard insisted and the doctor went down. The moment Brother Francis received the message, he got out of bed as well as ever and went upstairs. In a tone of mock annoyance he was reprimanded for allowing the fever to attack him and keep him from doing what he had been sent out to do. He was now charged not to let the fever return, and on his promising obedience, Gerard told the doctor to feel Brother Francis' pulse. There was no trace of fever. On seeing the general amazement, the saint said : " You wonder at this, and perhaps you look on it as a miracle ; well no ; but such is the power of obedience."[2] It was his way of putting things.

Meanwhile the real patient—this extraordinary physician who could so readily heal others—evidently had no intention of healing himself. Eight days had passed since his return to Oliveto, and he grew steadily worse. He saw his own approaching end. However, as soon as he was able to move about, he made up his mind to go home, that he might die amongst his brethren. He had a few good-byes to say before leaving Oliveto and amongst others he called on the Pirofalo family, with whom he was very friendly. Signor Angelo Antonio

---

[1] Landi.
[2] *Ibid*.

Pirofalo, when giving testimony in the apostolic process in 1850, tells us what happened on that occasion : " When the Servant of God was leaving my family for the last time, he told them that his death was not far distant. ' Look,' he said, ' from your window towards our house in Caposele. As long as you see a white cloth unfurled at a window, I shall be still alive. When the cloth shall disappear, I shall be dead.' Now from Oliveto to the house of *Materdomini* is a distance of over six miles, and it is impossible to make out with the naked eye even the window, let alone a cloth. Accordingly, it was to the amazement of my family that both the window and the cloth were seen, the cloth disappearing on the day Gerard died. It was a wonderful and notorious occurrence and was in everybody's mouth in Oliveto."[1]

Though Gerard was a welcome and an honoured guest under the archpriest's roof, still his host did not let him depart altogether free of charge. Gerard had to pay for his keep in prayer, and not satisfied with a mere verbal promise on the part of the Servant of God, the archpriest suggested a written pact of mutual spiritual aid. We give it as we find it in Benedetti :— (pp. 378-379).

JESUS—MARIA

A PACT AND COVENANT BETWEEN " IL VENERANDO " BROTHER GERARD MAJELLA OF THE MOST HOLY REDEEMER AND THE R.D. ARCHANGELO SALVATORE, ARCHPRIEST.

" In presence of the Most Holy Trinity and Most

---

[1] In Apost. no. 18, § 75.

Holy Mary and of the whole Court of heaven, the aforesaid 'venerando' Brother Gerard binds himself -:—

"1. Earnestly to beg the Lord in a special way in all his holy prayers, that we may see each other for all eternity in the glory of Paradise in the enjoyment of God.

"2. To help me, even from afar, both in all my spiritual and temporal needs by recommending me to God either by word of mouth or mentally.

"3. To obtain for me strength to fulfil my duties holily, to sanctify everybody, to shun offences against the Lord, and to be purified from every imperfection.

"4. To pray to God for the temporal and especially for the spiritual welfare of the members of my family, and for the general peace of Oliveto.

"5. He binds himself, moreover, to give this spiritual help in this and the next life.

"6. Also to obtain perfect obedience for all those penitents well-known to him.

"7. And I, D. Arcangelo Salvatore, who have written these presents, bind myself to correspond with all the lights the Lord will give me, to pray and to get prayers to His Divine Majesty for the aforesaid 'venerando' Brother Gerard."

One day, when on her death-bed, the Little Flower turned to the Mother Prioress and said: "Mother, I beg of you, give me leave do die." It was even so with Gerard: he still lived, for he had not leave to die.

Gerard left Oliveto on the morning of Sunday, August 31st, and arrived at Caposele about noon, "so exhausted," writes Tannoia, "that he looked more like

a dead than a living man."[1] " The moment I laid
eyes on him," Caione records, " I could scarcely restrain
my tears."[2] When his brethren gathered around him
with their words of sympathy and encouragement, it
was he who bade them be of good cheer : he was doing
the Will of God, and he was going to God. Two excellent
reasons for Gerard's cheerfulness. He was at once put
to bed.

Three things he asked to have in his cell : a much-
loved large wooden crucifix showing vividly the wounds
of Jesus, to be hung where he could see it on the wall
facing the bed ; a picture of Our Lady beside him ; and
a sheet of paper to be fastened to the door, bearing
these words in large characters : " The Will of God
is done here, as God wills it and as long as He wills it . . .
*qui si sta facendo la volontà di Dio, come vuole Dio, e
per tutto quel tempo che piace a Dio.*"[3]

The doing of God's Will in every conceivable circum-
stance and at every conceivable cost had been the master-
passion, so to speak, of Gerard's life ; and if ever the
ruling passion was strong in death, it was strong now.
That this Will might be done was a prayer ever on his
lips and often would he be heard saying : " Lord, I wish
for nothing but to do Thy holy Will." In life he often
repeated : " I live only to please Thee, to give Thee
pleasure and always to accomplish Thy Will."[4] It was
the same now when that life was drawing to its close.
In the course of his frequent visits Father Caione once

---

[1] English Edit. p. 426.
[2] Cfr. Tannoia, cap. xxxiv.
[3] Tannoia, cap. xxxiv.
[4] In Apost. no. 11, § 128.

asked him if he were perfectly resigned to God's Will.
" I imagine that this bed is the Will of God for me,"
was the reply, " and that I am nailed here to the Will
of God. I imagine and I trust that God's Will and mine
have become one."[1] He spoke the same language to his
brethren whenever they sympathised with him : " I am
doing the Will of God. I rejoice to be doing the divine
Will and to go and be united to God."[2] Doctor Santorelli
once asked him whether he wished to live or die. " I
wish neither to live nor to die," came the answer, " I
wish only what God wishes. I should like to die in order
to go and be united to God ; I should like to live as
I have not yet suffered anything for Jesus Christ."[3]
His ancient foe from hell, with whom he had so often
measured swords and whom he had so often worsted,
dared to try to shake his resignation by an offer of life
and health. " Away, filthy beast," he cried out, " I
wish only what God wills, and I command thee to molest
me no further."[4]

Conformity with Christ Crucified had been another
passion of his life, or rather another aspect of his love.
It was the same now. It was no mere devotional ornament he asked for in that wooden crucifix. He could
not take his eyes off it. Whenever allowed to do so,
he would rise and kneel before it for a short time, that
he might unite his pains to the pains of his Lord. Often
would he be heard repeating : " I suffer, my God, because
I do not suffer." And going even a step further in

---

[1] Tannoia, cap. xxxiv.
[2] Benedetti, p. 383.
[3] In Ord. no. 20, § 86, 110.
[4] Tannoia, cap. xxxiv.

heroism than the great Teresa of Avila, he would cry out : " May I suffer, my Jesus, and not die." And again : " I suffer much, O my Jesus, but everything is little for Thee Who didst die on the cross for me. Oh ! it is little indeed ! "[1]

Canon Bozzio, his old friend and a constant caller, writes of him : " During his last painful illness, I visited him almost daily. I noticed that he often wandered, but on coming to himself his soul was always in union with God . . . . With regard to his sufferings during his illness, never did I see his countenance ruffled, never did I hear a murmur pass his lips . . . . . It was a maxim of his that no prayer can sway the heart of God like that for suffering. ' God,' he would say,, ' willingly grants all graces that further the saving of our soul ; but in order that they may be valued as they ought, He wishes us to keep asking for them a long time. This is not so, however, when we ask for suffering. God grants this request at once and most surely.' "[2] No doubt he spoke from experience. The Lord heard this prayer of His servant and sent him suffering in " good measure, and pressed down and shaken together and running over."[3] The disease that was now rapidly killing him proved that. The hæmorrhages grew in frequency and abundance, heavy sweats wore down his already enfeebled frame, fever and dysentery racked him, and he fell from one fainting fit into another. In the soul of Gerard it was all a strange mysterious criss-cross of contradictory yearnings : he longed to die and go to God,

---

[1] Benedetti, p. 383.
[2] In Ord. no. 7, § 544 seqq.
[3] Luke, vi, 38.

" to be dissolved and to be with Christ "[1]; he longed to suffer and so not to die ; he longed to do nothing but the Will of God. One day, the rector found him in what seemed to be his death agony. He was deadly pale. Suddenly the crucifix caught his eye. He revived at once, his cheeks glowed, and on being asked what had caused the change, he replied with great earnestness : " Ah ! my Father, my longing to be with my dear God is very great."[2] " Many thought he would spring from the bed as he rose from it repeatedly stretching his arms heavenward," says another ; " he was like one who had been invited to some splendid feast."[3]

As soon as it got about that Brother Gerard was seriously ill, the monastery of Caposele became a place of pilgrimage. The last days of a saint were not a thing to miss. Not a day but brought its quota of callers clerical and lay. As many as could do so gathered at the foot of the bed and went home the richer for what they heard and saw. He never lost a chance of pleading God's cause with individuals when occasion offered, and exhausted and suffering as he was, he managed even to write several spiritual letters to those who had put themselves under his direction.

As his condition grew alarmingly worse, it was thought advisable to give him Holy Communion as Viaticum, though he received daily. As Father Caione was away attending a general chapter of the Congregation, Father Francesco Buonamano, the minister, took his place. Father Caione and Brother Gerard never met again. It

---

[1] Phil., i, 23.
[3] Tannoia, cap. xxxiv.
[3] In Ord. no. 20, § 127-128.

was the 5th of September. His confrères gathered round
the saint's bed. Before giving him the sacred Host,
Father Minister held It aloft before him, saying :
" Behold that Lord Who is now your Father and Who
will shortly be your Judge. Renew your faith and make
the proper acts."[1] With great reverence and humility
Gerard spoke : " Thou knowest, my God, that all I have
ever done and said I have done and said for Thy glory.
I die happy, for I trust that I have never sought for
anything but Thy glory and Thy Will." He then
asked to be left alone with his Lord.

Next morning, September 6th, they found him worse,
and as they feared he would not pass the night, decided
to anoint him. He had now neither eaten nor drunk
anything for several days. The dysentery and the sweats
left him utterly prostrate. It was clear that the end
could not be far off. Then something happened. The
Saint of obedience was to give men one last amazing
exhibition of it. The wonder-worker who had healed
so many miraculously was now miraculously to heal
himself.

That same morning a note was handed to him from
his spiritual director Father Fiocchi, from Naples,
containing a truly extraordinary mandate : he was to
stop spitting blood and to recover ! Gerard read the
letter and quietly placed it on his breast. Doctor
Santorelli called at his usual hour and found Gerard
in a state of profound recollection, holding the letter
in his hand. On being asked what it was all about, the
saint replied : " Father Fiocchi has given me an

---

[1] Tannoia, cap.xxxiv.

obedience. He says I am to spit no more blood."
"Well," asked the doctor, "and what do you intend
doing?" Gerard replied by turning to the infirmarian
and telling him to put away the basin he had been using
during his hæmorrhages. From that moment the
hæmorrhages ceased. But as the doctor noticed that the
dysentery continued, he said: "What good is there in
the hæmorrhages stopping if the dysentery continues?"
Gerard replied: "I have got an obedience concerning
the hæmorrhages but not about the latter." Santorelli
thereupon hurried off to Father Garzilli and asked him
to let Brother Gerard see that he had not fully obeyed
the command he had received, which meant that he
should be wholly cured and not partially. Father
Garzilli went at once to the sick man's room. "Is this
the way you obey, Brother Gerard?" he said, "have
you no scruple about this? Father Fiocchi wishes you
not only to stop spitting blood but also to get rid of
the fever and of every ailment and to get well and get
up." Gerard replied humbly: "Since this is so, Father,
I will obey in everything."[1]

When Santorelli saw him again in the afternoon,
he was met by these words: "Doctor, I must get up
to-morrow." The good doctor laughed at what he took
for a little witticism on the part of the dying man. But
Gerard repeated the announcement: "Yes, I must get
up to-morrow, and if you wish to give me something
to eat, I am ready to take it."[2] It was probably the
first time poor Gerard ever asked for anything to eat.
Santorelli hesitated, but seeing his patient so sure and

---

[1] Tannoia, cap. xxxiv.
[2] *Ibid*.

noticing a basket of very choice peaches on the table —a gift from the Salvatore family in Oliveto—he told Gerard he might have one if he promised to obey Father Fiocchi. " Very good," Gerard replied, " let the dictates of obedience be fulfilled and let God be glorified."[1] There and then he eat a peach, and a second, and a third, the doctor eyeing him nervously the while. Santorelli then left, fearful of the consequences. But nothing untoward happened. On the contrary, there was an immediate and a marked improvement. Indeed so rapid had been his progress that next day the saint seemed fit to resume community life. Next morning Santorelli called. He went straight to Gerard's room. It was empty ! On asking where his patient was he was informed that he was walking in the garden ! The good man could only exclaim : " I can't explain such a recovery except by a miracle of holy obedience."[2]

A miracle indeed his recovery seems to have been, a miracle wrought by Gerard on himself. He afterwards confided to the doctor that the Nativity of the Blessed Virgin was to have been the day of his death and of his entrance into paradise, but that he had begged Our Lord for the grace to die the following day, as his death on the feast itself would have caused much inconvenience to the community on account of the numerous pilgrims.[3] Father Fiocchi's command had indeed deferred his death ; but it was deferred for more than a day. We read in Caione's *Notes* that on Saturday, September 13th, he remarked to a certain Philip Galella, a carpenter

[1] Tannoia, cap. xxxiv.
[2] Benedetti, p. 390.
[3] This feast was celebrated with the greatest pomp in *Materdomini*.

who happened to be working in the house at the time, and a townsman of his own : " I was to have died on the feast of the Nativity of the Madonna, but through obedience I am to live for thirty-three days more." When his confrères saw him in the refectory again, on Our Lady's feast and during the octave, and following all the exercises of the community, great was the rejoicing. The hæmorrhages, the fever, the dysentery, everything had ceased, and he was seemingly as well as ever. He was even given some light work to do.

Meantime, though snatched from death himself, Gerard gave still further evidence of his supernatural knowledge by announcing the death of others which, humanly speaking, he could not possibly have heard of. On the 14th September, the feast of the Exaltation of the Cross, as we have already recorded, he announced the holy death of Mother Maria Celeste of Foggia.

Some days later, a painter named Caifi came from Oliveto to do some work in Caposele. He called to see Gerard and give him the kind wishes of the Archpriest Salvatore. It was early morning. Gerard opened the door to him and spoke first. " The archpriest is greatly upset by his father's death,"[1] he said. " That can't be," Caifi replied in astonishment. He then told the Brother that he had left him the day before full of life in the midst of his family and that he had joined the rest in sending his respects to the community. The saint, however, re-asserted the fact of his death, adding that the old man had succumbed to an apoplectic stroke. When Caifi said that in that case he should have to

---

[1] Benedetti, p. 392.

réturn to Oliveto to offer his sympathy and pay his respects to the deceased, Gerard told him to let the archpriest know that he had good reason to rejoice, as his father had escaped purgatory. On his arrival at Oliveto, Caifi found the old man dead and the household in mourning. But the saint's message put a new complexion on matters.

In Gerard's own case, however, death had concluded no permanent peace ; the respite was merely a truce imposed by obedience. It seems to have entered into God's plans for the career of this extraordinary man to postpone his passing from this world just long enough to prove conclusively to men what obedience could do, and no longer. According to Landi, after about a week it became clear to all that Brother Gerard was once again a very sick man. All the old symptoms returned, all the old complaints fastened their grip once more upon his frame. When the community congratulated him on his recovery, he said : " God has thus disposed for His greater glory and to show forth the power of obedience. But I must die, and in a few days I shall be in eternity."[1] At the beginning of October he remarked to Santorelli : " Doctor, I have carried out the obedience, but I have told you I must die soon. The time has come and no remedies can now cure me."[2] This was the 4th October. Meeting him again on the morrow, he said with the same explicitness : " My time has come, my dear doctor, I shall die in a few days."[3] Next day he had to take to his bed again.

---

[1] Tannoia, cap. xxxv.
[2] *Ibid*.
[3] In Apost. no. 20, § 62.

With the new approach of death the old longing for suffering showed itself afresh and became if anything more heroic and intense. He now prayed to be associated with the internal and external pains of Christ in His Passion and Death. His prayer seems to have been in some measure heard. One day Doctor Santorelli entered his cell and caught the following words addressed to the crucifix : " O Lord, help me in this purgatory in which Thou hast placed me."[1] On being asked what he meant, he replied that he had asked of Jesus Christ the grace to suffer for His love, and that his Lord had been pleased to hear him. " I am experiencing purgatory in this life," he said, " and the thought that I am giving pleasure to Jesus Christ consoles me." On another occasion he remarked : " I am suffering much. I am going through a real martyrdom and am scarcely able to speak." And to a priest named Gerard Gisone, who later became a Redemptorist, and who had come to consult him on spiritual matters, he remarked : " I am constantly in the wounds of Jesus Christ, and the wounds of Jesus Christ are in me. I suffer unceasingly the pains and sorrows of the Passion of Jesus Christ."[2] It was truly a touching sight to see this dying lover of the Crucified lifting his pallid and emaciated face to gaze with weeping eyes on the image of his suffering Lord and to hear him gasping out the words : " What I suffer for Jesus Christ is always but little. God died for me, and if it be His good pleasure, I am willing to die for Him."[3] It was only to intimate

---

[1] Tannoia, cap. xxxv.
[2] Landi.
[3] In Ord. no. 20, § 88.

friends that he thus laid bare the sufferings of his soul ; to others he made light of everything, and an extra-ordinary joy seemed to flood his soul.

Besides this great physical and mental anguish, his illness gave him occasion for suffering in other ways. Santorelli had given orders that a Brother should stay up with him for the purpose of giving him certain medicine about midnight. With tears in his eyes he said : " Oh ! doctor, this gives me real pain."[1] And he repeated the words several times with a distressed earnestness that showed how truly he meant them. And there was something else that disturbed him much : the expense to which he was putting the community. One day he sent for Santorelli. The doctor found the patient very depressed. Gerard begged him to let him know what the chemist's bills would have come to so far. He knew well the straitened circumstances of the Caposele community, and he had it in mind to write to his family and ask their help in the matter. When Santorelli tried to re-assure him on this score, he re-joined : " Of what use have I been to the Congregation ? And why should it be burdened with such expense ? " Even the thought that prayers were being said for his recovery in the community distressed this profoundly humble man. " I am a useless subject," he would exclaim, " and I don't deserve all this."[2]

" He spoke continually," says a witness, " of the love of Jesus and Mary and of the glory of heaven."[3] But at times, as he was too exhausted to speak, he

---

[1] Tannoia, cap. xxxv.
[2] *Ibid.*
[3] In Apost. no. 20, § 32.

would ask Brother Stefano to say aloud acts which he would follow in a low voice. One day the Brother asked him if any fear or temptation worried him. He got this answer : " I have done everything for the love of my God. I have seen Him in all things and have always walked in His presence. His Will has been my will. I have desired only what He wished. And so I die in peace."[1] And peaceful must be the death closing a life that can be summed up thus.

The supernatural atmosphere that surrounded him in life and showed itself in so many prodigious ways did not desert him in his dying hours. One humanly inexplicable phenomenon noticed by everybody who came in contact with him during his last illness was, that in spite of his physical condition, the air that filled the sick room was always remarkably fragrant. Even while he was in Oliveto this phenomenon was noted. Caione writes : " Gerard's room was filled with a heavenly fragrance ; and Don Giuseppe Salvatore has testified to me that in Oliveto, when people called to see him, they could find his room by the fragrance that emanated from it." A laybrother who lived with him in Caposele has recorded : " His person, his clothes and his whole room gave out a pronounced and extra-ordinary fragrance. As I could not analyse this perfume, I one day said to him : ' Brother Gerard, you are carrying perfume about you against the rule.' He assured me he was not. Then, noticing it still stronger, I got a scruple and went off to tell the rector. He, however, informed me that Brother Gerard had got great graces

---

[1] In Apost. us. 20, § 38.

from God and added nothing more. Thinking the matter over, I noticed that even the blood that came from the hæmorrhages had the same fragrance. Finally, his sorrows and sufferings were most acute on Fridays, and it was on those days that the fragrance was strongest."[1] When the end was near, and when we should naturally have expected a different state of things in the sick room, the perfume was so sweet that it surpassed all earthly fragrance. In this phenomenon God seemed to have renewed a wonder wrought in the case of certain other saints, *e.g.*, St. Joseph Cupertino, in order to testify to the outstanding purity of His servant. Caione adds that on the day preceding the night of his death heavenly and enthralling harmonies were heard in his room.

A striking incident occurred almost on the very eve of his death, probably on October 14th. A learned ecclesiastic named Prospero dell' Aquila, coming from Sant' Andrea di Conza, joined Doctor Giuseppe Salvatore at Oliveto, whence they both proceeded to Caposele to visit Gerard. On arrival they went straight to his room, leaving outside the door a peasant lad whom the priest had promised to show a living saint. Now Gerard had not seen the boy or been told of his presence in the house. He suddenly interrupted the conversation by expressing a wish that the boy should be brought in. The latter entered and glanced timidly over at the bed. On realising that a saint was not such a terrible person to look at, he plucked up courage and allowed his eyes to wander about the room. They were quickly

---

[1] Cfr. Benedetti, p. 398.

arrested by a harpsichord in a corner, which had been put there to cheer the patient. Here was something altogether new and strange, and the lad's interest was at once aroused. Gerard watched him and now invited him to play on the instrument, assuring him he would hear beautiful sounds. The boy shyly demurred, especially when he noticed that the bystanders were laughing. According to a witness, he told them he had never handled anything but a spade. The saint, however, kept urging him to play. The lad looked inquiringly at the priest, who smilingly nodded encouragement. At last he sidled across the room, sat down and touched the strings with his heavy uncouth hands. Instead of the awaited dissonance, he dumbfounded the company by producing delightful harmonies, and, as the witnesses in both processes have testified, afterwards declared that he felt an unseen force guiding his fingers. This instrument was later preserved with religious veneration by the Santorelli family and was still in existence in 1843.

October 15th, the feast of his beloved St. Teresa, dawned in Gerard's cell. " Doctor," he said to Santorelli, who had called early in the morning, " recommend me to St. Teresa and receive Holy Communion for me."[1] Though showing no immediate signs of death, he asked for the Viaticum himself and received it with such ecstatic joy that in the eyes of those present he seemed like a seraph being united with the divine essence. As if to bear away a souvenir of this last sacramental visit of his Lord, he asked for the corporal on

---

[1] Tannoia, cap. xxxv.

which the sacred Host had rested and laid it on his breast, over his heart, where he kept it till he died. The wonderful harmonies which had been heard on the preceding day through the instrumentality of the peasant boy were now heard again.

As the night drew on, he said to Brother Stefano : " Brother, I am to die to-night (he named the hour, which the witness forgets). Dress me, as I wish to recite the Office for the Dead for my own soul."[1] Landi writes : " The fervour and humility with which he prepared to appear before his divine Judge cannot be described. His purity of conscience was extreme, and he had preserved his baptismal innocence unspotted ; and yet, seven or eight hours before his death, sitting up in bed, he began to recite the *Miserere* with such fervour and humility as to move deeply the Brother who was nursing him. He would recite a verse first slowly and with great earnestness and then make an act of contrition, while the tears streamed from his eyes. Then, after every other verse, he would repeat, with a pause : *Tibi soli peccavi et malum coram te feci ;* and that other : *et a peccato meo munda me.* He uttered the words plaintively, sighing profoundly and weeping, and moved by such a lofty idea of God and of His infinite sanctity that the Brother infirmarian was seized with a holy dread."

Hearing from his friend Philip Galella that it was the hour of the evening *Angelus* he said : " We have six hours more."[2] In the meantime Santorelli had come in. He noticed the extreme prostration of the patient,

---

[1] In Apost. no. 20, § 98.
[2] *Ibid,* § 40.

but had no idea that death was imminent ; in fact, he thought he saw a slight improvement. As he moved away to leave, Gerard, contrary to his custom, requested him to stay. The doctor excused himself on the grounds that he had other patients to see in Caposele. Gerard did not then insist, and Santorelli left. They never met again. We can imagine how keenly poor Santorelli regretted his going when, on calling the following morning, he found Gerard dead and understood how he had wished him to be present at his passing.

To the same Galella the saint had remarked on that 15th October : " Today is a recreation day for the Fathers, and to-morrow they will have another." " How is that ? " inquired Philip. " Because;" Gerard replied, " I shall die to-night."[1] Perhaps for all his prophetic powers, he did not foresee that in every Redemptorist house and church, as well as in churches innumerable throughout the Catholic world, October 16th, the anniversary of Gerard's death, would be a day of high and holy festival to the end of time.

He was often heard repeating the words : " My God, where art Thou ? Let me see Thee."[2] Turning to Brother Januarius Rendina and Brother Carmine Santaniello,

---

[1] St. Alphonsus had quite an extraordinary devotion to St. Teresa of Avila and made her one of the Patrons of his Congregation. Hence the recreation day referred to by Gerard. In a letter (*Corr. Gen.* vol. 1, p. 7) he speaks of her as " la seconda mamma " ; the first being of course his Mother Mary. The second recreation day is explained in this way : the Church looks on the day of a saint's death as his real birthday, since it is the beginning of his eternal life. Following up this idea, and in the belief that they who persevere to the end in religion likewise enter into eternal life, the Founder had made it traditional in his Institute to look upon the day when any of its members die as a day of recreation.

[2] Tannoia, cap. xxxv.

he said : " Help me to unite myself to God."[1] And
when the former, his old friend and confidant said to
him : " Brother, we have always been good friends ;
remember me when you stand before God," he replied
in a tone of tender affection : " *E vorro io dimenticarmi
di voi* . . . . and would I forget you ? "[2]

It may be that his recent repeated and precise pre-
dictions concerning the hour of his death were not taken
seriously. Perhaps they were looked upon as the
wanderings of a dying man rather than the genuine
prophecies of a saint. Besides, the doctor's departure
had no doubt re-assured them. It is otherwise hard to
explain why the community did not realise that the
end was near and why they retired that night at the
usual hour, leaving only a brother—Brother Xavier
d'Auria—to watch by the patient. Perhaps the best
explanation is that Gerard had prayed to die forsaken
and that God brought these circumstances about in
order to answer that prayer.

Between ten and eleven o'clock he fainted. Suddenly
coming to, he exclaimed in great agitation : " Quick,
quick, Brother Xavier, drive away these gentry (*questi
milordi*). What do these two impudent fellows want
here ? "[3]   Hell had evidently shot its last bolt. Shortly
afterwards his countenance glowed with an unearthly
splendour. Kneeling on the bed, he cried out ecstatically : " There is the Madonna ! Let us honour her ! "[4]
Mary had come spectacularly into his life at its opening ;

---

[1] Tannoia, Cap. xxxv.
[2] *Ibid*.
[3] Benedetti, p. 403 ; Tannoia, cap. xxxv.
[4] Tannoia, cap. xxxv.

it was fitting that she should so come into it at its close.

The night wore on. During the two remaining hours of his life he kept invoking the holy names of Jesus and Mary and making acts of faith, hope, contrition and love. " My God," he would say, " I wish to die to give Thee pleasure. I wish to die in order to do Thy most holy Will."[1] And when he could no longer articulate, his moving lips showed what was going on within his heart. One half hour before the end, Gerard, " devoured by a thirst caused more by his burning love than by his illness,"[2] as a witness puts it, asked for a drink of water. The Brother went away to fetch it. He found the refectory locked and it took some time to get the key. On returning he found the saint lying on his side and facing the wall. The Brother thought he was asleep. In a few minutes he revived and turned to the other side. Realising that he was in his agony, Brother Xavier hurried away to call the minister, Father Buonamano, and another Brother. The Father entered the room just in time to see Gerard breathing his last. As the final absolution was being given, he died, and a new star of unusual magnitude and brilliance came out in the firmament of the Church. Brother Gerard Majella was dead ; as Father Ripoli put it in his juridical deposition : " consumed more by love than by disease."[3] It wanted a little of midnight, on October 15th, 1755. Gerard Majella had lived twenty-nine years, six months and nine days in this world ; he had lived five years, five months and fifteen days in his Congregation.

---

[1] Tannoia, Cap. xxxv.
[2] In Apost. no. 20, § 67.
[3] *Ibid.*, § 19.

" Being made perfect in a short space, he fulfilled a long time."[1] In the neat phrasing of the official document, " in life he surpassed others in holiness, in death he surpassed himself."[2]

The saint's remains at once exhaled an amazingly sweet fragrance—" *odore di Paradiso* "[3] as it was truly described by a witness—which permeated the whole house. As soon as they were laid out, Father Buonamano made an incision in the arm. Fresh blood flowed at once, though the poor body must have had very little in it ! He had the community called and ordered the discipline to be taken as an act of thanksgiving to God for Gerard's holy death and to petition Him for the success of a similar test to His servant's sanctity which he had in mind. According to Tannoia, three hours after his death, the community gathered around the body laid out in the saint's room. Father Buonamano raised the right arm and spoke thus : " Gerard, you have always been obedient. I now bid you in the Name of the Most Holy Trinity to give a sign of your virtue and work one of your accustomed miracles."[4] The Father then took a razor and opened a vein. Once more there was an abundant gush of bright red blood, " more than two pounds of it,"[5] as Tannoia puts it. There was a rush for linen cloths to dip in it, and these were distributed amongst Gerard's many friends, who showed great eagerness to possess them.

Later in the morning, the Brother sacristan went to

---

[1] Wisd. iv, 13.
[2] *Positio super Virtutibus*, § 302.
[3] In Apost. no. 21, § 8.
[4] Tannoia, cap. xxxv and Landi.
[5] Tannoia, *ibid*.

ring the dead bell in the church. But it was a merry peal he found himself chiming, such as is heard on days of high festival. On hearing it, Brother Januarius ran over to stop him, but the sacristan told him that when he rang as he did, he was only obeying an uncontrollable impulse. He was unconsciously echoing the *carillon* in heaven. And indeed it was attuned to the hearts of his confrères, for we are told that these hearts were filled with an unwonted joy such as would be felt at the canonisation of a saint.

"As soon as the news became known," writes Tannoia, "people of every rank hurried to our house. Rich and poor, young and old, lay and clerical—all crowded about the bier. One took delight in telling of some prophecy made by the Brother and verified in his own case ; another told how the secrets of his heart had been read ; whilst a third described how Gerard had led him back to the path of virtue and reconciled him with the God he had offended. The poor especially (towards whom Gerard had been a father) filled the church and house with their wailing and weeping. The people not only exalted him as a saint, but began to cut off his hair and tear up his habit, so that the Guards had to be sent for to surround and protect the body."[1] For two whole days it remained exposed to the veneration of the faithful. They came in their thousands, from a dozen miles they came. They surged around the bier, praying, lamenting, struggling to touch the holy remains. Never before had such crowds been seen in Caposele.

The sweet fragrance and the flow of fresh blood were

---

[1] Tannoia, cap. xxxv.

not the only phenomena after death that testified to Gerard's holiness. The body remained flexible to the end. Moreover, the face and forehead were constantly covered with beads of moisture giving out a heavenly fragrance, and this though the people were constantly removing it with their handkerchiefs, which they afterwards preserved as precious relics. Indeed Gerard was quite lavish of himself in this way after death. As in life, so now he showed his readiness to help those who were in difficulties. One good woman named Rosa Sturchio, who had often sought his advice in spiritual things, was most eager to possess some relic of him. Whether she arrived too late or whether she did not know how to set about it, she had evidently not succeeded in her quest and was kneeling in tears beside the body, secretly petitioning her holy friend. Her niece, Teresa Gasparri Mazzoni, tells us what happened in her deposition : " While she was thus praying, she saw to her great amazement the mouth of the deceased open and a tooth fall from it, which she reverentially picked up and treasured as long as she lived. When dying she bequeathed it to my mother, who wore it with great devotion round her neck to her last breath ; and after her death, this miraculous tooth was preserved by my brother, though half of it only remained, since the archpriest Frangi, of holy memory, wished to get half, as he had a great devotion to Brother Gerard."[1]

Before the holy remains were committed to the tomb, Father Buonamano was most anxious to procure for posterity an authentic likeness of the saint. Unfortun-

---

[1] Benedetti, p. 407.

ately no competent painter could be brought to Caposele in time. However, two casts in wax were taken, one of which remained in the community, while the other was given by request to the Salvatore family in Oliveto. Tannoia states that later on the Fathers tried to have a portrait made from their cast, but that the first attempt proved unsuccessful. On his return, Father Caione once more exploited Gerard's obedience and thus addressed him : " My dear Gerard, you see the portrait is a failure. You are to make it a success."[1] The painter set to work again and declared that he heard a voice telling him how he should hold his brushes and what strokes he should make. This second picture gave general satisfaction. It depicts the saint as the archpriest Salvatore saw him in Oliveto, in ecstasy, raised to a considerable height from the ground, holding a crucifix in one hand and with the other crossed upon his breast.

Before this took place, Father Buonamano, wishing once again to draw blood from the body of the saint, once again gave his orders. He met with the same success. Thirty-five hours after death fresh blood issued in abundance from the same vein of that " incredibly extenuated and fleshless frame."[2] Gerard's members were still flexible, and the miraculous moisture still flowed abundantly.

At last, on Friday evening, October 17th, the sacred remains were laid quietly to rest in a special place in front of the sacristy door, with nothing but the bare essentials written on the slab. Presuming that Gerard would one day be raised to the altars, Father Buonamano

---

[1] Tannoia, cap. xxxv.
[2] In Apost, no. 21, § 31.

had an official report drawn up, on the day of the funeral, of the various extraordinary phenomena—the fragrance, the fresh blood, the unusual moisture, the flexibility of the body—that had been observed between death and burial. He and Father Strina and ten laybrothers, together with ten lay people from outside gave sworn testimony before a notary.

Meantime Gerard himself, now living his true life in heaven, had been appearing on earth. Tannoia writes : " We have it on the testimony of a holy person who was much attached to Gerard that immediately after his death he appeared full of joy and clothed in his ordinary habit. He then appeared a second time richly clad and resplendent with glory. He encouraged this person to suffer willingly for Jesus Christ. ' God,' he said, ' richly rewards in heaven the slight trials we suffer for His love on earth.' He was also seen by Father Peter Paul Petrella, to whom he showed the glory he was enjoying in heaven."[1]

No tomb is deep and dark enough to imprison the memory of a saint or quench his light. Gerard had ever been regarded as a walking saint on earth ; no sooner had he left it than he was looked upon and invoked as a glorified saint in heaven. In doing him honour in Gerard's own Congregation St. Alphonsus himself—no mean judge—led the way. By reason of the innocence of his life, his spirit of penance, his union with God, as well as his countless miracles, he would speak of this his great son as the second St. Paschal Baylon. Barely three months after Gerard's death he

---

[1] Tannoia, cap. xxxv

writes to Father Caione : " I am sending you Father
Giovenale's *notes* on Brother Gerard. Keep them and
copy them as well as you can, as I have asked you to
do, according as your time will allow. It would be better
if you gave not more than a quarter of an hour to it
daily ; thus you will gradually get through the work.
I am sending you your own manuscript also ; it will
help to recall things to you." It is a far cry from this
anxiety to procure the highest possible honours for his
saintly son to his attitude towards the alleged seducer
of less than two years ago.[1] He distributed his portrait
everywhere. Writing to Mother Mary of Jesus, on
July 2nd, 1757, he says : " I am sending you a picture
of Brother Gerard which Don Benedetto (Grazioli)
sent me and which he got printed."[2] In the apostolic
process Father Giuseppe Papa thus deposes : " Our holy
Founder had the highest opinion of the venerable Servant
of God, and so, when dying, he took the portrait of
this holy Brother into his hands and recommended
himself to him. A short time previously he had decided
on writing his life, but, prevented by death, his holy
purpose remained unfulfilled."[3] The introduction of
Gerard's cause had always been uppermost in his mind
but illness and a multiplicity of duties never gave him
the necessary time.

The sons of St. Alphonsus gladly followed the example
set them by their Father. On their missions they
lavishly distributed the pictures of their confrère
and urged the people to have recourse to him in their

---

[1] *Lettere, Corrispond. General.*, ccxxvi.
[2] *Ibid.*, cclxxxii.
[3] In Apost. no. 22, § 92.

needs. Forty years after his death, in 1796, the room
he had made sacred by his last days was converted
into a chapel in honour of St. Stanislaus Kostka. Near
the entrance we read an inscription in Latin of which
the following is a translation :—

" This is the cell which Brother Gerard Majella of
Muro, religious of the Congregation of the Most Holy
Redeemer, a man of outstanding innocence and piety,
once honoured by his dwelling in it and made illustrious
by dying in it the death of the saints. The Fathers of
the same Congregation, living in this house, converted
it into a chapel and dedicated it, on the 13th July, 1796,
to the Flower of youth—St. Stanislaus Kostka, who,
by the beauty and fragrance of his angelic virtues,
blooms in heaven like a lovely flower."[1]

Father Ripoli, who became Superior-General of the
Congregation, wrote as follows : " If I am wearing the
habit of St. Alphonsus, I owe it to the high opinion I
formed of the Venerable Brother Gerard. . . . . I can
also testify that in our chapters all our old superiors
used to hold up the Venerable Servant of God as a model
of virtue and regular observance to the laybrothers,
just as our holy Founder was held up as a model to
the priests of the Congregation."[2]

We have entitled this final chapter of our book *The
Passing of a Saint*. But the saints do not pass. They
do indeed pass out from the sight of their generation,
but only to return after a longer or a shorter period,
arrayed in all the might and splendour of their canonised holiness, to live again in the minds and hearts of

[1] Benedetti, p. 448.
[2] In Ord. no. 22, § 79-81.

generations unending that have never known them in the flesh and that now give them a reverential love and turn to good account their powerful mediation with Heaven.

There is surely something not of this world, something eternal in the Church's undying remembrance of her saintly dead. As soon as she is satisfied that the odour of sanctity has been emanating from the grave of the humblest of her children, slowly, solemnly, hopefully she sets to work. With an unhurrying industry, and an unimagined thoroughness, and a patience that no delay or difficulty can exhaust, she unearths the story of that life. She may have to dig deep for its details ; years upon years, whole centuries even of human history may have to be sifted in order to reach them, and that individual career of that holy man or woman disentangled from a vast and tortuous accumulation of events. But the Church is never wearied or daunted in her seeking. Time means nothing to her. When those to whom she has entrusted her task have passed away, she hands it on to others. Tranquil yet expectant she prays and waits for God to speak His approval of her verdict ; and then, with certainty and decision in her voice, she proclaims the sanctity of her child, puts the halo of sainthood on his head, turns his grave into a shrine, and allots him a niche in her temples. So it was to be now with Gerard.

It is almost superfluous to say that his renown after death spread fast and far. A member of the Benedictine community of Atella states : " I have seen people who, at the mere mention of his name, would uncover their head."[1] " It is impossible," writes Tannoia, " to describe the confidence the people have in this servant of God. They invoke him as a canonised saint. Everywhere his picture is eagerly sought after and it is impossible to satisfy all demands. And convinced that they have received a great treasure, some kiss it and press it to their heart and head ; some bring it home and hang it over the door or on the wall of their room ; others fix it to buildings in danger with the assurance that this wonderful Brother could not, so to speak, grant any small grace, but could only work great wonders in cases of great danger."[2]

Gerard's response from heaven to all this trust and veneration was generous and immediate. Miracles came at once and in abundance. " There is a real rivalry," writes Don Angelo Salvatore the Archpriest of Oliveto, some time after Gerard's death, " between Gerard and his friends : they honour and invoke him more than any other saint in heaven, while Gerard unceasingly distributes the most marvellous gifts. Who could count all the miracles that occur almost daily in our arch-diocese of Conza and in the neighbourhood through his intercession ? "[3] Tannoia is frankly annoyed that a better effort was not made to count and register them : " I cannot but blame our Fathers," he writes, " for their carelessness in not putting together the accounts of all the prodigies he wrought. I should fill volumes if I had them all."[4] A biography of the saint published

---

[1] In Ord. no. 22, § 56.
[2] Cap. xxxvi.
[3] Tannoia, English Edit., p. 444.
[4] Cap. xxxvi.

in 1875 mentions seventy of the most striking.

However, more than enough miracles had become public to serve the interests of Gerard's cause. His first stay in his native Muro as a Redemptorist had been marked by so many miracles that his fellow-citizens already entertained the hope of honouring him one day on the altars. One of them, with more enthusiasm than discretion, one day expressed this hope to Gerard himself. The saint replied that he would be a saint in heaven, but that he would put every obstacle in the way of his canonisation.[1] Fortunately he failed. His cause was formally introduced in 1847. This was eventually followed, in 1893, by Gerard's beatification by Leo XIII. Finally, on the 11th December, the name of Gerard Majella was written by Pius X on the register of the saints.[2]

Now all the saints are eminently lovable, for they were all essentially eminent lovers—of God and their fellowmen. All the unlovely things in fallen human nature—self-seeking, duplicity, meanness, arrogance, harshness, resentment and the like—that sever friendships and hold men apart, were eradicated from the character of the saints to an extraordinary degree. Their official sainthood supposes this. On the other

---

[1] In Apost. no. 6, § 87.

[2] On the day following the feast of St. Alphonsus, in the year of the beatification, 1893, a great-grandson of Gerard's intimate and lifelong friend Doctor Santorelli—another Santorelli—regaled the Redemptorist community in Caposele with a poem in Italian on the *Beato* containing no fewer than 584 stanzas ! We give the opening one.

> " Musa Siderea,
> sai ch'egli è bello
> in versi sciogliere
> lodi a Majello ! "

hand, all those gracious and alluring qualities that bind heart to heart were theirs pre-eminently. And yet, curiously enough, out of the mighty host of the Church's canonised men and women a mere handful are venerated and loved and prayed to by the masses of the faithful as " popular " saints. Apart from those who are the object of a local cult in places associated with their earthly career and those who are particularly honoured by isolated groups, such as the members of a religious Order, the universally popular saints are few. Though they are one and all duly venerated and invoked when the liturgy ordains it, few, very few are taken to the heart of the Catholic world at large. This may be due to their very number and to the necessarily stereotyped character of their fundamental sanctity, or to ignorance of their individual lives, or to the unattractive manner in which these lives are told. Anyhow, from the multitude the few emerge. Whether it be their human personality that sets them apart, or some distinctive feature of their sanctity ; whether it be the story of their career as a whole, or some fascinating and unforgettable incidents in it ; whether it be the special flavour of their spiritual teaching, or just their incidental sayings ; whether it be just their youth, or even their physical traits—at least as the artists have handed them down to us—or even their very name ; whether it be a few or many of these things, or a combination of them all—whatever it is, the individual appeal is there, and a saint leaves the serried ranks of the canonised to join the little company of saints who may almost be said to monopolise the hearts of the faithful. His name leaps from mouth to mouth ; it crosses con-

tinents and seas ; books and pamphlets tell his story
in a dozen tongues ; painters and sculptors get busy
and make his features familiar the world over ; his
name becomes a household word in the homes of
Christendom ; his shrine is raised in hundreds of churches,
and the faithful gather lovingly about them to sing his
praises, to lay their sorrows and perplexities at his
feet, to crave his patronage in their cause. He becomes
the property, the pride, the joy of every nation, a free-
man of every city and country-side in the Catholic
world. Such a saint has Anthony of Padua, for instance,
long since been ; such a saint, too, has Thérèse of Lisieux
become with an unprecedented rapidity ; and such a
saint the lowly but wonderful Redemptorist laybrother,
Gerard Majella, who died in Southern Italy nearly
two hundred years ago is fast becoming. Speaking in
the process between 1848-1856, a witness declares :—
" There is not a corner of the world in which his sanctity
is not spoken of."[1] How far more true is this in 1946 !
Some details of this universal cult will not be amiss,
before we have done, and will, we hope, further the
interests of our saint. They are far from being
exhaustive, and where continental countries are concerned, are necessarily limited and unfortunately subject
to revision as far as the present goes, as they have been
drawn from pre-war publications. This, however, in
no way takes from their value as evidences of the place
St. Gerard holds in Catholic circles.

It would be superfluous to enlarge on devotion to
St. Gerard in Italy—his own fatherland, and still more

---

[1] In Ord. no. 22, § 131.

so to detail the enthusiastic love for him witnessed in *Materdomini*, where his blessed bones repose and which is the heart and centre of a devotion that is now general. There are, however, a few items of interest we should like to record. In 1902 the *Pious Union of St. Gerard* was inaugurated. It was later raised to the dignity of an archconfraternity, which in four years had a membership of 40,000 and in twenty-one years a membership of 119,000. In 1904 the State made *Materdomini* a Postal and Telegraph Office of the second class : an eloquent tribute to its importance. In 1905 a printing-press was set up in *Materdomini* for the purpose of spreading devotion to the saint. The periodical *S. Gerardo Majella* appeared in four languages : Italian, French, English and Spanish, and in 1929 had a circulation of 26,000. The same year saw the birth of an association of boys and girls, whose members were known respectively as *Gerardini* and *Gerardine*, and which in one twelvemonth had fifteen thousand names on its register. The original church has since been enlarged to meet the ever-growing numbers of the pilgrims and decorated becomingly. On February 18th, 1930, Pius XI gave it the title and status of a minor basilica. To emphasise Our Lady's ancient claim to the place, the dedicatory words are : DEIPARAE AC DIVO GERARDO DICATUM. Amongst the pilgrims who visited the shrine in 1938 was the then Crown Prince Humbert, son of King Victor Emmanuel III. Fortunately it has been spared the ravages of war.

Germany and Holland, where we should not expect such a typically Italian saint as Gerard to find such favour, present us with some striking facts.[1] In the *Westfälisches Volksblatt*, of the large industrial town of Bochum, in Westphalia, a correspondent writes in 1927 as follows : " It is eight o'clock on Monday morning. The vast Redemptorist church—the *Klosterkirche* —is so crowded that the very passages are filled. What is the secret attraction that draws so many Christians to it every Monday ? What urges us to begin each week with Mass in the *Klosterkirche* ? Look at the altar of St. Gerard Majella ablaze with lights and bedecked with flowers ! Look at all those people praying and singing before it ! A Father ascends the pulpit and reads out a list of acknowledgments and of various needs that had been entrusted to St. Gerard during the previous week : the conversion of a certain sinner, the cure of a sick person, peace in a home, the end of a distressing case of unemployment, a mother's happy delivery . . . . Then the priest and the congregation kneel together and give thanks for petitions granted during the previous week and beg for fresh favours. He alone who has been one of that praying multitude can know how moving is this corporate thanksgiving and supplication. Soon the endless filing up to the Eucharistic Table begins. The Saviour Himself, the Author of all grace, draws our hearts.

" When Benediction is over, a wonderful sight keeps you in the church. A Father takes a small reliquary from St. Gerard's altar containing a particle of the

---

[1] It is now known definitely that the Redemptorist church and monastery both in Bochum and in Aachen (Aix-la-Chapelle), of which we are about to speak, have been destroyed. God grant that they may soon become again what they have been before, centres of striking devotion to our saint.

saint's bones, from which even in our own day the miraculous oil still flows, and gives it to each one to kiss. Look at that unending line : in the faces of people of every age may be read the hard struggle for a livelihood, the manifold miseries of present-day life. But listen to the comforting words of the hymn :—

> O Thaumaturge, exaudi
> Clamores supplicum !
> Quid valeas, ostende,
> Amorisque impetum ![1]

" Throughout the following week we enjoy and live, as it were, on the heavenly blessing brought away from that blessed spot." So far the correspondent.

During the octave preparatory to the saint's feast the people come in all weathers to the daily sermon in his honour, many of them arriving two and three hours before in order to secure a seat. On the last Sunday (1930) there were about 3,000 present, and in the eight days 12,000 Communions were distributed. In the course of one year 7,443 people called at the monastery to present their petitions to St. Gerard, and of these 572 returned to give joyful thanks for the hearing of their prayers.

Speaking of the miraculous oil mentioned above, or " manna," as it is called, the *Analecta C.SS.R.* add that the same phenomenon observed in the case of the saint's relics in Caposele are seen in the monastery in Bochum, *viz.*, the slow flow of miraculous liquid, which, in the latter place, had already penetrated most

---

[1] O Wonder-worker, hearken to the cries of thy suppliants ! Show thy power and the might of thy love.

of the surrounding silk. When in May, 1926, the Bishop of Paderborn had witnessed this phenomenon himself and had prayed fervently before the reliquary, he gladly gave leave for the weekly Mass before the Blessed Sacrament exposed.

In Aachen (Aix-la-Chapelle) the weekly Mass in honour of St. Gerard is said at 6.30 in the morning to meet the requirements of working-people and servants. There are from 200-300 communicants each time.

In Heiligenstadt, a town with a Catholic population of 9,000, a Confraternity of St. Gerard was canonically established on October 16th, 1925, and in 1939 had a membership of 3,673.

Nor is devotion to the saint in Germany restricted to Redemptorist churches. Thus, for instance, in the Rhine town of Siegburg, at the request of his clients, the Benedictine monks have Mass in honour of St. Gerard. Moreover, his cult is most marked in many communities of nuns.

The saint has responded lavishly to all this devotion. The following is a remarkable case of it. The pastor of the country parish of Wettrup, in the diocese of Osnabruck, who had heard a good deal about St. Gerard's activities in favour of those in need, was in great difficulties over the building of a church. It had long been badly wanted and the bishop had given orders for its construction. But funds were exceedingly low. However, the good priest put the whole business in Gerard's hands, presented a statue of him to our house in Glanerbrucke (perhaps recalling Gerard's holy bribery at Monte Gargano), promised to make him the joint-patron of his parish with St. Anthony the Hermit, and every

Monday had public prayers recited in his honour. On June 19th, 1932, the foundation-stone was laid ; and on the 9th November of the same year the new church, complete in every way, was solemnly consecrated by his Lordship the Bishop !

This achievement was universally regarded as one of Gerard's miracles. What bears this out is the remarkable fact that it was almost invariably on a Monday —the day when devotions were held in honour of the saint—that gifts and contributions came in. So true was this that after some time the workmen would ask the priest : " And what has St. Gerard brought you today ? " Thus on one Monday he received the sum of 1,680 marks from six or eight different benefactors ; on another the price of fourteen Stations of the Cross from fourteen different families ; on another Monday the high altar was presented ; on another the communion rails ; on yet another a statue of the saint. Now previous to this the priest had promised to procure a relic of St. Gerard by the 16th October for another church in the diocese dedicated to him. He succeeded. The following day was a Monday, and the priest looked forward to Gerard remembering the new church. He was not disappointed. As he was leaving his presbytery in the morning for the new building, a man handed him twenty marks ; on his return another benefactor handed him twenty more ; a few minutes later he was called to the 'phone and the promise of one hundred and twenty more marks came over the wires ! Three gifts in a quarter of an hour ! The tables were well turned on the holy briber of Monte Gargano ! To conclude. On yet another Monday a timber-merchant called on the pastor. On learning in the course of conversation that the flooring of the new sacristy was not yet forthcoming, he exclaimed : " I meant to present the flooring for the new church. My gift has also reached you on a Monday ! I intended calling last Friday, but was prevented."

It we turn to Holland, we find that St. Gerard is immensely popular. In the Redemptorist church in Wittem a second Monday Mass at a later hour had to be added. On each of the nine Sundays before the saint's feast there are between 800 and 1,200 communicants. These later years, during the octave, the eight confessionals in the church are so crowded that men's confessions have to be heard in the rooms of four of the Fathers of the community. Writing in 1939, a correspondent tells us that there is an unceasing pilgrimage to the saint's shrine all the year round. On the Sundays of the spring and summer months ten confessors are kept busy for three hours. On the feast itself, the communicants numbered 4,000 ; fifty large buses and two hundred motor cars were counted. In May, August and October the pilgrims came from all parts of Holland—driving as many as 164-165 miles and walking as many as thirteen. If needs be, they travel by night and fasting, in order not to miss Holy Communion. On one 16th October Holy Communion had to be distributed to men and boys in the community oratory and in the neighbouring Redemptoristine convent chapel, in order to relieve the pressure.

As we should expect from the highly active Catholicism of the Dutch, devotion to the saint is not limited to prayers and pilgrimages. The press is enlisted in its favour. Prayers, novenas, calendars, periodicals pour from it to further his cause. Thus there is the *S. Gerardus-bode* (St. Gerard's Messenger), contributed to mainly by our Fathers, though edited by a parish priest ! There is the *S. Gerardus-Klokee* (St. Gerard's Bell), a monthly publication begun in 1920, which, towards the close of 1930, had a circulation of 30,000 and early in 1931 bade fair to reach the 33,000 mark.

Here again, in Holland, devotion to the saint is far from being confined within Redemptorist circles. Since his canonisation thirteen parochial churches have been built under his patronage. The churches that contain his statue and, generally speaking, have weekly devotions in his honour, especially on Mondays, are almost innumerable. To say nothing about Redemptorist churches, in very many others the feast of St. Gerard is solemnly honoured either by a *Missa Cantata*, or by special prayers, or by a general communion, or by public devotions for three or eight days before.

Again leaving out of account the centres of Redemptorist influence, confraternities or pious unions bearing his name exist in several places, especially where the saint is the official patron. Gerard has been made patron of religious communities devoted to works of charity ; moreover, five hospitals, more than a score of Catholic schools, as well as a Girls' Training College thrive under his auspices. Under the name and patronage of Gerard are seven societies of young men and one of girls called *Patronaat*, besides various societies for making vestments and clothing the poor. Many trade-guilds bear his name. Not rarely is it seen over hostels, studios and workshops. Two Vincent de Paul conferences have publicly placed themselves and their activities under his protection. In one district a Rifle Brigade wages a peaceful war under Gerard's standard ! We must add that an amazing number of Dutch children are given his name in baptism.

In North America there is the League of St. Gerard with an ever-growing membership, whose object is to make known the wonderful story of his life and his great power with God, especially as " The Mothers' Saint," " The Patron of a Good Confession," and " The Patron of a Religious Vocation." With regard to mothers, we quote from the pamphlet issued in connection with the League : " Never perhaps has there been such an organised attack on the very well-springs of human life as today. Statistics on this point are staggering. Something must be done quickly to smash the army of anti-lifers if the white races are to continue to exist. It is our hope that St. Gerard's tender yet powerful assistance to mothers in the hour of need will prove to be the bulwark of the Church in Her battle to preserve Christian mothers in a pagan world. Our hope is shared by many priests and laity alike." There is, moreover, the Guild of St. Gerard, whose specific object is to provide hospital accommodation for mothers.

This speciality of the saint, if we may so call it— the miraculous aid given to mothers in danger—begun in his lifetime, has continued ever since his precious death and is now meeting with a recognition that is world-wide. Already during the process of his beatification a witness stated that even in his day Gerard was spoken of as : *Il Santo dei felici parti* . . . the Saint of

happy deliveries. Today he is such more than ever.
Countless mothers have lived to bless him and countless children have been gratefully given his name. Before
going further, we must mention here that as the patron
of a good confession St. Gerard is still more widely
known, and his activities in this direction, so phenom-
enonally displayed while he was on earth, are continued from heaven in favour of that most pitiable
of sinners, whom fear or false shame keeps from using
the great sacramental remedy for his sins, or from using
it aright. And surely, too, St. Gerard has a special
claim to the allegiance of Christ's consecrated spouses,
in whose interest he worked so hard and whose religious
perfection he had so much at heart, and who was so
zealous and so successful in recruiting for the cloister.

Let us return to devotion to the saint and let us come
to Ireland. (Again, we say, our survey is not meant
to be exhaustive). It would be strange if Gerard were
not popular in Ireland. But his Irish clients are innumerable, especially in Redemptorist centres. In the
Redemptorist church in Limerick his shrine is unusually
large and rich in mosaics depicting scenes from his
life on its walls. In Clonard, Belfast, the saint's shrine
is seldom without clients, and each day numbers call
to the monastery to be blessed with his relic. The novena
preceding his feast is made with enthusiastic piety,
more than 3,000 attending each night and about 5,000
coming each day to venerate his relic. 10,000 copies
of a novena booklet were printed in 1944 and were
sold out in a couple of weeks.

But where devotion to St. Gerard in Ireland is concerned, it looks as if the palm must go to the people

of Dundalk. The cost of the new shrine in St. Joseph's church was paid off within a year by local subscription alone. A perpetual novena to the saint was begun some years ago, and a very large congregation attends the Tuesday morning Mass at seven o'clock, at which there is an average of 400 communicants. The attendance during the novena before the feast is really extraordinary. In 1940 the communions during the nine days totalled 9,226, and in 1945, 15,839. And this in a town with a population of 13,000 souls! So great is the congregation at night that some years ago special services had to be arranged for the children, as well as for the old and infirm, in the afternoon. In 1944 (and again in 1945) two separate services for adults had to be held. At one of these a Father fell to counting the number present. He stopped when he came to 1,450. And the church seats 750! Generosity, need it be said? is not all on the people's side, and extraordinary favours are reported, some of them having all the appearance of the miraculous. But perhaps the most distinctive feature of the devotion of the people of Dundalk to the saint is their ordinary everyday attitude towards him. They look on him and speak of him as their constant unfailing friend, who understands their daily needs and is ever ready with his sympathy and help. Hence their confidence in him is unbounded.

With regard to devotion to St. Gerard outside Redemptorist circles, one item is of interest. The young resident tailor in Malpiedi's notorious high school— now a canonised saint—has given his name and his patronage to a select school for boys, under lay management, in the outskirts of Dublin. October 16th is a gala day for them and is usually spent picnicking in the country.

If we look for an explanation of Gerard's popularity, apart from God's designs and the saint's lavish intervention in behalf of his clients, perhaps we shall best find it in his love for God—rapturous, trustful, all-embracing—loving everyone and everything that God loves. All the world loves a lover, we are told, and we know with what sympathy the fortunes of youthful lovers are followed in fact and fiction. It is even so with those ardent and youthful lovers amongst the saints. Our heart goes out to them and we love to have them for our friends. Thus it is with Thérèse of Lisieux ; thus it is with Gerard of Muro. With our own solicitude for the morrow in mind, we love his joyous trustfulness in God. We love him as he walks through life with the heart of a child, his hand in his heavenly Father's, his eyes looking upwards in every emergency. We love him in spite of his austerities, for we know that towards himself alone is he austere, and that his heart melts with pity at the sight of the distressed. Moreover, for all his penitential rigours, there is nothing about Gerard that repels, and there clings to him an atmosphere of childlike joyousness reminding us of what man must have been before he fell.

And now, before we conclude, we should like to answer a question which we feel more than one reader must have put to himself as he perused our pages. Had Gerard Majella any faults ? He had, for he was human and, for all his tremendous sanctity, a fallen child of fallen parents. We dare not think or say otherwise.

But further than this we really cannot go. Frankly we are unable to specify and can only conjecture. The only witness against him is himself, and the evidence of saints against themselves is unreliable and mislead-ing. Their keen vision of the greatness and holiness of God, their realisation of the meaning of sin, their sensitive and loving hearts, their abysmal humility—all these things made them see stains quite beyond our dull sight and feel guilt that does not penetrate our callousness. As we have seen, Gerard could wax eloquent against Gerard, and at times he did so in letters to intimate spiritual friends and whenever his virtues were unwisely referred to in his presence. And that is really all we have to go by. Superiors, directors, confrères, visitors to the monastery, as well as all with whom he was brought into contact without its walls, are unanimous in their enthusiastic praise of him. The acts of the process are an unbroken pæan. Here is some of the language we meet with in their voluminous pages. Gerard was " the perfect man," " a compendium of all the virtues," " a prodigious man lavishly favoured by God," " a prodigious saint," " a saint by excellence," " a living saint who could not be reproached with the smallest fault," " a portent of virtue," " an incarnate angel," " a spotless angel," " his life was more angelic than human " ; " he was the jewel of his superiors and of his brethren," " the wonder of contemporaries and posterity " ; his reputation was " *colossale.*" Now, when we have deducted from these words what is due to the overstatement of enthusiasm, we have more than enough left to show that Gerard Majella was an extra-ordinarily sinless man, even for a saint. He is brilliant even amongst the stars.

And since this is so, we may find ourselves putting a further question : what purpose can the example of such a man, whose life is packed with amazing miracles and with still more amazing virtues, serve in our work-aday world of ordinary men and women ? We may as well ask what is the purpose of the stars in the sky. And perhaps we have asked that question as we stood beneath them and looked up and recalled what the men of science tell us of them. When we think of their incalculable numbers, their bewildering immensities, their unimaginable yet ordered speed ;—when we remember that there are stars so distant that they are pouring their effulgence on an unseeing world, we may be tempted to ask : *To what purpose is this waste ?* Is this colossal multitude of shining spheres a vast futility, a gigantic but ineffectual expenditure of magnificence and power ? The Psalmist has the answer : *The heavens show forth the glory of God : and the firmament declareth the work of his hands.*[1] If the firmament did nothing else, it would do this. In its stupendous script the name of its Architect is plain to eyes that want to see.

It is something like this with the stars in the firma-ment of God's Church, with the great saints. If a saint like Gerard Majella, who seemed to live more in heaven than on earth, who glitters with every rare gift, who seems so hopelessly beyond our world, did nothing else than " show forth the glory of God "— show forth His power by miracles and His holiness by

---

[1] Ps. xviii, 2.

virtues, he would justify his presence amongst those whose lives we write and read. And he would be what the readers of such lives are anxious to find : a practical saint. But it does not call for a particularly close study of Gerard's twenty-nine years to realise that he is as imitable in all sorts of ways as he is admirable. We refer our readers again to that body of resolutions of his—so many of them commonplace, if we like—and there they will see the foundation on which the towering structure of his canonised sanctity has been reared. However high, by God's grace and our own efforts, our sanctity is to go, it must be built on the same foundation. Every page of Gerard's life shows how he loved God and men, how he suffered and how he worked. And these are things we have all to do.

Appendix A

Some of our readers may like to see the original of St. Alphonsus'
beautiful hymn.

Fiori felici, voi che notte e giorno
Vicino al mio Gesù sempre ne state,
Nè vi partite mai finchè d'intorno
Tutta la vita alfin non vi lasciate :
Oh ! potess'io far sempre il mio soggiorno
In questo luogo bel dove posate !
Ahi ! qual sorte saria la mia, qual vanto
Finir la vita all mia vita accanto !
Faci beate, e voi che così ardete
In onore del vostro e mio Signore ;
Vorrei mirari un dì, come voi siete,
Tutto luce ed ardor fatto il mio core.
E insiem con voi, che tutte vi struggete,
Struggermi anch'io vorrei di santo amore :
Quanto v'invidio, oh Dio, quanto io saria
Lieto in mutar con voi la sorte mia !
Sacro vasello, tu più fortunato
In te nascondi e chiudi il mio Diletto :
Chi più nobil di te, chi più beato,
Che giungi a dare al tuo Signor ricetto ?
Oh ! se l'ufficio tuo fosse già dato
Per un sol giorno al mio povero petto
Tutto fuoco, ed amor sarebbe il core,
Fatto casa del fuoco e dell'amore.

Ah ! che fiori ! che faci ! ahi che vasello !
Quanto di voi felice più son io,
Quando l'amato mio sen vien da agnello
Pien d'affetto e pietà nel petto mio :
Ed io misero verme accolgo in quello
Piccolo pan tutto il mio Bene e Dio :
Ahimè ! perchè non ardo allor, non moro,
Che tutto mio si rende il mio tesoro ?

Anima, vanne, e alla tua luce amata,
Qual farfalla d'intorno ognor t'aggira :
Vanne, di fde e amor tutta infiammata,
E a vista del Diletto ardi, e sospira :
E quando giunge poi l'ora bramata
Che a te si dà quel che il cielo ammira,
Stringilo teco, e con divoto ardore
Digli che altro non vuoi che amore, amore !

480

Appendix B
DEVOTIONS IN HONOUR OF ST. GERARD
NOVENA PRAYERS

First Day—St. Gerard, ever full of faith, obtain for us, we pray thee, that believing firmly all that the Church of God proposes to our belief, we may strive to secure through a holy life the joys of eternal happiness.

Nine Hail Marys.

V. Pray for us, St. Gerard,

R. That we may be made worthy of the promises of Christ.

LET US PRAY

O Almighty and Everlasting God, who didst draw to Thyself St. Gerard even from his tenderest years, making him conformable to the Image of Thy Crucified Son, grant, we beseech Thee, that imitating his example we may be made like unto the same Divine Image, through Jesus Christ, Our Lord. Amen.

Second Day—St. Gerard, most generous saint, who from thy tenderest years didst care so little for the goods of earth, obtain for us that we may place all our confidence in Jesus Christ, our true treasure, who alone can make us happy in time and in eternity.

Nine Hail Marys, with V. and R. and Prayer, as above.

Third Day—St. Gerard, bright Seraph of Love, who, despising all earthly love, didst consecrate thy life to the service of God and thy neighbour, promoting God's glory in thy lowly state and ever ready to succour the distressed and console the sorrowful, obtain for us, we beseech thee, that loving God, our only Good, and our neighbour for His sake, we may be hereafter united to Him for ever in glory.

Nine Hail Marys, etc., as above.

Fourth Day—St. Gerard, spotless Lily of Purity, by thy angelic virtue and thy wondrous innocence of life thou didst receive from the Infant Jesus and His Immaculate Mother sweet pledges of tenderest love ; grant that we may ever strive manfully in our life-long fight and thus win the crown that awaits the brave and the true.

Nine Hail Marys, etc., as before.

Fifth Day—ST. GERARD, Model of Holy Obedience, who throughout life didst most heroically submit thy judgment to those who represented Jesus Christ to thee, thus sanctifying thy lowliest acts, obtain for us from God cheerful submission to His holy will and the virtue of perfect obedience, that we may be made conformable to Jesus, our Model, who was obedient even unto death. *Nine Hail Marys, etc., as before.*

Sixth Day—ST. GERARD, most perfect imitator of Jesus our Redeemer, do thou whose greatest glory was to be humble and lowly, obtain that we, too, knowing our littleness in God's sight, may be found worthy to enter the kingdom that is promised to the humble and lowly of heart.
Nine Hail Marys, etc., as before.

Seventh Day—ST. GERARD, unconquered hero, most patient in suffering, do thou who didst glory in infirmity, and under slander and cruel ignominy didst rejoice to suffer with Christ, obtain for us patience and resignation in our sorrows, that we may bravely bear the cross that is to gain for us the crown of everlasting glory.
Nine Hail Marys, etc., as before.

Eighth Day—ST. GERARD, true lover of Jesus in the Blessed Sacrament of the Altar, do thou, who didst kneel long hours before the Tabernacle and there didst taste the joys of paradise, obtain for us, we pray thee, the spirit of prayer and an undying love for this Most Holy Sacrament, that thus receiving frequently the Body and Blood of Jesus we may daily grow in His holy love and merit the priceless grace of loving Him to the end. *Nine Hail Marys, etc., as before.*

Ninth Day—ST. GERARD, most favoured Child of Heaven, to whom Mary gave the Infant Jesus in the days of thy childhood, to whom she sweetly came before thou didst close thine eyes in death, obtain for us, we beseech thee, so to seek and love our Blessed Mother during life, that she may be our joy and consolation in this valley of tears, until with thee, before the Throne of God, we may praise her goodness for all eternity. Amen. Amen. So I hope, so may it be.

Nine Hail Marys, etc., as before.

LITANY OF ST. GERARD

(For private use only)

Lord, *have mercy on us.*
Christ, *have mercy on us.*
Lord, *have mercy on us.*
Christ, *hear us.*
Christ, *graciously hear us.*
God, the Father of Heaven, *have mercy on us.*
God, the Son, Redeemer of the world, *have mercy on us.*
God, the Holy Ghost, *have mercy on us.*

Holy Mary, Mother of Perpetual Succour,
St. Joseph, Foster-Father of Christ,
St. Alphonsus, Founder of the Congregation of the Most Holy Redeemer,
St. Gerard, endowed with extraordinary graces from early childhood,
St. Gerard, perfect type of a faithful servant,
St. Gerard, shining example for the labouring classes,
St. Gerard, great lover of prayer and work,
St. Gerard, seraphic adorer of the most Blessed Sacrament,
St. Gerard, living image of the Crucified Saviour,
St. Gerard, most devoted client of the Immaculate Virgin Mary,
St. Gerard, bright mirror of innocence and penance,
St. Gerard, admirable model of heroic obedience,
St. Gerard, silent victim of ignominious calumny,
St. Gerard, great before God by thy deep humility,
St. Gerard, truly wise by thy childlike simplicity,
St. Gerard, supernaturally enlightened in divine mysteries,
St. Gerard, solely desirous of pleasing God,
St. Gerard, zealous promoter of the conversion of sinners,
St. Gerard, wise counsellor in the choice of vocation,
St. Gerard, enlightened guide in the direction of souls,
St. Gerard, kind friend of the poor and distressed,
St. Gerard, safe refuge in sickness and sorrow,

Pray for us

St. Gerard, wonderful protector of unbaptised children, ⎫
St. Gerard, compassionate intercessor in all our wants, ⎪
St. Gerard, exalted by God through astonishing miracles, ⎬ *Pray for us*
St.Gerard, ornament and glory of the Redemptorist Order, ⎭

Lamb of God, who takest away the sins of the world, *Spare us, O Lord*.

Lamb of God, who takest away the sins of the world. *Graciously hear us, O Lord*.

Lamb of God, who takest away the sins of the world, *Have mercy on us*.

V. St. Gerard ,pray for us.

R. That we may be made worthy of the promises of Christ.

Let us pray.

O Almighty and Everlasting God, who didst draw to Thyself St. Gerard even from his tenderest years, making him conformable to the Image of Thy Crucified Son, grant, we beseech Thee, that imitating his example we may be made like unto the same Divine Image, through Jesus Christ, Our Lord. Amen.

PRAYER FOR THE GRACE TO MAKE A GOOD CONFESSION

O Great Patron of a Good Confession, Saint Gerard ! O thou who didst give courage to souls whom fear and shame had overcome ! O thou who didst make known to poor sinners the sins wilfully concealed from the minister of God ! O thou who didst give sorrow to their heart, resolution to their wills, truth to their lips, help me ! I wish to make a good confession. If there be any mortal sin which, through my own fault, I have not confessed, bring it clearly before my mind. Help me to know my sins. Obtain for me true sorrow for them, and a firm purpose never to offend God again by mortal sin. And when I am kneeling in the confessional, be with me, and help me to tell all my sins in spite of fear or shame. Saint Gerard, in thy hands I place this confession. Be thou to me what thou wast to many another poor soul, " an Angel of God sent to deliver me from hell." Amen.

PRAYER IN TEMPORAL NEEDS

O God, Who didst so often give to St. Gerard power to succour those in need, grant me the grace which I implore of Thee (*here mention it*), through the intercession of Thy most charitable Servant, that being helped in my present need, I may with my whole heart love and serve Thee, my only Treasure in time and eternity. Amen.

PRAYER FOR MOTHERHOOD

O good St. Gerard, powerful intercessor before God and Wonderworker of our day, I call upon thee and seek thy aid. Thou who on earth didst always fulfil God's designs, help me to do the holy Will of God. Beseech the Master of Life, from Whom all paternity proceedeth, to render me fruitful in offspring, that I may raise up children to God in this life and heirs to the Kingdom of His Glory in the world to come. Amen.

PRAYER FOR EXPECTANT MOTHERS

O Everlasting and Almighty God, Who, through the operation of the Holy Ghost, didst prepare the body and soul of the glorious Virgin Mary, Mother of God, to be a worthy dwelling for Thy Son, and Who, through the same Holy Ghost, didst sanctify St. John the Baptist before his birth ; deign to hear the prayer of Thy humble servant. I implore Thee, through the intercession of St. Gerard, to protect me (her) in motherhood and to safeguard against the evil spirit the child which Thou hast given me (her), that by Thy saving Hand, it may receive Holy Baptism. Grant also that, having lived as Christians on earth, we (they) may attain to everlasting bliss in Heaven. Amen.

PRINTED BY
JOHN ENGLISH & CO.,
WEXFORD.